A TERRIBLY SERIOUS ADVENTURE

A TERRIBLY SERIOUS ADVENTURE

Philosophy at Oxford 1900–60

NIKHIL KRISHNAN

P

PROFILE BOOKS

First published in Great Britain in 2023 by
Profile Books Ltd
29 Cloth Fair
London
EC1A 7JQ
www.profilebooks.com

Typeset in Sabon by MacGuru Ltd

Lines from *Autumn Journal* by Louis MacNeice (Faber and Faber),
reproduced by permission of David Higham Associates.

Lines from *The Less Deceived* by Philip Larkin (Faber and
Faber), reproduced by permission of Faber and Faber.

1 3 5 7 9 10 8 6 4 2

Printed and bound in Great Britain by
Clays Ltd, Elcograf S.p.A.

A CIP catalogue record for this book is available from the British Library.

ISBN 978 1 80081 236 9
eISBN 978 1 80081 237 6

Those who know they are deep strive for clarity. Those who would like to seem deep to the crowd strive for obscurity.

Nietzsche

There is no philosophical idea, however deep or subtle, that cannot and should not be expressed in everyone's language.

Bergson[1]

Contents

Dramatis Personae

Principal characters

R. G. Collingwood (1889–1943). English philosopher, historian and archaeologist who made serious contributions to all three disciplines. His philosophical work concerned questions in all branches of philosophy, but his work on the philosophy of history was especially influential. Major works: *The Principles of Art* (1938), *An Autobiography* (1939), *The Idea of History* (1946).

Gilbert Ryle (1900–76). Pioneering philosopher of mind and a foundational figure in the tradition of 'ordinary language philosophy'. Waynflete Professor of Metaphysics at the University of Oxford and editor of *Mind*, an influential philosophical journal. Major works: 'Systematically Misleading Expressions' (1932), *The Concept of Mind* (1949).

Isaiah Berlin (1909–97). Émigré from the Russian Empire after the Bolshevik Revolution; historian of ideas, liberal and anti-Communist political thinker. Major works: *Karl Marx: His Life and Environment* (1939), *The Hedgehog and the Fox* (1953), 'Two Concepts of Liberty' (1958).

A. J. Ayer (1910–89). Influential figure in the reception of Austrian logical positivism in the English-speaking world. Public intellectual, secularist, liberal and rationalist. Major works: *Language, Truth, and Logic* (1936), *The Problem of Knowledge* (1956).

J. L. Austin (1911–60). Pioneering figure of 'ordinary language philosophy', aiming to 'dissolve' philosophical problems by showing them to emerge out of misunderstandings of language, as well as the theory of 'speech acts'. Major works: 'Other Minds' (1946), *Sense and Sensibilia* (1962), *How to Do Things with Words* (1962).

G. E. M. (Elizabeth) Anscombe (1919–2001). Student of Ludwig Wittgenstein at Cambridge. Later, his literary executor and the English translator of his later works, including the *Philosophical Investigations*. A convert to Roman Catholicism. Major works: *Intention* (1957), 'Modern Moral Philosophy' (1958).

R. M. Hare (1919–2002). Moral philosopher associated with a 'prescriptivist' theory of morals, according to which moral language is understood not as describing the world but as prescribing courses of action. Major works: *The Language of Morals* (1952), *Freedom and Reason* (1963), *Moral Thinking* (1981).

Iris Murdoch (1919–99). Moral philosopher and novelist best known for her work on moral psychology and an approach to ethics inspired by Plato. Major works: *Sartre: Romantic Rationalist* (1953), *The Sovereignty of Good* (1970), *Metaphysics as a Guide to Morals* (1992).

Mary Midgley (1919–2018). Philosopher and public intellectual best known for her work at the intersection of zoology and moral philosophy. Major works: *Beast and Man* (1978), *Wickedness* (1984).

Peter Strawson (1919–2006). Philosopher of logic and language who did pioneering work in reviving metaphysics and on the theoretical philosophy of Immanuel Kant. Major works: *Individuals: An Essay in Descriptive Metaphysics* (1959), 'Freedom and Resentment' (1960), *The Bounds of Sense* (1966).

Philippa Foot (1920–2010). Moral philosopher best known for her contribution to the revival of Aristotelian approaches to ethics and her original work in applied ethics. Major works: 'Moral Arguments' (1958), 'Morality as a System of Hypothetical Imperatives' (1972), *Natural Goodness* (2001).

Bernard Williams (1929–2003). Moral philosopher best known for his sceptical views about the authority of morality, and for his conception of philosophy as a humanistic discipline whose concerns are continuous with those of history and literature. Major works: 'A Critique of Utilitarianism' (1973), *Moral Luck* (1981), *Ethics and the Limits of Philosophy* (1985).

0

Giddiness

One may as well begin with Socrates. And with Socrates, it always begins with a boy and a question. This boy is sixteen. He likes to wrestle, and he likes geometry; he will die one of the greatest mathematicians of the age. He is called Theaetetus, and he gives his name to a dialogue by Plato about an episode, very possibly historical, when he, an adolescent mathematical prodigy, meets a Socrates who is shortly to be charged with heinous crimes – impiety, corrupting youth – and sentenced to death.

Theaetetus is not beautiful, but he is bright, even-tempered and intellectually eager, which makes him just Socrates's type (Socrates was a soul man). In his usual way, he asks the boy, 'What is knowledge?'

Theaetetus would like to play, but he doesn't know how. 'I assure you, Socrates, that I have often tried to think this out, when I have heard reports of the questions you ask. But I can never persuade myself that anything I say will really do … And yet, again, you know, I can't even stop worrying about it.'[1] Sometimes, he admits, 'when I'm looking at them' – Socrates's questions – 'I begin to feel quite giddy.'[2]

'I dare say you do, my dear boy,' says Socrates. 'For this is an experience which is characteristic of a philosopher, this wondering: this is where philosophy begins and nowhere else.' Where philosophy begins: in wonder, giddiness and sleepless nights.

*

Reading a book without a preface, the logician Michael Dummett (b.1925) once wrote, 'is like arriving at someone's house for dinner, and being conducted straight into the dining-room'. No one is required to read it, but a reader 'who wants to be personally introduced has ... the right to be'.[4] Even an impersonal history needs a personal note to set off the rest; even Oxford's short, packed terms have room for a 'noughth' week, when introductions are made, and the quaint ways of a strange town explained to the newcomer.

This book is a history of philosophy at Oxford in the mid-twentieth century. Who would want to write the story of such a thing, and why? The question might be asked with either curiosity or disdain: disdain from those who come to the subject armed with strong prejudices, curiosity from those persuaded the history needs to be written but surprised to see it written by someone with so exotic a name.

I arrived in Oxford in 2007, on a scholarship that paid for me to do a second undergraduate degree. Having completed one already, in economics, a moderately useful subject for which I had little affection, I was resolved not to waste a chance to study something I might, recklessly, enjoy. But at that stage, 'philosophy' was a subject about which my ideas were vague and largely romantic. I had grown up in India, a country with a long and sophisticated philosophical tradition honoured today chiefly as a piece of inert heritage. One was glad to know it was there; few people were particularly inclined to study it. Still less was there any inclination to treat it as a going concern. Few universities offered it as an option, and those that did taught it as history, as if it were part of the essence of the subject that a philosopher must be not only wise but dead.

What I associated with the word philosophy was a particular quality, call it *depth*. Philosophy was (as the etymology of the Sanskrit word for it suggests) *vision*, the philosopher a sort of seer (or, see-er). Abstraction was the mark of philosophy, and outlandishness the sign of a philosophical claim worth taking seriously, the more radical its rejection of common sense the better. I was drawn, before I had read very much of it, to a view of philosophy as mystery, as poetry, as paradox. The idea that philosophy was about solving problems – as in, say, trigonometry – would have struck me then as both vulgar and silly.

My undergraduate tutor at Oxford did not share my view. He picked on what I had thought an innocuous line in an essay. 'Now what *exactly* do you mean by … ?' I cannot remember the sentence that provoked the question. It was probably the sort of thing I used to think made for a good, a philosophical, sentence: figurative, allusive, oblique, long, and entirely indeterminate in meaning. I offered up my paraphrase, equally figurative, allusive, etc. 'But what does that mean, *literally*?'

'Well,' I said, being young, a little cocky and very ignorant. 'Aren't these sorts of things essentially … *ineffable*?' He paused, as one might at a swear word from an altar-boy. Then, shortly, 'On the contrary, these sorts of things are *entirely* and *eminently* effable. And I should be *very* grateful if you'd try to eff a few of them for your essay next week.'

How I resented it at the time. The demand for the explicit statement of theses, for arguments laid out in steps, for claims backed up with evidence, all felt like they belonged to the world of economists, accountants and engineers that I had hoped to leave behind. Why must essays have these unimaginative structures, giving away the game at the start? And why the infernal symbolism, all Greek letters and arrows pointing both ways?

Because I was earnest and anxious to please, I did as I was told. It helped a little that I had a native impulse to pedantry that could be put to useful work. My essays became tamer and shed their attempts at poetry. There was a great deal more 'I shall argue that' and rather less mystery. That much was part of a quite familiar undergraduate experience, of learning the rules of a game, the conventions of a genre, the norms of a discipline. But there was something else about these norms that I resented: their

3

insistence on making flights of philosophical fancy accountable to something variously called (impressively) 'intuition', (earthily) 'common sense' and (prosaically) 'the ordinary'. The idea that philosophy might have to doff its cap to such things was, to me, not so much objectionable as contradictory. It was as if the queen had to seek permission to rule from a mere pawn, or – to change the metaphor – as if the astronomer had to run his calculations by the local palm-reader.

Week after week, I had it put to me that the views I was defending – with increasing confidence and adeptness – didn't ring true. That the man or woman on the street would find them absurd. That they were pushing against the boundaries of what our words usually meant. My essays came back with dozens of little scribbles in the margins – '"the" or "a"?', 'necessary or sufficient?', 'does this really follow?', 'loose', 'obscure' and (most damningly of all) 'unclear'. These criticisms were delivered with the wit and gentle English cruelty that made them hard to ignore. My reports ended with sentences like, 'Mr K. is yet to learn the difference between truth and beauty, open-mindedness and vacillation, the provocative and the absurd.' Here, I found myself not an outsider to philosophical conventions so much as on one side of an old disagreement about philosophy itself.

I found the point well stated in an essay by the philosopher-novelist Iris Murdoch, in whose divided self I found my own ambivalences reflected. 'There is a two-way movement in philosophy,' she wrote, 'a movement towards the building of elaborate theories, and a move back again towards the consideration of simple and obvious facts. McTaggart says that time is unreal, Moore replies that he has just had his breakfast. Both these aspects of philosophy are necessary to it.'[5] I did not then know who McTaggart and Moore were; I thought perhaps they might be dummy names, variations on the generic 'Jones' and 'Smith' familiar from the reading list.

I suppose that what I was rejecting was the idea that Murdoch had put so well: that philosophy is flight of fancy as well as curt reminder. I desired the fantasy and resented the grunt work, and most of all, the idea of having to be accountable to so lowly a thing as common sense. Today, many years of education later, I teach students in whom I recognise some of my own impulses. And now, it is me with the gentle put-downs, the red pen running wild in the margin of essays that tell me how ineffable it all is.

I had thought, in my initial resentment, that my tutors were telling me, absurdly, that nothing was ineffable, that everything could be put into sentences that might be written by a well-trained bureaucrat. That claim would have been a mistake, but that wasn't their point. Some things may well be impossible to put into words. But most of us are bad at telling those things apart from the ones we simply haven't yet found the right words for – because we lack the wisdom, the clarity of vision, or perhaps the purity of heart. That was the moral lesson of my cruel tutelage, and it was several more years before I understood that a *moral* lesson is what it had been.

Plato, of course, had anticipated it all a couple of thousand years ago. It now seems to me grimly ironic that the scene had to be re-enacted before its lessons could be absorbed. So many of Plato's dialogues are versions of the same parable of the older man and the younger. Old Socrates claims to know nothing at all and speaks only in questions; the young man blithely professes knowledge of all the answers. It takes him a while to learn he should not be so blithe.

The young man is exposed for not knowing what he claims to know. But something else is also exposed, something about the distinctive style of the philosopher. What must have struck the cocky youths in their first encounters with Socrates is the unsettling effect of being taken at their word; not at being taken seriously – rich and glib, they were used to that – but at being taken literally.

The second surprise was that of being called to account.

Philosophical questions – are we free? can we know? – seem accountable to nothing. What conceivable experiment could prove, or disprove, an answer? How would we even know if we got it wrong? Moreover, little seems to hang on getting the right answer. Indeed, the very idea of a right answer seems to bring in standards improper to a question of that kind. The natural temptation is to take the question not as a request for a straight answer, but as an invitation to be interesting. Before one has been exposed to Socrates's questions, it is natural to think that the only demands philosophical chat makes are expressive ones. The most common folk model of the philosopher's style is not that of the weatherman telling you to leave your umbrella at home, but that of the oracle, whose power relies on its every utterance being able to mean itself, its opposite and everything in between. The folk idea of philosophy, sometimes to the credit of the subject and sometimes to its discredit, finds its essence in complexity and ambiguity, not in simplicity and clarity.

The peculiarity of Socrates, and what people must have thought his vulgarity, lay in his insistence that we say no more and no less than we mean. Also in his insistence that we stand by what we have said, until we can no longer mean it. A Socratic education in philosophy is, above all, an education in responsibility. I had thought at first that the technicality of the philosophy I was being taught, its desperate fealty to common sense and its clinical literal-mindedness were signs of its betrayal of the Socratic legacy to which it laid claim. I was wrong.

*

This book is a history of something sometimes called 'linguistic philosophy', or – to a use a term in one way broader and in another narrower – 'analytic philosophy'. More precisely, it is a history of some strains of this style of philosophy, as practised by a dozen or so figures at Oxford between 1920 and 1960. On any account, that style took a central concern of philosophy to be language. Most people in that tradition had high hopes for a philosophy done in that style, most ambitiously, that their new linguistic methods would simply 'dissolve' traditional philosophical problems. Even those without such ambitions shared a commitment to using language in a distinctive way: as free of jargon as possible, and with a vigilance to subtle verbal distinctions that outsiders couldn't always distinguish from pedantry.

As in any intellectual tradition, the differences within it are as significant as the differences between it and its rivals. Where it is debatable whether some particular figure or text belongs in this tradition, I have erred on the side of inclusion. I tend to take the view that a tradition is composed of both establishment and rebel, legitimate heir and pretender. A tradition without a heterodoxy is only half a tradition.

The reader should be warned that most of the figures in this tradition were white men, most of them at least middle class, their cosy common-room repartee only occasionally disrupted by the appearance of a woman, or an émigré from central Europe. Under whatever name, linguistic philosophy – or something descended from it – still dominates the academic philosophy of the English-speaking world. Rumour has it that brave evangelists have even managed to find converts in deepest France. In any case, it was – or had shaped – the kind of philosophy that I was taught to do, the kind that I in my turn teach my own students.

I have tried to keep the story short, which has meant leaving out many books and many people.[6] Not all have received their due; in particular, there is a good deal more to be said about the *arguments* of the philosophers than I have said here. But there are many books that cover the texts and arguments, rather fewer that make anything of what is called the human drama of the story.[7] I have tried to make more of that drama, if only as compensation for the cold impersonality of the conventional histories, where idea communes with idea, argument clashes with argument, without anyone having to stop for lunch. Because it is roughly chronological, this book cannot avoid being a work in two parts: one part full of travel and youthful uncertainty, the other full of men and women in their thirties and forties settling down to write the books and essays that have been many years in the making. What I have sacrificed in depth and detail, I hope to have gained in scale and pace. If I am not always explicit in my defence of a particular interpretation of this history, it is because I hope to allow my readers to spot the patterns for themselves.

That phrase – 'Oxford philosophy' – evokes something of a bygone age, the age commemorated in the row of photographic portraits in the seminar room (the 'Ryle Room') at 10 Merton Street where I spent so many hours of my youth, and the crisp English names of the philosophers under them: Ryle, Foot, Strawson, Anscombe … But by the time I got there, the subjects of the portraits were all dead or dying. The elbow patches of the old days were gone, as were the patrician vowels and the smoke that made Oxford philosophy the thing it was.

In the beginning, I found it a nuisance to be surrounded by people for whom 'Gilbert' and 'Philippa' and 'Peter' and 'Elizabeth' (and others you will meet in the following pages) were not only items in a bibliography but the names of teachers, friends and unforgiven nemeses. Now, I'm rather inclined to make a virtue of my never having met them. Coming to this terrain from another country, another language, and another generation, I have ended up feeling something like the proprietary entitlement to it that Jorge Luis Borges, speaking as an Argentine, felt about all Western culture: 'We have a right to this tradition, greater than that which the inhabitants of one or another Western nation might have.'[8]

The sense of a proprietary right came to me in slow degrees, beginning in resentment and culminating in an affection and loyalty that are all the fiercer for having come so slowly. I wouldn't want to tell the story of people I did not like, or at least like to read. Nor, equally, would I be able to write about people against whom I refused to hear an ill word. I can't claim to be impartial about Oxford philosophy. It has made me, to the point that I couldn't reject it as worthless without rejecting myself with it. But I do believe I possess what Susan Sontag once said was an essential qualification in the historian of a sensibility: 'a deep sympathy modified by revulsion'.[9] I needn't say that the sympathy heavily outweighs the revulsion. But I hope to have given the prosecution all the evidence it needs to make the case on the other side.

The critics shall, then, have their due. But the many people who have decried Oxford philosophy have decried it for different and often incompatible reasons. Oxford philosophy, it has been said, was pedantic yet amateurish, made a fetish of science yet showed an ignorance of it, was too secular, too reductively materialist, too reactionary and somehow also too blandly moderate. The critics can't, surely, *all* be right.

Others before me have defended Oxford philosophy against these charges.[10] But there is a specific sort of critic who has not, to my knowledge, been adequately addressed. The sort of critics I have in mind hold Oxford philosophy up to standards of a broadly humanistic sort. Their challenge to this philosophy is that it fails to be humane, as philosophy ought to be: to provide insight into something called 'the human condition'. To critics of this stripe, Oxford philosophy's emphasis on questions of language and meaning, its disclaiming of the speculative ('metaphysical') aims of the philosophy that came before it, are a betrayal of the tradition whose name it claims for itself.

The critics appeal to a standard I share, and they are certainly right to find particular works in this tradition wanting. But I think they are quite wrong in their stronger criticism that nothing in this tradition *could* ever answer to these humanistic standards. I want to say something in defence of Oxford philosophy that isn't typically said of it. I want to praise it for a quality it has never claimed for itself: that of being edifying.

I admit this is a peculiar strategy, a little like praising the

Spanish Inquisition for its clemency. Few people have come away from reading the philosophy of this period with a sense of having been edified. I suppose I think such readers are missing something important about it. I was one of those who was improved, morally and (one might say) spiritually, by my immersion in the philosophy of this period.

One of the understated heroes of the following pages, J. L. Austin, is best known for what he did to sharpen our eyes to the difference between what one says, what one does in saying it, and what one's saying it brings about. 'Fire' can be the name of one of the elements, a warning to leave the theatre, and the inadvertent cause of a stampede. In the same spirit, I am interested not only in what the Oxford philosophers in my story were saying but also in what they were doing in saying it and what their saying it brought about. Oxford philosophers rarely claimed to do more than clarify a couple of ideas, to make a couple of distinctions. But I shall be arguing that they delivered vastly more than the little they promised. Some philosophy can edify without meaning to. Indeed, some philosophy is all the *more* edifying for not trying to be anything of the sort.

I need to convince humanistic critics of Oxford philosophy to accept an unfamiliar description of it. The trouble is that Oxford philosophy comes, to such readers, weighted with a received interpretation. According to the received view, Oxford philosophy is the most regrettable stage in a regrettable shift in the history of philosophy: the 'linguistic turn'. At a certain point in the nineteenth century, European philosophers decided to abandon the worthy metaphysical speculations of their predecessors and to turn their attentions instead to the *language* of that speculation. In the beginning, the 'turn' produced a certain amount of ingenious technical achievement in symbolic logic and the foundations of mathematics. In the form it took in inter-war Austria, the 'turn' had the modest effect of getting philosophers to think seriously about the significance of scientific discoveries. But by the time the 'turn' reached Oxford, it had been reduced to a debased kind of amateur linguistics that could keep the Bertie Woosterish types who practised it occupied in verbal puzzles while fancying themselves the inheritors of the Socratic mantle. Only the conceit, the imperial hubris of its practitioners – upper middle class, and privately educated nearly to a (white) man – could have sustained them in this delusion.

For now I shall do no more than propose an alternative description of the same tradition. My own origins, in a world utterly unlike mid-century Oxford, make it hard for me to take seriously the idea that its appeal must be restricted to the white and expensively educated. Moreover, the notion of a 'linguistic turn' is in my view a red herring. The idea of a 'turn' is only one of many ways in which the story can be told; my reservations about the conventional way of telling that story come down to the fact that it obscures the many continuities between what came before the turn and what came after.

My own view is that Oxford philosophy was just one more stage in the slow evolution of a basically Socratic picture of philosophy, one that views philosophy as concerned with the pursuit of truth through rigorous, self-aware dialogue. That original picture, captured in Plato's famous depictions of Socrates interrogating young Athenians about their beliefs, adapted like any living tradition to the demands and structures of modernity. Like Socrates did in his day, the tradition distinguished itself from the sophists and rhetoricians of its own. The central idea in this tradition is that of *philosophy as responsible speech*, and of *responsibility as accountability*.

The challenge of philosophy is that the standards of argument themselves are up for grabs. By contrast, modern science in its everyday form makes itself accountable to the results of experiments and the law makes itself accountable to authorities. Nothing in philosophy counts uncontroversially as either an experiment or an authority. What then makes one philosophical claim any worthier of assent than any other? The 'linguistic turn' proposed a sort of answer: at the very least, what we *should* say should be held accountable to what we *do* say.

To put it another way, I propose to understand Oxford philosophy not in terms of shared doctrines (there were none), nor a shared canon (always contested), or a shared 'methodology' (the very word would have induced nausea). I propose to understand it in terms of the particular virtues it aspired to embody. Some of these virtues were, by any reckoning, moral ones: humility, self-awareness, collegiality, restraint. Others are better thought aesthetic: elegance, concision, directness.

The greatest works of this tradition, which you shall meet in the following pages, are some of the great works of twentieth-century literature. In them, abstraction is balanced by a striking attention to particulars, impersonality by moments of dramatic individuality. There are passages in them that have moved me as much as anything in music or poetry, and they possess the power to move or enthral because of, and not despite, the constraints under which their authors labour. If one wants a low-brow example, one might consider a claim that has been made about the fiction of Agatha Christie: that in her love of formal complexity, her perfunctory way with traditional ideas of character and incident, the endless range of experiments she pulled off even within a circumscribed world of vicars and village gossips, she belongs with Gertrude Stein, Virginia Woolf and James Joyce.[11]

For a higher-brow example, one might turn to such composers as Bach and Schoenberg, about whom it has been suggested that their achievement consisted in reconciling the apparent tension between the baroquely formal and freely expressive. The closest analogy I can find in my own experience is that of classical Indian music, especially in the highly formalistic southern variation that I studied in my childhood: 'It is strange, but right,' says one writer of this music, 'to think of ecstasy not as a function of breaking out (as the Greek word would suggest) but as breaking *into* bonds.'[12] There are passages in *The Concept of Mind, Sense and Sensibilia, Intention* and *Individuals* – to name only four of the books I shall discuss in these pages – for whose effect there is no better analogy.[13]

To put the same point another way, this is a history of philosophy written as a history of people, their dispositions, their habits, or more precisely what the French sociologist Pierre Bourdieu called a *habitus*: their habits of thought, speech, accent, cadence, their physical postures as they walked and talked and wrote, and their more abstract habits: how they saw, heard, felt.[14] Its basic unit of organisation is not the argument but the anecdote, and what it is concerned to understand is not just what people thought but what they were like. I should be happy if some readers finish the book finding themselves agreeing with some of their conclusions or persuaded by some of their arguments, but I should be happier still if they came away simply admiring them.

1

Fog

Gilbert Ryle (b.1900), the first-born of the protagonists of this story, grew up in Sussex, sunniest of English counties. In later life, he told a sort of origin story for himself. A bright young schoolmaster at young Ryle's school, just 'down from Oxford', asked his class the kind of question Socrates would have relished: 'What is colour?' 'Paint,' replied one unassuming lad. Ryle smirked knowingly. Asked if he could do better, he said something to the effect that a colour is the power of an object to produce a certain kind of sensation in us. It was what, a few years later, he knew to call 'a Lockean sort of answer'. 'I scored five marks for my sapience,' the grown-up know-it-all recalled in his memoir.[1]

Ryle belonged to a generation of men who had just started to call each other by their Christian names, but he was inconsistent on the matter.[2] We had better play it safe and call him 'Ryle'. His grandfather was the first bishop of Liverpool, and the author of a steady stream of readable theological treatises with titles like *Knots Untied*. Old Bishop Ryle sought salvation in the Word of God, 'the Word made clear to the head and applied to the heart'.[3] Woolliness was the chief instrument of the devil, his way of dividing Christian from Christian; God's work called for his servants to do better. 'If men would only define with precision the theological terms which they use, many disputes would die. Scores of excited disputants would discover ... that their disputes have arisen from their own neglect of the great duty of explaining the meaning of words.'[4]

He managed to raise an agnostic son – Gilbert's father – who became a prosperous general practitioner with a sideline in philosophical speculation; he was one of the early members of the Aristotelian Society. His own ten children, clever and variously gifted, never had a faith to lose. Gilbert Ryle repudiated the evangelical inheritance but imbibed the family manner and always wrote in the punchy style of his grandfather.

He was born in the late summer of 1900, a lucky year to be born an English boy. Just a year older and there was every chance that he would have been one of the 149 boys from Brighton College who died at Ypres, the Somme or in Palestine, and whose deaths were announced at school assembly. As it was, Ryle survived, eighteen years old at the Armistice, and ready to head for – or 'go up to' – Oxford, armed with the confidence of a happy childhood spent under a Brighton sun.[5]

His Oxford college was Queen's, on the High Street, dubbed by Pevsner 'the grandest piece of classical architecture in Oxford', a product of 'the short phase which one has a right to name English Baroque, i.e. Baroque with English reservations'.[6] A surviving photograph of Ryle in his twenties could be that of an officer on leave, or a young schoolmaster capable of going from joshing to sternness in a blink. His jaw is set, his eyes hardened; the high forehead portends the baldness of middle age. The one decorative touch is the wet gloss of the Macassar oil holding his immaculate side parting in place.

The degree for which he was 'reading' was Literae Humaniores, with its two phases, 'Moderations' and 'Greats'. Mods – Oxford leaves nothing serious without a nickname – ended with a gruelling set of exams, two a day on average, in Greek and Latin language and literature. It has been said that only the ten-day ordeal that is the Chinese civil service entrance exam is harder. Ryle was half-hearted for those first five terms, a succession of eight intense weeks punctuated with long vacations. He achieved distinction as a rower, rising, as he later put it, 'to the giddy height of Captain of Boats'. But he found also that he 'lacked the ear, the nostrils, the palate, and the toe' of the real classical scholar.[7] It didn't stop him getting a first-class degree anyway, in the only way one is supposed to get a first at Oxford: without trying.

Ryle's one early classical love was Aristophanes, whose bawdy plays spared no one but were especially rude about philosophers. (Socrates in *The Clouds* is mostly interested in examining the rear end of a gnat.) His other early love was logic, 'a grown-up subject, in which there were still unsolved problems'.[8] 'Unsolved' meant, among other things, that the only advantage the old had over the young was that of having had longer to think about the questions.

Greats was a peculiar and somewhat unsystematic coupling of history (ancient Greek and Roman) with philosophy (ancient and modern). Ryle 'did think that the Academy mattered more than the Peloponnesian War' – the Academy in question being Plato's original – but was left cold by his tutors' attitude to the *Republic*. They treated it, he recalled, 'like the Bible, and to me most of it seemed, philosophically, no better'.[9]

His tutor at Queen's was Herbert James 'Hamish' Paton (b.1887), a Glaswegian in his early thirties who had arrived in Oxford on a seventeenth-century scholarship that had once been held by Adam Smith. Paton had a keen but, as Ryle remembered it, 'unfanatical' interest in the philosophy of an Italian contemporary, Benedetto Croce (b.1866), himself an unfanatical follower of Hegel (b.1770).[10] Hegel's cult in Germany had tended – or so it certainly seemed in England – to fanaticism of one kind or another. But Croce, by then the author of a sprightly little book called *What Is Living and What Is Dead of the Philosophy of Hegel*, preferred the Hegel who decried the more mystical sort of philosophy, 'with its frenzies, its sighing, its raising the eyes to heaven, its bowing the neck and clasping the hands, its faintings, its prophetic accents, its mysterious phrases of the initiates'. No, said Hegel-as-presented-by-Croce, 'philosophy should have a rational and intelligible form'. It should be 'exoteric', that is to say open to public interpretation, 'not a thing of sects, but of humanity'.[11]

When Ryle started at Oxford, Paton was just returning from Versailles, where he had attended the Paris Peace Conference as an expert on Polish matters. He had picked up his expertise as a member of the intelligence division of the Admiralty, where he, like a few other lucky dons of the decade who managed never to see the inside of a trench, had spent his war years. His students often found him 'unforthcoming', but that could mean simply that he refused to give them the answers.[12]

Not giving students the answers was at the heart of the distinctive style of teaching Ryle would have encountered at Oxford. From being one of a few dozen boys at Brighton College, he found himself alone in a study with Paton – or occasionally, with one other student – with his opinions being given the closest attention by someone vastly better informed on the subject. There have always been many ways of running an Oxford tutorial, but Paton's model for the task was that of the courtroom cross-examiner. Ryle was among the few to find provocation and excitement in his almost-catchphrase, 'Now, Ryle, what *exactly* do you mean by ... ?'[13]

*

Ryle was lucky to have had Paton easing his path into philosophy and Oxford. Paton was one of the few members of 'the lost generation' to be found in the senior common rooms of Oxford in the early 1920s. R. G. Collingwood (b.1889) was one of the few others; as Paton's memoir had it, 'generals had not then discovered that brains may have a greater military value than can be displayed in trench warfare by platoon commanders'.[14] The two of them were 'a slender bridge between predecessors at least ten years older and successors at least ten years younger'.[15] 'For good and for ill', Ryle remembers 'the traditions and the habits of pre-1914 Oxford philosophers were, by say 1925, hanging by a very thin thread.'[16]

In Ryle's remembering of the twenties, 'the philosophic kettle in Oxford was barely lukewarm'.[17] This was in spite of the presence there of sectarians of at least three stripes. And in other climes, the battle between sharply distinct worldviews is the stuff of *Sturm*, *Drang* and excited undergraduates. There was that lonely 'pragmatist', F. C. S. Schiller (b.1864) at Corpus Christi, who took truth to be a matter of practical usefulness and devoted himself to such useful tasks as managing the finances of the Mind Association (formed to oversee the running of the flourishing journal of the same name), ghost-hunting (still a respectable occupation for gentlemen), and the sterilisation of the poor. Then there were the last of the Victorian 'idealist' metaphysicians, greatly interested in the gap between Appearance and Reality, the manifold and the Absolute (and much given to Germanic capitals). At its ascendant in the nineteenth century, idealism spoke in the inspiring tones of Thomas Hill Green (b.1836), much loved by his students for liberating them, as one put it, 'from the fear of agnostic mechanism. He gave us back the language of self-sacrifice, and taught us how we belonged to one another in the one life of high idealism. We took life from him at its spiritual value.'[18]

The philosophical, argumentative voice of British idealism was that of Francis Herbert Bradley (b.1846), who declared in 1893 that 'reality is sentient experience'. The famous lines continue: 'What I repudiate is the separation of feeling from the felt, or of the desired from desire, or what is thought from thinking or the division ... of anything from anything else.'[19]

Reality, Bradley was saying, is not something distinct from and outside the mind; the mistake of both philosophy and 'common sense' (which is almost as bad) is to separate the inseparable. In his youth, he was a formidable polemicist and a stylist of great talent. But Bradley had by 1920 turned into a recluse, his ears and kidneys failing, his polemical instincts sublimated in armed nocturnal expeditions around the grounds of Merton College that ended in a tally of dead cats. (He loved birds.)[20] Collingwood, a kindred spirit who 'lived within a few hundred yards of him for sixteen years', didn't see him at all; Ryle saw him once, but they said nothing to each other.[21]

Certainly, there were such figures as Paton and Collingwood, and some of their teachers keeping the old Bradleian spirit, if not the old Bradleian fire, alive, but they seemed, even to a sympathetic Collingwood, 'the *epigoni* of a great movement; and like all *epigoni* they felt that what needed to be said had been said, and need not be repeated'.[22]

The whole set of them would get labelled 'idealists' or, worse, 'Hegelians'. The label was applied principally by sectarians of the third Oxford school: the 'realists'. At the notional head of this school was the redoubtable John Cook Wilson (b.1849) – in Collingwood's description, 'a fiery, pugnacious little man with a passion for controversy and an instinctive eye for its tactics'.[23] Cook Wilson took up what he saw as the central idealist claim: the interdependence of knower and known. As the idealists saw it, there is no reality separate from the mind – and so knowledge could not be understood as a simple matter of 'mind' coming into contact with 'world'. Among the many subtle arguments Cook Wilson presented against the idealist view, the most effective was the simplest: suppose we think of knowledge in terms of an analogy with the collision of bodies: 'the very nature of the collision between two bodies, A and B, necessitates itself that A and B should be different from one another'.[24]

This was Cook Wilson's doctrine, and the remark also embodies his unconcessive style, with its '*necessitates*' and the unnecessary algebraic notation. The style didn't make for easy reading, but the difficulty was not that of the subject matter. Cook Wilson's student and colleague H. A. Prichard (b.1871) put the point more fluently:

If there is to be knowledge, there must first *be* something to be known. In other words, knowledge is essentially discovery, or the finding of what already is. If a reality could only be or come to be in virtue of some activity or process on the part of the mind, that activity or process would not be 'knowing', but 'making' or 'creating'.[25]

A young Ryle esteemed Prichard for his provocations, his 'vehemence, tenacity, unceremoniousness, and a perverse consistency that made our hackles rise, as nothing else at that time did'.[26] He even went so far as to dub himself a 'fidgetty Cook Wilsonian'.[27] In time he would disclaim all labels, dub the standard histories of philosophy chronicles 'sham crusades', and simply dismiss those who wondered, 'How can one advance except behind a banner?'[28]

True, there had survived into the 1920s 'the tail end of a party-contest between something called "Idealism" and something called "Realism"' that the young had to make up their minds about, but the important thing to them was not what it was called.[29] Ryle had the advantage of regular challenges from his siblings, none of them philosophers but none the stupider for that. 'I remember thinking that it would be rather hard to convince my sceptical brothers that my peculiar subject of philosophy could matter very much if it only amounted to championship of realism, or alternatively, championship of idealism. They would have said, "Why not just stop bothering about both -isms?" and I pretty soon did.'[30]

'For good and for ill,' Ryle had said. His generation's 'questions, accents and impatiences' were not those of their 'pedagogic grandsires'. The 'pieties, lores, sagacities, equipments – yes, and fetishes too' of antebellum Oxford:[31] these would not make it to the other side of the 'boundless military cemetery' that separated the generations.[32] The war had had something to do with it, even for the lucky few, like Ryle, for whom it had meant not trench foot but the near-daily announcement at school assembly of another dead prefect: 'Our often brash personal ambitions, aspirations and resolutions were those of young men who knew that there might not be very much time.'[33]

Among these brash aspirations was the aspiration to write, and even the ambition to be published and read. The old tended not to trouble themselves with such vanity; every word published was another confession of vulgarity. 'The (printed) letter killeth,' Cook Wilson had said. An encomium for a recently deceased colleague, H. W. B. Joseph (b.1867), read: 'His best memorial, unlike that of many other teachers, perhaps consists in the books that his pupils refrained from writing.'[34]

This suspicion of the written word goes back, like so much else in the period, to a belief put into Socrates's mouth in Plato's dialogue the *Phaedrus* that philosophy is *too* accessible when written down, even to those 'who have no business with it'. Much better 'the living, breathing discourse of the man who knows', a discourse written down only figuratively, 'in the soul of the listener'.[35] Plato's chosen form, the Socratic dialogue, may have been an attempt to square the circle: to write, but only as a way to evoke that superior thing, conversation.

Conversation, rather than mere speech, was the thing. Were it otherwise, philosophers might have made more of that other possibility for quasi-publication: the lecture. But lectures were never popular at either Oxford or Cambridge, possibly because it was never made in anyone's interests to do them better: no lecturer's job depended on his lectures being well attended, and no undergraduate's examination results depended on his having attended the lecture. Yet they persisted. Maybe to abolish them just because no one attended them would have set a dangerous precedent.

At Cambridge, the lecture had formidable opponents: the academic reformer Henry Sidgwick (b.1838) had made the case for getting rid of them, or at any rate, for transforming them into something more Socratic. But the most he managed to achieve was the reform of the supervision (the Cambridge word for the tutorial), from another occasion to deliver an impromptu lecture to a chance for a confusion to be clarified. Progress in philosophy, he wrote, came from 'stating perplexities clearly and precisely. The art that has to be learnt in order to achieve this result has been called the art of "concentrating fog".'[36]

Intellectual fogs, said Sidgwick, were 'liable rapidly to envelop large portions of a subject'. The pedagogical challenge was not to dispel it – an impossible task – but simply 'to concentrate it'. How did one do that? By forcing the student 'to state the difficulty on paper. Sometimes, in the mere process of writing it down, the difficulty will disappear like the morning mist, one does not know how.'[37]

But the writing down had never been the point. The ulterior aim of the exercise was a clearing of the mind, and minds could be cleared as well in a sentence spoken as in one written down. But either way, it was the undergraduate and not the don who spoke first; and in this, too, the tutorial encounter was, and was recognised to be, Socratic.

The temptation among the dons to play Socrates must have been strong. The tutorial system at Oxford certainly encouraged the image: the old man in conversation with the young; wisdom and naïvety; sophistication and earnestness. The tutorial was supposed to be, and in the hands of some dons succeeded in being, co-operative. But other conversational practices existed, especially when the match was between supposed equals. These non-tutorial conversations were reminiscent not of a friendly chat with Socrates but of the pseudo-gladiatorial practices of ancient 'dialectic'. But antagonistic or not, the idea was that philosophy thrives in conversation.

Sometimes, the conversation needed kindling, and the job was done by the student's essay, placed in the don's college pigeonhole a few hours earlier or, more likely, read out during the tutorial itself. But the essay wasn't the point: it served the same function as the naïve remark of one of Socrates's young interlocutors that sets off the dialogue that bears his name. 'Knowledge is perception,' says Theaetetus. Is it then? Socrates wonders.[38] And off we go, on a journey of clarification, counterexample, objection, until we're left with our original question, 'What is knowledge?', knowing only that we don't know the answer.

The institution of the tutorial had, notoriously, erotic possibilities (Plato makes much of them). But there is little evidence that the Oxford philosophers of the early twentieth century ever availed themselves of what opportunities the tutorial system afforded them. Tutorials were a lot of work. Many a philosopher's obituary noted, with a combination of envy, pride and pity, the sheer number of hours he had devoted to delivering them. Such discipline made enormous demands on body and soul, 'even of the most robust' (latter-day practitioners will confirm that it still does).[39] But the focus on tutorials tended to encourage 'the belief that philosophy lives in the intercourse of mind with mind rather than in books and systems'. There's something to that, though it did tend to 'lead to a dangerous dissipation of effort'.[40] To put it more bluntly, tutorials often proved a terrible (and expensive) waste of time, conveying in an intimate setting with a senior statesman what could have been done as well or better in a lecture delivered by a competent journeyman.

The ubiquity of the tutorial also had a dangerous effect on people's conceptions of getting it right. 'It is far too easy', Paton wrote, 'for a body of clever men … to arrive after discussion at some conclusion which they take to be final.'[41] It had an equally chilling effect on people's anxieties about getting it wrong: 'The practice of dialectic may also become too gladiatorial and may produce in the timid a fear of publication which naturally increases with advance in years and in local repute.'[42] And the thing devolves into a vicious circle: one is too exhausted to think a new thought, and so one fears to write; in panic at the thought of not writing, one takes on more teaching to fill up the evening hours. The tutorial system had much to answer for, for good and for ill, and it didn't get better with the changing of the guard.

＊

Ryle triumphed at Greats; so much so that he was asked to stay on for a couple of years and sit the exams for a new degree course, to set the standard for a first-class performance in 'Modern Greats', or 'Philosophy, Politics and Economics'. Oxford had started to admit students to read PPE in 1920; the first students arrived in the Michaelmas – autumn – term of 1921, and in 1924 were preparing to take their final exams. The demand for such a course had been felt for a while, not least among the philosophers of Oxford. J. A. Smith (b.1863) – Paton's old tutor at Balliol College – was the likely author of an anonymous pamphlet published in 1909 titled *Wanted! A New School at Oxford*.

'School' was being used in its Oxford sense of 'degree course'. The pamphleteer made the case for taking philosophy to the Greekless. Philosophy, the pamphlet said, 'alone forces on the mind a systematic analysis of the ordinary terms employed'.[43] And in so much of life, and more to the point, in much of politics, 'the common disputes and misunderstandings are due to the absence of the habits of mind thus produced'.[44] Why restrict the opportunity for acquiring these happy dispositions to those who wish to study – and are therefore required already to know – ancient Greek?

The author noted, dispassionately, that 'in increasing numbers men are coming up to Oxford with but a very slight knowledge of Greek', and they were choosing – alas – history. Which meant that 'a large and growing number even of those who would profit most by an element of Philosophy in their education are deprived of all chance of receiving it'.[45] But what of the old Greats? Well, those who wanted to study Greek and Latin would do it anyway, having been prepared for it through years of schooling. And would this draw students away from history? Perhaps, the pamphleteer conceded. But the champions of history had it easy: 'Nothing will be easier than to appeal to the rooted distrust of Philosophy and Logic which the British parent shares with the greater part of the nation.'[46] And thus, ten years later – lightning quick for Oxford – the promulgation of that fateful regulation, Statt. Tit. VI. Sect. 1 C: 'The subject of the Honour School of Philosophy, Politics, and Economics shall be the study of the structure, and the philosophical and economic principles, of Modern Society.'[47]

The new school would come to be the salvation of Oxford philosophy, it having hitched its wagon to the newly ascendant disciplines of economics and politics and advertised itself as essential training for the future statesman, civil servant and man-about-the-empire. The advertising was not blatantly false, nor did the advocates for it seem insincere, but the point, debatable from the start, seems to have been widely accepted.

More students meant more jobs for teachers. Ryle, without a postgraduate qualification to his name, graduated straight into a job as lecturer at Christ Church. His new college lay a little way down and off the High Street from Queen's, where it occupied an idyllic expanse of land along the Isis, the name the Thames takes for the first part of its course. The retirement of the senior philosophy tutor there put Ryle in charge of the teaching of philosophy in the college. Now himself a don, Ryle attended the weekly Thursday Teas where the Prichards and Cook Wilsons and the other philosophers of their generation prosecuted the old battles over crumpets at four o'clock. The meetings were 'crowded and hurried'. By the time the crumpets had gone around and the tea had been poured, it was already half past four, and that left twenty minutes before the junior dons had to rush off for their five-to-seven tutorial shift. The younger philosophers rarely felt emboldened to make more than the occasional deferential remark.[48]

'One couldn't start,' Ryle complained, 'or anyhow maintain, a discussion about anything without the subject being changed before long to "Which dialogue did Plato say that in and did he really mean it?" and "Could the Greek be interpreted in another way?"[49] The 'great and glorious dead' haunted the living, and no one was quite ready to exorcise their spirits from the conversation. There were rumours that things were done differently at Cambridge; the names of men called Russell and Moore came up every now and then, talk of developments in something called 'symbolic logic', and there were murmurs that a certain young man of Austrian extraction had written an interesting book – a *Tractatus* something-or-other. A young Welshman and contemporary of Ryle's, Henry Price (b.1899), had gone so far as to visit the other place to find out if the rumours were true. But there was no appetite for news from Cambridge at Thursday Tea. If the old logic had been good enough for Aristotle, it was good enough for Oxford.

Ryle and Price were freer to speak when the elders were tucked safely into their beds, and the tables stacked with better food and stiffer drinks. This happened at the fortnightly gathering of younger philosophers in a club that called itself the Wee Teas (a donnish joke playing on the folksy name for the Free Church of Scotland – 'the Wee Frees'). One fellow had to host the dinner and stand the drinks (beer, not wine, and never more than three courses). After everyone was properly lubricated, the host gave a paper, and then the discussion began. 'Our tongues wagged more freely and our wits moved less deferentially,' Ryle said.[50] The Wee Teas, over the course of their forty years of existence, had many influential members. Other than Price, there was Frank Hardie (b.1902), later the author of two fine books on Plato and Aristotle; and in subsequent years, they would be joined by William Kneale (b.1906), who would write, with his wife the Leibniz scholar Martha Kneale (b.1909), an authoritative history of logic; John Mabbott (b.1898), who would be Ryle's ally in the reform of postgraduate education at Oxford; and Oliver Franks (b.1905), a philosopher who could never resist the call to public service and served, at one point or another, as 'don, mandarin, diplomat, banker, provost, pillar of state'.[51]

Also among the original Wee Teas was a man better known for his connections to a different donnish club. But the time that C. S. Lewis (b.1898) spent with a literary group called the Inklings – and the association with J. R. R. Tolkien (b.1892) – would come a little later. Lewis was a couple of years older than Ryle and had shown similar academic promise as an undergraduate studying Classics and philosophy. Where Ryle had gone in for an additional couple of years of politics and economics, Lewis did a further year of English language and literature (like PPE, a relatively new subject at Oxford and regarded with comparable disdain). Appointed first to teach philosophy at University College, where he had been an undergraduate, he eventually became fellow and tutor in English at Magdalen College, where he stayed for the next thirty years.

The Wee Teas had the same spirit of 'absolute candour' as the Conversazione Society of Cambridge, better known as the Apostles. In the words of Henry Sidgwick, writing in the last years of the nineteenth century, its spirit was that of 'the pursuit of truth with absolute devotion and unreserve by a group of intimate friends, who were perfectly frank with each other, and indulged in any amount of humorous sarcasm and playful banter, and yet each respects the other, and when he discourses tries to learn from him and see what he sees'.[52] 'We never aimed at unanimity,' said Ryle of the Wee Teas, 'or achieved it; but we could try out anything on one another without anyone being shocked or rude or polite. Each of us had five friends and no allies.'[53] The Wee Teas had no idealists, no realists, indeed no permanent factions and no 'hustings-words'. Friendship, as Lewis would write, begins with the thought, 'What? You too? I thought I was the only one.'[54] 'We discovered', said Ryle, 'that it was possible to be at once in earnest and happy.'[55] Only his marriage, John Mabbott said, had been happier.[56]

The early years of the Wee Teas coincided with those in which the beginning sections of Evelyn Waugh's *Brideshead Revisited* are set. The Oxford of Waugh's memories – made sentimental by the privations of the war – 'was still a city of aquatint'. In autumn it was misty, in springtime grey and in summer glorious, exhaling 'the soft vapours of a thousand years of learning'.[57] The youth of Waugh's memory is the youth of young men, happiest in each other's company.

*

By the time Ryle entered the world of academic philosophy, it had already changed in one important respect. A young F. H. Bradley, not yet the cat-murderer of his dotage, lived at a time when the fellows of Oxford colleges had all been in holy orders; most undergraduates were destined for the life of the vicarage and pulpit. When Ryle became a fellow, his colleagues were scientists, mathematicians, historians and literary scholars. At Christ Church, whose chapel is also the cathedral of the Oxford diocese, there would also have been a steady stream of theologians around him, but heavily outnumbered by those teaching secular subjects. At other colleges, founded as theological institutions, it was entirely possible for there to be no theologians at all.[58] The controversies of Bradley's youth were fired by anxieties about liturgy and the origins of Christianity; when one of Ryle's colleagues talked of going over to Rome, he was likelier to be planning a holiday than a conversion.[59]

Something else had changed since the High Victorian age of Bradley's youth. John Stuart Mill, T. H. Huxley, Leslie Stephen – the leading lights of Victorian philosophy – had kept a cautious distance from the universities, and published in such organs as the *Westminster* or *Edinburgh Review*. They wrote not 'papers' but essays, and the readership they assumed was that of the educated layman. Their vocabularies were wide but untechnical, their syntax complex but idiosyncratic. They had individual styles that no teacher had tried to clip according to the demands of some disciplinary convention.

By the mid-1920s, the old Reviews were gone, or at any rate, denuded of academics, who preferred now to publish in things called 'journals'. They wrote for each other: that meant, on the one hand, the need and the tolerance for specialist vocabulary, and on the other, a deep self-consciousness about both being and seeming rigorous. Taken together, it made for a new and strikingly unessayistic style of prose. 'Eloquence will not silence rival experts and edification is not palatable to colleagues,' Ryle remarked about the shift. 'Philosophers had now to be philosophers' philosophers.'[60]

The most illustrious of the journals was *Mind*, founded in 1876 as a quarterly. The papers presented at the weekly Bloomsbury meetings of the Aristotelian Society for the Systematic Study of Philosophy were published in their annual *Proceedings*. The Mind Association and the Aristotelian Society had been teaming up since 1910 for the annual 'Joint' Sessions, held each year at a different venue. The senior Oxford philosophers rarely deigned to attend these meetings; well supplied with the audience they wanted for their philosophy at Oxford, they saw no reason to go. With Ryle and his generation, this began to change. The young dons of Oxford saw for the first time the energy of philosophy elsewhere as they met and chatted with Scottish philosophers, Irish philosophers, Welsh philosophers, even philosophers from exotic lands as far abroad as Cambridge.

From Henry Price, Ryle had already learnt of the legend of George Edward Moore (b.1873) of Trinity College, Cambridge. But the Joint Sessions gave him his first glimpse of the unicorn. 'He reminded one,' Ryle wrote in a posthumous encomium for *New Statesman*, 'in quick succession, of a Duns Scotus, a ton of bricks and one's farmer uncle on a holiday.'[61] Some saw him as a holy fool; others thought him Christ-like, or – what was to a philosopher an immeasurably higher compliment – the second coming of Socrates.[62]

His lectures at Cambridge were thought a model of the form: everything had obviously been gone through with care and attention, again and again, but the lecture itself was no mere recitation. He would arrive, a student recalled, 'with his head evidently full of the problem'.[63] Then he would abandon his manuscript and try to think through the problem afresh, on his feet before an audience. There was no explicit counsel of perfectionism, none of the sonority of the headmaster's sermon exhorting the sixth form to the pursuit of truth. He simply lived his dicta, looking for better words for his ideas, never satisfied with any formulation. What oh what was the best way of putting it? His audiences, a member recalled, 'were not left out as mere spectators, but would become caught up in his activity', each one asking himself, what oh what was the best way of putting it?[64]

In his youth, he had been a man of great, 'almost ethereal' beauty, and retained to his old age 'an extraordinarily loveable smile'.[65] But his face was capable of enormous expressiveness: an absurdity from an interlocutor could set off all his features at once, eyes opened wide, eyebrows bouncing into his hairline, tongue shooting out of his mouth. He could exhaust a whole box of matches trying to light a pipe in the middle of an argument.[66] He had no wit; no one could remember him telling a joke. His genius consisted in an instinctive grasp of what was important and what irrelevant; 'he pursued truth', said Leonard Woolf (b.1880), a Cambridge undergraduate when Moore was at the peak of his influence, 'with the tenacity of a bulldog and the integrity of a saint'.[67]

Moore had had a youthful fling – like many – with idealism in its most pungent Hegelian variety, as incarnated by the slightly older J. M. E. McTaggart (b.1866). McTaggart wore his eccentricities with pride. He rode a tricycle. He walked 'with a curious shuffle, back to the wall, as if expecting a sudden kick from behind', a fact that may or may not be explained by his having been bullied at boarding school.[68] He saluted every cat he met. His dissertation for a fellowship at Trinity, later published as *Studies in the Hegelian Dialectic*, had elicited from that older Apostle, Henry Sidgwick, the remark, 'I can see that this is nonsense, but what I want to know is whether it is the right kind of nonsense.'[69] Apparently, it was.

'How clear he was, compared to the majority of philosophers,' said Moore of McTaggart, damning with faint praise.[70] He was grateful for McTaggart's attempts to make Hegel clearer, to translate the German's vatic sonorities into sentences of clean(ish) Anglo-Saxon, and found that 'he did succeed in finding many things precise enough to be discussed'.[71] If they were precise enough to be discussed, then they were also precise enough to be refuted. C. D. ('Charlie') Broad (b.1887), McTaggart's executor, would write, 'If Hegel be the inspired and too often incoherent prophet of the Absolute, if Bradley be its chivalrous knight, McTaggart is its devoted and extremely acute family solicitor.'[72] Moore was no less acute: his own writing certainly had the flavour (as one unsympathetic reader put it) of 'a canny solicitor blocking loopholes in a piece of conveyancing'.[73]

But Moore also had a forensic persona, and his weapon in all conversations with idealists was the devastating formula: 'I *simply* don't understand *what* he means.'[74] Time, McTaggart had claimed following Bradley, was unreal.[75] Moore greeted such pronouncements with the question: what did that mean? Perhaps a translation out of the Hegelian might help. Suppose we replaced that upper-case abstraction Time with 'before', 'after', 'past', 'future', 'now', 'then'. 'If Time is unreal,' he said, 'then plainly nothing ever happens before or after anything else; ... it is never true that anything is past; never true that anything will happen in the future; never true that anything is happening now; and so on.'[76] But – and here we might imagine Moore with that seraphic smile for which he was so loved – surely it is undeniable that I had breakfast *before* I had lunch.[77] And if so, some things really do happen before others. And is there much more to the claim that time is real?

Moore wielded his naïvety like a dagger, exploding, puncturing, deflating anything he suspected of being hot air. But nothing about this was mere technique. If his literalism meant he was missing something, then he let it be known that all it would take to persuade him was a simple explanation of what he was missing. Perhaps time was unreal in some highly abstruse sense, in which case our everyday thoughts involving time are unthreatened by metaphysics. But what is this new and abstruse sense? Why use the everyday words to make an unquotidian-sounding point?

Bradley's defenders 'may say that he is using the word "real" exclusively in some highly unusual and special sense', making the apparent conflict with the commonsense view of time and its passage to be born of misunderstanding. But Moore was unpersuaded. 'What, however, I cannot help thinking is that, even if he means something more, he *does* mean what ordinary people would mean *as well*.'[78]

The words had to be simple, hence the novelty of their claims, their radicalism, their unsettling strangeness. But the arguments pointed towards some more technical, obscure point, something a long way from common sense and as such utterly unthreatening to everyday conceptions. The idealists were caught on the horns of a dilemma. Either they meant something so obscure and technical that its truth was of no real interest, or they meant something so far away from the everyday that it was impossible to accept. The plausible thesis was uninteresting, the interesting thesis implausible.

The same was true of the philosopher's nightmare, at least as old as the seventeenth century: the sceptic. What was one to say to those who denied that we could know the first thing about the 'external' world? Wouldn't the world look just the same if it were the product of a hallucination engineered by an evil demon? And what proof was there that all this – mountains, rivers, breakfasts – wasn't part of a very elaborate dream? The argument was irresistible: Only if I know I'm not being deceived by an evil demon can I know anything at all about the external world; I don't know I'm not being deceived by an evil demon. So, I don't, *can't*, know anything about the external world. Where's the flaw?

Moore had an answer. Here, he said, is a hand. And here is another.[79] That much I know. And if I know those things, I know at least two things about the external world. And if I know those things about the external world, I know I'm not being deceived about it by an evil demon. The ball was back in the sceptic's court.

No one was spared Moore's explosions of 'genial ferocity'.[80] When his brother, the poet Thomas Sturge Moore (b.1870), wrote a book containing the words 'I conceive the human reason to be the antagonist of all known forces other than itself',[81] G. E. Moore sent a letter to his fellow Apostle Leonard Woolf, then a civil servant in Ceylon, as it was, to say, 'I do wish people wouldn't write such silly things … vague, and obviously inconsequent, and full of falsehoods.' They claimed to be philosophy but really, they aspired to be, and to sound like, 'a sermon – to make you appreciate good things; and I sometimes wonder whether it is possible to do this without saying what is false. But it does annoy me terribly that people should admire such things.'[82]

Ryle found him 'a dynamo of courage': he emboldened the youth, not by letting them have an easy time of it, but by giving them exactly as hard a time as he gave everyone: the old, the famous, even himself.[83] His severity when confronted with evidence of his own past muddles was infamous. At one symposium, a speaker quoted approvingly some remarks of Moore's from an old paper. Moore admitted that the words were his, but announced that he thought it a shame that the symposiasts were expending so much attention on them. For one thing, he simply couldn't understand what his younger self had been on about. To the extent that he could understand them, the words seemed to him simply false. What *had* he been thinking? At lecture after lecture, the voice of dissatisfaction sounded.[84]

The demand to make oneself clear could not, as such, have been new to Ryle, a veteran of Paton's persistent question, 'Now Ryle, what *exactly* do you mean by … ?' Nor could the opposition to idealism, after all those Thursdays buttering crumpets for Cook Wilson. But Moore seemed to embody quite unselfconsciously in his personal style something the Oxford realists lacked: an alternative *moral* vision.

Here, the idealists – their metaphysical idealism sitting nicely with a political idealism – had more to offer in the way of what is ordinarily thought 'a philosophy'. Even in the nineteenth century, there were those who thought such aims dubious in a real philosopher. Moore's old teacher, Henry Sidgwick, wrote of his feeling that 'the deepest truth I have to tell is by no means "good tidings"', and so, 'I naturally shrink from exercising on others the personal influence which would make men [resemble] me'.[85] The polemics of Bradley were repellent to him, lapsing 'into mere debating-club rhetoric'. Bradley, it seemed to him, was a rhetorician, that is to say, a false philosopher: 'for really penetrating criticism … requires a patient effort of intellectual sympathy which Mr Bradley has never learned to make, and a tranquillity of temper which he seems incapable of maintaining'.

The sonorities of T. H. Green had as little appeal for him: 'I would not if I could, and I could not if I would, say anything which would make philosophy – my philosophy – popular.'[86] Charlie Broad, a younger colleague of Moore's at Cambridge, saw the problem: 'Even a thoroughly second-rate thinker like T. H. Green, by diffusing a grateful and comforting aroma of ethical "uplift", has probably made far more undergraduates into prigs than Sidgwick will ever make into philosophers.'[87]

The old idealists had taken care to deliver their metaphysics in the voice of Dickens's Mr Pecksniff: doctrines about the spiritual nature of reality went down better when served with a morally uplifting call to arms. Moore had nothing comparable to offer, but somehow, his youthful treatise of 1903, the grandly titled *Principia Ethica*, did have something of an impact on the youth of the incipient Bloomsbury Group – John Maynard Keynes (b.1883), Lytton Strachey (b.1880), Leonard Woolf – who read it as Cambridge undergraduates. Keynes thought the appeal had something to do with the book's thesis as they interpreted it. In his (idiosyncratic, partial) summary:

> nothing mattered except states of mind ... These states of mind ... consisted in timeless, passionate states of contemplation ... The appropriate objects of passionate contemplation and communion were a beloved person, beauty and truth, and one's prime objects in life were love, the creation and enjoyment of aesthetic experience and the pursuit of knowledge. Of these love came a long way first.[88]

At least, this was how Keynes seems to have read the book: as a romance, a bible for secular aesthetes, indifferent to questions of what was usually called morality.

For Leonard Woolf, on the other hand, the real effect of Moore and the *Principia* had nothing to do with their doctrines. Rather, 'they suddenly removed from our eyes an obscuring accumulation of scales, cobwebs, and curtains, revealing for the first time to us, so it seemed, the nature of truth and reality, of good and evil and character and conduct'.[89] It wasn't so much that Moore was instating a new metaphysics in place of the old. The place where the old metaphysics had sat was a place where nothing need be, nothing but 'the fresh air and pure light of plain common sense'.[90] Moore's only demand of the youth, Woolf said, was to 'make quite certain that we know what we meant when we made a statement'. Do that, and a divine voice will answer all questions: not Jehovah or Christ, just 'the more divine voice of plain common sense'.[91]

In the 1920s, common sense began to be heard at the Joint Sessions and its utterances were faithfully relayed back to those who had missed Moore's latest explosion. The taboos of the old were failing to take hold among the young, and thus ended the unhappy sequestering of Oxford philosophy from what was happening only a few hours' bus journey away. Price had been the first to fall; now it was Ryle who 'went all Cambridge'.[92]

*

Moore's personal example could only have strengthened the impulse towards clear and precise statement already implanted in Ryle by five years of tutorials. Where Cambridge did offer something entirely new was in the work of Moore's more urbane friend and colleague, Bertrand Russell (b.1872). Word had reached Oxford that a certain Russell was ploughing his own anti-idealist furrow out in the Fens. The realism was all to the good, but why did the man have to spoil things by putting in all that maths? Ryle was three when Russell published his *Principles of Mathematics* (1903), but even in 1928, no Oxford philosopher of the previous generation seemed to have read it.[93] 'Partly powered by some native recalcitrance towards the official line,' Ryle said, he picked up some Russell 'lest I miss something that ought not to be missed'.[94]

In Russell's account of his youth, he too had briefly succumbed to the siren song of idealism, but he and Moore managed to climb 'out of this mental prison and found ourselves again at liberty to breathe the free air of a universe restored to reality'.[95] Russell was the hare to Moore's tortoise. His mathematical abilities were vastly superior to Moore's (and indeed, to those of nearly everybody else). The problems that exercised him lay at the underexplored intersection of mathematics and philosophy.

The idealist, Russell took it, was denying that we could have direct access to reality; he proposed that we could, by means of a relationship with it he called 'acquaintance' (the word came to be a term of art in his usage).[96] I could be acquainted with 'sense data' – the patches of colour, snatches of sound, the smells and textures of the world; I could also be acquainted with concepts – say, 'brotherhood'.

This led him to the second plank of his realism: the solution to the problem of *aboutness*. The idealist, recall, repudiated 'the separation of ... what is thought from thinking'; all thinking is, in a sense, about thought and all knowledge self-knowledge. The realist disagreed. Our thoughts about mountains were about mountains, not about thoughts. That meant the realist had to say something in answer to the question of how it was that our thoughts and words could be *about* things other than themselves.

Countless new students of philosophy are puzzled by the heavy weather made of such questions as 'How is my *thought* about Cambridge a thought about *Cambridge*?' But the preoccupation with the question makes rather better sense once we see it as something the realists of the early twentieth century had to answer before the idealist could finally be consigned to the rubbish dump of intellectual history. And Russell's answer was simple: my thought about Cambridge – say, 'Cambridge is quiet in the winter' – is a *proposition*, 'composed wholly of constituents with which we are acquainted',[97] such as 'Cambridge', the concept 'quietness' and alas, 'winter'.

But where does that leave our thoughts about things we are *not* acquainted with through our senses? Say I think, 'Bertrand Russell is rather good at mathematics': my thought is about a man I have never met. Russell proposed that the name – in this case, 'Bertrand Russell' – corresponds to an associated 'definite description': usually a phrase of the form 'the such-and-such'. Bertrand Russell might be, for me, associated with a certain description: say, 'the godson of John Stuart Mill' or 'the first president of the Campaign for Nuclear Disarmament' or 'the man who refuted idealism'. That allows us to rewrite our original sentence, replacing the name 'Bertrand Russell' with the associated definite description, say: 'The first president of the CND was rather good at mathematics.' But there is another step, because something in the new sentence now raises questions. 'It might be thought excessive', Russell wrote in his *Introduction to Mathematical Philosophy*, 'to devote two chapters to one word, but to the philosophical mathematician it is a word of very great importance.'[98] The word was 'the'.

Russell proposed that a sentence containing the definite article, of the form 'The *F* is *G*', could be, as it were, decomposed further, into this set of sentences: 'At least one thing is *F*; no more than one thing is *F*; whatever is *F* is *G*.'[99] Or, to apply the point to the present case: 'At least one person was the first president of the CND; no more than one person was the first president of the CND; whoever was the first president of the CND was rather good at mathematics.' This could equally well be rendered in the still-new formal notation at the cutting edge of German logic: $\exists x \forall y ((Fy \leftrightarrow y = x) \wedge Gx)$. Who would have thought the old 'the' to have had so much blood in him?

The promise of the new logic, at any rate its philosophical promise, was unobvious. Which of the traditional problems of philosophy did the new methods help with? Russell and Moore had seen it first, and now Ryle was about to see it too: all of them. The special business of philosophy, on this view, was to scrape away at sentences until the content of the thoughts underlying them was revealed, their form unobstructed by the distorting structures of language and idiom. The activity felt, Russell said, rather 'like that of watching an object approaching through a thick fog: at first it is only a vague darkness, but as it approaches articulations appear and one discovers that it is a man or a woman, or a horse or a cow or what not'.[100] The agreed term for this activity was 'analysis'.

The essay in which Russell aired these ideas filled Ryle with mounting excitement and the sense of radical new possibilities.

The logical notation was new; Ryle, no mathematician, didn't care much for the symbolism.[101] But the notation seemed to him only a new way to further an old, perhaps the oldest, aim of philosophy: to make clear what is muddled. Was this not what Socrates had been seeking? 'What is knowledge?' he had asked, but might he not as well have said, '*Analyse* knowledge'? And might he indeed not have done even better not to take up the single word, 'knowledge', as the target of his analysis, but rather the full sentence, 'I know that …', much as Russell had proceeded with 'the'? No one was likely to get far with completing the sentence, '"The" means …', but one *could* paraphrase the standard kinds of sentence in which 'the', or for that matter, 'a' or 'know' appeared so as to exhibit their 'logical form'. Finally, it seemed, philosophy had found the keys to the kingdom.

Ryle kept working at his German, indispensable to stay in touch with the philosophy coming out of Germany and Austria. He travelled there often, usually for walking holidays, and worked his way through new publications with a dictionary by his side, just as he had done with Italian a few years before, when he attacked the works of Croce similarly armed. He was eager to share his discoveries, volunteering lectures on such figures as Bernard Bolzano (b.1781), Franz Brentano (b.1838), Edmund Husserl (b.1859) and Alexius Meinong (b.1853) – or, as the Oxford wags had it, 'Ryle's three Austrian railway-stations and one Chinese game of chance'.[102]

In time, he was ready to go up before the Jowett Society of Oxford – named after the Victorian Master of Balliol whose translations of Plato had done so much to revive both philosophy and classical scholarship – armed with foreign names, tricky paradoxes, clever arguments and a radical new conception of philosophy. Socrates, he announced, had been on the right track: analysis was indeed the proper business of philosophy. But it was a shame that Plato had got lost in the thickets of metaphysics, looking for incorporeal 'Forms' behind the everyday terms, 'justice', 'piety', 'knowledge'. The real task, he announced with the hubris of a young man with a new idea, was to examine the *meanings* of expressions. But Hamish Paton, a little older, and wiser now to the excitements of youth, was ready with his customary caution: 'Ah, Ryle, how *exactly* do you distinguish between philosophy and lexicography?'[103]

At the time, Ryle would have had to admit that he didn't, and couldn't, or not exactly. Maybe philosophy *was* a kind of lexicography (and what of it?). Or maybe it was the lexicography of a language no one spoke but in which everybody thought. A few more years of reading lay between Ryle and the view he would come to adopt. It had been a mistake, he eventually decided, to think the point of philosophy was to pick up this or that expression and ask, 'What does it mean?' or, 'Does it make sense?' The real questions, he came to think (and found that Russell and Moore had got there first), were, 'Why does this or that expression make nonsense?' and, 'What *sort* or nonsense does it make?'[104]

By 1932, Ryle was ready to throw down the gauntlet. 'Philosophical arguments', he said innocently enough to his audience at the Aristotelian Society which met at Russell Square in the early spring of that year, 'have always largely, if not entirely, consisted in attempts to thrash out "what it means to say so and so".'[105] Thus was everyone from Russell back to Socrates enlisted into the new project of analysis: after all, philosophers had always asked to know what things meant. But that was to say very little.

Ryle was ready to be more specific, describing 'a whole class of expressions of one type which occur and occur perfectly satisfactorily in ordinary discourse, but which are ... systematically misleading'. Systematically misleading expressions, as he defined them, 'are couched in a syntactical form improper to the facts recorded and proper to facts of quite another logical form than the facts recorded'.[106] For instance: 'Carnivorous cows don't exist.' The sentence seems to give carnivorous cows the property of nonexistence – but things must surely exist to have any properties at all. A moment's reflection can give the (unobjectionable) statement the air of paradox; another moment's reflection, and a handy translation ('There are no carnivorous cows', or better, though more clunkily, 'It is not the case that there exists something that is both a cow and carnivorous') will suffice to dispel it.[107]

Ryle dealt with 'Unpunctuality is reprehensible' the same way: there was no such *thing* as unpunctuality, just people who weren't ever on time and other people who reprehended it. And indeed 'Poincaré is not the king of France', insofar as it implied that there was such a position that he *might* have held. Our language, he thought, was inadequate to the form of the facts.

There was no need to change our language in consequence; after all, no one had really been misled as a result. But we did need to be vigilant about the antics of philosophers, who were too apt to infer from the clothing of our language the existence of a spectral universe of invisible things: 'Partly through accepting the grammatical *prima facies* of such expressions, philosophers have believed ... devoutly in the existence of "ideas", "conceptions" and "thoughts" or "judgements".'[108] But there were no such things, and no point at all in inquiring into what sort of thing they were.

Philosophers had to be translators – if that wasn't what they'd always been. When they found an expression that failed to exhibit, or even actively 'concealed or disguised', the 'real form of the fact', they knew what they had to find: 'a new form of words which does exhibit what the other failed to exhibit'. The conclusion was in a way disappointing. Was this all they were here to do? Ryle concluded with a confession: 'I would rather allot to philosophy a sublimer task than the detection of the sources in linguistic idioms of recurrent misconstructions and absurd theories.'[109] Philosophy as he now was compelled to think about it felt like it had been taken several pegs down from its once exalted sense of itself. But there it was: philosophy was *at least* this, and only the soppy and the nostalgic could find in this fact cause for serious regret.

And thus were the lines drawn in the proverbial sand. You could be on the side of the old idealists (who indulged, it was said, in 'talkie-talkie') or you could be on the side of the new realists, Cook Wilsonians with Cambridge features (the idealists accused them of 'argy-bargy').[110] The argy-bargy faction were winning. The few surviving idealists might still emit sporadic puffs of gas, but with the dawn of analysis, surely the long night of fog was finally over.

2

Nonsense

Alfred Jules ('Freddie') Ayer (b.1910) turned nineteen on 29 October 1929. It was a date remembered as the beginning of the Great Depression, perhaps one of the few ills for which no one in later years tried to blame him. Ayer was not yet, at this stage, what he would later be called: 'the wickedest man in Oxford'.[1] A first-year undergraduate reading Classics at Christ Church, he was assigned a set of oak-panelled rooms in a corner of the college's eighteenth-century Peckwater Quad. Their previous occupant had been W. H. Auden (b.1907).[2] In Auden's day, the room was kept permanently dark. It was rumoured that the mantelpiece had been adorned with a mouldering orange – a symbol of the West – and a loaded revolver to save time once its owner had decided, as he (being a poet) surely must, to end it all.[3]

Ayer, inspired by the artistic girlfriend he had met in Paris, kept his curtains open and his walls adorned with prints of the still-controversial Cézanne (*The Railway Cutting*) and Van Gogh (*Portrait of Patience Escalier*), aesthetic choices that signalled his idea of modernity.[4] A few hundred yards away, the poet Stephen Spender (b.1909) was doing the same with prints of Gauguin and Klee. Affectation it certainly was, but what is affectation – Spender later asked – if not 'an aping of the hidden, outrageous qualities which are our real potentialities'?[5]

Not so long before that, Ayer had been a schoolboy at Eton, to which he had won a scholarship at the age of twelve, coping well enough with the daily diet of classical authors, sadistic masters and casual antisemitism (his mother's family were Dutch Jews).[6] He had discovered Bertrand Russell's *Sceptical Essays* (1928) at school, embracing the 'wildly paradoxical and subversive' doctrine announced in its opening paragraph: 'that it is undesirable to believe a proposition when there is no ground whatever for supposing it true'.[7] He had even managed to discover Moore's *Principia*, and accepted (for a time) its most famous thesis, that goodness is a real quality but undetectable by scientists, a view that had the advantage of giving philosophers something they alone could study.[8]

Like Auden before him, Ayer went to Gilbert Ryle for tutorials in philosophy.[9] Just shy of thirty now, Ryle still had the frame of the rower and a bluff officers' mess manner that occasioned surprise once it came out that he had never in fact seen the inside of a trench. He was cultivating a pipe, and a non-judgemental philistinism: 'No ear for tunes,' he liked to say when music was mentioned.[10] Before one heard him speak, and sometimes even after, it was easy to mistake where he fell in the old Oxford divide between athlete and aesthete. His manner was that of the 'hearty', just as Auden's was that of the 'pansy'.

Future annals of the 1920s would paint the streets of Oxford as the battlefield for a long campaign of the one set, swilling beer, muscles rippling even under heavy woollen scarves, against the other, admiring their silk and porcelain in tasteful solitude. Encounters between the sets usually ended in a 'ducking' in the nearest college fountain.[11] The gloriously camp Anthony Blanche in *Brideshead Revisited*, a distillation of a whole decade's worth of Oxford aestheticism, was more articulate than most when he told his assailants, 'Nothing could give me keener pleasure than to be manhandled by you meaty boys. It would be an ecstasy of the very naughtiest kind.'[12] One could reject both options, but that only left Communism, and for most undergraduates of the 1920s, drawn from the comfortable middle classes, that wouldn't have done at all.

By the time Ayer arrived at Christ Church, the old divisions were weakening. There were more scholarship boys from working-class families. Lacking the funds, elan, introductions and confidence about future solvency that might have allowed them to make something of Oxford's hedonistic possibilities, they devoted themselves to their essays, setting standards of diligence and scholarship their tutors were consequently able to enforce more generally. With the Depression, the would-be aesthetes' parental allowances had been cut and dandyism on the cheap looked an awful lot like simple intellectualism. Like other university fads, the onslaughts on aesthetes came to seem like a lot of effort for little reward, especially now that the aesthetes knew the score and didn't step out unless armed with their chosen weapon, a lavatory chain.[13] Soon, the would-be hearties began to feel too much like they were simply playing a part scripted by some long-graduated third-year. They 'lacked conviction', said Stephen Spender about the late 1920s, 'and there was a certain hysteria about their athleticism'. Meanwhile Oxford, with its lorries and smokestacks, was growing: the motor cars manufactured in its factories ran every hour of the day and night down the High Street, reminders to the dreamers of what lay beyond the spires.[14]

Ayer – lover of Impressionism, women and football – was caught awkwardly between the groups. As, indeed, was Ryle, for the hearty carapace went with a scrupulosity of diction and great respect for intellectual achievement. Despite a face that brought to mind Colonel Blimp as a junior officer, he was the least parochial of Englishmen. Where philosophy was concerned, he was cosmopolitan, unafraid of being thought pretentious. A competent reader of German and Italian (in addition, of course, to the Latin and Greek he couldn't afford to forget), he was already serving up, to any student with a daring enough palate, an exotic philosophical diet.

Ayer was started off, like everyone else, on the selections from Selby-Bigge's classic anthology of *British Moralists*. But it became clear from their conversations that Ryle had horizons broader than the Greats curriculum.[15] A few months before Ayer arrived at Oxford, Ryle had met and befriended, at the Joint Session of 1929, an Austrian with the grand name of Wittgenstein, whose enigmatic first book, the equally grandly titled *Tractatus Logico-Philosophicus*, had many pioneering things to say about the kind of analysis that Ryle was beginning to practise.[16] At any rate, it said a good deal about what analysis might be but didn't provide very many actual analyses for readers to taste the proof of the pudding. Later the same year, Ryle met a German philosopher teaching in Vienna, of a different temper but sympathetic views: Moritz Schlick (b.1882). To talk to Ryle was to get a whiff of a philosophical breeze from foreign places.

Ryle was also beginning to talk of another kind of 'phenomenological' analysis being hawked by a Professor Husserl of Freiburg – whose 1927 *Encyclopaedia Britannica* article on the subject made it sound very exciting indeed: it was, the article declared, 'a new kind of descriptive method which made a breakthrough in philosophy at the turn of the century'. Phenomenology promised answers to old questions about the mind and the body, perception and knowledge, by applying methods that involved paying close attention to states of mind and the contents of experience.[17]

The summer before Ayer arrived at Oxford, Ryle had volunteered to review a certain new book in *Mind* – the venerable journal was now edited by G. E. Moore. The book that had caught Ryle's attention was a still untranslated German tome by a certain Martin Heidegger (b.1889), successor to Husserl at Freiburg. Readers picking up the newest issue of *Mind* in Christ Church library would have seen Ryle pronounce Heidegger 'a thinker of real importance'. He commended 'the immense subtlety and searchingness of his examination of consciousness, ... the boldness and originality of his methods and conclusions, and ... the unflagging energy with which he tries to think behind the stock categories of orthodox philosophy'. But there was a barb to come: something about the style of the book, and its inheritances from previous German philosophy, made him think the whole tradition of phenomenology was 'heading for bankruptcy and disaster and will end either in self-ruinous Subjectivism or in a windy mysticism'.[18]

Ryle knew next to nothing about the political direction in which Heidegger was travelling. His review made little of the book's ethical concerns, its talk of authenticity and guilt and fallenness. He didn't detect what some later readers would judge to be its implicit politics.[19] Even in *Being and Time*, as Ryle had noticed, Heidegger evinced a desire to purge language – or more specifically, to purge his German – of the legacies of the philosophy he rejected. That desire let him take on 'the hard task of coining, and [placed] on us the alarming task of understanding, a complete new vocabulary of terms – mostly many-barrelled compounds of everyday "nursery" words and phrases – made to denote roots and stems of Meaning more primitive than those in which Plato, Aristotle, and subsequent scientists and philosophers have … taught us to talk and think'.[20] But why, Ryle objected, think these new coinages were any freer of the accretions of confused philosophy?

In 1933, the year that Hitler became chancellor, Heidegger showed what his sternest critics thought to be his true colours. He accepted the position of rector of the University of Freiburg, where he demonstrated a striking willingness, if not always to champion the Nazi cause openly, to enable it, by innumerable acts and omissions. He was observed at a book burning, and delivered explicitly pro-Nazi speeches to students. His own notebooks, only widely available since 2014, are full of unambiguously antisemitic remarks. His attempts to protect the interests of Jewish colleagues and mentors were, at best, half-hearted. Asked by a student, a few decades later, if he had retained his interest in Heidegger after that review, Ryle is supposed to have answered: 'No, because when the Nazis came to power, Heidegger showed that he was a shit, from the heels up, and a shit from the heels up can't do good philosophy.'[21]

The old battle of hearty against aesthete was turning into something darker. Auden, who had been watching events in Berlin from the 1920s, noted that the anti-intellectualism of British, even Oxford, life, was taking on a distinctly minatory aspect. Every issue of *Punch* seemed to have caricatures of intellectuals, 'spectacled, round-shouldered, rabbit-toothed'. Might that not be a portent of something darker? 'Cross the channel and this dislike, in more countries than one, has taken a practical form, to which the occasional ducking of an Oxford aesthete seems a nursery tiff.'[22]

Freddie Ayer didn't really catch the political bug as a student. When he joined the Canning Club – where the most glamorous young Conservatives were to be found – it was its social possibilities that seem to have been the appeal. He became club secretary, reading a paper – as he later recalled, 'not without shame'[23] – on the trouble with democracy, a little inspired by the arguments of that original anti-democrat, Plato, on which he was weekly writing essays for tutorials with Ryle's colleague Michael Foster (b.1903). But the flirtation with authoritarianism was brief and never more than a flirtation. Ayer's commitments were, a friend recalled, 'fairly middle of the road',[24] and he frustrated the more partisan of his friends with his moderation, and his preference for philosophy and friendship over politics.

In any case, Ayer's gifts were not those of the orator but that slightly different thing, always popular at Oxford: the talker. There was healthy competition. Next door at Corpus Christi was that other Jewish boy from London, Isaiah Berlin (b.1909) – the son of émigrés from the USSR, his father like Ayer's a timber merchant – whose rapid-fire speech, full of learned allusions, would be much imitated as representing the voice of Oxford itself. He was also taken up by the notorious Maurice Bowra (b.1898), a survivor of the Western Front who ruled the scholarly end of the Oxford social scene, reputed as a purveyor of bleak epigrams not equalled since the time of Oscar Wilde. In his later incarnation as the warden of Wadham College, he made his preferences clear: he wanted to admit, in that order, 'clever boys, interesting boys, pretty boys – no shits' (when it was a realistic possibility, he was the first to come out in favour of admitting girls as well – but that was nearly forty years away).[25] It was as well that he put cleverness first, or neither Ayer nor Berlin would have had a chance.

Bowra's dinner parties were his way of bestowing, or denying, favour. He sought friendship, and from his friends, absolute loyalty. He had decided likes (Symbolist poetry, the Mediterranean, paganism) and dislikes (Christian morality, academic scholarship, public life).[26] To a generation of favoured undergraduates, he was *the* bachelor don, availing himself fully of the privileges of college life – in particular, the retinue of cooks, servers and 'scouts' with brooms and mops who made his hospitality possible. Philosophy, to which he had been introduced by a deeply pious tutor of the Cook Wilsonian persuasion, had made no impression on him; of all the legacies of ancient Greece – apotheosis of civilisation – it was his least favourite. What Ayer and Berlin brought to his parties was not philosophy but vitality.

Many things about him struck the young Ayer: the 'massive head, small watchful eyes, and a resonant voice, delivering words like rapid musketry'.[27] Then there was the contempt for conventional pieties (seeing his college flag at half-mast, the usual indicator of the death of a college fellow, he told the porter, 'Don't tell me. Let me guess.')[28] And above all, he exuded a sense that what mattered was not duty or virtue but *life*. Ayer would come to model his own wit on Bowra's, striving in his speech and prose to emulate the fluency of Bowra's conversation.[29]

Some of this may even have translated into better philosophy. Ryle thought well of Ayer: 'extremely penetrating, and unsentimental',[30] he wrote in his report after his first term teaching him – by which he may have meant that Ayer showed the attachment to arguments over conclusions, the willingness to let a refuted thesis go unmourned, that distinguishes the philosopher from the dogmatist. At the end of his final term at Oxford, he went as far as to call him 'the best philosopher that I have yet been taught by, among my pupils'.[31]

Stephen Spender, having his tutorials with E. F. Carritt (b.1876), a fellow at University College at roughly the same time, came out with no affection for the subject. Week after week, it seemed, another philosopher of the canon would be wheeled out for ritual humiliation on a philosophical obstacle course: John Stuart Mill would be exposed as confused, Locke and Hume as simply wrong, Kant as less simply (but still) wrong. On this obstacle course, he later wrote, 'Some of them get further than others but they all fall sooner or later into the traps which language sets for them. It soon occurred to me that it was useless to enter a field where such distinguished contestants had failed.'[32] That was, at any rate, Spender's response, explained in part perhaps by talents that lay elsewhere (for instance, in poetry) and in part by the over-modesty that came of belonging to that Oxford underclass, the young man from the *minor* public school.

To Ayer, the failures of the canonical heroes had the opposite effect. Far from putting him off philosophy, they spurred him on – there was evidently work yet to be done – and gave him a new focus for his curiosity: if not the great and glorious dead, then perhaps someone from the ranks of the living.

Ryle was ready with a suggestion: perhaps young Ayer was in the right frame of mind to take on Wittgenstein's *Tractatus*. It was the first Ayer had heard of the man or the book. When he picked it up, he found it utterly unlike anything he had read before. He had acquired a little German at school but not enough to cope with stuff like this. He had to rely, for the moment, on the translation attributed to the Cambridge linguist and eccentric Charles Kay Ogden (b.1889), but which was in fact primarily the work of the precocious mathematician and philosopher who had been even younger than Ayer himself when he had done it: Frank Ramsey (b.1903).[33]

The style of the *Tractatus* – numbered sentences and virtually no explicit argument – had nothing in common with anything in Oxford philosophy, and very little in common with anything in contemporary Cambridge philosophy either. This fact was in spite of its being published with a foreword written by Bertrand Russell. The book began with a declaration both emphatic and enigmatic – 'The world is everything that is the case' – that could be read either as a preliminary definition of terms or as a controversial statement about the nature of what exists.[34] No clarification or argument was immediately forthcoming, giving the opening statement the flavour of a mystery that only the whole book, fully understood, would solve.

And on the propositions went, setting out an account of facts, a position about how language represented reality, a theory of what propositions are, and some more technical material on 'the general form of the truth-function'. It concluded, surprisingly, with a section that seemed to belong to another book, about mysticism, the ethical, the aesthetic and the ineffable. Who knows what the young Ayer actually made of it, how much of it he understood? But the book hit him with the force of revelation. 'This was exactly what I wanted,' he later wrote, 'the very conclusions I had been groping towards on my own. All the difficulties that had perplexed me were instantly removed.'[35]

In his final undergraduate term, the early summer of 1932, Ayer felt ready to deliver a paper on the *Tractatus* to a meeting of the Jowett Society, to be followed by a response from Berlin, who hadn't yet read the book. Ryle was there, but none of the older folk were. The meeting was very possibly the first time the book had been publicly discussed at Oxford (it had been available for ten years). Ayer appeared in a dinner jacket, carnation in buttonhole, to fire what he would later call 'the opening shot of the great positivist campaign' that was to dominate at least the next decade of his life.[36]

Shortly after Ayer's exams, Ryle drove him to Cambridge. He

was taken up a long flight of stairs near the entrance to Trinity College and into a small room, monkish and barely furnished, to see Wittgenstein for the first time. Ayer must by then have known a little about his childhood in one of the wealthiest families of Europe, his early fascination for engineering, the sudden turn when studying the subject at Manchester to mathematics, and soon, to the philosophy of mathematics. He certainly knew of the fabled encounter with Russell in Cambridge when the older man, unsure if this gauche young engineering student with his peculiar ideas was a genius or a crank, decided to take a punt on him.[37] Ayer knew too that Russell had gone on, though perhaps a little prematurely, to declare the young Austrian his intellectual heir, the man to take forward the logical inquiries that Russell had initiated with his early work, even as Russell himself was moving into a life dominated by politics and society. To know all this, and to have read the *Tractatus*, was one thing; but it was still something to see the man in the flesh.

Wittgenstein was in his early forties. Slim and energetic, he looked not much older than Ryle. His English, awkward and thickly accented when he had first arrived at Cambridge asking to meet Russell, was now fluent and idiomatic. He pulled out a couple of deckchairs from a cupboard for his guests and offered them a box of biscuits. Ayer was introduced and was asked what he had been reading. A play, Ayer replied, *La vida es sueño* – an allegory from seventeenth-century Spain full of philosophical reflections on the difference between dreams and reality. And what did he think of it? Ayer said he had not understood it very well – meaning that he'd found the archaic Spanish difficult. Wittgenstein seemed pleased, perhaps supposing Ayer to be one of those earnest, thoughtful young men he particularly liked. (Ayer later decided, out of vanity or insight, that Wittgenstein may have had a bit of a crush on him.)[38]

Despite a string of 'beta' marks on his papers, Ayer got his first-class degree – no thanks to the philosophy examiners, figures of the old school who were unlikely to be impressed by his combination of logical acumen, disdain for Plato and sympathy for John Stuart Mill.[39] The ancient historians came to his rescue, deciding after a second look at his papers that he was 'first class' after all, their phrasing suggesting that they were not so much classifying exam scripts as giving the once-over to souls queueing up at the gates of heaven.[40]

He was elected to a temporary lecturership at Christ Church, and was given his first two terms off, which left him time and money to get married to Renée, his girlfriend of the previous three years, and perhaps to study somewhere other than Oxford. He asked Ryle for his advice: ought he to go over to Cambridge to sit at Wittgenstein's feet? Ryle didn't think Ayer was the sort to be happy sitting at anybody's feet. He pointed him instead to a less obvious place, one that had the advantage of doubling up as a honeymoon location (as Cambridge, whatever its other virtues, did not): Vienna.

*

The May 1931 issue of the *Journal of Philosophy* had brought Ryle news from New York of 'Logical Positivism: A New Movement in European Philosophy'. The authors were Albert E. Blumberg (b.1906) and Herbert Feigl (b.1902), writing from their respective perches at Johns Hopkins and Harvard (where Feigl, the Viennese visitor, was spending a year on a Rockefeller Foundation scholarship). The label, they agreed, was less than ideal, but it was better than any other they could think of. 'Positivism' was supposed to invoke the tradition – just as often termed 'empiricist' – of David Hume, John Stuart Mill, Auguste Comte and Ernst Mach, whose attitude to philosophy might be summed up in the slogan, 'all knowledge is based upon experience'. You perceive, you make your inductive inferences, you generalise, you theorise, but it all starts with experience, and never stops being accountable to it.

The trouble with the old positivism, they thought, was the silly extreme to which it was led by its reliance on the rudimentary shape of the logic available at the time. Mill took his empiricism too far, believing it to offer a perfectly adequate account not just of the natural sciences but also of mathematics and logic, which come out in the old positivist view as extensions of psychology. That view could no longer be sustained, not once we had understood – really understood – what Albert Einstein and Jules Henri Poincaré had shown in physics and what Russell, and his German correspondent, Gottlob Frege, had shown in mathematics.[41]

What was needed now was 'a unified theory of knowledge in which neither logical nor empirical factors are neglected'.[42] And that was what the new philosophy aimed to provide: philosophy as done by people at the frontiers of both logic and physics. Philosophy, as the new positivist conceived of it, aimed at no more (but, equally, no less) than 'the clarification of the meaning of propositions and the elimination of just such meaningless pseudo-propositions'.[43] What was meaningful in our talk and thought would survive, clarified; the rest would be destroyed, and would deserve no better.

The authors singled out four names for special mention: there was of course Wittgenstein, Viennese but presently at Cambridge; then there was Hans Reichenbach (b.1891) and his circle at Berlin; and there were the two philosophers in Vienna itself, Rudolf Carnap (b.1891) and Moritz Schlick. Ryle had met and got along with Schlick, but his encounters with Wittgenstein left him with serious reservations. This was evidently a man who needed acolytes, not colleagues, someone always on the brink of an explosion, too quick to divide the world into the saved and the damned.[44]

Wittgenstein was, in any case, rumoured to be shedding the views of the *Tractatus*, discussing (more often, dictating) his repudiations and new views to a narrow circle at Cambridge and forbidding its members, on pain of wrathful excommunication, from disclosing the contents of the discussions to anyone outside. He had an intense anxiety about the possibility of being plagiarised, or worse, of being misrepresented. For the chumminess of the common room (Ryle's natural habitat) or cocktail bar (Ayer's) he had only contempt. Ayer's natural schoolboy cheek and big mouth could only be suppressed so long. However much he might try to accommodate himself to the ways of such a teacher, nothing good was likely to come of the association.

Where then ought Ayer to go? Better by far, Ryle said, that Ayer enrol at the University of Vienna and work under Schlick. If the *Journal of Philosophy* article was to be believed, Wittgenstein was really a fellow traveller of the Viennese philosophers, the *Tractatus* distinguished from (say) Carnap's *The Logical Structure of the World* (1928) only by the tone of quasi-religious solemnity into which its concluding sections regrettably lapsed. Ayer had little interest in the mysticism ('Whereof one cannot speak, thereof one must be silent,'[45] etc.). He had, rather, taken the point of the book to lie in its classification of 'significant propositions' into two classes: 'either they were tautologies, like the propositions of logic and pure mathematics, or they were empirically verifiable. Everything else, including metaphysics and theology, was literally nonsensical.'[46]

If that was Wittgenstein's point – and it was possible in the 1930s, if not later, to think it was – then Schlick and Carnap seemed to be saying the same thing that Wittgenstein was, stripped of the embarrassing mysticism. Vienna offered the chance of regular conversations with scientists and mathematicians, and a new house journal (*Erkenntnis*, which Carnap and Reichenbach had been running together since 1930) that was open to everyone to read and be published in, but without the Delphic air. Moreover, Ryle could confirm that Schlick had excellent English, and exuded a geniality, kindness and open-mindedness that had nothing of the stereotypical Teutonic *Meister* about him. Ayer would not be forced either to draw on his school German, or bend his personality to the dictates of a dominant teacher. He was persuaded. His plans for his first year as an Oxford graduate fell into place. He would get married; he would take the exam for a fellowship at All Souls College; he would go to Vienna.

*

All Souls was a disaster. His dismissal of metaphysics as nonsensical (for roughly the reasons given in the *Tractatus*) was unpopular with the examiners; his argumentative style was pronounced by one to show 'a lack of worldly wisdom'.[47] The fellowship went instead to Isaiah Berlin. At Renée's urging and despite his qualms, the wedding was a Catholic ceremony at the Brompton Oratory in London's Knightsbridge.

Renée's arguments seemed to him decisive. Her family would be severely distressed if it was anything else; he would at worst have to repeat words that he thought were meaningless anyway; she wouldn't actually try to enforce the undertaking that their children be brought up Catholic. And so, Ayer coped manfully with the sprinkling of holy water. The next day, the couple were on a boat from Harwich to Ostend. There they took the long train ride through Germany to Vienna, where a pianist friend had already found them lodgings in Wieden, with an American English teacher, Frau Jones, who seemed to have forgotten her English from living so long in Vienna.[48]

Ayer found the city, no longer an imperial capital, 'a little run to seed'. But he loved 'the heavy baroque architecture of the old imperial buildings' and sat for hours at the cafés where no one expected you to order a second cup of coffee while you made your way through the newspapers, keeping to his budget by eating every day at a cheap restaurant near the university where he could order boiled beef and noodles. He also discovered the possibilities of dance-halls, acquiring a love of dancing that he retained for the rest of his life, and a consciousness that it didn't matter that he was small (five foot seven) and unremarkable-looking as long as he turned on the metaphysical quality he had in oodles: charm.[49]

He and Renée spent their free moments looking at the Bruegels at the Kunsthistorisches Museum and developed a special affection for Tintoretto's *Susanna and the Elders*, in which the biblical Susanna is observed bathing by men concealed behind a rose trellis. His German got better with the combination of private lessons, readings from the plays of Arthur Schnitzler, afternoons at the cinema and evenings at the opera, where he saw for the first time a production of *Don Giovanni*, taking special delight in the bit of Leporello's aria where he tells us how many women his master has loved in Spain: *tausend und drei*, as the translated libretto went. Ayer the young don (of a different kind) would come to take the number and diversity of the Don's conquests as a target and challenge.

Armed with a letter of introduction from Ryle, he walked up the Prinz Eugen Strasse to the apartment of Moritz Schlick, Chair of the Philosophy of the Inductive Sciences. Schlick was fifty, and debonair, rather like Ayer's idea of an American senator. He read the letter from Ryle and conversed with Ayer, in English, for half an hour, then decided Ayer could attend lectures at the university. Schlick would make the necessary arrangements. He would also be welcome to participate in meetings of what was being called the *Wienerkreis*, the Vienna Circle. The Circle had produced an intellectual manifesto in 1929 ('The Scientific View of the World: The Vienna Circle') and were bringing out a series of pamphlets under the title *Unified Science*. Such a combination of confidence, organisation and efficiency was unheard of at Oxford.

The small room in which the Circle met was located in a building a little way removed from the university itself. Members of the Circle sat around a (disappointingly) rectangular table. Carnap, alas, wasn't there, having accepted a chair at the University of Prague. That left Schlick in Vienna to keep the Circle going, and he always sat at the head of the table. Across from him sat a large, pasty man with the smiling eyes of an ageing vaudeville star and strongly held political views, in his case, of a socialist character: Otto Neurath (b.1882).

To his left sat Schlick's teaching assistant, Friedrich Waismann (b.1896), an ardent Wittgensteinian eking out a living as a *Privatdozent*, a teacher whose income relied on the number of students enrolled in his classes, never large. It was rumoured that this meagre income was occasionally supplemented by Schlick's personal largesse. To Schlick's right sat the mathematicians, the old Hans Hahn (b.1879) and the young Karl Menger (b.1902). Often, they were joined by a third, a young Kurt Gödel (b.1906), who listened intently but almost never spoke. Ayer remembered him as a 'dark and small and silent and self-contained' young man, still waiting for the world to notice the significance of the 'incompleteness theorems' he had published two years before.[50] And then there was Olga Hahn-Neurath (Hans's sister and Otto's wife, b.1882), a mathematician who had been blind since her early twenties, and who filled the seminar room with smoke from her Virginian cigarettes.[51] It would be a while before there would be much chance of seeing, in Vienna or elsewhere, not one but two women in the same seminar room.[52]

Ayer found himself the youngest in the room, the only other person roughly his age an American with a PhD (whatever that was) from Harvard called Willard Van Orman Quine (b.1908). Quine was a quicker study than Ayer, picking up enough German in his first months in Vienna to give a talk to the Circle on his Harvard dissertation on logic. Quine also took in a good deal more than Ayer did from Schlick's lectures on the philosophy of science. Ayer was initially befuddled by them: Schlick's German was hard and spoken in a bland monotone while the content presupposed a detailed knowledge of science he did not have.

Why then were the lectures, quite unconcerned with matters of social or political significance and with nary a concession to the attention span of the young, so packed? Why were his seminars standing room only? Schlick was, of course, a sort of socialist, but not a word of socialist theory, still less injunctions to socialist praxis, escaped his lips. He had published on ethics, applying his ideas about sense, nonsense and verification to ethical statements. He had concluded that the best way of dealing with ethical thought was to think of it as a (heavily disguised and regrettably metaphysical-sounding) form of *empirical* thought.[53] As Mill and Hume had thought before him, he regarded ethical thought as concerned with claims about human happiness, which made it, pleasingly, something that could be studied by the natural sciences. But he made no systematic attempt to connect these claims to his socialist commitments; that was not where he seemed to think the intellectual action was.

Schlick's ethical theories wouldn't in any case have explained the zeal of the students crowding into lecture halls to hear his disquisitions on the theory of meaning and the verification of propositions. If they had come hoping that the theory of linguistic meaning would reveal the meaning of something more obviously interesting (for example, life), the very first lecture would have made it clear that it would do no such thing, perhaps even pointing out that windy talk about the meaning of life was a perfect specimen of the metaphysical nonsense at the top of the positivists' hit list. The puzzle remained.

The question was raised again when, a couple of years later, another English-speaking philosopher arrived in Vienna, this time from New York, on a philosophical Grand Tour of Europe (Cambridge, Vienna, Warsaw, Lwów, Prague). Ernest Nagel (b.1901) had heard a good deal of talk about the new 'analytic' philosophy that was so much the rage in Europe, and was looking to get a sense of the whole thing so he could take the news back to his colleagues at Columbia. At Lwów in Poland (later, Lviv in Ukraine), Nagel sat through the lectures on logic of Leon Chwistek (b.1884). The lecture room was uninviting: heated only by a coal stove, floors creaky and walls showing signs of decay under the whitewash. But the benches were crowded with young men writing papers that would be thought worthy of publication back home. Nagel asked the students if they hoped to land academic jobs afterwards. Of course not, they weren't silly enough to think there was any chance of that. Nevertheless, they continued to scribble away at their proofs. The old professor had no idea what he was doing right.[54]

At Vienna, there were young men *and* women at Schlick's lectures, the devotion to the teacher and subject matter comparable to what Nagel had seen in Poland. Outside the lecture hall, things were not so good: the economy foundering, reactionary parties in power, and, after Hitler's accession in 1933, the odd Nazi *Hakenkreuz* beginning to appear at Viennese windows, the occasional riot temporarily closing down the university.[55]

Maybe that was it, Nagel speculated. Maybe this was 'at least the partial reason for the vitality and appeal of analytic philosophy'. On the face of it, and in its official pronouncements, it was ethically neutral: 'its professors do *not* indoctrinate their students with dogmas as to life, religion, race, or society'. But the very refusal to indoctrinate was a way of signalling an allegiance to the anti-clerical tradition in Viennese thought.[56] What felt revolutionary was what was being left unsaid: 'if the way of intelligence becomes part of the habitual nature of men, no doctrines and no institutions are free from critical reappraisals'.[57]

Nagel concluded that the excitement surrounding analysis came about because of its ability to serve two ends at once. On the one hand, it offered its practitioners 'refuge from a troubled world', a place to 'cultivate their intellectual games with chess-like indifference to its course'. On the other, it was 'a keen, shining sword helping to dispel irrational beliefs and to make evident the structure of ideas'. Analysis could be, at once, 'the pastime of a recluse and a terribly serious adventure'.[58]

*

Ayer went to Vienna already half a logical positivist. Nothing he heard there put him off the doctrine, and given his wobbly German, it isn't clear how much he absorbed there that he hadn't already got from his reading of the *Tractatus*. In the summer of 1933, after he had returned to England having 'gone all Vienna', as Ryle might have put it, Ryle took him to Birmingham for the year's Joint Session.

He had sharply divided opinion by the end of the conference, showing little tact and no deference towards any elders he suspected of metaphysical proclivities. But a few senior philosophers liked him or at any rate sympathised with the project. One of them was Richard Braithwaite (b.1900), an exact contemporary of Ryle's whose interest in the philosophical questions raised by probability made him curious about what Carnap was doing in the same field. Ayer had liked him when Ryle had introduced them, but remained a little in awe of his knowledge of mathematics and the sciences: though at least this put them on the same side.[59] Another was Susan Stebbing (b.1885), whom Ayer with his customary eye had noted was 'a handsome woman, though careless of her appearance', who had been fighting a lonely battle over the preceding decade to get Viennese ideas taken more seriously in Britain.[60]

Stebbing had started her philosophical life as an idealist. She had read history at Girton College, an all-women's institution sprawling at the north-western edge of Cambridge, until she happened upon a copy of F. H. Bradley's *Appearance and Reality*. She had her Damascene conversion to a different style of philosophy after what might, to a lesser soul, have been a traumatic encounter. It happened in 1917 at a meeting of the Aristotelian Society. A youngish man she didn't know picked up on a remark she had made in her paper ('Relation and Coherence') and asked her, repeatedly and with several thumps on the table, 'What *on earth* do you mean by that?' To her alarm, she realised she wasn't at all sure. But a moment later, to her relief, it became clear that the man was not interested in humiliating her after all. By the end of the session, Stebbing was both convinced that her main theses in the paper had been simply mistaken and confident of their having had a grain of insight she needed to work at spelling out a little better. The man's name, she learnt, was Moore.[61]

And Moore was still there in 1933, no longer even youngish but still exploding at the errors of the old and young alike, wondering what *on earth* something or other could mean. Early that year, Stebbing had read a paper to the British Academy in which she tried to connect the kind of 'analysis' Moore had been urging with the empiricist project of Schlick and Carnap in Vienna. She saw promise in both, but her sympathies were ultimately with Moore: we start with the things we know (I had breakfast before I had lunch; I have hands), which rules out certain outlandish metaphysical theses (time is unreal; we can't have knowledge of the external world). And then we get down to the hard task: to explain what we mean by what we ordinarily say.

The trouble, of course, was that 'what we ordinarily say, we say unclearly. We speak unclearly because we think unclearly. It is the task of philosophy to render our thoughts clear.'[62] But how was philosophy to do that? By thinking about thinking? By thinking about logic? That is what Stebbing took the positivists, including Wittgenstein, to be saying. We start from large, very general principles about the nature of language and use them 'to draw limits with regard to what we *can* think'. But that project, she thought, was a mistake. The positivists were wrong to 'seek to make *everything* clear at once'. We needed to take things – expressions – one at a time; in other words, *piecemeal*. And we clarified our thoughts about things by thinking 'about what we *were* thinking about' – goodness or time or colour or knowledge or whatever – and trying to find alternative expressions that say '*more* clearly what the original expression said *less* clearly'.[63] Ploughing her lonely furrow, she had reached a conclusion much like Ryle's. Philosophers had to be translators.

Stebbing was no positivist, nor was she a fellow traveller, but she did see the need to work through their views in detail, getting clear on what they had in common with those of the Cambridge analysts as well as where they diverged. She had no interest in a pointless scrap between Vienna and Cambridge. She too had been at the Seventh International Congress of Philosophy in 1930 where she, like Ryle, had first met Schlick. Like Ryle, and indeed Schlick himself, she was – as most academics are not – an efficient organiser who made things happen quickly. She had arranged for Schlick to visit London the previous year, and was soon to bring Carnap over from Prague to talk about his most recent book, not yet available in English, on 'logical syntax'. She made sure Ayer met him. Ayer found him intellectually impressive but humourless, an unfortunate cross to bear among the English.[64]

At the Joint Session, the younger philosophers with analytic sympathies decided that they needed a journal that advanced their point of view. *Mind* remained a formidable institution, but it came out too infrequently to serve their needs, and the average paper published there was too long. They needed something that could be produced cheaply, quickly and often, its default mode not the discursive essay but the 'note'. Another young turk, Austin Duncan-Jones (b.1908), soon to take up a position at Birmingham, agreed to be editor. Ryle, Stebbing and a colleague of Stebbing's called Cecil Mace, would be the editorial committee.[65]

The group moved quickly, with the energy that marks excitement about something new, and the first issue of *Analysis* (as the new journal was inevitably christened) came out in November 1933. The issue had papers by Ayer ('Atomic Propositions'), Ryle ('"About"'), Braithwaite ('Solipsism and the "Common Sense View of the World"') and Helen Knight (b.1899), a Cambridge philosopher who was then part of Wittgenstein's secret circle ('A Note on "The Problem of Universals"'). All this was prefaced with a brief 'Statement of Policy': *Analysis* would publish *short* pieces, their aim being 'the elucidation or explanation of facts, or groups of facts, the general nature of which is, by common consent, already known; rather than with attempts to establish new kinds of fact about the world, of very wide scope, or on a very large scale'.[66] Which was all a polite way of saying: metaphysics unwelcome.

*

Christ Church was a good place for Ayer to be while all this was happening. Cardinal Wolsey, effectively its founder, had intended for it to impress with the handsomeness of its proportions, that sense of everything being bigger, more spacious, more generous than it needed to be. One walked in through the formidable gates on St Aldate's into Tom Quad, with its central fountain where generations of mewling aesthetes had been ducked. And just across, the cathedral, and beyond it, the (rebuilt) cloisters, and just a few hundred yards away, the Meadows, a rural idyll rudely plonked beside a busy road. Here, field after fenced field full of cows gave way to the river path, where one could sit watching mallards and swans and crews of rowers grunting their way down the Isis.

Ayer was treated to free dinners in college hall, all five courses included with the lecturership, though the booze and guests (only men allowed) were charged to his accounts, or 'battels'. There was excellent company to be had: Ryle was there, drinking like a champion (he set a record at the Sportsman, necking a pint of beer in five seconds),[67] the wit honed among the Wee Teas expressed in naughty but learned epigrams in dead languages. Ryle generated anecdotes: once asked by an earnest Christian undergraduate visiting Oxford if he could explain the difference between the soul and the intellect, he replied, beer mug of course at hand, 'The intellect is that part of you with which you read books other than the Bible.'[68]

A steady stream of Jewish academic refugees and exiles from Germany and Austria had begun to appear in Oxford. Ernst Cassirer (b.1874), a man of enormous erudition and humanity, gave a class on Leibniz. He knew no English, so the thing had to be restricted to the Oxford philosophers with decent German, which turned out to be a sizeable number (Ayer, Ryle, Price and Berlin were there, and several others). However, the experience was unedifying for everybody. The Oxford philosophers pressed their usual questions: is this statement true or false? Consistent or inconsistent with this other sentence?[69] Cassirer seemed quite shocked: surely the question was 'what does this statement mean?', and really, one shouldn't take the statements quite so precisely. He was unwilling to debate, and seemed to be interested in the problems as such, without having the slightest desire to solve them. It appeared to the unhappy participants that his questions were a historian's questions, not a philosopher's – though Cassirer would no doubt have thought that this way of marking the distinction rather begged the question: perhaps philosophers should *be* historians. 'That is a very interesting question' were not words generally to be heard at Oxford, except as a polite way of saying, 'That is a thoroughly wrong-headed question.'[70]

Albert Einstein (b.1879) too was at Christ Church, on a research studentship before he was to move to Princeton where he would spend many productive years at the Institute for Advanced Study. The great inspiration of Einstein's youth had been the physicist Ernst Mach. On learning that Ayer had been in Vienna studying with Schlick, who was among other things the president of the Ernst Mach Society, he sat Ayer down to discuss – in a mixture of English and German – the doings of the Circle.[71] A young Theodor Adorno (b.1903), a decade and a bit away from being the dominant figure in German Marxism, was at Merton College, working, improbably, with Gilbert Ryle on a dissertation about Husserl. He acquired a reputation as a dandy among Oxford contemporaries who didn't know enough about Husserl, Marx or jazz to be able to keep up a conversation with him.[72]

Adorno didn't take to analysis; no Marxist of the decade did, preferring history and economics to this style of philosophy. One of the very few even to join the debate was a young man called Maurice Cornforth (b.1909).[73] Cornforth had joined a symposium at the Joint Session of 1934 – 'Is Analysis a Useful Method in Philosophy?' Cornforth, announcing that he was speaking as a Marxist, pronounced that analysis – and the style of philosophy devoted to it – was 'useless, harmful and impossible'.

Analysis, he said, was a way of 'cloaking the real character of our knowledge, and obscuring the import of discovery, in the interests of the bourgeoisie, and the international reaction in its struggle against revolutionary materialism'. Real (i.e. Marxist) philosophy had higher aims than clarifying the logical syntax of propositions. It too sought clarity, of a kind, but the aim was 'the emancipation of the human race'.[74] Moore, with his customary vehemence, repeated Cornforth's epithets back to him: 'useless, harmful and impossible'? How *on earth* could anything be all three at once?[75]

Meanwhile, the positivists at Vienna, never idle, were organising congress after international congress to propagate their views. Ayer travelled to Paris for the congress of 1935 to talk about 'The Analytic Movement in Contemporary British Philosophy', to find that everyone who was anyone was in the audience. Russell was there, eliciting great warmth by replying to a French questioner in French and a German questioner in German. Neurath was there, informing a (for once) befuddled Susan Stebbing that he had 'always been for the womans'. Ayer found that the diffident man in his early thirties he had met was Karl Popper (b.1902), who had recently published *Logik der Forschung*, which had shown sympathy for some positivist ideas. And there was a Polish logician called Alfred Tarski (b.1901), a member of the Lwów–Warsaw group that Ernest Nagel was to be so impressed by. Tarski presented a paper on truth, a systematic alternative to the theory Carnap had been defending. But Carnap, to everyone's surprise, treated the paper not with anger at the prospect of a public humiliation, but with the awe owed to a revelation.[76]

Back at Oxford, Ayer was ready to start preaching the Viennese gospel. He had been doing his duty by the official curriculum and saw his students, a mix of classicists and those reading for the now well-entrenched PPE degree, on tutorials about Plato's views on the structure of the soul (it has three parts) and Aristotle on the types of friendship (also three) and Descartes (the mind and body are distinct substances) and Leibniz (space is an illusion and the universe is made of immaterial 'monads') – no doubt tempted to yell, 'Nonsense, nonsense, the purest nonsense.'[77]

On Saturday mornings, Ayer lectured on Russell, Wittgenstein and Carnap, a radical venture, and proof that Ryle's affection for foreigners (from Germany, Austria, Cambridge) was contagious. Ryle had at least had the courtesy to begin his eccentric series with the long-dead Bolzano; here was a man with the temerity to lecture on three philosophers who were not only still alive but still writing. Ayer lectured in the quick, chatty patter that was to remain his characteristic mode of speech. It wasn't clear to him how much the students were taking in, but they did keep coming, even though they didn't have to. After all, Wittgenstein wasn't going to be on the exam. In tutorials, his students, only a year or two younger than him, were inclined to be overfamiliar: 'What great sad dark brown eyes you have, sir.'[78]

Ayer was writing with industry. Moore had accepted for publication in *Mind* an ambitious paper titled 'Demonstration of the Impossibility of Metaphysics'. He expatiated on his Viennese discoveries to anyone who would listen, until Isaiah Berlin suggested, controversially, that he really should get all this written down before the energy began to sap.[79] Ayer didn't want to be another of those Oxford philosophers reduced to silence by the demands of the term-time tutorial load. Also, who knew how much longer the Circle would stay together in Vienna? The days of Jews, Socialists and freethinkers in Austria were surely numbered. Berlin, refugee from Bolshevism, knew a thing or two about that.

By a stroke of luck, Ayer found himself at a dinner party

thrown by another well-travelled young philosopher. Dick Crossman (b.1907) at New College was supposed to be working on a book about Plato, but he was also in with the *New Statesman* crowd and had views on German fascism that he was anxious to share. Like Auden, Crossman had spent his first years as a graduate travelling in Germany. At the party was Sheila Lynd, an influential figure in publishing who worked at the London offices of Victor Gollancz, the publisher of the moment (George Orwell's *Down and Out in Paris and London* had been getting some excellent reviews). Perhaps Gollancz might be interested in publishing something by an up-and-coming philosopher about a fashionable new intellectual movement. Ayer called on Gollancz shortly after that encounter. He left his London office with a contract.[80]

Deadline in sight, Ayer acquired a typewriter, although he hadn't got beyond hunt-and-peck. The *Mind* essay could be the basis for chapter one, but from then on, he was composing from scratch, and slowly, so there was little need to edit. It took him eighteen months to produce the promised manuscript, the last full stop placed three months before his twenty-fifth birthday. Victor Gollancz was a little nonplussed at the sight of the manuscript: page after page of abstract, slightly technical prose wasn't quite the sort of thing he was used to publishing. But he kept his promise and did it justice: Bauhaus typeface – an appropriate choice given Carnap's sense of allegiance with the architects and designers of the school[81] – with generous spacing that gave a short book of 60,000 words a sense of real heft. It was sold for nine shillings in a first edition of 500 copies. Gollancz seemed to think it unlikely there would be any further editions of *Language, Truth, and Logic*.

Shortly after the book's publication, Ryle was in Blackwell's bookshop next to Trinity College where he found two of the last survivors of the old guard, Prichard and Joseph, talking in scandalised tones of their shock that such a book should have found a publisher. (It was unclear whether they had read it.) Prichard in his previous encounters with Ayer could barely stand to address his words to him directly, preferring to address Joseph, who was to convey them to the upstart. Ryle was wondering if he should join the conversation when Ayer's book found an unexpected, though hardly sympathetic, champion. Robin Collingwood, by now very possibly the last survivor of the idealist generation, appeared all of a sudden to deliver a prophecy, cruel but accurate: 'Gentlemen, this book will be read when your names are forgotten.'[82]

3

Argy-Bargy

'A Portuguese Jew, by the look of him,' wrote Virginia Woolf (b.1882) in a letter after she had met Isaiah Berlin (b.1909) in Oxford for a dinner at New College. 'A communist, I think, a fire eater.'[1] Her dining companion was in fact born in Riga, then in the Russian Empire, and was a life-long anti-Communist. Shortly after the Bolshevik revolution, the young Berlin had been brought to London and sent to St Paul's School, where his masters found him rather 'inclined to write about ultimates'. His friends, even then, were struck by the way he spoke, 'like playing an instrument ... like a fountain', seemingly for the sheer pleasure of it. About the only time he was silent while others spoke was at chapel. 'O Lord, open thou our lips,' said the chaplain, and Berlin was, with a small number of other Jewish boys, one of the few whose mouths didn't shew forth His praise.[2]

Berlin went to Corpus Christi, where the offices had no typewriters and undergraduates were not supposed to read anything so extravagantly modern as the new degree in philosophy, politics and economics. He learnt the Latin grace in case he was ever called on, as a scholar, to say it at dinner, but he never was. Berlin took on the editorship of a fashionable student magazine, *Oxford Outlook*, and used the perch to acquaint himself with the best undergraduate talent. His college rooms on Magpie Lane, just off the High Street, were the site of a permanent salon, where political chat was studiously avoided. He read constantly and into the night, his rooms in a state of constant chaos – books, letters, records and forgotten cups of tea.[3]

His tutor at Corpus Christi was Frank Hardie, one of Gilbert Ryle's Wee Teas. The gentle Scotsman wouldn't let him get away with airy talk of 'ultimates'. A few tutorials in, Berlin knew that the slightest hint of pretentious obscurity would invite a rap on the figurative knuckles.[4] Maurice Bowra collected him for his 'immoral front' of non-conforming students and dons, letting him correct his Russian and showing the precocious talker how the real maestri did it.[5] Stephen Spender, still an apprentice poet, took him to Austria, the attraction being not logical positivism but the Salzburg Festival, at which, between 1930 and 1938, he watched revivals of *Don Giovanni*, *Don Pasquale* and *Fidelio*, while eating at cafés into which every so often would barge packs of ruddy louts in *Lederhosen* sporting swastikas on their arms, noting darkly that the café's clientele looked distinctly *cosmopolitan*.[6]

Berlin was sexually reticent, but – committed to liberal ideals – didn't judge. He was amused, but not offended, when someone took him for Spender's boyfriend. He couldn't accompany Spender into the Communist Party but respected the commitment: it was almost (one of his highest terms of praise) *Russian*.[7] When Spender graduated and made a trip to Germany, Berlin stayed behind at Oxford. Spender worried for his friend, so sophisticated and yet such an innocent. He worried in particular that Berlin might be one of those promising young men so entranced by Oxford that they could never leave. He wrote from Germany with warnings: 'If philosophy withdraws to the seclusion of Oxford and is studied by people who see nothing outside of Oxford, it will create a remote idealistic world, which is quite as cloistered as the Church ever was, but which provides a trap for people with brains.'[8]

Spender's warnings went unheeded. When Berlin finished Greats, he stayed on to do PPE for a year and caught the eye of Dick Crossman, fellow in philosophy at New College. Spotting an opportunity to shed some of his burdensome teaching load, Crossman had contrived to get his college to create a position for a second tutor in philosophy. He preferred lecturing on radical topics before adoring audiences to going through the daily grind of listening to essay after mediocre undergraduate essay read out loud to him. Young Berlin would do that for him. There was neither application nor interview, nor any requirement of having published in a scholarly journal (Berlin's bibliography consisted at the time of a few reviews of books and music for *Oxford Outlook*). All it took was a testimonial from Hardie and the assurance provided by a good first at Greats, and Berlin went, seamlessly, from being a promising undergraduate to being a don.[9] Spender despaired.

The experience was disappointing at first. The main subject of conversations in the New College senior common room was cars. Crossman, far from being the committed Russian-style intellectual one might have supposed, struck Berlin as a cynic with contempt for the humane values that Berlin prized. Worse, he gave the impression of being a sort of 'left-wing Nazi'.[10] Frank Hardie, aware that Berlin was unhappy where he was, suggested that he should try out for the All Souls Prize Fellowship.

Berlin found the experience of applying for the fellowship an ordeal. First, there were the nine hours of exams (philosophy, economics and 'general' topics). Then he was paraded before the entire fellowship and asked to do a sight translation of a German passage. Old Lord Chelmsford, the warden of the college and former Viceroy of India, was visibly unimpressed. Another fellow, Arthur Headlam, the Bishop of Gloucester, wondered – though not in Berlin's hearing – if it was *quite* suitable for the fellowship to go to a Jew. After all, there had never been one at All Souls before – a compelling consideration at a college whose motto was *semper eadem*, 'always the same'.[11]

Convinced he had no chance, Berlin resigned himself to another year as Crossman's underling. And then the news came:

he had been elected. The *Jewish Chronicle* announced the news with jubilation: another bastion of English life breached. The Chief Rabbi wrote to congratulate him; Baron Rothschild to invite him to his country home (he accepted). Once he was allowed into the most exclusive of its institutions, he never again felt excluded from the British establishment. One day he would be dining with Goronwy Rees (b.1909), another prize fellow, who had grown up in Aberystwyth, the son of a Welsh schoolmaster; the next he might find himself drinking with the editor of *The Times* or the Foreign Secretary.[12] He came to feel at ease in such encounters, confident his silver tongue would earn him his keep, and never in doubt that he was there on merit.

All Souls was odd even by Oxford's high standards. It was beautiful, no doubt of it, and very old; it had been founded by Archbishop Chichele in 1438. The front quad, largely unchanged since its foundation, was a little Gothic with unexpected classical elements.[13] The North Quad was eighteenth-century; Nicholas Hawksmoor had been called in to advise (the college, he wrote, should preserve 'antient durable Publick Buildings ... instead of erecting new fantasticall, perishable trash').[14] The Codrington Library, named after a benefactor and sometime fellow whose family wealth came from slave-worked sugar plantations in Antigua, Barbuda and Barbados, was a handsome affair, well stocked in law and theology, and with more than respectable collections in Classics, history and aesthetic criticism ('*belles-lettres*') built up over the centuries. It was a collection that evoked a Pall Mall club more than a college library.[15]

For indeed a club is just what it was, and the clubman's life suited Berlin just fine. The place was, one need hardly say, all male, and staffed by porters even more deeply committed to the college and its ways than the fellows were. He wrote to Spender a few years later, about his loathing of all discontinuities, of deracination. That was why he was such a passionate champion of small societies – such as those he knew at Oxford. Perhaps, he wondered, it was all a longing for 'a womb with a view, a womb of one's own'.[16] His friends called him by his family nickname, 'Shaya'.[17] Virginia Woolf eventually took to him, deciding that he reminded her, in his quickness, of John Maynard Keynes as a young man, and sending him flirtatious notes: 'If you knock on my little grey door, I shall open it.'[18]

In 1933, as Freddie Ayer was settling into his lodgings in Vienna, Berlin received an offer from the warden of New College. H. A. L. Fisher (b.1865) was a retired Liberal politician then serving as the general editor of the Home University Library of Modern Knowledge series. Would Berlin write the volume on Karl Marx? He wasn't Fisher's first choice, but more illustrious writers had declined.[19]

Berlin accepted, although he was far from any kind of expert on the subject. *Capital* was, of course, on the PPE syllabus, but the full corpus (some of it available only in German) still awaited his attention. He worked his way through volume after volume, German dictionary at hand, always grateful when there was an English translation he could use as a 'crib', or (and here he had a real advantage over most British Marx scholars) a commentary in Russian, which he read fluently.[20]

Marx turned out not to be a congenial subject for Berlin. Berlin found himself constantly drawn away from Marx and Marxist writers to those who articulated and defended (and not only in argument) the liberal – bourgeois – civilisation he valued. The critic Alexander Herzen became a particular favourite, as did Ivan Turgenev.[21] Both knew full well the evils of tsars, but were equally anxious of the threat of the mob that might take their place.

All Souls was not, in the 1930s, a place where one could be uncommitted on such questions. The matter of appeasement was always in the air, the older fellows dividing themselves neatly into pro and anti. Among the elders the pros had it, while it was mostly anti among the young. Every now and then, the fellows would welcome a visiting German, probably selected for being the sort of

Bertie Woosterish type it was thought the British would like. Why on earth, one pro-German visitor said to the assembled fellows, was it any less reasonable for Germany to have imperial ambitions than for Britain? A man in the corner memorably growled back: '*Wir Juden und die anderen Farbigen denken anders.*'[22]

'We Jews and the other non-whites think otherwise': the man was Lewis Namier (b.1888), who had emigrated from Russian-controlled Poland and had taken British citizenship before the First World War. His studies of eighteenth-century English politics would set the gold standard of the history of Realpolitik, his approach strongly opposed to the 'history of ideas' that Berlin was trying to write. On this occasion, and perhaps for the last time, Berlin and he were on the same side. The remark – and perhaps the prospect of war itself – had created an unexpected alliance, of imperial Britain, its Asian and African subjects, and the Jews of Europe, all temporarily on one side against Germany. The idea of such an alliance, however fantastical, served its purpose. For Berlin, it put him, and fellow members of the 'Pink Lunch Club', on the right (that is to say, the left) side of history.

The club was the idea of G. D. H. Cole (b.1889), a fellow in economics at University College who had just published *The Intelligent Man's Review of Europe Today* (1933). Berlin liked him, for all his bad jokes, schoolboyish air and visceral hatred of bankers and Americans.[23] The club brought together the anti-appeasers of Oxford and became, for a time in the mid-1930s, the place where one could listen to the leading lights of the British left, trade union leaders, Spanish Republicans and German refugees, Jews, socialists and, sometimes, Jewish socialists. The lunch was emphatically not the point, Cole arranging the meetings at cheap restaurants where bread, cheese and beer could be had for a shilling – more appropriate settings for conversations about the soul of the left than the hall of All Souls.

*

Berlin's intellectual life improved immeasurably a year into his fellowship, when another young philosopher was elected to All Souls. He came from Balliol, an unusual place for an All Souls man to originate. Balliol had, after all, been the home of T. H. Green and his worthy band of Victorian idealists, and its dons were said to dissuade their undergraduates from succumbing to the lures of that den of vice. Fellows at All Souls, it was said, ate but did not work; they drank at all hours of the day; strange men came to dine with them from London. But John Langshaw Austin (b.1911), more than most, could be trusted to keep his head amid such temptations.

Austin came from solidly middle-class stock. His parents, both English, lived then in St Andrews in Scotland; he had shone as a classical scholar in the fresh air and almost-pastoral playing fields of Shrewsbury School in rural Shropshire. He liked the school well enough, and made his peace with its demands. His work in Greek was judged 'far above the usual level even of an able Sixth Form'.[24] As house monitor, he was decisive (which probably included the use of the birch) but regarded as fair, and elicited from the small boys the same awed respect he commanded for the rest of his life. He was never found guilty of the slightest eccentricity and no one was surprised when he was elected to a scholarship at Balliol College. He would read, of course, Classics.

At Balliol he kept his head down, but he did just enough – a little acting, a little sport – not to acquire a reputation as a stick-in-the-mud. He read a good deal of Aristotle, took no strong views on the matter of idealism or realism, and turned out essays as required in a predictably tidy hand.[25] Austin's first tutor was a man called C. G. Stone (b.1886), the author of *The Social Contract of the Universe*. It was a work of unblushing metaphysics, published when Austin was just beginning Greats and taking on the question, by then quite unfashionable, 'What must there be … if there is to be reality at all?'[26] A reviewer commended the book for 'the austerity, simplicity, and conciseness of [its] style', but went on to deliver a quietly damning compliment: 'It is sometimes complained of Cambridge philosophers to-day that they pursue simplicities so resolutely as to become wholly unintelligible; and therefore it is a pleasure to record that the same type of complaint may now be levelled against certain Oxonians.'[27] Austin's affection for Stone didn't extend to accepting either his methods or his preoccupations.

Austin's other tutor, H. A. Prichard, had more of an influence on him. Prichard was of the 'realist' party of Cook Wilson. But Prichard still struck Austin as the most impressive of the old guard. Austin participated so vigorously in discussions at his lectures that Prichard tried to stop him coming – he was putting the other students off.[28] He surprised no one with his *proxime accessit* – honourable second place – in the Ireland and Craven prize, or in the Gaisford Prize for Greek Prose, or his firsts at both Mods and Greats. When he was elected, a few months after his final exams, to the All Souls fellowship, he was informed by a telegram sent to his parents' home in St Andrews that the college hoped he would be available to dine on Monday. He replied nonchalantly to say he'd been intending to be in Oxford on the day anyway.[29]

Berlin and Austin, chalk and cheese, hit it off. For several hours every day after breakfast, the two men would talk philosophy. When Austin accepted a teaching fellowship at Magdalen two years later, the men continued to meet for long walking conversations. Magdalen lay a couple of hundred paces east from All Souls along the High Street. A little removed from the High Street was Addison's Walk, a quaint footpath around an island in the Cherwell, the minor river that meets the Isis just outside the college; Austin's conversations with Berlin would take them on long circuits along the Cherwell. Berlin came to think Austin 'the ablest [philosopher] I ever knew intimately'.[30] To Berlin, terrified by the sight of a blank page and dependent on the provocations of earlier writers to set his pen going, Austin's ability to think without a text marked him as a real philosopher.[31]

When Austin spoke, there was nothing between him and his subject, no traditional commentary, no -ism, no special theoretical lens. It felt rather like 'the question was being posed clearly for the first time: that what had seemed blurred, or trite, or a play of conventional formulae in the books had suddenly been washed away'.[32] Here was the problem, by itself, shorn of accretions: 'clear, unanswered and important'. And what's more, the whole thing had an air of a virtuoso performance of 'fascinating assurance, apparently effortless skill'.[33] Those who walked past Austin's windows in the evening would hear strains of Bach being played, solo, on the violin.

Austin's temper was not Berlin's: not for him the temptations of literary life and the company of poets and Cabinet ministers. His speech was deliberate, every syllable enunciated, every phrase considered. His sense of humour tended towards the schoolboy-ish, his diction lapsing every so often into the Edwardian. Freddie Ayer, who came to know him at the same time, though never as closely, found him 'impersonal. With his steely spectacles, his slightly taut figure, and the light belted mackintosh he often wore, he made me think of a gunman,' not so much a gangster as a sort of Irish nationalist 'fighting against the Black and Tans'.[34]

But his capacity for sympathy seemed infinite. He could take in everything Berlin said (and Berlin was capable of saying a great deal per minute), without judgement, without dismissal, without any demand for things to be paraphrased in some preferred idiom. He listened, he understood, and when he started to speak, with the piercing clarity he brought to all things, philosophical or not, it 'made one's thoughts race'.[35] But like G. E. Moore – whom he, of course, admired – what he dispensed was common sense in generous portions.

What, Berlin once wondered aloud, ought one to say to a child who wanted to meet Napoleon at the Battle of Austerlitz? How to explain why it couldn't be done? Was the point verbal, as some philosophers were suggesting? Could one really say that 'it does not make sense, as we use words, to say that you can be in two places at once or "go back" into the past'? But in that case, Berlin went on, why couldn't a precocious child reply that if it was all a matter of how we use words, well, we could start to use our words differently. And then perhaps we might shake hands with Napoleon at Austerlitz? How to get the child to see the utter folly of confusing what Carnap called the 'material' and 'formal' modes? Austin, a little wryly at the sight of Berlin's agitation, said he didn't think there was any call to bring Carnap into it. 'Tell the child to try and go back into the past. Tell it there is no law against it. Let it try. Let it try, and see what happens then.'[36]

Here was a clever man who showed no desire to preach to one, to convert one, to bully one, to trip one up.[37] Austin was not an expressive man. He was not warm, and had few friends. By some odd alchemy, he had found in Berlin exactly the qualities he most needed in an interlocutor: Berlin said what he thought, and was clever enough to understand what Austin was saying.[38] For a time in the 1940s, Berlin displayed on the mantelpiece of his New College office a two-foot by six-inch piece of cardboard, presumably acquired from a car dealer, that said simply: 'AUSTIN'. It was a reminder, Berlin explained to any who asked, that 'there are acute critics at work'.[39]

The capacity for sustained argument, step by step by step, was familiar to anyone who had seen Prichard in action. The ability to live without -isms may have been a sign that Ryle's example was beginning to corrupt the youth of Oxford. But Austin, barely twenty-five, seemed to have achieved the freedom from dogmatism that Prichard, a man of decided prejudices, only preached. Austin was, even then, a temperamental – if not yet doctrinal – realist. The world was resolutely there, there *anyway*, and it was possible to get it wrong. Equally, it was possible to get it right. But getting it right involved walking up the steep path of labour; there was no shortcut for the genius.

Austin's model for philosophy was not, as in Vienna, physics or mathematics. To his frustration, he didn't know enough about the sciences, his parents having fallen prey to the delusion, then common among the middle classes, that Classics was the only thing for a clever boy.[40] He worked in his first couple of years at All Souls to remedy his scientific ignorance, making his way conscientiously through several textbooks of mathematics. But he didn't need maths or science to teach him that insight came only from the expenditure of blood, sweat and close attention to detail. That he had learnt – as Nietzsche (b.1844), and closer to home, A. E. Housman (b.1859) had done before him – from the discipline of philology, the historical study of languages.

Housman applied his philological learning to the task of textual criticism, preparing authoritative editions of Latin texts. Textual criticism, Housman once said in his usual deflationary way, was what we do when we 'notice and correct a misprint'.[41] The activity was unglamorous, the critic 'a dog hunting for fleas'.[42] Scientists in their laboratories had the enormous advantage of being able to 'bring their opinions to the test of fact, and verify or falsify their theories by experiment'. But how was a critic, trying to decide between a dozen small variations in different pieces of papyrus purporting to be editions of the same Latin poem, to test a hypothesis about the correct line reading? There being no such test, the critic needed to take care: 'We should look sharp after ourselves; … we should narrowly scrutinise our own proceedings and rigorously analyse our springs of action.'[43] Was this not as good a motto for the philosopher? And was this not the spirit, if not quite the letter, of the verificationists of Vienna?

Housman died in 1936, a world-weary old don, in Cambridge. Two months later, Moritz Schlick was shot in Vienna, four times in the abdomen and legs, with a 6.35 mm pistol. He died on the spot. The shooter was a former student, Johann Nelböck (author of a doctoral dissertation titled 'The Importance of Logic in Empiricism and Positivism'). His motivations were never entirely clear. He had been, for a time, in an institution, diagnosed with paranoid schizophrenia. He was sentenced, nevertheless, to ten years in prison. Two years later, after the German annexation of Austria – the *Anschluss* – he sought a pardon. Had he not, he said, by eliminating 'a Jewish teacher who propagated doctrines alien and detrimental to the nation ... rendered National Socialism a service'?[44] (Schlick was not Jewish.)

Two days after the assassination, Berlin was writing to a friend of 'a really valuable philosopher ... a man of great beauty' who had just been assassinated – 'murdered' didn't seem quite enough. The letter was apprehensive; there were Fascists abroad in Oxford. Just the previous month, Oswald Mosley of the British Union of Fascists had come to the Carfax meeting rooms, where the heckling from a couple of Communists in the crowd had set off a riot that ended in the anti-Fascists being put on trial for 'acting in a disorderly manner'.[45] Berlin was at the trial: the Fascists who testified there, reminiscent of Goebbels, were 'terrifying neurotic figures'. The police appeared to be on their side.[46]

To be a young don in those days was to be politicised, whatever one's prior attitudes to politics. And the politics of the youth were, for the most part, left-wing. The Pink Lunches continued, now with Austin in attendance, and the long post-breakfast conversations continued. But it occurred to both Berlin and Austin that they should open out the conversations to others. There were, by then, quite a few young philosophers around – a generation younger even than the Wee Teas – and it seemed like a good idea to get them into the same room.

An excuse for the exercise came when Berlin discovered at Blackwell's bookshop, quite serendipitously, a book by a Harvard logician, C. I. Lewis (b.1883), called *Mind and the World Order: Outline of a Theory of Knowledge* (1929). The book came out of a quite different tradition, the American pragmatism of the nineteenth century, but was evidently concerned with questions of interest at Oxford, Cambridge and Vienna, questions about the nature of knowledge, reality and the proper aims of philosophy. He passed it on to Austin, who was distracted by it from his violin (he was working, in his usual systematic way, through Bach's unaccompanied partitas).[47] They decided to offer a joint class on the book, a rare instance of a class given at Oxford on a single book by a living author. That sort of treatment was typically reserved for someone dead and (usually) Greek. The class was listed, optimistically, on the undergraduate lecture list. If the worst came to the worst, and no one came, Berlin and Austin would simply have to fill the silence by themselves.[48]

But the students came, drawn there perhaps by the reputation Austin had begun to acquire as a tutor at Magdalen. The small lecture room at All Souls seemed even smaller for the presence of a dozen or so undergraduates. By some unspoken agreement, no one invoked the names or the authority of the great and glorious dead. The conversation was restricted to the book and its themes. About six pages in, even the book was left behind. The atmosphere was one of complete relaxation, unsolemn and lively, with no one allowed to hog the floor with displays of erudition. But Berlin discovered another side to Austin's personality that hadn't come through in their tête-à-têtes. With an audience to play to, Austin turned into another, scarier, person. Berlin came to dread the moment when Austin would turn to him with a deadly glare and ask, ever so politely, 'Would you mind saying that again?'[49]

Sometimes, Austin's predatory eye would leave Berlin for a moment and turn to the class with a question. If the question was greeted with silence, as was sometimes bound to occur, the class having seen what had happened to Berlin every time he spoke, Austin would 'extend a long, thin finger, and after oscillating it slowly to and fro for a minute, like the muzzle of a pistol, would suddenly shoot it forward, pointing at some hapless youth, chosen at random, and say in a loud, tense voice, "*You* answer!"'[50] Somehow, the students kept coming.

'He dominated the class', Berlin remembered, 'through sheer force of intellect.' He 'had to win'. Berlin, happy enough to be outshone by someone he acknowledged as the superior philosophical intellect, played up the sense of a fight to the death, or a game of American football, drawing up 'argumentative plans' where the Balliol undergraduates would be arranged as protection 'against Austin's onslaughts'.[51] 'I would have been glad', Berlin later said, 'to have been much cleverer than I was. I knew that I wasn't first rate ... but I was quite respected. I wasn't despised ... I was one of the brethren.'[52]

*

Beginning in the spring of 1937, on Thursday evenings after dinner, Berlin's rooms at All Souls hosted, at Austin's instigation, meetings of young philosophers. Freddie Ayer, still at Christ Church and now a minor celebrity after the first run of *Language, Truth, and Logic* had sold out, was a regular. Another was Stuart Hampshire (b.1914), one of the Balliol undergraduates who had come to the Lewis class and was now a fellow of All Souls himself. There was also Donald MacNabb (b.1905) of Pembroke, Tony Woozley (b.1912) of Queen's, and Donald MacKinnon (b.1913) of Keble. They were all too young for the Wee Teas, but there was a sort of apostolic succession (Berlin's tutor was Frank Hardie, Woozley's Oliver Franks and Ayer's Gilbert Ryle). The former young turks, most of them still shy of their fortieth birthdays, were now senior statesmen.

The meetings were even more informal than the class on Lewis. The men addressed each other by their Christian names – with the exception of Austin, whom no one then or later (save, possibly, for his wife) dared call anything other than 'Austin'.[53] No term-cards were distributed with plans or syllabi, and meetings did not end with an announcement of the plan for the next. The participants were content for things to happen organically. A few topics kept coming up. One was whether we could have knowledge of other minds: could I ever know, really know, that you have a headache, with the same certainty that *I* know that I do? Another was what it took to be 'the same person' despite having undergone radical changes. Yet another was counterfactuals: what did it mean to say things like, 'If Chamberlain hadn't gone to Munich, Hitler would have invaded Britain'? The phrase 'sense data' was much bandied about, much taken apart; ditto 'a priori'.[54]

There were large questions in the background (is metaphysics possible? what distinguishes sense from nonsense? what is philosophy anyway?) and here, Ayer was at a distinct advantage, having just published a book whose chapters briskly went through answers to all those questions (no; verifiability; handmaiden to the sciences). Everyone had read *Language, Truth, and Logic*. The thrill of its iconoclasm made it *the* book to cite for the undergraduate who wanted to provoke his tutor, and *the* book to own for the layman who wanted his bookshelves to hint at transgressive opinions. But the book deserved to be read too, and its arguments accepted (or rejected) on their merits. No one at Oxford accepted its doctrines *in toto* – not even, it soon transpired, Ayer himself – and each man had his own particular line of objection to push. Still, the group was grateful that the book existed, if only as a focus for discussion: someone had to say the silly thing so it could be put right.

And so it went. Ayer's book was full of provocations. Philosophy is analysis, not speculation. Metaphysics is folly. There is no knowledge to be had of any 'transcendent' (what does that even *mean*?) reality. To try to gain such knowledge is to disobey the rules that determine what language is meaningful. Any genuine statement of empirical fact must be verifiable through experience. Any non-empirical truth, say a truth of logic or mathematics, is true in virtue of the meanings of the terms involved. Historical truths are tricky: the number of hairs on Caesar's head as he crossed the Rubicon had to be either odd or even, but how could one ever verify such a claim? But there was a way around this: truths about history were meaningful to the extent that they were about the archaeological and textual traces that they had left behind. Ayer seemed to have an answer to everything.

The provocations went further, extending to things even non-philosophers could care about. Assertions of value – good, beautiful, and so forth – were, Ayer proposed, best understood as 'emotive', expressive of the speaker's attitudes and emotions, attempts to get others to share them. There were no moral facts, nor any aesthetic ones, except those that described, as an anthropologist might, what human beings actually do with those parts of language. Despite appearances, there wasn't any genuine moral disagreement. To the extent that it was *disagreement*, it was disagreement over the empirical facts being assumed; to the extent that it was moral, it amounted to little more than shouting, 'Boo murder, hurrah kindness!' Theology was meaningless. It wasn't so much that there was *no* God and *no* immortal soul and *no* ego – that would have been to concede too much, i.e. that there might have been. It was rather that those statements, being so obviously *metaphysical*, could mean nothing at all, and if they meant nothing, they couldn't be true, or for that matter, false. Ayer seemed to pride himself on having gone further even than the common or garden variety atheist.

The 'positivism' Ayer had brought back from Vienna was no longer a mere mood: it consisted in *those* theses, clearly stated (by Ayer, in a lucid and surprisingly stately English) and explicitly argued for, open to revision, qualification and – maybe – refutation. One didn't have to reject the whole -ism at once, nor to dismiss it as shallow or wicked. One could say, quite simply, that it was false for such-and-such reasons, or that this argument for this thesis failed at this point. 'We felt', Stuart Hampshire said later, 'that we'd left the past of amateurishness and indeed of a certain provincialism of the Oxford of Prichard and Joseph.'[55]

Everyone spoke, and there was rather a tendency among the

'brethren' to leap in before the last speaker had completed his sentence. Austin loathed the anarchy and tried to introduce rules of order and a buzzer to enforce them.[56] Berlin managed to persuade him that the four pages of parliamentary-style rules he had drawn up were a little excessive for a group of seven people. Despite the persistent disagreements, there were no stable factions. The group was young, no one's mind fully made up. But one thing remained constant: Ayer and Austin were not going to agree on anything.

Ayer, for all his official opposition to metaphysics, was really a metaphysician at heart. His positivism hadn't turned him, as it had some others, into a hater of theories. On the contrary, as Susan Stebbing had pointed out about Carnap, positivists suffered from the same tendency as the metaphysicians they attacked: they too wanted to squeeze the world into their scheme. If this meant that some piece of common sense came out as disreputable or nonsensical, well, so much the worse for common sense. But Austin was, like Stebbing and Moore, if not quite a *defender* of common sense, unwilling to give it up at the first whiff of positivist opposition. Like Moore, and indeed his old tutor Prichard, he 'disliked and distrusted … the rhetoric, pretension, and obscurity that are apt to accompany metaphysical ambitions'.[57]

The 'workshop, no-nonsense atmosphere of the Vienna Circle' was congenial to him. But it came to seem to him that the Viennese philosophers simply weren't no-nonsense enough. They were, rightly, opposed to metaphysical nonsense. But in their 'addiction to quasi-scientific technical jargon', they were falling prey to another kind of nonsense. As a later critic complained, positivists never 'wrote "later" if they could write "at time $t_2 > t_1$"'.[58] The positivists, Austin concluded, were defenders of 'just another ambitious philosophical theory, marked scarcely less … for all its down-to-earth intentions, by mythology and obscurity'.[59] As such, the positivist, for all his public denunciations of metaphysics, was really – as the old idealist Bradley had once said

– no more than 'a brother metaphysician with a rival theory'.[60] Austin wanted none of it.

A pattern emerged at the Thursday evening meetings. Ayer would speak up for (say) *sense data*, the immediate content of experience. The concept was essential both to the Cambridge analysts and the positivists, who needed it as the foundation of their theory of knowledge. Austin would push him to clarify what he meant by this, with a literalism and persistence that Moore would have envied. Suppose the visual field had seven black and seven yellow strips. Did that amount to fourteen pieces of sense data? Or just one tiger skin? How large was the average sense datum, what its lifespan? How did one count sense data? Did they depend on perceivers? And what was a perceiver anyway, just more sense data, or something of a different kind? And so it went: Ayer would propose, Austin dispose; Austin was the almost irresistible force, Ayer the almost immovable object.[61]

Ayer had picked his side, and he seemed faintly irritated at Austin's attempt (as he saw it) to resurrect the antiquated theories that his 'phenomenalism' about perception had been devised to supplant. Was Austin trying to revive some Aristotelian theory of 'substance'? Or Locke's 'corpuscles'? Come, come, he said, let's not hide our true colours behind the Socratic pretence of only asking questions. Let him come out with an alternative: if not sense data, then what?

At that stage, Austin was quite sincere in his eschewal of alternative opinions. He wasn't even convinced that a theory was called for. What was wrong with our ordinary talk of seeing objects? Certainly there were such things as optical illusions and tricks of perspective, but one didn't need to create a whole new category of 'sense data' to describe what we see when we see a straight stick seeming to be bent in water. We could keep our talk of sense data – a special dialect carved out of ordinary language – for the occasions that called for it, for describing one's symptoms to a doctor, say, or the look of an Impressionist painting of London in the fog.[62]

Austin was not one to join Ayer in explaining away the apparent counterexamples to the sense data theory. He pressed them, relentlessly, against Ayer. What indeed were we to say about – to pick a sentence Berlin had proposed – 'Pink is more like red than it is like black'?[63] It's true, if anything is, and it's patently meaningful. But observation could not verify it (could the positivist allow that one can perceive a *similarity*?), nor was it a tautology where the meanings of the words (pink, red, more, like) would imply that the sentence had to be true. Positivism not only seemed to have nothing to say about such cases, it seemed not to be able to make sense of them at all.

Another troublesome case for the positivist was talk about the mental states of others. The sentence 'Freddie has a headache' was evidently meaningful. But how was one to verify it? Maybe talk of other people's headaches was really a disguised way of talking about the (observable) way in which they behaved when they had headaches – groaning, clutching at their temples, turning out the drawers hoping to find an aspirin. But is that what I meant when I said, 'I, Austin, have a headache' – that 'I, Austin, am disposed to groan, clutch, etc.'? And if that is not what I mean, why such an asymmetry between the meaning of the two sets of sentences?

For Austin, when the general principle clashed with the particular case, it was always the general principle that had to yield. And if that left one with no general principles, well, there were worse things. In this, he was entirely with Ryle and Price and the spirit of the Wee Teas. Philosophy was best done 'piecemeal', the problems taken up one by one, and neither positivism nor any other of the available -isms were willing to do that.

Why should we think (as C. I. Lewis had suggested) that everything that existed was either a universal or a particular? Why need all language be divided into descriptive and emotive? Why need all statements be divided into empirical and logical, verifiable and unverifiable? How could we be so sure, in advance, that these dichotomies were exhaustive? As Susan Stebbing had put it just a few years before, the mistake of the positivists was to 'seek to make *everything* clear at once'.[64] Well, it wasn't going to be as easy as that.

Austin shared with Moore, as a later colleague of his put it, the view that 'if progress was to be made', then '*many* questions would have to be raised, *many* facts surveyed, *many* arguments deployed step by step and narrowly criticised'.[65] For the point *was* to make progress, not to pirouette on the spot. It would be slow; it would be toilsome. But then, philosophy was no place for the lazy, nor for the easily bored.

'Temperamentally', Berlin later said, 'some people like mending the wall and some people like knocking holes in it. Austin was ... a hole-knocker, and Freddie was a mender.'[66] The destructive talents of Austin came to seem to Ayer almost a moral vice (to the extent that his positivism allowed him to speak of such things). At one meeting, Donald MacNabb of Pembroke remarked that their Thursday discussions made him think of 'a pack of hounds in full cry' (the fox in the analogy being, one hopes, the truth).[67] Ayer pounced on the comparison.

He must have been a little exhausted. He had proposed four successive formulations of his phenomenalist thesis – that tables, rocks and so on are simply constructs out of our perceptual experiences – each one designed to plug a chink Austin had found in the last. It was to no avail; Austin was fully equal to the latest iteration, a counterexample ready to hand. Ayer snapped. 'You are like a greyhound who doesn't want to run himself, and bites the other greyhounds, so that they cannot run either.'[68] There may have been something to the accusation, and Berlin was one of those who thought so.[69] But on the other hand, why run at all when the kennel was so warm?

The ad hominem was unusual for the setting. The group was committed to the idea, without anyone ever having had to state or enforce it, that – as Hampshire later put it – 'we should always discuss philosophy in a very quiet and if possible ironical or at any rate unexcited and unrhetorical [way]'. Rhetoric 'would have been thought just absurd. And Austin carried this to an extreme. Even the most solemn questions … had to be disinfected by a very calm, committee man's tone of voice in speaking about them.'[70]

This quality went with something else about Austin's character. All he wanted to be, all he wanted other people to be, was *rational*. Life had rational ends; one sought them (a good reason to do philosophy in the first place) and then pursued them. He could give no higher praise than to dub a man 'sensible'. An education in philosophy, he had believed even before he had decided to dedicate his life to it, was a good thing for the young. It made them rational, critical, sceptical: the alternative, as he liked to put it, was 'being chuckle-headed'. It was a shame that philosophy was not more powerful against the 'traditional pieties' of his students, who remained, despite his best efforts to play Socrates, 'incurably respectable and dully virtuous'.[71] The sudden hint of iconoclasm seems to fit awkwardly with the obsession with the sensible, but 'sensible' in Austin's idiolect was never a byword for conservatism. So few people were, by his lights, sensible.

But politics offered nothing but chuckle-headedness. Susan Stebbing turned away from *Analysis* – and indeed, analysis – to try to bring logic to the masses. 'I am convinced', she wrote in a popular manual on logical thinking published as a cheap Penguin paperback, 'of the urgent need for a democratic people to think clearly without the distortions due to unconscious bias and unrecognized ignorance. Our failures in thinking are in part due to faults which we could to some extent overcome were we to see clearly how these faults arise.'[72] And all the while, outside, there marched Mosley's blackshirts, no committee men they, and unlikely to pick up a copy of Stebbing's *Thinking to Some Purpose* at a railway station bookshop. Everywhere, the clever hopes of a low, dishonest decade were expiring. Government-issue gas masks were making their way to each household, just in case. And a few weeks before the start of the Michaelmas term of 1939, Germany invaded Poland.

4

Blood

Mary Scrutton (*mariée* Midgley, b.1919) arrived at Somerville College in the October of that fateful academic year, 1938–9. Being an institution for women, it wasn't yet entitled to call itself a 'college'. She had good reason to be nervous. Somerville was a place for *serious* young women. It didn't make allowances for the inevitable gaps and deficiencies in the education of most of the girls who applied to study there. How would she find it, studying for a Classics degree – Literae Humaniores – without the grounding in the ancient languages the young men starting the degree in the same year could take for granted? It would be especially embarrassing for her as a scholarship girl to reveal just how unprepared she was for the rigours of the Lit. Hum. course.

She had, it was true, had some advantages. The Scruttons were the sort of parents who subscribed to *New Statesman*, called themselves 'internationalists' and vocally supported the League of Nations, and voted of course for the Labour Party.[1] Tom Scrutton, Mary's father, had for a time in the early 1920s been the chaplain at King's College, Cambridge. When other families declared themselves scandalised at the sight of the philosopher G. E. Moore rather than his wife wheeling his children around in a perambulator, the Scruttons let their children know they thought such attitudes silly.[2]

Young Mary spent her early childhood in the civilised gentility of a country rectory in Greenford, to the west of London. Her clergyman father had the characteristic opinions of a man of his class and station: ecumenical, but only to a point. His children got a sense of the limits of his tolerance when they showed him a book they had fished out of a garden pond while looking for newts: *The Spiritual Exercises of St Ignatius*. The Church of Rome was all very well, but one's children were better off protected from its influence.

The word 'philosophy' cropped up early in Mary's life in the scoldings of a Miss Annie, her school headmistress, disapproving of her struggles with the cabbage on her plate. She ought, the headmistress said, 'to be more philosophical about these things'. What was 'philosophical', the child asked? It was, the headmistress replied, 'eating up your cabbage and not making a fuss about it'.[3] Here was the sort of definition that might have made a good beginning, if not quite an ending, to a Socratic dialogue.

Miss Annie also conveyed to the young Mary another Socratic lesson. When the girl protested that she *did* know the answer to a question put to her in a lesson but couldn't put it into words, Miss Annie replied with a principle that could have come from an Oxford philosopher: 'If you can't say a thing clearly, then you don't actually know what it is, do you?'

At twelve, Scrutton was sent to Downe House School, an idyllic place in the countryside of Berkshire, where the teachers were liberal (if not, in educational terms, progressive) and allowed the girls many hours of unstructured, unsupervised time in which to do what they liked.[4] In her time there, she picked up very little science, though a good deal of French, a fair amount of Latin and even a little Greek, the latter only because a keen teacher offered to teach it to a small set of enthusiasts. University was always held up as a possibility, and Scrutton was initially drawn to English Literature. But she decided, on a teacher's urging, that she was bound to read literature anyway; why not study something she wouldn't otherwise get to know?[5]

She was discovering Plato and, in his dialogues, the idea of philosophy as a special kind of literature. Her teacher informed her that Oxford offered a course that combined the study of the ancient languages, for which she had an evident aptitude, with the study of philosophy, in which she was beginning to show an interest.[6] Despite her small Latin and less Greek, it was going to be Classics that Scrutton applied to study, and Oxford where she would study it.

Downe House had led her to the classics in the best possible way: not as part of the conveyor belt that took the brightest among the sons of gentlemen through scholarship examinations and university to the civil service or the professions, but as a response to the naïve interests of the young in reading interesting books. She was seriously behind in comparison to the men she would be studying the subject with; on the other hand, she hadn't been drilled in her declensions to the point of boredom. Moreover, unlike the men who studied it with a sense of fatalistic inevitability – what other subject was there? – she could say what it was about the classics that fascinated her.[7]

Scrutton, having already taken the entrance exam, went to Oxford to be interviewed for a place at Somerville. She was nervous, and made to feel desperately underprepared by a girl boasting loudly about the impressive things she had said in her meeting. But a mistress at Downe House had prepared her charges well for the 'General Paper' by assigning them large, indeed philosophical, essay questions to answer, with no prior preparation, in forty minutes ('Nature is too green and badly lighted. Discuss.') The quality of her General essay seemed, in the minds of the Somerville tutors, to outweigh whatever difficulties would be caused by her relative lack of linguistic training. She was offered a place, with a scholarship, and found herself with nearly a year in which to prep for the rigours of Mods.[8]

Scrutton went first to a Mrs Zvegintzov in Chiswick for language lessons, but found that there might be time still for a little Continental travel before the Michaelmas term. Her Downe House mistress waved away any idea that she should try to improve her

French at Grenoble: German was the language to learn. And if Germany itself was too ghastly – Scrutton's parents would have been following political developments there closely – surely Austria was stable enough to visit, even in the March of 1938.

She arrived in Vienna on 1 March to stay with a family friend – Professor Jerusalem, who helped her with her German and armed her with Baedeker guides with which to navigate the city. She took in, as Ayer had done only a few years before, the Bruegels at the Kunsthistorisches Museum. Less uplifting were the posters outside that read '*Großdeutschland Ja!*', the two words separated by a sea of disembodied arms doing Sieg Heil salutes.

'*Ja*' was one of two permissible responses to the question on the imminent referendum: 'Do you agree with the reunification of Austria with the German Reich that was enacted on 13 March 1938 and do you vote for the list of our leader Adolf Hitler?' On the streets were young Aryan men, singing from the Hitler Youth songbook, '*Denn heute gehört uns Deutschland/Und morgen die ganze Welt.*' Today, Germany belonged to them; tomorrow, the world. By the time the referendum took place in April (99 per cent for Ja; the ballot was not secret), Chancellor Schuschnigg had resigned, the *Anschluss* was a done deal, and Austria part of the Third Reich. Professor Jerusalem was arrested, then released, and Scrutton went home to Berkshire, her German not much improved.

*

In October, with her dramatic sojourn in Vienna now a fading memory, Scrutton found herself at Somerville. The college had been founded in 1879 and was named after the mathematician Mary Somerville. The architecture was Victorian, the buildings largely unromantic. Still, the place had its charms: unpromising archways could lead to quadrangles full of trees and neo-Georgian buildings. To the south of the college was St Aloysius, where the Catholics of North Oxford would appear for Sunday mass, making the Woodstock Road heave for a moment with children. The college had its own chapel, only a few years old when Scrutton arrived. It was described by an observer as 'bleakly classical, ashlar ... bleak also inside – unloved-looking somehow'.[9]

A medical student took her in hand early on and told her to stop doing her hair like a girl guide, and that she really had to do something about her shoes. The dean of the college was the sort of sensible, downbeat academic who might have won even J. L. Austin's approval. She told the students that they had to mind their Ps and Qs as if the future of women's education depended on it. Because it did: 'The women are still on probation in the university,' she said, and a single indiscretion by a single female undergraduate would be wheeled out decades later as decisive, told-you-so evidence that women didn't belong at Oxford after all.

The question before the first meeting of the Junior Common Room committee, into which Scrutton was co-opted in her starting term, was whether they might have male undergraduates to tea not only on Saturdays (as the regulations already permitted) but also on Sundays. Despite the President's earnest urgings against deciding on anything drastic that they might come to regret, the committee approved the proposal. Men could come to tea on Sundays too; *vive la révolution*.

For meals at the college's dining hall, the women divided themselves by year, the oldest students sitting at the long tables nearest the windows. But each table was more subtly divided. At the one nearest the dons sat the studious women in navy and beige, disinclined to linger at meals, each wearing a frown of perpetual anxiety. At the table farthest from the dons sat the long-haired beauties, their experiments in fashion not yet constrained by the demands of wartime rationing. They were often late to meals, and not because they'd lost track of time at the library. Scrutton sat, though not by any conscious choice, at the middle table, where everyone was, or seemed, middling.[10]

One undergraduate was an exception to the general rules of segregation. Iris Murdoch (b.1919), with her blonde fringe, and skirts that called to mind an Alpine peasant-girl, was easy to mistake for an art student. 'She was never beautiful', Scrutton later wrote, 'but always attractive.'[11] Scrutton was struck by her liveliness, her swinging gait, her willingness to sit wherever she liked, seemingly indifferent to the rules rather than in revolt against them. She was at ease with everyone and able to put everyone at their ease. She turned out to be another classicist, and Scrutton was to see a good deal of her.

Murdoch was the daughter of Irish Protestants, born in Dublin but brought up in Chiswick in west London. Her confidence and indifference to hierarchy may have come of her having been educated in two progressive schools, the Froebel Demonstration School in London and later, as a boarder, Badminton School in Bristol. It was English she had first thought to study, but it was Greats that she decided on in the end.

Murdoch and Scrutton's first five terms would be devoted to the study of Greek and Latin language and literature, on which they would be examined at Mods. Murdoch and Scrutton shared a tutor in Mildred Hartley (b.1904). Hartley was a woman of modest eccentricity – she smoked a pipe and celebrated the start of the vacation by putting on a pair of trousers and reading a thriller. She made no concession to the poverty of her wards' previous training in classical languages. No doubt it was unfair that women, coming from schools where the classical languages were taught badly if at all, had to do the same exams as men who had been reciting their declensions since the age of six. But there was nothing to be done about it, and she would cut them not the slightest slack.

If the men were opting for papers in Greek and Latin verse composition, Hartley's girls would take them too. Her girls would be exposed to the most exacting classical scholarship, and if they didn't understand what she was talking about, that was just too bad. They were to be *credits* to Somerville. In principle, her attitudes were egalitarian. In practice, they were less so, producing bafflement and resentment on the one side, frustration and wasted effort on the other.

Many of the lectures Scrutton attended on classical philology occasioned similar bafflement. One concerned the spelling of the name 'Pyrrha' in the famous Horatian Ode ('For whom bind'st thou / In wreaths thy golden hair,' as it goes in Milton's rendering). There were dozens of variations, the lecturer said, introduced by copyists. 'Absolutely insoluble problem', he said, 'of not the slightest importance.' The unimportance of the question gave him no pause. He had a captive audience; why should it? The poetry went unmentioned; no one spoke of beauty or goodness.

Scrutton and Murdoch got a better sense of what the point of studying the classical world might be in the lectures of E. R. Dodds (b.1893). Dodds had been a surprise election to the Regius Professorship in Greek, for which he had been up against Maurice Bowra. He had come to Oxford a relative outsider: Irish, socialist and with an unimpressive war record. Isaiah Berlin wrote to a friend declaring his election in 1936 as much of a *catastrophe* for classical studies as the assassination of Moritz Schlick had been for philosophy.[12] And yet, shy and retiring, Dodds had bedded in, and classical studies had survived. Scrutton enjoyed his lectures on Plato, even though their focus was more on his literary qualities than his philosophical ones. Murdoch was unconvinced by Plato: 'the old reactionary', she decided. Why read him with his bad arguments and cheap rhetoric when one could read Marx instead?

Murdoch joined the Communist Party, a zealous convert to the cause. Scrutton demurred: her *New Statesman*-reading parents had been members of the Left Book Club, created by Victor Gollancz the same year he had published Ayer's *Language, Truth, and Logic*, and was well informed about Stalin's show trials of the 1930s. Communism would never be for her.

*

Scrutton and Murdoch were able to put aside internecine squabbles to work together on the extraordinary by-election campaign of October 1938. Oxford, usually a safe Conservative seat, was up in the air: the sitting MP had just died; the Labour and Liberal candidates had stood down to make way for one who promised to unite the left. Improbably, it was going to be a philosopher, Alexander ('Sandy') Lindsay (b.1879), Master of Balliol and the author of books on Kant, Plato and Henri Bergson, on whom it fell to defeat Quintin Hogg, thirty-one, fellow of All Souls. Hogg was a doughty defender of Prime Minister Neville Chamberlain and his claim to have brought 'peace in our time' home from Munich in the September of 1938. Hogg was isolated at All Souls among the younger fellows, most of whom were ardently opposed to the Munich agreement, but he began the campaign a firm favourite. A by-election in a small university town was turning into a referendum on appeasement itself.

Lindsay was Glaswegian, 'a tall, shambling, bear of a man', as the politician Denis Healey would later describe him. 'Wisps of white hair floated round a large pink head. He lectured in a light, sing-song voice, twisting the ends of his gown in front of him.'[13] He managed to inspire an extraordinary coalition. When, on 13 October, a Balliol undergraduate called Ted Heath (b.1916), who had spent the previous summer talking to Republicans in Spain, broke ranks with his friends at the Conservative Association and opened a debate at the Oxford Union on the mock-parliamentary motion, 'This House deplores the Government's policy of peace without honour', it was carried by 320 votes to 266.

Undergraduates and dons found themselves united campaigning for Lindsay – Gilbert Ryle signed letters supporting him, as did Maurice Bowra. J. L. Austin went to Hogg's meetings to heckle. He may have come up with the Lindsay campaign's most memorable slogan, 'A vote for Hogg is a vote for Hitler', a play on Hogg's

'A vote for Hogg is a vote for Chamberlain' (it was condemned by Lindsay himself, who preferred 'Save Peace, Save Czechoslovakia').[14] Scrutton and Murdoch stuffed envelope after envelope. Louis MacNeice (b.1907) in his long poem *Autumn Journal*, the best piece of writing to come out of Oxford in those years, captured the sense of an honourable compromise felt by many of Lindsay's supporters:

> The perfectionist stands for ever in a fog
>   Waiting for the fog to clear; better to be vulgar
> And use your legs and leave a blank for Hogg
>   And put a cross for Lindsay.[15]

Shortly before election day, Robin Collingwood wrote to Lindsay, 'I do not think that the country has ever in all its history passed through a graver crisis than that in which it is now involved ... Your candidature shows that the spirit of English democracy is not extinct. I hope that it still survives even among those who have to vote next week.'[16]

It didn't, and the more observant campaigners saw it coming. Roy Jenkins (b.1920), who spent that October 'canvassing up sodden and leafy half-drives in North Oxford' discovered, to his enormous dismay, 'that Conservative loyalty to Chamberlain and Hogg was rather stronger than academic solidarity with Lindsay'.[17] The Lindsay faction sat dejected outside the town hall on St Aldate's, where the votes were being totted up, their red-and-yellow rosettes tattered after a day at the polling stations. Hogg had won, with – small comfort – a halved Conservative majority.

'We felt glum that night,' wrote Frank Thompson (b.1920) – an undergraduate shortly to fall in love with Murdoch; 'we were like rags soaked in cold vinegar.' The Lindsay campaign had seemed to contain 'the creative, the generous, the imaginative'. The Hogg faction, he thought, was all 'selfishness, stodginess and insincerity'.[18] Louis MacNeice, in his poetic rendering of the by-election, called it a 'coward vote', the work of 'profiteers, the dunderheads, the smarties'.[19]

Yet another undergraduate, M. R. D. Foot (b.1919), announced that there were only two alternatives left, 'to join the Communist Party or abdicate from politics. I can't swallow communism so I'll abdicate and take up psychology.' But the dominant tone was one of indignation, against the selfish, stodgy and insincere who had voted for Hogg. 'I hope North Oxford gets the first bombs,' said another undergraduate, 'but it would be rough on the Pekinese.'[20]

*

In the November of 1938, Picasso's *Guernica* was shown in Oxford, and the academic *beau monde* went to see it.[21] But it wasn't long before the prospect of bombs in North Oxford was no longer an idle fantasy. When the war began, in its ominously quiet early ('phoney') phase, twenty was the age of conscription. That meant a boy admitted to Oxford could have a few terms' worth of tutorials before the front beckoned. But no one expected that number to stay fixed. The young men had heard that one before, or rather their fathers had. Between tutorials, lectures, the river and rugby pitch, there was also the Officers' Training Corps, where those who hoped to become officers drilled half a day every week.

Ministry of Food regulations later came into force. Not even the canniest gourmet could find plovers' eggs to serve at luncheon, not even at the well-stocked Covered Market. Sometimes college dinners had no meat. Would-be aesthetes were reduced to wearing the same coarse tweed as the rest. For a time, there was at least coal to heat the students' rooms, but soon that too was gone when fuel rationing started. There was cake, though, and even the occasional cigarette, for those willing to queue in the autumn cold.

The old distinctions – who the scholar, who the commoner; who the freshman, who the elder statesman; who the Etonian, who the Wykehamist; who the Balliol man, who the damned – were dissolving. At some colleges, there were so few servants left, and those left put to darkening the windows at dusk in preparation for air raids, that students were sent to the kitchens, or armed with dust mops. The college gardens were commandeered for potatoes, the dreaming spires for fire-watching. Some colleges were taken over entirely by one government ministry or other, the men evacuated down the road to a neighbouring institution. Everyone was a transient in the last days of arcadia.

Degrees were shortened by a year. Medical students from London took over Wadham, Keble and St Peter's Hall, the Royal Institute of International Affairs part of Balliol, the Directory of Fish Supplies St John's. Tutorials were less intimate than before; students were sent to other colleges, put into little groups (there were not enough hours in the day for the solo tutorials of the old days). The younger dons were disappearing, to fight, or be useful in some way better suited to their talents (breaking codes, making up numbers at the civil service). The old, and those who'd failed their physicals – the myopic, the arthritic, the asthmatic – were left to pick up the slack.

All of a sudden, Oxford was not much fun: no cigarettes, no razors, no soap, vegetarian dinners and the prospect of having to wipe one's bottom with scraps of old newspaper. Even Maurice Bowra, veteran of another war and now warden of Wadham College, was beginning to lose his high spirits: 'One's job is to stay here and stick it out.'[22] His letters began to sound positively homiletic: 'One's chief duty is to be sane, and not indulge in hate, which only creates lies and trouble for the future. (How very moral all this sounds, but it is so extremely real now.)' But there were comforts: 'We are all in it together, old and young, men and women. The sacrifice is equally shared.'[23]

And suddenly, in a stark inversion of the usual order of things at Oxford, there were barely any men to be seen. Female clerks and civil servants were soon walking busily in the town centre. The academic women who'd been there all along, both tutors and students, became more visible, after decades of being hidden away where they could do, and be done, no harm: at St Hilda's at the eastern end of the High Street beyond Magdalen bridge, Lady Margaret Hall near the Parks, Somerville at the southern end of the Victorian suburbs of North Oxford, and St Hugh's, so far north one may as well be at the university of Birmingham (that is to say, it was a twenty-minute walk from the centre). Dr Pusey had in 1884 described the establishment of the women's colleges as 'one of the greatest misfortunes that has happened even in our own time in Oxford'.[24] Until 1920, women who passed the same exams were not entitled to Oxford degrees, and even in 1939, there were still people who held Dr Pusey's view of the matter.[25]

The lectures and classes the women attended for Mods in the year after the declaration of war had a peculiar feel. There were about as many women there as men when it began, but by the time Murdoch and Scrutton were attending lectures for Greats – the second part of the Classics course – the women were in the majority (the men being required elsewhere), and the men remaining were unusual for Oxford: disabled, conscientious objectors, ordinands, few of them likely to have known each other from school or rowing. Scrutton would remark, many years later, that conditions were ideal for the women to speak, and, what was rarer, to be heard.[26]

*

By the time the Michaelmas term of 1940 began, there was nothing phoney about the war. Paris had fallen. The Thursday evening group of the late 1930s had abruptly been dissolved. J. L. Austin was in training at Aldershot. A. J. Ayer had managed to wangle a commission in the Welsh Guards (the bowler hat and old school tie he wore to his meeting with the colonel might have helped), and was learning to ride a bicycle in preparation.[27] Tony Woozley was in the King's Dragoon Guards, dividing his time between tutorials on logic at Queen's in the morning and instructing student cadets in tank-driving as a member of the Armoured wing of the OTC in the afternoon; he would soon be deployed to North Africa.[28] Stuart Hampshire was shortly to be sent to Sierra Leone.[29] Isaiah Berlin was off to Washington, soon to be doing something very secret for the British Information Services. That left Donald MacKinnon, suddenly alone, nearly the only philosopher his age at Oxford.

Iris Murdoch appeared at his rooms in Keble in 1941, a spartan chamber in a Victorian-Gothic tower with a battered armchair and a table messy with papers. Sometimes, he was still in the boiler suit he had worn the previous night for fire-watching.[30] Sometimes he was lying under the table, sometimes he rolled himself up in his carpet, like a living mummy. Sometimes he shouted his questions out of one of his windows, the student to respond through the other. Sometimes, he would teach from the bath, the student reading his essay from atop the toilet.[31] (He did not do this if the student was female, which suggested some minimal awareness of the norms of propriety.) One male student was dragged to the Lamb and Flag next door, was bought a whisky, then made to walk up and down the bar while MacKinnon talked, his oration *full* of audible *italics*, about *Kant*. The soldiers drinking at the bar clapped when he'd finished. MacKinnon blushed – as if he hadn't realised they could hear him.

He sometimes taught, probably had to teach, on Sundays, but insisted his students never miss church for a mere tutorial. His dentures – he was twenty-eight, but this was 1941 – seemed always about to pop out. His students tended to assume he was much, much older than he was. With his enormous shoulders, the quaint burr of his native Argyllshire creeping every so often in his otherwise Winchester College vowels, the physical clumsiness that meant he was always breaking things, he seemed more prophet than philosopher, something out of Dostoevsky, or the Old Testament itself. He sometimes admitted he felt guilty about not being in uniform like other men his age, and seemed to think it might be easier on his overdeveloped conscience if he worked himself literally to death.

Who knew if the sudden movements of the body, the grimaces that sometimes took over his countenance, the long, long silences, were pathological symptoms or expressions of philosophical anguish? The eccentricity that had marked him at the Thursday sessions of positivists and positivists *manqués* was his unabashed commitment to the possibility of metaphysics. He taught with passion, seemingly without regard to the formal (or even informal) requirements of his job. Mary Scrutton was summoned back for additional tutorials on some thorny passage of Kant (on top of his already excessive burden) until they had 'got to the bottom of this'.[32]

Iris Murdoch, after a few weeks of tutorials with him, wrote to her boyfriend, Frank Thompson, about her extraordinary tutor: 'It's bucked me up a lot meeting him.' For what seemed like the first time, a good moral philosopher was also a morally good man. She had lately given up on the traditional categories of value, but meeting MacKinnon had made it possible for her to think in terms of such old-fashioned categories again.[33]

*

MacKinnon's eccentricities coexisted with an extraordinary capacity for thoughtful consideration. When students came to him, anxious and depressed, he spoke to them with kindness and sensitivity. He saw each student as an individual (he saw so many every week that one wonders how he managed it). When he learnt that a certain student was confined to bed in her room in North Oxford in 1942 with tuberculosis trying to prepare for her Finals, he let Murdoch know that 'Philippa might appreciate a friendly visit'. Murdoch took the hint and appeared at her door, a rustic bouquet of wildflowers in her hand.

The Philippa in question was Philippa Bosanquet (*mariée* Foot, b.1920). A year younger than Scrutton and Murdoch, and having come up to Oxford in 1939 to study PPE, she was treated to the full range of MacKinnon's eccentricities: the pokers waved, the interminable silences, and the respectful attention to the works of Kant, Hegel and F. H. Bradley. It mightn't have been obvious that Bosanquet would appreciate friendly visits. She was shy and far from confident but didn't always look it. Even as an undergraduate, Bosanquet seemed halfway on the road to being a *grande dame*. Scrutton found her 'a little formidable', the sort of person with unmeetable standards.[34] She looked like the sort of young woman who knew how to get a boisterous dog to sit.

Bosanquet was very well-dressed and remained so even after clothes rationing began. She had no need to make do and mend. She'd had a more privileged upbringing than most of her fellow Somervilleans, but it was a privilege of the wrong sort for what she wanted. Her father was the prosperous manager of a steelworks in Yorkshire and she was brought up in a world of hunting balls. The young Philippa had been educated (or left uneducated) by her governesses, who had tended to be the sort of women well-informed about a lady's comportment but unsure who had come first, the Greeks or the Romans.

When, for once, she found herself with a governess with a university degree, there occurred to her for the first time the idea that she might go to university too. Against her mother's wishes, she worked for a year with a correspondence course and a tutor, intending to apply to Somerville. When she was admitted, her dismayed mother – the daughter, as it happened, of the American president Grover Cleveland – feared for her prospects. A friend offered reassurance: 'At least she doesn't *look* clever.'[35]

*

Lunch at Somerville always brought the chance of a serendipitous encounter with a new person. One day, Mary Scrutton found herself at lunch with a student in the year above, Jean Coutts (*mariée* Austin, b.1918), who had brought a friend, another Classics student from St Hugh's. The conversation turned to Plato. Scrutton, who didn't agree with Murdoch in dismissing him as an old reactionary, thought that he'd been on to something with his talk of 'Forms', immaterial, immutable and 'behind' all their visible manifestations. Of course there had to be such things: what else could be behind what made all men men, all beautiful things beautiful, all good things good?

What else indeed. But the guest had a different question. Maybe so, she said, but what does it *mean* to say 'the good itself'; and what sort of *behindness* is it? What could it mean to say they must *be*, to say they *must* be? Other people had been raising similar questions: Moore with his 'what *on earth*', and the positivists with their hair-trigger sensitivity to anything in the ballpark of nonsense. This young woman's words, their demand for clarity and meaningfulness, sounded similar. But the tone was different, and not only because it was spoken in so beautiful, so gentle a voice. It was a real question: what did it mean? What could it mean? What might it mean?

The point of asking the question was, if possible, to answer it. The possibility that it might be answered, indeed that it might be answered in Plato's favour, wasn't closed off in advance. The question wasn't being asked rhetorically as an excuse for consigning another body of nonsense to the bonfire of metaphysical vanities.

The thoughtful visitor was Gertrude Elizabeth Margaret Anscombe (b.1919), known to all as Elizabeth. She had always been a serious girl, and had always looked it. One student, introduced to her a few years later, found her eyes drawn away from the shapeless trousers, baggy jumper and the hair ('longish, greasy and of no particular colour, held back in some kind of "bun"') to her face, 'of astonishing serenity and beauty'.[36] People craved her favour, as of the Holy Virgin.

She was brought up, Anglican and middle class, in south London, where her father, a soldier turned schoolmaster, taught physics at Dulwich College. At twelve, she discovered Catholicism in heroic stories of the recusant priests of the Elizabethan age; her life-long refusal to give in to the demands of the supposed spirit of the age may have had something to do with her taking the recusants as her models.[37] She cut her philosophical teeth while trying to repair an argument for the existence of God she found in a Jesuit text: the crucial premise was that everything that happens has a cause, but this seemed to her to contain within it what it was supposed to prove. She thought it was a simple matter of tidying it up a little so that it didn't commit a fallacy. Like a one-woman Socratic dialogue, she brought herself to the realisation that the argument would need rather more work than that. Without any explicit idea that this was what she was doing, she turned herself into a philosopher.

In her first year at Oxford, she started taking instruction in the faith from a Dominican. At a Corpus Christi procession in the summer of 1938, she had met a fellow convert, a young man at Balliol College, a few years older and fresh from success at Greats, who was receiving instruction from the same Dominican.

Peter Geach (b.1916) was the son of a man who had studied the Moral Sciences tripos (as the philosophy course at Cambridge was then called) but who settled for sending his son to Oxford because Balliol offered the better scholarship. He arrived there with his dialectical skills well honed by his father's training, and an adolescence spent reading Russell, Moore and McTaggart. The place suited him just right.

Balliol offered the young Geach exactly the sort of stimulation he needed: clever chaps with whom to argue the night away. It was the sort of place where he might find other young men willing to join him in editing a Jacobite publication (*The White Rose:*

For English Liberty). When Edward VIII abdicated in 1936, Geach had raised a Jacobite flag on Balliol tower and asserted the claim of Rupprecht of Bavaria, a Stuart descendant. Many of his fellow Jacobites were, as he was not yet, Catholic. In their arguments, Geach was cleverer, but the Catholics (he later said) were right. And then, it happened: 'My defences quite suddenly collapsed: I knew that if I were to remain an honest man I must seek instruction in the Catholic Religion.'[38]

Then came the climactic Corpus Christi day procession. The young woman was beautiful, and spoke beautifully, but was she – he had to ascertain – 'reliably Catholic'? On it being confirmed she most assuredly was, he initiated the courtship that would culminate in marriage a few years later: 'Miss Anscombe,' he is supposed to have told her, 'I like your mind.'[39]

*

Sequestered in distant St Hugh's, Anscombe did not come to know either Murdoch or Scrutton well as an undergraduate. They were left to figure things out for themselves at Somerville. Things got better for them once they moved on from Mods to Greats. Their tutor for history was now Isobel ('Iso') Henderson (née Munro, b.1906), less anxious and less obsessive in her demands of her students than Mildred Hartley. Scholarship was one part of what made life enjoyable for her, and she felt an acute sense of continuity between what was best in the civilisation of the ancient world, and the (embattled) European civilisation of which she felt a part. She lived with her family at Lincoln College, a little way south of Somerville (her father was the rector, that is, the head of house). She had taken in Oxford politics with her mother's milk. Fair-haired and confident, she spoke with conviction and clarity about the things that interested her: music, horses, cricket, sailing and Spain.

A suggestion or recommendation from Henderson counted for

something with students and fellow dons alike. When Murdoch and Scrutton were told they should 'go to Fraenkel's classes', there was no question of declining. The girls took it that this was supposed to be a special honour, from the man generally thought the greatest classical scholar living.

Eduard Fraenkel (b.1888) was a German Jew from a long-assimilated line of wine merchants. Their Jewishness only became a part of their self-image when Hitler forced it onto their attention. In his youth he came under the influence of the great Ulrich von Wilamowitz-Moellendorff (b.1848), a philologist best known for being one of Friedrich Nietzsche's sternest scholarly critics. Yet, he had something of the same intense relationship with his subject matter as Nietzsche had with his. One had to *get it right*, at any cost.

Here was philology at its most full-blooded. There was no doubting the man's scholarship: not even the most demanding scholiast in Byzantium could have had a complaint against his rigour. The usual stuff of academic philology was all where it should be (variant line readings, notes on grammar, commentaries on the commentaries of older scholars, mild rebukes to inaccurate scribes). But how much more there was here. This was philology practised as history, archaeology, art criticism and theology all at once. The language was a way into a whole world.

Wilamowitz (as he was generally known) had the knack of turning the question, 'What does this text really say?' into a way of asking, 'What was it like to be *alive* then?' 'The tradition is dead,' he famously remarked. 'Our task is to revivify life that has passed away.' But to make the ghosts speak, we had to feed them with our blood.[40] The methods of science, patient and meticulous, were only worth setting to the task if there was some chance of bringing 'that dead world to life ... to recreate the poet's song, the thought of the philosopher and the lawgiver, the sanctity of the temple and the feelings of believers and unbelievers, the bustling life of market and port, the physical appearance of land and sea, mankind at work and play'. Philology, much as Socrates once remarked of philosophy, begins in wonder, 'wonder in the presence of something we do not understand'.[41]

Fraenkel took it all to heart, the letter and the spirit, the sense that in philology lay all the secrets of life and death. He shared the energy and intensity of his master without being as physically imposing. A childhood infection of the bone marrow had left him with a deformed hand and a withered arm, but his disability appears to have made no difference to his feverish work ethic. His academic career, which he did not care to advance by being baptised, began in the shadow of the slow decline of the Weimar Republic. His reasons for not being baptised, he later explained, were 'a sort of family pride, and ... a sense of tradition'.[42] The freedoms and relative tolerance for Jewish scholars in these years were sufficiently robust for him to ascend to a full professorship in 1923. His career appeared to be flourishing when, in 1935, the shocking news of the Nuremberg laws came to him. He was forbidden to teach. The rector of Freiburg, as it happens a certain Martin Heidegger, tried to make a case for him as belonging to the right category of Jew: '*edle Juden von vorbildlichem Charakter*', as he put it in a letter to the Ministry of Culture. But 'noble Jew of exemplary character' or not, he had, by the end of the year, been dismissed with a modest pension. Fraenkel began English lessons.

On A. E. Housman's recommendation, he was offered a temporary fellowship at Trinity, Housman's college in Cambridge, and then a Chair in Latin at Oxford. Early on during the English half of his life, he was taken to visit Winchester College during the summer term: the sight there of schoolboys sitting outdoors composing – at any rate, claiming to be composing – Greek verse under the sun, impressed and moved him. Perhaps the move to England wasn't such a climb-down after all.[43]

Fraenkel arrived in Oxford to take up the Chair in Latin at Corpus Christi College in 1935, with testimonials from Maurice Bowra and Housman – the latter professing an ironic gratitude to Hitler for his gift to British academia. As an academic émigré, Fraenkel was far from alone. The 1930s saw perhaps as many as 70,000 European Jews migrate to Britain. Oxford naturally attracted the most prominent academics among them. (Ernst Cassirer had briefly been one.) A. L. Rowse of All Souls reported feeling sometimes like he was 'inhabiting a bit of old Vienna or some Central European university town', such was the tower-of-Babel quality of some streets.[44] One Sudetenland refugee started something called a 'Delikatessen' in the Covered Market. Clever, industrious and grateful, the refugees picked up English with an impressive rapidity, but the official language was 'Emigranto': a German speckled with the odd piece of useful English idiom, an English haunted by the German of their thoughts.[45]

With Fraenkel and fellow refugees from German universities came that peculiar Germanic institution, the 'seminar'. Fraenkel quietly ignored the usual Oxford deference to the needs of undergraduates and started a set of seminars to which tutors were invited to send their most talented students. There was no promise that the seminars had much to do with the undergraduate syllabus. They would help no one get a first at Greats. And perversely, as he was the new Professor of Latin, they would concern a play in Greek.

Fraenkel had been working on the *Agamemnon* – the first tragedy in Aeschylus's *Oresteia* cycle – on and off, since the 1920s. He would eventually publish his edition of the play in 1950, the text and notes ultimately comprising three large volumes, weighing nearly half a stone. (A 'Teutonic monster', said someone at Oxford University Press, referring to the book rather than its author.) This was no Pelican paperback, and no one was likely to pick it up after a casual browse at Blackwell's bookshop.

King Agamemnon of Mycenae is home from ten years' fighting in Troy. The Greeks have won, and Agamemnon is now prepared to regard the sacrifice of his daughter to the goddess Artemis as having been worth it, all things considered. At home waits his queen Clytemnestra, with vengeance for her daughter in her heart, and a lover, Aegisthus, who has his own grudge against Agamemnon (his father having been tricked by Agamemnon's into eating two of his sons). Very little happens, in any narrow sense. Agamemnon returns, a concubine by his side, the mad prophetess Cassandra. Off-stage, he is stabbed in his bathtub. Clytemnestra is remorseless, and talks about the killing in loving detail. Her exiled lover bursts into the palace; their revenge is sweet, for now. How much could there be to say about this meagre plot? It turned out, roughly, 1,100 pages' worth.

The book came out of the seminar, a roving affair that began in Germany many years previously, but which was now putting down new roots at the long table in the austere ground-floor room at Corpus Christi. Attending were somewhere between twelve and twenty people, a mixture of undergraduates and dons, with Fraenkel himself always presiding, for two hours between five o'clock and seven, every week in term time. It was to these seminars that Murdoch and Scrutton were urged by their tutors to go.

It all took place, Scrutton later recalled, in a room with Tudor windows, so 'visibly ancient ... that one had a strong impression of forming part of a timeless sequence of scholars'.[46] And that, in a sense, was what it was: in Fraenkel seemed to coalesce the whole tradition, from archaic Greece through the chaos of the Peloponnesian wars, to Rome and its fall, through the dark middle ages with their wanton destruction and ignorant transcriptions and the rediscoveries of the Italian Renaissance, all this channelled through the scientific methods of the German Enlightenment and barked out in weekly doses to the terrified spectators at Corpus Christi.

The seminar felt, and in a sense was, endless. It became very quickly apparent that there was no prospect of their being done with the text this term, or the next, or indeed the one after. They were to keep going until they had got it right, *perfectly* right, which translated to a pace of just around ten lines an hour. It took him as long to get through the play, it was pointed out in tones of amusement and awe, as it had taken Agamemnon to capture Troy.

For Murdoch, watching the proceedings with terrified awe, this was a vision of scholarly excellence. The atmosphere, she recalled, was tense, as if the place were an interrogation chamber, the pregnant silences unbroken by any human voice, the reflective quietness interrupted only by the clock of Merton College next door striking the quarters.[47] The dons were no less in awe of their master than the undergraduates; in some ways, they had more to lose when their ignorance was exposed by the superior scholar.

Fraenkel needed to be right. The seminars were, as one uncharitable observer put it, rather like 'a circle of rabbits addressed by a stoat'.[48] In his need for the upper hand, Fraenkel could be reminiscent of J. L. Austin, that least Germanic of scholars. Austin's seminar with Isaiah Berlin on C. I. Lewis (what he would unGermanically have called his 'class') had had something of the same flavour of urgency and power play. It had been to an earlier generation of inter-war Oxford undergraduates a more modest version of what Fraenkel's was to the students of the war years. Like Austin, Fraenkel could eventually be brought to concede a point, once he had had the chance to sleep on it and could point it out himself, in his own way, without any concession that anyone else had got one over on him.

Naturally, the murmurings in the senior common rooms of wartime Oxford were not kind to their friendly neighbourhood refugee. Stuart Hampshire thought him 'Germanic, [a] show-off, dominant, boastful',[49] a formulation that risks suggesting that it would have been all right for Fraenkel to have been a dominant, boastful show-off as long as he had had the grace to be English while doing it.

There were other qualities Fraenkel shared with Austin. As one later participant at the seminars put it, 'He could certainly be alarming when presented with a rash or pretentious error, but the quality he conveyed in his teaching and taught one to respect was humility in the face of dense and complex philological fact.'[50] But what kept his audiences coming back (after all, there was no compulsion to attend) was not the command over philological minutiae, but that extraordinary 'gift for drawing general significance from detail'.[51]

Murdoch recalls him beginning with some isolated fact – a possible reading of an obscure line, an alternative sense to some familiar verb – but as he spoke, like a camera shifting focus, that fact would acquire a new aspect as its background began to appear: a patch of landscape in the middle distance, and the hills beyond.[52] Scrutton saw soon enough that this was, among other things, an education in humane scholarship, an education by example. What was it like to do it, to dedicate one's life to it? In one word, in one pause, in the difference between an iota and an eta, an omicron and an omega, was the story of many generations of scribes and scholars, and through them – their triumphs and their errors – Fraenkel told what amounted to a secret history of the Renaissance itself. The ancient ghosts were baying for blood, and for two hours every week, Fraenkel kept them well nourished.

The *Agamemnon* is about evil. It is about history. It is about curses and grudges and the endless cycle of vengeance. It was something to read such a play in 1939. W. H. Auden wrote that year of the eternal pattern whereby the victims of evil 'do evil in return'.[53] There was no need to underline this moral, no need to put into words what all could see of the parallel between the fate of Europe and that of the House of Atreus, this cycle of wronging and avenging and not quite forgiving. People could make those connections for themselves. The seminar was not about Versailles or Hitler or Neville Chamberlain. It was about Aeschylus and his words.

The form of the class was simple enough: a short passage of text was chosen for the week and assigned to two participants, one undergraduate and one don. It was a solemn duty, fraught with peril, and it can seem from their reminiscences that no one ever forgot the lines they were assigned. Fraenkel's English was improving, but it retained some unexpected Germanisms. He persisted in pronouncing Zeus as 'Tsois'; he garbled his metaphors ('as flat as a pikestaff'); and on one occasion, a student had to point out gently that the usual translation of the Greek word for Zeus's pickaxe was his 'mattock' and not, as he had puzzled his audience by saying, his 'buttock'. But the comic moments came seldom, no one inclined to laugh in the presence of this German mage with his withered arm, enormous head and motile eyebrows that could transform in an instant from expressing fury to laughter or a conspiratorial smile. The scholarship, in the end, had to serve the poetry, and no scholar had a more poetic sense: he recited it with an expressiveness and vitality absent from the Anglican cadences of the British scholars. Undergraduates at his lectures would be treated every now and then to musical interludes – Horace sung to a tune he must have learnt at school, or a full-throated rendition of the chorus from Aristophanes' comedy *The Frogs: brekekekex, ko-ax, ko-ax; brekekekex, ko-ax, ko-ax.*

That was the public man. There was also the man one got to know if one was specially picked for individual instruction. It seems to have struck few people as potentially objectionable that it was usually the female students at his *Oresteia* lectures who were picked for this special honour. In the war years, most of the students attending were women, and Fraenkel was only interested in the ones wearing scholars' gowns (billowy and covering the arms, as opposed to the sleeveless gowns permitted the 'Commoners'). It was well enough known that the instruction would be accompanied by energetic 'pawing', as the grim Somerville vernacular had it. But these things, it was implied, had to be borne as the price of proximity to greatness. One could hardly expect such men to be without the odd eccentricity.

Reports from the many women who studied with Fraenkel paint different pictures of the sessions. Mary Wilson (*mariée* Warnock, b.1924) found herself led from the lecture room in Corpus Christi to the roof, with its view of Christ Church meadow. There she was castigated, first for the deplorable state of her Greek, then for her poor musical taste (Brahms, he declared, was a fraud). Then, to what she described as her embarrassment, there began a long series of fumblings with the buttons of her blouse. It was the 1940s and she did not feel she had a right to complain or even resent it. Warnock tried to forestall the unwanted attentions by inviting a friend to join her, but Fraenkel was simply grateful for another target for his ministrations, dubbing the pair – one dark, the other fair – his two sheep, black and white.

One of the many things to have unnerved those who later learnt of Fraenkel's conduct was the tendency of the targets of his unwelcome attentions to stick up for him. Perhaps it was a way to deal with the trauma, or an aspect of the power he continued to exert even posthumously – a pattern we are better at recognising today. Warnock claimed to have come out of the encounters unhurt and armed with the stuff of a dozen comic anecdotes, the basic currency of academic conversation. Iris Murdoch found nothing to dislike in her evenings with Fraenkel. Her descriptions, as her husband's memoir reported them, were 'fond and reverential'. She had found nothing 'dangerous or degrading' in his behaviour, and seemed happy to accept his attentions as he sat beside her over a passage of text, dividing his concentration between her and the word under consideration, 'as lovingly keen on them as he seemed to be on her'.[54] She published little that was explicitly a memoir of Fraenkel, but in a way, virtually everything she would ever write was about him, pervaded by a sense of eroticism as an exercise in power as much as in love. The fiction she was a decade away from writing would circle obsessively around such figures: mages, gurus, enchanters. Some of them are abusers, but they have known abuse too, from those who jeered at their physical deformities or their Jewishness.

At worst, the attitudes Murdoch expressed were mixed. It was as if justification were beside the point. As Warnock recorded their conversations about the man, they agreed that 'the impropriety of his sexual behaviour seemed utterly trivial compared with the riches he offered us, and the vast horizons he opened up'. So what if he ran together 'the physical with the intellectual'? It was, surely, 'the most natural thing in the world, a conjunction of mind and body which it would have been silly and ungrateful to attempt to disjoin'.[55] That, at any rate, was one woman's way of thinking of it many years later. Warnock's friend, a visiting Cambridge student called Imogen Wrong (*mariée* Rose), who tried to laugh it off at the time later came to see the experience as traumatic. In her view the man was no harmless eccentric but part of a long line of academic predators allowed to get away with it, his predations defended by his admirers as the concession owed to genius.

The atmosphere around Fraenkel was, in the strict sense of the word, *dread*ful. There was the quotidian dread of failing to parse a sentence to his satisfaction, which merged into dread of other things: the death of a brother or a lover, or the destruction of Europe itself. Many decades later, Murdoch would try to recapture what it had been like in a poem titled 'The Agamemnon Class, 1939', where the anxieties of war and the anxieties of scholarship are one. There were times, Murdoch wrote, when it seemed that what they feared was not death but that it would be publicly revealed that they were ignorant of the 'Aorist of some familiar verb'.[56]

∗

Murdoch and Scrutton sat for Greats together in the summer term of 1942; Bosanquet had to do her final exams the same summer – she had started later, but her course was a year shorter; Anscombe, only a few months older, had started and finished a year earlier. Their immediate future was settled: they had, like the other Somerville women in their year, applied for civil service jobs. The assignments began to arrive in the post. Someone was going to the

Board of Trade, someone to work on the artificial insemination of pigs. Scrutton was sent to the obscurely named Ministry of Production. Murdoch had to wait longer, and somewhat ambivalently (did the government want a card-carrying Communist in its ranks?), but was in the end sent to the Treasury. That matter settled, they could look forward to Greats.

The exams passed without mishap, though Scrutton was subjected to a three-hour *viva voce*. Murdoch, receiving no similar summons to an oral exam, assumed this meant she hadn't got a first. Their tutor, Iso Henderson, insisted that her two Greats candidates be given a proper send-off and arranged a special dinner where they would dine with the scholar of Spanish music J. B. Trend from Cambridge, and A. L. Rowse, who had just published an exciting work of medieval history, *Tudor Cornwall* (to be followed, as the donnish All Souls joke went, by a sequel titled *Stuart Hampshire*).[57]

The women dressed with due deference to the august company and listened attentively to the opinings of the men. As they walked back to Somerville afterwards, St Giles' bathed in moonlight, Scrutton asked, 'Did we learn something new this evening?' 'Oh yes,' said Murdoch dissolving into mirth, 'I do think so ... *Trend is a good man and Rowse is a bad man.*' The adjectives were quaint at a time when no sophisticated philosopher would be caught uttering anything so uncouthly old-fashioned. Cats fled in alarm at their laughter.[58]

Both women got their firsts, managing, when it counted, to remember the aorists of all the necessary verbs. Murdoch's war was spent as a civil servant in London, in what she described in a letter to Philippa Bosanquet, now a close friend, as 'a fantastic world, ringing with telephonic voices, & peopled by strange fictional personalities such as Lords Commissioners of his Majesty's Treasury'.[59] She was not the most natural of civil servants, feeling throughout these years a sense of dissociation, as if the peremptory voice of her official letters was part of an elaborate playlet that everyone else was taking far too seriously. She messed things up often enough, losing a file here, forgetting a letter there, but also acquiring a genuine respect for the business of bureaucracy, the stakes at least as high as they had been in the construal of a line of Aeschylus. She wrote to her then lover, Frank Thompson, to say how much she was learning, and how interesting she found administration.[60]

Still, she longed to be somewhere else. She was chafing – as everyone in London seemed to be – at the cushiness of her war while others elsewhere were, as she once put it, 'taking it on the chin'. She wanted desperately to be abroad, and was ready to volunteer for anything that would take her to the Continent.[61]

Some of Murdoch's time, in her early days in London, was spent with her colleagues in the civil service. One of them, Peggy Stebbing, was the niece of the logician and *Analysis* co-founder Susan Stebbing, who had died during the war. The rest of her time was spent with her acquaintances among the wartime literary *demi-monde* in Chelsea, Bloomsbury and Soho, hovering about the offices of Cyril Connolly's short-lived journal *Horizon*. These creatures had the 'redness of blood' she didn't see in the Treasury. They knew and cared nothing for politics. T. S. Eliot, on the other hand, they could respect, the magazine intended as a sort of continuation of the *Criterion*, the periodical devoted to the unity of European civilisation that he had run for the previous seventeen years.

Her to-do list after Finals was long: learn ju-jitsu, learn to draw, learn about comparative mythology, America, psychology, animals … She did get around to learning some Russian from an émigrée living near Sloane Square: it went with her politics and the spirit of the recent alliance with the Soviets, and would no doubt prove useful in the new Europe that would (surely) rise from the rubble of the war. Her family's home in Chiswick was bombed during the Blitz but her parents were safely stowed in Blackpool. In the summer of 1942, she went flat-hunting, getting lucky when she found a studio not far from Buckingham Palace, 'of quite indescribable charm ... of utterly irresistible personality'. A little while later, she would share it with her friend Philippa Bosanquet, by then in London too and working at Chatham House. The pair named the studio Seaforth.

*

The place was quaint, in every sense of the word, and seemed to exist in a parallel dimension where no German bombs could reach. There was a modest little gas-fire that had to do for both heating the flat and making toast. They managed to divide the space so that it had something just about deserving to be called a kitchen – though its poorly fitted glass-paned greenhouse roof made it useless for keeping out the heat in summer, the cold in winter or the rain any time of year. Things were never quiet: if it wasn't bombs – the women would hide in a bathtub, which they hoped might protect them from shrapnel – it was the rumbling of the Circle and District Line trains far below. The bombs did indeed come close to Seaforth, but the place, and its inhabitants, survived.

Murdoch remained a Communist, but no longer carried a card – perhaps to disarm suspicion at the Treasury. The East End had been more or less destroyed in a series of air raids and the Tube stations were full of the newly homeless. Men in uniform marched the streets; men whom Murdoch admired, despite her politics. She thought highly of William Beveridge's plan for a post-war welfare state, declaring it 'a fine piece of work, thorough and equitable'.[62] And, as she wrote solemnly to Frank Thompson as if reporting that she had finally finished *War and Peace*, she lost her virginity.

Philippa Bosanquet's work involved research into economics, one of the subjects of her Oxford degree, specifically into the prospects for post-war reconstruction funded by an inflow of American capital into Europe. Every morning's walk to work felt like stepping into a new city: no building or square could be trusted to have survived the night. At dusk came the daily chore of putting up the blackout materials, which could double on the coldest nights as an extra blanket. They slept in their overcoats, clutching hot-water bottles just as the pre-war aesthetes had clutched their teddy bears. Occasionally a kindly, or lustful, male friend would buy them a restaurant meal (it was illegal to spend more than five shillings), or they would splurge on sticky buns at the Lyons tea-shop nearby.

The flat had three pairs of shoes that the women shared between them. They exchanged literary enthusiasms, with Murdoch converting Bosanquet – poorly read despite her Oxford degree – to the pleasures of Samuel Beckett's *Murphy*. They shared secrets too, and conversations about men, comparing lists of marriage proposals (Bosanquet told Murdoch it would be quicker if she, Murdoch, named the men who *hadn't* proposed to her). The rumour went that the collection of empty hock wine bottles on Murdoch's mantlepiece represented the number of wartime proposals she had declined.

Letters came for both the women from Donald MacKinnon, still in Oxford and still worried for their souls. He thought he saw in Murdoch a certain destructiveness that could hurt the ones she loved. There was a complicated business – the full facts of which aren't easy to disentangle even from the detailed surviving correspondence – involving the relationship between the two women and two men: Tommy Balogh and M. R. D. Foot, the latter a fellow volunteer on the Lindsay campaign during what had come to be called the Munich by-election and now a captain in Army Intelligence. Murdoch began with Foot, then left him (as it was vaguely alleged) for Balogh, who had an ongoing courtship with Bosanquet. In the course of consoling him for his heartbreak, Bosanquet found herself drawn to Foot. She decided later on that she came out the best from the love-quadrangle. For the entirety of her post-war academic career, she was always Mrs Foot.

*

Elizabeth Anscombe could not take the same enthusiastic part in the war effort. She had put down her position in a contribution to a pamphlet published in 1939, in the early ('phoney') days of the war. The pamphlet was to be called *The Justice of the Present War Examined: A Catholic View*, but the Archbishop of Birmingham denied it the *imprimatur* it needed to claim to be presenting a Catholic view; no doubt he took the same view of Catholics in England as the Somerville dons did of women at Oxford: still on probation and required to be on their best behaviour.

The pamphlet was eventually published with the subtitle, *A Criticism Based on Traditional Catholic Principles and Natural Reason*. Anscombe's section, 'The War and the Moral Law', allowed that there was, in the invasion of Poland, a genuine *jus ad bellum* – grounds for war. All the same, there was good reason to expect that the Allies would not observe *jus in bello*, the rules governing the conduct of war. No matter how just the grounds for making war, one could not be confident that the war would be prosecuted justly. That was enough for it to be a mortal sin, and simply forbidden.[63]

Her husband Peter Geach tried, but failed, to join the Polish Army (his mother was Polish and he felt a great identification with the country and took a special interest in its achievements in logic).[64] He declared himself a conscientious objector in the end, and spent the war years working in pine forests in the south of England. Anscombe and Geach married in 1941, at the Brompton Oratory – where nine years before them, Freddie and Renée Ayer had said the same words, if rather less sincerely. For one reason or another, a good deal of their married life ended up being spent apart. Geach is supposed to have called it 'telegamy', marriage at a distance.[65]

Elizabeth Anscombe, never Mrs Geach, got her first too, but that, like everything she subsequently said or did, was divisive. She had found her *métier* early, and rather resented the time she was asked to spend on the ancient history component of Greats. She ended up failing the Roman history paper, but her performance in the philosophy exams was so spectacular that her examiners wanted to give her a first anyway. The philosophers were arranged against the historians, and the latter demanded a viva where she might redeem herself by showing some knowledge of ancient history, however minimal.

Anscombe gave them nothing. To question after question, she responded with stony silence. Eventually, one examiner lowered the bar to the floor: 'Miss Anscombe, can you name a governor or procurator of a Roman province? *Any* Roman province?' – perhaps hoping that a recent convert would at least be able to volunteer the name of Pontius Pilate. She said, 'No.' 'Miss Anscombe,' he continued, 'is there *any fact at all* about the history of Rome which you would like to comment on?' And again she said, 'No.' Somehow, and in spite of her refusal to give them material to work with, the philosophers prevailed.[66]

Married now, though to a man constantly called away to one or other forest for his wartime duties, Anscombe began to seek an institution that would support her research. She was awarded a fellowship that took her to Newnham College, Cambridge, in 1942. Even then, it was not common for an Oxford graduate hoping to pursue philosophical studies to go there. Tutors, now of an age to have shed the prejudices of the Cook Wilson years, still warned their students of the risk of corruption. But what other way was there of learning what Wittgenstein had lately been up to? News had trickled in of a radical change of mind, of a total abandonment of the doctrines of the *Tractatus*, of new methods, and a new style. But trickles and rumours were all they were. The man published nothing in the usual sense of the word, and his students guarded the contents of his lectures jealously. Bold young men had tried and failed to gain admission to the inner circle. How likely was a young woman of twenty-three to get any further with the magus?

5

Saturdays

Robin Collingwood spent most of his philosophical life as what Nietzsche might have called an *untimely* man. He was one of several philosophers of the old school dubbed 'the last British idealist'. In fact, he rejected the label 'idealist', but made things hard for himself by not suggesting an alternative.[1] Maybe there was no single word that could capture what he was. That left him, a reluctant recluse for much of his life, an outsider to everything.

He was a creature of the nineteenth century cursed to spend most of his life in the twentieth, a metaphysician among positivists, a cosmopolitan among little Englanders, an aesthete among philistines, a philosopher among historians and a historian among philosophers. His 1930s were not spent discovering the joys of analysis with the ageing Wee Teas. Nor had he the slightest interest in joining the younger turks in debating the ins and outs of whatever was coming out of Vienna.[2] His contemporaries didn't know what to make of him, and he decided to make nothing of them.[3]

He had spent the First World War working on intelligence at the Admiralty.[4] The post-war years up to 1927 had been tiring, his days filled up in the usual way of Oxford dons with the tutorial teaching load of both Lincoln and Pembroke College.[5] Things eased a little when he was appointed university lecturer in philosophy and Roman history, even then an unusual combination. It was a vindication of his undergraduate resolve to neglect neither the history nor the philosophy components of Greats. He was unusual even as an undergraduate in not adopting the customary strategy of the Greats student: to find a furrow and spend the next years carefully ploughing it.

He had never taken the Cook Wilson view of (that is, *against*) publication; nor had he embraced the atheism of the younger realists. He was an Anglican, of the conventionally unorthodox sort. Religion, he had argued in a short book published during the war, was a genuine form of knowledge, which put him at odds with the positivist leanings of the new analysts.[6] When Gilbert Ryle was telling the Aristotelian Society about the logical form of 'Unpunctuality is reprehensible', Collingwood was writing *An Essay on Philosophical Method*, claiming that philosophy had little to do with 'analysis', as Moore, Russell and Susan Stebbing understood it. He saw analysis as the most recent manifestation of an old sceptical tendency in philosophy, now being extended to the aspirations of philosophy itself.[7] The analysts claimed, as the original mission statement of *Analysis* had put it, to lack any interest in establishing 'new kinds of fact about the world'. All they claimed to want to do was to elucidate a body of facts, 'the general nature of which is, by common consent, already known'.[8] Collingwood refused his consent.

Like sceptics through the ages, the analytic philosophers claimed to have no doctrine, only a method. But a method must be based on a principle, which needs defending no less than a doctrine does. To his mind, no analyst, not even the redoubtable Susan Stebbing, had managed to come up with one. No, philosophy was not what the analytic philosophers called 'analysis'. Philosophy was, as Hegel had more or less correctly said, consciousness striving to understand itself.[9]

While producing a steady stream of contrarian philosophical writings, Collingwood kept up his study of Roman history, turning himself into the country's leading authority on Roman inscriptions in Britain. He travelled to the north of England regularly to direct excavations, bringing to archaeology a conjectural brilliance that helped make sense of his suggestion that it shared with philosophy a commitment to the 'logic of question and answer'.[10] One did not simply point and dig, hopeful that something would turn up. Nor did the things one turned up on a dig come neatly individuated, like the 'propositions' that the analysts claimed to analyse. Facts came bundled together, in complex structures that had to be understood as wholes. The analytic aspiration to divide reality into 'atomic facts' seemed to him futile, an attempt to divide the indivisible.[11]

Collingwood, never in the mainstream of anything, managed to draw attention to himself at least as a provocateur. His ideas about philosophy and its relation to history began to appear in lectures, and the more intellectually ambitious of his students recognised in him a spark of originality absent in the plodders who otherwise taught them. But he didn't seek influence in any more programmatic way. He took on no administrative tasks if he could avoid them, and earned his colleagues' resentment by electing to spend his vacations in his own house in rural Oxfordshire.[12]

The year 1935 saw him elected to the Waynflete Chair in Metaphysics, succeeding John Alexander Smith, who was now in his seventies and doubtless pleased that the PPE degree he had helped to found was flourishing. The Chair required Collingwood to move to Magdalen College, around the same time that a 24-year-old J. L. Austin was a tutorial fellow there.[13] While in the Chair, a year short of fifty, he had a stroke, and was ordered by his doctor to take a year's leave. He returned to the Lake District of his childhood, where the games he had played with his playmates had provided the inspiration to a family friend, Arthur Ransome, for that future classic of children's literature, *Swallows and Amazons*.[14] This time, his days were spent not on swimming and playing at pirates but on composing *An Autobiography*, a quite singular work that was less concerned with recounting events than it was with tracing the origins of his own ideas. After all, he explained, 'the autobiography of a man whose business is thinking should be the story of his thought'.[15]

An Autobiography showed a more explicit awareness of the political direction of the age than anything else written by an Oxford philosopher at the time. It frustrated him that few of his colleagues at Oxford shared his sense of the dangers of Hitler and Mussolini.[16] When A. D. Lindsay stood in the 'Munich by-election' of 1938, Collingwood was an enthusiastic supporter.[17] Other philosophers had, of course, supported Lindsay's doomed campaign, but Collingwood seemed to think an interest in politics not just a desirable supplement to workaday philosophising, but an essential part of it. One of the many things he held against the realists, Cook Wilson and G. E. Moore, was what he saw as the unimaginativeness of their conception of philosophy, their denial of (or more often, their indifference to) any role it might play in politics and the world outside the university.

The tone of the last chapter of *An Autobiography* darkens steadily, beginning with a denunciation of British indifference to the Spanish Civil War and the subsequent policy of appeasement towards Hitler's Germany, then turning sharply to direct its righteous ire at the realists of his youth for making such things possible. 'I know now', he wrote in the book's grim concluding paragraph, that the philosophers he had known in his youth, 'for all their profession of a purely scientific detachment from practical affairs, were the propagandists of a coming Fascism'. He knew, he continued, 'that Fascism means the end of clear thinking and the triumph of irrationalism. I know that all my life I have been engaged unawares in a political struggle, fighting against these things in the dark.'[18] But from then on, he declared, he would fight in the daylight.

*

The news came to Oxford in 1943 that Robin Collingwood was dead, two years after he had resigned his professorship, following a series of strokes. He had asked to be taken up to the Lake

District, his family transporting him north on a train full of soldiers.[19] He died in Coniston, leaving behind a large body of writing, increasingly frenetic in his final years. He left behind also a vacant Chair in Metaphysics at Magdalen College, for which his colleagues would eventually need to find a suitable successor. It would have to be someone eminent, but with his best work plausibly still ahead of him.

Naturally, it was Gilbert Ryle who was offered the Chair: eleven years younger than his predecessor and on the verge of finally doing the interesting things he'd been promising since he was a strapping young captain of boats. And so it happened. The 'last British idealist' had been ushered off the scene. In 1945, Mr Ryle of Christ Church – having only recently been Major Ryle of the Radio Security Service – was to become Professor Ryle of Magdalen.[20]

Ryle had had an excellent war. Part of the little-known MI8, the signals department of the War Office, he had worked out of the headquarters at Arkley View near Barnet in Hertfordshire, north of London. He was one of several Oxford dons working there, including Stuart Hampshire, and the historian Hugh Trevor-Roper. Theirs was not the task of the journeymen in wartime intelligence, to discover German intelligence 'secrets'. With enough work, the order of battle, logistics, manpower could be discovered. Much harder was the business of solving intelligence 'mysteries'. How did Hitler and the Nazi high command think? What was their outlook? Without that broader understanding, a secret was in itself useless. As Trevor-Roper later put it, 'it was only by understanding the general character of the German Secret Service – its organisation, personnel, nomenclature [and] style – that we could judge the significance of particular actions or projects'.[21] This was a project of decryption beyond the best machines that Alan Turing, working not far away in Bletchley Park, could design.

The Oxford to which Ryle returned, in the Michaelmas term

of 1945, was bursting with youth. A hothouse of transients during the war years, the city was abuzz again. Young men who had survived years of combat or had just been released from prisoner-of-war camps were returning to complete the degrees they'd had to abandon. Those old enough to remember the returning men of the last war were struck by the unexpected sanity of the returners.

In 1919, one observer remembered, the returning men 'jumped when a door banged; they could not sleep without a night-cap of whisky; they awoke shouting in nightmares'.[22] Desperate 'to recover the *douceur de vivre* of the Edwardian years', the tone they had set was one of 'febrile gaiety'.[23] The generation returning in 1945 were less jumpy. Their memory of the time before the war was not of an Edwardian summer but one long winter of discontent and menace. Their wars had not been spent in trenches, waiting for orders or a fatal bomb. They had been busy, and when not busy, mostly safe.[24] Their tutors found them 'forward-looking and entirely serious; there was no line between workers and play-boys'.[25] John Mabbott, an associate of Ryle's from the inter-war Wee Tea dining club, found them 'a delight to teach'.[26]

Faced with this surfeit of students, the colleges of the city started hiring again. And suddenly, the fossils of the senior common room found themselves sharing their port with young men and women, who had seen more of life than they ever had: code-breaking, military intelligence and death camps. Khaki doffed, Ryle arrived in a repopulated Oxford. His accession to a Chair in Metaphysics had an irony that he was the first to remark upon. Collingwood, as befitted a holder of that Chair, had actually believed in the possibility, even the desirability, of metaphysics. Ryle was on the record as thoroughly sceptical of the whole enterprise. The proper analogy, he is said to have quipped, was a Chair in Tropical Diseases: the holder was committed to eliminating his subject.[27] Two years later, G. E. Moore gave up the editorship of *Mind*, and Ryle was anointed his successor.[28]

Old Hamish Paton, his undergraduate tutor at Queen's, was

still there, and asked Ryle to contribute a book to a new series of which he was serving as a general editor, *Hutchinson's Philosophical Library*.[29] Ryle was forty-five and had published only papers until then. He agreed, but with no precise idea at the time of what it was to be about.

Too long, he had to admit, he and his allies had been pontificating about the nature of philosophy and the methods appropriate to it. Too long they had mocked and knocked. All this was congenial enough when the enemies were besieged and running out of supplies, while one's own side was young, well armed and well fed. But now the old were dead or had been pensioned off. The citadel had fallen, the insurgents were in charge, the foot-soldiers waiting for orders. The cathedrals of metaphysics had been demolished, by evangelists from Vienna who had sneaked past the frontlines long before the Luftwaffe came roaring in. Ryle's generation, if not Collingwood's, was well prepared for this possibility, and no tears were shed when the edifice came tumbling down. The great question of the thirties had been: what, if anything, should be erected in their place?

Crude forms of Viennese positivism had left the anti-metaphysicians with an awkward question about their own identity. As Ryle put it, 'Where then do we anti-nonsense philosophers belong?'[30] Were their no-nonsense tracts against metaphysics themselves pieces of metaphysics? Ayer's *Language, Truth, and Logic* was, after all, hardly filled with sentences of zoology. Had they been fighting nonsense with nonsense? The answer in Wittgenstein's *Tractatus* had seemed to be 'yes', leaving his acolytes to wonder if there could after all be good, therapeutic nonsense.[31] There was also the option of reducing philosophical theses, even of the anti-nonsense sort, to expressions of attitude (positivism, on this view, would be most honestly expressed as 'Boo metaphysics, hurrah science!') The pages of *Analysis* were devoted to the activity described in the title, which also seemed to be permitted even under the most rigorous of prohibition laws. But Ryle was coming to think that 'the Viennese dichotomy "Either Science or Nonsense" had too few "ors" in it'.[32] Non-scientific modes of discourse were patently meaningful and the task for philosophy was to find ways of making sense of their meaningfulness.

The invitation from Paton was a chance for Ryle to go beyond the discussion notes of *Analysis*. 'It was time, I thought, to exhibit a sustained piece of analytical hatchet-work being directed upon some notorious and large-sized Gordian Knot.' It was time to cease the endless chatter about 'methods' – always a vulgarism at Oxford – and to *apply* them. The naysayers and the faithless were owed 'an example of the method really working'.[33] The discoverer of a new cure-all, Ryle sought a specific illness to cure with it.

His first inclination was to take up the old problem of 'the Freedom of the Will' (the upper-case F and W a sure symptom of metaphysical excess). He settled in the end on 'the Concept of Mind', the old set of problems about mind and body that went at least as far back as René Descartes in the seventeenth century: are the mind and body distinct entities? What is the relationship between mind and body? What is thought? How can thought lead to action? How does the mental act on the physical? Can we know the minds of others as reliably as we know our own? Can we know the minds of others at all?[34] Descartes was to play villain in Ryle's story. His main weapon against his formidable foe was not the 'verification' principle, nor was his war cry the Viennese chant of 'Science or Nonsense'. Ryle's silver bullet, devised over the 1930s, was the idea of a 'category mistake'.

Ryle explained it best with examples. A foreigner is visiting Oxford. He is taken to see the cathedral, Magdalen Tower, the Bodleian Library, the Ashmolean Museum and the Clarendon Laboratory. All this is very nice, he says, but what I want to see is the *university*. Where is it? Ah, says his host, though he should be used to it by now. You see, it's like this …

The foreigner is taken then to a game of cricket. Eventually, he can distinguish batsman from bowler from fielder from umpire.

But who, he asks, pleased to show that he does know something, is in charge of the famed *esprit de corps*? Or do they not have that in England? Again, he is looking in the wrong place, and for the wrong sort of thing. Or perhaps, the mistake is to look for a *thing* in the first place. But how to avoid it, when our language treats universities and team spirit (and indeed, constitutions and parades) as if they were things of the same kind as the things they are made of – colleges and libraries and cries of howzat?

The foreigner will learn; he is new to this. And he will learn too, in time, that he should not go looking in bookshops for a copy of the British constitution, nor seek a postal address for the Church of England. But Ryle's flippant examples were building up to a more subversive point, and not about foreigners. There are facts about ourselves that we understand perfectly well until we are asked to state them. And then, it's like asking for directions from a fellow tourist.[35]

Ryle's topic was the mind, but he didn't like to call it 'the mind'. It encouraged the mistake he was trying to diagnose to talk of such a thing as *the* mind, or to talk of the mind as *a* thing, possibly a thing 'inside' another thing, 'the body'. Instead, he started from this idea: we know all sorts of things about minds, none of it learnt from philosophers, and we demonstrate that we do in the ways we talk to and about each other. We can tell how people are feeling from looking at their faces, understand their intentions when we see what they do and how they do it. We can change other people's minds by arguing with them or laughing at them. In all of this, we're using the concept of mind. And then we're asked to wear our philosophers' hats, and we start to gibber nonsensically: the mind is this, that and the other. And what we gibber, Ryle thought, deserved a rude nickname: 'I shall often speak of it, with deliberate abusiveness, as "the dogma of the Ghost in the Machine".'[36]

The philosopher wants to speak sense about the mind. And he starts, sensibly enough, from some of the deliverances of common sense. What does common sense tell us about the mind? Well, it tells us that minds are not like bodies, in the sense that they're not made of the same stuff. From which it must follow that they must be made of different stuff – spooky, immaterial, 'mental', stuff. After all, bodies are visible, minds not. Bodies are public, everyone can see them. By contrast, minds are private. I have a privileged access to my own mind that no one else could ever have. I know I have a headache; you can only *infer* that I do from what I do, and fallibly at that. For how can you be so sure all that groaning and clutching of the temple, the hunting in the drawers for aspirin, is not just part of an elaborate pretence? My body is a machine, my mind the ghost that haunts the machine. Tempting, natural, and yet, Ryle thought, quite wrong.

How did we come to make such mistakes about ourselves? The villain of Ryle's story was Descartes, the originator of a historically influential 'dualism' of mind and body. But Descartes scarcely appears in the pages of *The Concept of Mind*. The confusions of some dead seventeenth-century Frenchman would have been, in themselves, uninteresting. But they were not only *his* confusions. His name granted an unearned authority to a confusion to which we are all prey.

We are all 'dualists' sometimes; our language makes it hard not to be. We talk, after all, of 'the mind' using a noun, a habit that inclines us to treat it as a thing of the same sort as 'the body'. We speak of 'doing sums *in* our heads' and distinguish between what we really think and what we say out loud. Now, our language is what it is, and Ryle had no interest in changing it. After all, we can talk sense enough 'with' our concepts. The lapse into nonsense, Ryle thought, starts when we're asked to talk 'about' them. Our talk about our concept of mind – and indeed, of imagination and will and intention and belief and knowledge and so much else – is shaped by a myth. And we may as well call that myth, as we call other things that are allegedly the doing of Descartes, 'Cartesian'.

In calling it a 'myth', Ryle had something specific in mind: the Cartesian myth, he said, involves 'the presentation of facts belonging to one category in the idioms appropriate to another' – looking for the team spirit at mid-off or the British constitution on the shelves of the Bodleian Library. 'To explode a myth is accordingly not to deny the facts but to re-allocate them.'[37] We are, all of us, Cartesians without knowing it. What we need is a re-education in our own concepts, a remedial course in thinking about ourselves. The campaign would be scattershot. There would be no final battle, just a piling on of analogies and instances and aphorisms designed to surprise the Cartesian enemy and divest him of his convictions. If he succeeds, you will talk and think just as you did before, but you'll do a better job of distinguishing what you actually think from what you think you think.

The Concept of Mind came out in 1949. A crowded Oxford swooped on it as it had swooped thirteen years before on *Language, Truth, and Logic*. This was the work of a rather older man, a *professor*, even, but one who wrote with the elegance of middle age and the gumption of youth. The book had arguments aplenty, but its basic argumentative unit was the epigram – appropriately enough, for a book one reader described as a piece of therapy that was also a piece of guerrilla warfare, and another as an exorcism.[38] Ryle's epigrams were simultaneously spells and war cries. Stuart Hampshire, tasked with reviewing the book for *Mind*, found that long passages of argument consisted simply 'of a succession of epigrams, which ... explode on impact, shattering conventional trains of thought'.[39]

Epigrams there were indeed in profusion. 'Philosophy is the replacement of category-habits by category-disciplines.'[40] 'Misinterpretations are in principle corrigible, which is part of the value of controversy.'[41] 'There is no incompatibility between being well-informed and being silly.'[42] And examples that were both striking and utterly ordinary: what distinguishes the 'trippings and tumblings' of clowns from those of the clumsy?[43] Why is it that sailors find it so hard to describe in words the knots they tie?[44] Is it possible to sneeze voluntarily?[45]

In all of this, there was always the threat of being caught out in that terrible thing, a 'category mistake' – the mistake of treating concepts belonging to one category as if they belonged to a different one. Mental arithmetic is not 'in the head' in the same way that the medulla oblongata is.[46] Tides, hopes and the average age of death can all rise, but not in the same way.[47] What I handle is where my hand is but what I see isn't usually where my eye is.[48] 'Some readers may think', Ryle said, 'that my tone of voice in this book is excessively polemical. It may comfort them to know that the assumptions against which I exhibit most heat are assumptions of which I myself have been a victim.'[49] But Ryle's 'heat' didn't sound so much angry, as bluff. His opponents were not so much knaves as patients. And Professor Ryle had the cure-all.

The bluffness of Ryle's style served as an antidote to what he liked to call the 'occult' tone of the Cartesian. The Cartesian approach to psychology, he thought, created a mystery about the most everyday of things. It made the knowledge we have, and know we have, of other people's minds – that they're happy or sad or scared – seem like an impossible achievement, like sneaking into a locked dark room without a key. Ryle wished an end to that mystery. *Inner* this and *private* that were to be replaced with *outer* that and *public* this. There were not two worlds – a covert world of the mind and the overt world of the body. There was just one world, and it could be described in one language. The 'hidden inner' was to be replaced, wherever possible, with the 'obvious outer', and the 'less workaday with the more workaday'.[50]

This still left a substantial remainder: things that resisted attempts at reduction to the outer. What, for instance, was Rodin's *Thinker* doing exactly? It was hardly enough to say that his thinking *just was* his sitting in silence with a furrowed brow; he could be doing that without thinking any thoughts. In the beginning, Ryle professed impatience with the question. The 'privacy' of thought was not its essential attribute: one could think aloud as well as in silence. Indeed, one could think in diagrams or gestures. Further, he said, we don't learn to think in private before we learn to do so aloud with others, just as it took many centuries of people reading aloud before they learnt to read in silence.[51] Philosophers seemed puzzled about how we learn to communicate our thoughts to others. They should really have been puzzled about how we ever learn to keep our thoughts to ourselves.[52]

Unusually for a book of philosophy, *The Concept of Mind* left one with memories not of arguments but of characters. Its pages were populous, but not with philosophers; a few were mentioned, but much less often than one would expect. There were not even footnotes for them to be relegated to. The book felt, if anything, like a novel set at the village fête, where we run into foreigners adrift, mapless parishioners, runaway donkeys, 'warm and active' kittens, clowns tumbling, sailors tying knots, children learning their times tables, drunkards playing chess, dipsomaniacs hallucinating serpents on the eiderdown. And somewhere someone sees distant Helvellyn in his mind's eye and hears 'Lillibullero' in his inner ear. It is what they used to call a very English scene.[53]

Among the reviews that set the tone for the reception of *The Concept of Mind* was the one published in the *Times Literary Supplement*. There was no byline, in the usual way of the *TLS* in those years, but the identity of the reviewer was an open secret. J. L. Austin managed the feat, a useful skill in an academic reviewer, of spending most of his essay on criticism while sounding rapturous in his enthusiasm. The criticisms ranged in their intensity from complaints about terminology (why this needless talk of 'logical grammar' and 'logical syntax' when plain old 'grammar' and 'syntax' will do?) to a suspicion about the neatness of Ryle's picture of 'one world, not two'. Why, if we really did have to count worlds, did it have to be either one *or* two? What if there were really *nineteen*? Ryle's arguments, if they succeeded, left the human being – once thought a weird mind–body chimera

– alone and undivided. But his arguments, once the final score was totted up, seemed to point not to a vision of the body as a lonely landlord now that his ghostly tenant has been evicted. Rather, it suggested a tenement's worth of lodgers, none ghostly, all entirely real. The mind had been not so much eliminated as multiplied.[54]

Stuart Hampshire's review in *Mind*, by his own admission 'one-sidedly critical', took issue with Ryle's history, such as it was. The ghost in the machine was supposed to be a creature of 'Cartesian' dogma. One could allow him his lack of interest in the history *qua* history (as they liked to say at Oxford), but the reader was owed some acknowledgement that the ghost was not a fiction devised by philosophers. 'So far from being imposed on the plain man by philosophical theorists … the myth of the mind as a ghost within the body is one of the most primitive and natural of all the innumerable myths which are deeply imbedded in the vocabulary and structure of our languages.'[55] The folk didn't seem to need the help of philosophers to be corrupted.

Even more serious was the refusal to come clean about the hauntings that persisted even once the ghost was supposed to have been expelled. Ryle suggested that it was misleading to speak of 'seeing' Helvellyn in one's mind's eye; it would be better to speak simply of imagining it, which is more like pretending than it is like seeing. But is that what it is like to see Helvellyn – or indeed anything else – in one's mind's eye? Many people, and not just the dogmatic Cartesians, claim really to be seeing something. Maybe it isn't a *thing* they see, but does it follow that they see nothing? (What about after-images?)

Ryle denied that he was that disreputable creature of the psychology department, a 'behaviourist'. No, he had no wish to describe all human behaviour by reference only to the consequences of something called 'conditioning'.[56] Nor was he sceptical of the existence of thoughts and feelings, dismissing them as spooky, unobservable phenomena to be jettisoned along with talk of ghosts and spirits. He only wanted, as he had said, to 're-allocate' them. He was, at most, a 'logical' behaviourist – that word again, 'logical' – and all he wanted to do was to reinterpret the idioms in which we speak of the mind. What we said about it didn't mean what we thought it did.

That, at any rate, was Ryle's official line. But the inner world wouldn't be translated away so easily, and the style even more than the substance of his dismissals made his detractors, and no doubt some of his champions, wonder whether this wasn't so much bad philosophy as sincere autobiography. Perhaps Ryle denied, or deflated, the inner life so readily because he didn't have one. Stuart Hampshire, in his review, put this point in more neutral terms. *The Concept of Mind*, he said, 'conveys a sharply personal and definite view of the world: a world of solid and manageable objects, without hidden recesses, each visibly functioning in its own appropriate pattern'.[57] Austin declared the tone of the book endearing. Ryle showed 'a whole-hearted faith in the deliverances of his own personal experience'.[58]

On the other hand, the critics acknowledged the book's other excellences. 'Professor Ryle', said Hampshire, 'writes with Aristotelian pregnancy.'[59] His book was a happy return to the jargonless, unfootnoted, commonsensical fluency of philosophical writing in the eighteenth century.[60] Too long had intimations of a revolution in philosophy been restricted to vague hints. Finally, one bold soldier was willing to charge the fortress: 'Here at last is a book which actually uses the now rapidly changing methods of linguistic analysis to cut the root of a large metaphysical problem.'[61]

'Not only is the book stimulating, enjoyable and original, but a quite unusually high percentage of it is true, the remainder at least false.' And what a delight it was to read, as so little philosophy was and is. The syntax was simple, the vocabulary large and diverse. 'All,' said Austin, 'save those who have never learned to suspect solemnity, will join in [Ryle's] enjoyment of his numerous jokes ... *Le style, c'est Ryle.*'[62]

*

'The remainder at least false': nothing gives a better flavour of the intellectual climate of the time than the fact that this could be meant as a compliment. A whole book with not a line of nonsense! Whatever else there was to be said about Ryle, one had to give him that much. But former insurgent or not, Ryle was now in the ranks of the professoriate. However much he wanted this to be the start of something new, it was hard not to feel that it was really the punchline to a shaggy-dog story he had been telling since a junior don. Youth in search of novelties had to look elsewhere.

This came in the form of a mysterious card that arrived in the pigeonholes of the younger philosophers at the beginning of the Oxford term, inviting them to 'Sat. mng. mtgs'. The card specified a place, usually a middle-sized college room, and a time, usually 10.30 a.m. What would happen there? A seminar? Too German. A seance? Too Cambridge. If a novice dared ask, he would be told simply that they would be carrying on with what they had been doing the previous term. Or if they were done with that, they'd be starting something new, yet to be decided. In other words, it was best to turn up and see.[63]

It *looked* like a seminar, in that there were a group of people with roughly similar intellectual backgrounds and tastes. They had in common their relative youth and juniority (professors were pointedly not invited). But no paper was read out. Sometimes there was a text, as short as a single sentence, under discussion. Sometimes, the only book to be seen was a *Concise Oxford English Dictionary*. But sometimes there wasn't even that. The median age of the club's clientele was under forty, and the median sex male. What unified the proceedings was the oddly charismatic character at their heart, keeping order and a sense of purpose without ever seeming to do so. Lieutenant-Colonel Austin, as he could now be called (though he was happy to be plain Mr), had returned to Oxford in his mid-thirties, married with four children, and a war's worth of experience in running things.

Austin's war remains shrouded in secrecy, though some facts are reasonably well established. He had spent the summer of 1940 in preliminary training, first in Aldershot in Hampshire and then in Matlock in Derbyshire. Then, some perceptive person had arranged for him to get a commission in the Intelligence Corps, which took him to London and the War Office. There, he was set to work on the German Order of Battle: a massive project in military intelligence trying to work out, from bits and pieces of information, just what kind of military resources Hitler had at his disposal, what the command structure of the German armed forces was, the size of the different battalions, and where they had been deployed. The work had been difficult, the amount of detail overwhelming, and the costs of failure high. It was like classical philology, only no one had yet died of a mistake in construing a line from Catullus. There were no shortcuts, no theories. There was no room for mere approximations of the truth. Austin was in his element.

The following year, Austin got married, to Jean Coutts, a recent graduate of Somerville and a promising philosopher herself; they were to have two daughters and two sons. In 1942, he was put in charge of a small section tasked with doing the preliminary intelligence work for a land invasion of Western Europe. The section had been active before he took it over, but its organisation was shambolic, its methods amateur. Austin, with the brisk efficiency of a house monitor asked to whip the small boys into shape in time for a founder's day parade, set about putting his stamp on the place. Suddenly, there was a sense of purpose, of urgency, and the shocked realisation that better methods made for quicker results. Men superior to him in rank began to defer to him on all aspects of military intelligence. The amateur, an enthusiastic exile from academe, would teach the professionals how it was done.

In 1943, the section was enlarged and Austin was now a major.

As D-Day came nearer, the logistics for it reaching a complexity unprecedented in the history of war, Austin kept calm and carried on, an encyclopaedia of information. He seemed to know the German army about as well as any German general. He knew the civilian administration in occupied France almost as well. He knew where the guns were placed along the coast of Northern France. He knew too how to distinguish between the important and the trivial, preparing weekly reports that contained everything anyone realistically needed to know about the latest changes in the German dispositions. A guidebook was prepared – a *vade mecum* – with enough information for invading troops, but not so large it wouldn't fit into their rucksacks. It was almost certainly his idea that the book was called *Invade Mecum*: Invade with me. He was, an unnamed military colleague was later quoted as saying, 'more than anybody … responsible for the life-saving accuracy of the D-Day Intelligence'.[64]

In 1944, summer saw his section move to Normandy, and then to Versailles. The work got less interesting for a time, then got altogether too interesting once enemy prisoners began to be taken and interrogated. Austin took part in these interrogations, bringing to them – one imagines – the relentlessness of his tutorial teaching manner. The simple question, the pregnant pause; the demand for absolute accuracy, the imperviousness to bluster, an eye for evasion, and a willingness to go on for as long as it took to get it right. Wartime suited Austin, and at the end of it all, he told his colleague, with a slightly chilling eagerness, that 'if he were to become involved in another war', he would enjoy working on the logistics of supply.[65] Mr Austin, sometime fellow of Magdalen, returned to Oxford with a British OBE, a French Croix de Guerre, and an American appointment as an Officer of the Legion of Merit.

*

That was the war, but now it was peacetime. Yet, those returning from the front found themselves less exhausted than invigorated. Oxford, overpopulated with energetic youth, was the place to start new things and make new starts on old things. Ryle was in the Waynflete Chair and bringing to his role his own special bulldog energy. *Samizdat* copies of Wittgenstein's work from the 1930s onward were beginning to appear in discreet envelopes smuggled, no doubt at enormous risk, from Cambridge. Austin approved of Ryle's election, on the whole, but was ambivalent about the cult of Wittgenstein. Why did Wittgenstein have to make it all so personal? Why that stifling atmosphere, that demand for deference to the master, those comical performances of spiritual agony? And what exactly did the man have against stating things definitely, clearly, and fully?[66]

Philosophy needed a new start, and the first thing that would have to go was its traditional rhetoric. No doubt its questions were big and important but there was no need to carry on so. Po-faced solemnity was no guarantee of seriousness, nor laughter a symptom of triviality. They were to talk to each other as colleague to colleague, not as master to disciple, nor as sage to acolyte. Philosophy was a set of problems, which were not diminished in seriousness or difficulty by being presented as puzzles. You set them out in the smallest words that wouldn't distort them. Your choice of methods came after, and not before, the problem was examined, with the fewest possible presuppositions. There was no need to dismiss any method off the bat. What counted as a good method, that is to say an *effective* method, would come to light only once we tried a few. If not a hammer, maybe a screwdriver, or pliers, or a hardback edition of the *Oxford English Dictionary*.

Erudition wasn't called for, at least not yet. After all, we hadn't yet worked out just what sorts of erudition might be useful. Cleverness couldn't be scorned, but it couldn't be a substitute for hard work and patience. But most of all, one had to be honest. If a solution didn't work, there was no point trying to rescue it out of some misplaced idea of saving face. And behind all this was a more basic ideal of collegiality. If we were all in it together, then both success and failure could only be ascribed to the team, not to the individual. A single genius was not needed – philosophy wasn't that sort of thing. Its problems needed more workmanlike virtues: open-mindedness, diligence and a willingness to co-operate. Some of these principles, as always, were more honoured in the breach, but those were the principles. Or at any rate, that was the *mood*, and it was not only the mood at Oxford. Winston Churchill, recall, lost the election of 1945 in a landslide to that mild-mannered committee man Clement Attlee.

Perhaps it was inevitable that an age of orators was to be followed by an age of committee men, an age of grand designs by an age of modest five-year plans. The change was essentially a change in style, but it amounted to a change in substance. And it brought new risks that were not remarked upon at the time. After all, it was not orators but committee men who had made sure the gas chambers wouldn't run out of gas, who ensured the grand designs made the lengthy transition from the mind of the tyrant to the world of things one could see, touch and be killed by. There was of course no guarantee that these committee men would not turn out to be, in their innocently banal way, just as evil. But the evil of the Adolf Eichmanns of the world was the evil of their ends. For their efficiency and tenacity, it was possible – as a character in Albert Camus's novel *The Fall* noted acidly – to have a perverse admiration.[67]

In fact, Austin needed no models other than himself. The problems of military intelligence in the war had seemed intractable, but they were not. They had been solved, and they had been solved not by geniuses working alone but by the co-ordination of the labours of many. There were big truths to discover, certainly, but – as one of his colleagues wrote – 'the road to large truths runs through the patient accumulation of incalculably many small truths'.[68] Scientists knew this well enough now; the age of the Victorian great-man scientist, of Darwins and Faradays, was over. Science needed labs, teams, methods, journals. It needed not the blessings of a master but the review of peers. And what was good for the military or scientific goose should be good enough for the philosophical gander. Truth was found by teams working together, under an efficient, unbombastic leader keeping things ticking along by injunction and example. Austin saw himself as that leader (was there another candidate?) and the team would meet on Saturday mornings.

Of course, the Saturday morning meetings were not quite what Austin really wanted: the participants were not at his beck and call, being college fellows with an exhausting tutorial load. There was no way to keep them coming other than by making the meetings interesting. Austin never really got the philosophical counterpart to the Theatre Intelligence Section he wanted, generating reliable results week on week. But what he did get didn't feel to those attending like a second-best approximation. As Austin's colleague Geoffrey Warnock put it, they were, 'for many people and for many years, the best of all philosophical occasions'.[69]

*

An early topic in the sessions – chosen as if in contempt of seekers after Seriousness – was games. This was a few years before it became widely known, from Wittgenstein's discussion of the point, just how hard they were to define. What, after all, does rugby have in common with bridge? Wittgenstein was urging caution: 'Don't say: "There must be something common, or they would not be called games," but look and see whether there is anything common to all.'[70] Austin, at this stage unaware of Wittgenstein's example, did look and see, enlisting a platoon to join him. Participants were assigned particular games to investigate and become authorities on. One was sent off to the library to master the rules of an exotic thing called 'baseball'. Austin even invented one himself – a card game called CASE – partly as a challenge to himself to devise, single-handed, a set of rules to cover all cases and without ambiguity or conflict.[71]

The minions would return with their results, to be reported formally and recorded in writing. It was a wonder that it happened at all, that men – and they were nearly all men – so opinionated, so temperamentally undeferential, and, by Friday afternoon, dog-tired from a succession of tutorials, would leap when Austin blew the whistle. As a prefect at his old school, he was thought to have exercised without sentimentality the right to wield the birch on the insubordinate young.[72] In time, he had become the sort of person whose voice, as calm and measured as that of some comic-book archvillain, had much the same effect.

Austin saw that the early zeal wouldn't last for ever and was willing to make concessions. The meetings became more relaxed, postures less stiff, and the atmosphere less like a meeting of managers reporting on where they were with their sales targets. Despite Austin's preference for the snazzy modern room in St John's College with its executive chairs that made slouching difficult (no good philosophy was done in an armchair, he thought), the group generally ended up in the Old Common Room of Balliol next door: 'shabbily comfortable', remembered one participant approvingly, 'leathery, Victorian'.[73]

When they were done with 'games' and 'rules', they moved on to 'disposition', then to 'symbol' and then to 'class'. It felt like a radical shift when it was proposed that they discuss a book: Aristotle, naturally, but also Gottlob Frege (one of whose books Austin translated from the German), Wittgenstein (or as Austin had it, 'Witters') and at one point, a book on something called 'linguistics' by a young American named Noam Chomsky.

To the extent that the topics chosen had anything in common – apart from the fact that Austin had suggested, or at least approved, them – it was their position at the very edge of what generally counted as philosophy, their distance from what they discussed in the course of their Monday-to-Friday tutorial grind. If the topic itself was standard, then the approach was to be novel. What had to be escaped, at any cost, was the rut, the road more travelled.

And so, there was no official line, and no single method. In time, things got very loose indeed: people came in and left as they pleased and attracted no adverse comment for wanting an early lunch, or to catch up on the sleep sacrificed to another lot of essays. By the early 1950s, the meetings were extremely fluid, with nothing like formal rules of order, and consistently and sometimes uproariously funny. Austin, unlike Wittgenstein, liked jokes, jokes that could run the gamut from the wry to the surreal, and he liked other people to laugh at them.

At the surreal end was his attempt to mark the distinction between 'being an X' and 'pretending to be an X'. How much realism could there be in a piece of pretending before one wasn't pretending any more? The example concerned a game at (say) Christmas, perhaps in some big country house with a roaring fire behind you. You have to pretend to be a hyena for a forfeit. You decide to pull out all the stops: 'going down on all fours, you make a few essays at hideous laughter and finally bite my calf, taking ... a fair-sized piece right out of it. Beyond question you have gone too far. Try to plead that you were only pretending, and I shall advert forcibly to the state of my calf – not much pretence about that, is there? There are limits, old sport.'[74]

The effect was never simply relaxing, never simply to put people at their ease. Even the really bizarre jokes contributed to an atmosphere of slight danger. One was never entirely safe; things would never be entirely predictable. 'It was always just a little as if the headmaster were present,' one participant remarked.[75] The atmosphere might be informal, but that didn't mean casual. It was a subtle distinction, but a failure to observe it might result in the little card with an invitation to the next term's meeting going unfortunately missing. When Austin left early, as his growing administrative duties sometimes required him to do, the effect was tangible. Backs went just that little bit more supine, the talking became just that little less guarded, the laughter turned into giggling, the informality devolved into something more Bacchic.

Saturday mornings were, however informal, meetings of colleagues, not of friends; that was another distinction Austin observed scrupulously. Virtually no one knew what he was like at home. People tended to imagine his wife to be a woman of enormous discipline, their children in matching knickerbockers reciting the seventeen times table over perfectly poached breakfast eggs. It was hard to imagine them talking at mealtimes. The very few who ever penetrated the Austins' domestic sanctum were surprised at how relaxed and kindly the atmosphere in fact was.[76] But at work – and Saturdays *were* still work – the old-fashioned rules still applied. There was no question of anyone calling him 'John'. Notoriously, during the war, when a visiting American officer suggested that the group feel free to use Christian names, Austin reminded them that 'Austin is a Christian name too'.[77]

The lack of formality went with something else, unusual in philosophical settings: the absence of adversarialism. The usual seminars (the Jowett Society, the Philosophical Society) adopted forms that encouraged it, its format of talk, reply, question-and-answer session encouraging the adoption of attitudes more proper to a baying mob. The presence of a seminar guest visiting from elsewhere didn't arouse hospitable sentiments so much as the tribalism of the home team's supporters greeting a rival club. On Saturday mornings, disagreement was permitted, even encouraged; that was normal enough. What was abnormal was that *agreement* was permitted, too. It was all right to say that someone else was right, and to say this was neither flattery nor surrender as long as it was sincere.

The possibility of agreement was what Austin had pegged his hopes for philosophy on. Lacking the scientist's methods for decisive corroboration – philosophers don't typically make falsifiable predictions about how the world will turn out to be – one had to settle for other symptoms of progress, other criteria for correctness. Austin did once say that if philosophy had such criteria, they would consist in securing the agreement of a bunch of 'more or less cantankerous colleagues' to a thesis after they had heard one's arguments for it.[78] Such agreement was frequently secured, though at the time few seemed worried about the fact that their group was small, homogeneous, and may not prove anything at all about the prospects of their consensus once exposed to the glare of a non-Oxford sun.

Mostly, it was Austin whom people agreed with. Inevitably so, perhaps, because the chap was so often right, so seldom wrong. More precisely, it was because he was seldom wrong in ways that his fellow dons were able to detect until it was too late. Because he was generally right, it was easy for him to deal with disagreement. He was less good at dealing with refutation. He didn't like being wrong, and he didn't like being shown to be wrong. It was an open question which came first. Given his co-operative ideal of philosophy, his fondness for adopting the persona of a mere 'underlabourer' and his loathing of the magus postures old Witters adopted, he really should have been better at conceding a point, even one made against him. But in this respect, he was not very good at practising what he preached.

His colleagues all received a ribbing at least once. During one term they broke the usual taboo about 'moralising' and discussed some actual moral problems in, as one participant put it, 'an absolutely ground-floor, first-order way',[79] the point being to remind themselves how they usually talked about this sort of thing. One of the problems they discussed was how they should respond, say as examiners, to someone offering them a bribe. R. M. Hare of Balliol, fond of talking about (his) principles, said that he should reply, 'I don't take bribes, on principle.' 'Would you, Hare?' said Austin. 'I think I'd say "No, thanks".'[80] At another meeting, where the subject was Wittgenstein's obscure insistence on distinguishing between a report of pain and an expression of pain, Stuart Hampshire said something about the groanings and grimacings of those in pain being characteristic of what people in pain do, an example of 'pain-behaviour'. Austin disliked the example: 'Well, you'd be a tartar in the wards, Hampshire – "Lights out, and *no groaning!*"'[81]

Austin could be no less of a tartar where open displays of feeling were concerned. Wit was desirable, flamboyance not. And at all times, one had to be alert to the possibility of philosophers getting unmoored from common sense, of them starting to say things no one in his right mind should have said. The company of other bluff and commonsensical philosophers was no inoculation. It was all very well for Ryle to have replaced the old Cartesian talk of private theatres with 'behavioural dispositions': public, observable, unmysterious. But 'disposition' was not – not really – a term of ordinary speech. Ryle's use of it seemed to Austin at risk of blurring a number of distinctions already recognised in common speech.

Was a disposition the same thing as a 'trait'? A 'propensity'? 'Characteristic'? 'Habit'? 'Inclination'? 'Tendency'? 'Susceptibility'? 'Liability'? Wittgenstein compared language to a toolbox – many tools for many purposes. All very good, Austin thought. But what was a tool, exactly? How was it different from an instrument, an implement, a utensil, an appliance, a piece of equipment, apparatus, gear, kit, device … And was it ever simple to decide where some particular thing best fit? A pair of scissors say. To everyone's surprise, the answer was far from straightforward. By steady steps, they reached a consensus on the matter. Kitchen scissors? Utensils. Garden scissors? Tools, or maybe implements. And tailor's scissors? Unclear: maybe instruments, maybe even 'sewing materials', but definitely not utensils.

Each of these words could lead them into another, obscurely fascinating, rabbit-hole. Austin could uncover ambiguities in the oddest of places. When some object came with instructions on 'how to use' this or that, what was being promised? What we were to use it for – to cover a wound rather than insulate a frayed wire, for instance? Or the way to use it? And come to think of it, was there a difference between 'a way of using' and 'a way to use'?

The examples, produced in what seemed like divinely inspired bouts of good linguistic form, became Austin's favourite method. He could take the simplest, most everyday thing, and find a puzzle in our ways of talking about it. If a landlady complained about her lodger's 'nasty habits', would we take her to be complaining about the same kind of thing if she'd spoken instead of his 'nasty ways'? Why can we speak of someone as a 'good' batsman but not as a 'right' batsman?[82] Could someone complain of a pain in the waist?[83]

This was a kind of fieldwork, which had the great advantage that one need go no further than the Old Common Room at Balliol to find one's site. If one was suddenly doubtful about the terms of ordinary aesthetic appraisal, for instance, one need only cross Broad Street to ask a clerk at Boswells how he might praise a particularly shapely teapot, or walk a hundred paces to Blackwell's bookshop to ask an assistant for a manual of industrial design to see how the experts spoke of jugs, settees and the texture of bathroom tiles. But these things were for special exigencies. For the most part, one could be one's own native informant, one's own interpreter. And after a sweaty morning's work splitting hairs, there was a wife, or for the bachelor dons a member of the college staff, waiting with a hot lunch.

There was a phrase, repeated in one way or another, that gave the whole affair what unity it possessed – what should we say if … what should we say of … *what should we say when* … But who were 'we'? Oxford men? Philosophers? Human beings? Rational animals? And 'should' meaning *would*? Or 'should' meaning *ought to*? Or some mysterious third thing: neither purely fact nor purely norm, neither merely descriptive nor merely prescriptive? The question of why it mattered what we should say was not one that Austin ever addressed squarely. Others have since attempted to provide the answers Austin so vexingly withheld. But that is an account better discussed later in this story.

*

What did Wittgenstein make, if anything, of what was happening at Oxford? When he died in 1951, the work he had been doing since his return to Cambridge was far from widely available. He had shared it in lectures, dictations and the odd conversation with a student. But a *book* felt beyond him. Books had to begin and to end, and one page come after the other, the 'ideas' – whatever those were – arranged into something like a consecutive, or otherwise natural, order. But what was the natural order for his ideas, whose essence – if they had one – lay in their disorder? Wittgenstein didn't know.

Oxford had read the *Tractatus*, eventually, and heard murmurings of a radical change of mind. But no one was entirely sure what the change amounted to. The teachings were closely guarded, and Wittgenstein did not take kindly to publicity. An early missionary from the Fens was the excellently named John Wisdom (b.1904), whose paper at the Aristotelian Society in early 1937, 'Philosophical Perplexity', was the nearest thing people outside Cambridge had to a chance of hearing the authentic voice of the master. But Wisdom was, as he freely admitted, not a reliable messenger. Many of the examples in his paper were marked '(W)', for Wittgenstein; however, a minatory footnote warned, 'It must not be assumed that they are used in a way he would approve.'[84]

In Wisdom's telling, Ryle had got it right when he had decried the risks of taking language at face value. The surface features of language could be misleading indeed. But Ryle was still too close to Russell and Moore if he thought the way to avoid such error had to go through the royal road of logical analysis. Ryle seemed to take the question to be, 'This is what we say, but what do we really mean?' Wisdom proposed that the real question was, 'Under what circumstances are such things usually said?'[85]

Philosophers in the Cartesian tradition had wanted to distinguish sharply between what I know (authoritatively) about my own mind and what I can infer (fallibly) about the minds of others. Sometimes, that point was put in terms of a distinction between what I can know directly and what I can know only indirectly. But what, asked Wisdom, was a philosopher saying in affirming or denying that 'I know directly what is going on in Smith's mind'? Perhaps nothing. In other words, the statement is the purest nonsense. But what sort of nonsense is it? Is it like 'Cat how is up' – a nonsense born of a disrupted syntax? Or like 'All whiffley was the tulgey wood' – the nonsense of words with no conventional meaning? Neither, said Wisdom. What we should say about such sentences is that they lack a conventional usage. There's no human context in which that's the kind of thing one would say. But philosophy tempted people into thinking that there was a real puzzle about these things, that these provocative sceptical claims are ones that we could actually take seriously: 'We can't ever really know the causes of our sensations.' 'Inductive conclusions are never justified.'

Such statements have the air of laments, as if, Wisdom said, the philosopher 'can dream of another world where we can see our friends and tables face to face, where scientists can justify their conclusions and terriers can catch hares'.[86] But the accents of lament are misplaced. Nothing is being regretted. Indeed, there is nothing here to regret, any more than there is to regret in the fact that no one has yet managed to draw a pentagon with three sides, or score a try in a cricket game. Metaphysical theories are false; but 'there *is* good in them, poor things'.[87]

What good is that? Here, Wisdom took Wittgenstein to be giving one answer, and himself to be giving another. 'Wittgenstein allows that the theories are philosophically important not merely as specimens of the whoppers philosophers can tell. But he too much represents them as merely symptoms of linguistic confusion. I wish to represent them as also symptoms of linguistic penetration.'[88] Why do that? Because if all philosophers can do is cure the puzzled of their puzzlements, then surely, Wisdom thought, there are other ways of securing that end: drugs, for instance, or distraction.

In the world of his philosophical formation, where the dismissal of metaphysics as nonsense amounted to no more than the clearing of throats before the real point could be made, Wisdom found his *métier* in restoring metaphysical statements, if not quite to respectability, then at least to usefulness. Wisdom's rehabilitation of metaphysics was like the construction of a museum where such specimens of venality might be kept on display, a warning to future offenders and an inspiration to artists. Metaphysics could then have a kind of meaningfulness as a source of paradoxical illumination, reminders of truths overlooked, literally absurd but figuratively resonant. This gave philosophy a permanent task, for there would always be forgettings and exaggerations that needed curing with a well-placed reminder. The methods of philosophers needn't then be aligned only with those of scientists. Poets had something to teach them, as did lawyers, each with their special way of getting us to see one thing as similar to another, to see one thing *as* another. There was room in this picture for argument, and also for imagination.

Ryle liked Wisdom, as did Austin; he persuaded them that Cambridge may well be doing something interesting after all, however rebarbative the personal manner of the other principals. Their styles were, of course, different. If each was in his way aphoristic, each was drawn to aphorisms of different sorts: 'Stupidity is not the same thing, or the same sort of thing, as ignorance'; 'There are more ways of outraging speech than contradiction merely'; 'If you will excuse a suspicion of smartness: philosophers should be continually trying to say what cannot be said' (respectively, Ryle, Austin, Wisdom).[89] That stuff about saying the unsayable evoked, even as it seemed to deny, Wittgenstein, but the Austrian would not have prefaced his remark with an apology for 'a suspicion of smartness'.[90]

For a long time, Wisdom was indispensable as font of Wittgensteinian ideas, but his own distinctive style stopped him serving as mere spokesman. Like Wittgenstein's, it disdained mere argument and any appearance of offering proofs. Yet, its blokeish flippancy and fondness for English demotic ('whoppers', 'poor things', 'smartness') made for a mood quite unlike the one produced by the more Viennese cadences of Wittgenstein. Reading Wisdom felt like listening to some radical twelve-tone piece by Schoenberg played by an orchestra specialising in the pastoral symphonies of Vaughan Williams.[91] And Wisdom's reputation, and his usefulness, seemed always at risk of coming up against the inevitable facts: Wittgenstein would die, and what he had said would get out. Later, other people did start to return from Cambridge with rumours and carbon-paper copies of notes. But only the death of Wittgenstein opened up the prospect of some more direct contact with His Master's Voice.

*

Elizabeth Anscombe spent a good deal of her war at Newnham College in Cambridge. Not for her the civil service or the charms of wartime London. In 1944, she learnt that Wittgenstein was to start lecturing again. He had spent the previous two years working as a porter at Guy's Hospital in London, and then as a pharmacy technician in the hospital's laboratory, mixing – with great precision, it was said – zinc and salicylic acid ('Lassar's paste') for patients in the dermatology department.[92] She became an enthusiastic attender, saying enough to make him take notice of a mind he could respect, and an interlocutor who seemed to understand him.

Facts about this stage of their acquaintance are scarce. Anscombe may have been unique among those who knew him in resisting the temptation to serve the underground trade in Wittgenstein anecdotes. But in a letter written in November 1944, Wittgenstein noted the presence of 'a woman, Mrs so and so who called herself Miss Anscombe, who is certainly intelligent'.[93] By May 1945, he felt he had seen enough of her to be able to write a letter of reference for a research fellowship: 'undoubtedly, the most talented female student I have had since 1930, when I began to lecture; and among my male students only eight, or ten, have either equalled or surpassed her'.[94]

Wittgenstein has been described, not without grounds, as a misogynist, but the evidence is mixed: he had certainly had female students of enormous talent before, which makes his initial remark much more than faint praise. Margaret MacDonald, Alice Ambrose, Margaret Masterman and Helen Knight were among those who were privy to his lectures in the 1930s. Wittgenstein's letter goes on to list Anscombe's virtues – 'an excellent grasp of philosophical problems, great seriousness, and uncommon ability for hard work' – and explained away what he thought the immaturity of the essays she had submitted with the application. 'It is the unavoidable consequence of her having been, on coming to Cambridge, subjected to new philosophical influences which she has not had the time to digest' – the new influences being, presumably, his own.[95]

In the beginning, Peter Geach was jealous. Anscombe was moving, he thought, 'away from my tutelage; I am afraid that I resented that, but I could recognize this feeling as base and irrational, and soon overcame it'.[96] She became Wittgenstein's 'old man', welcome at classes where there were few women, allowed to suggest topics for discussion. Geach came to make the great man's acquaintance too, though Wittgenstein seemed ambivalent about him. Asked once by his landlady what Geach was like, he replied obscurely, 'He reads Somerset Maugham.'[97]

Over the subsequent few years, Anscombe and Wittgenstein became very close. Soon he asked her to be one of the executors of his literary estate. Then he asked her to translate the as-yet-untitled book he was then writing – or rather, trying to assemble out of fifteen or so years' worth of notes, written (usually in German) or dictated to students (usually in English). He encouraged her to go to Vienna to improve her German, and more to the point, her grasp of Viennese dialect.

Before she knew him, she later observed, the great philosophers of the canon – Plato, Aristotle, Aquinas – had seemed to her but statues, beautiful but inanimate. But here was someone who belonged in their company, a living man, conversing with her, someone in whom she could confide, someone she could find silly. Once, finding him in raptures about a profound phrase he had discovered in St Augustine, that God 'moves without moving', she was forthright enough to inform him that it meant no more than that God makes other things move without moving himself. He could be silly while trying to be deep, and deep while trying to be silly. A favourite proverb of his, an Austrian demotic expression, went, 'You can't shit higher than your arse.'[98] It captured, less obscurely, something of his own early philosophical views on the limits of language: there was no effing the ineffable.

Anscombe was offered a research fellowship at Somerville in 1945, but her trips to Cambridge continued. Her personal manner was changing. Despite her considerable talent as a linguist and historian of philosophy, she had started to dismiss the history of ideas as an affront to true philosophy. Her face would contort into grimaces of the purest agony when gripped by a philosophical thought, as if it couldn't be real philosophy unless it physically hurt. Her students heard every now and then in her vowels the hint of an Austrian accent; some must have been surprised to learn she had grown up in that exotic Viennese suburb, Dulwich.[99]

Once and only once was Wittgenstein enticed – Anscombe the intermediary – to Oxford. He would not give a paper, but he would reply to one. A willing sacrificial victim was found in Oscar Wood (b.1925), the undergraduate president of the Jowett Society.

His subject was to be the feted, notorious argument in Descartes, *cogito, ergo sum*, I think, therefore I am. Was this, or was it not, a valid argument? It was the middle of May 1947, and the meeting was to happen at Magdalen. The room was, inevitably, nowhere near large enough; there were people on tables, on windowsills and on the floor. Gilbert Ryle was there, as was Isaiah Berlin. Wittgenstein walked in, to the slight surprise of a crowd that had expected a larger man. He was wearing his customary open-necked shirt and a green pullover. The table was semi-circular and illuminated with candles; he was seated with Wood to one side and Anscombe to the other. Wood's words are lost to history but his paper, 'short and well-constructed', was well received. As he spoke, Wittgenstein listened with apparent absorption.[100] Then it was his turn to speak.

'Mr Wood', he began, 'seems to me to have made two points.' One, he said, was about knowledge, the other about 'substance'. It was unclear if this was intended as neutral summary or accusation. And from then on, both Mr Wood and Mr Descartes were left unmentioned as Wittgenstein broke free of the usual conventions of the respondent. Wood had shown nerves of steel, having read his paper with a calm he couldn't possibly have felt, knowing his respondent's reputation. The size of the crowd, well above the Jowett average, was daunting enough. But Wood had to deal also with the gaze of Wittgenstein's blue eyes, and the interruptions of an ancient man sitting at the table who lapsed into loud periodic fits of coughing.

Wittgenstein gave them the performance they had been expecting, or dreading. The long silences put in their appearance, the burial of head in hands, the pained moanings ('no, that's not right at all') directed as much at himself as at anyone else. 'No, no – that is wrong – what is to be done? It is all so difficult; how is one to approach it?' Wittgenstein didn't speak in paragraphs; every utterance seemed a false start, a red herring. Then others began to chip in. Anscombe, of course, found nothing peculiar in this way of going on; nor did Geach or Yorick Smythies, another Cambridge familiar. Others, Mary Warnock and Mary Scrutton, who both knew Anscombe, had an inkling of what might be to come. Wood managed at times to speak up for himself, or to encourage Wittgenstein to talk about knowledge and Descartes.

Every now and then, Wittgenstein said something that did sound like it might be about the *cogito*. 'If a man says to me, looking at the sky, "I think it will rain, therefore I exist," I do not understand him.' 'That's all very fine,' piped up the old man whose thunderous coughs had punctuated the meeting. 'What we want to know is: is the *cogito* valid or not?' This was old H. A. Prichard, the last of the survivors of the age of Cook Wilson. He was still alive, but only just.

Wittgenstein said something to the effect that Descartes was unimportant. 'With respect to you and your colleagues,' said Prichard – who disconcertingly insisted on calling their guest 'Mr Whittgensteen' – 'what Descartes said is of far more importance than anything you have said.' In one account of proceedings, he is said to have persisted: 'Mr Whittgensteen, Mr Whittgensteen, you have not answered the question. *Cogito ergo sum* – I think therefore I am. Is it true, Mr Whittgensteen, is it true – I think therefore I am?' 'I think', Wittgenstein is supposed to have replied, 'this is a very foolish old man; so I am – what?' The audience was left divided between those who thought this a marvellous bit of repartee worthy of the senior common room, and those who thought it simply rude. Prichard left early.[101]

No one was keeping minutes, and what seems to have survived in the memories of those present is the sense of an opportunity missed, a clash of philosophical styles that produced more heat than light. And perhaps that one extraordinary moment when Wittgenstein shouted at Wood, 'Say something crude, say what you really think, and we shall get somewhere!'[102] The remark was in one sense an attack on Oxford, its respect for the history of the subject that had survived all the scientific pretensions of the

1930s; but in another, it was the truest expression of one of the forms this respect took. Was it really Socratic to spend one's time reading the works of the glorious dead? Was it not Socrates who had first taken it as his motto to ask his young interlocutors to say what they really thought?

They continued the next day in All Souls. There was no pretence this time that Wittgenstein was going to be talking about Descartes or Oscar Wood. Instead, Wittgenstein and Anscombe put on a sort of double act, the latter adopting even more flamboyantly the accents of agony she had learnt from the former. There was an awkward moment when a glamorous young woman from London, brought there by an undergraduate no doubt promising her an 'occasion', said from the floor, 'Virginia Woolf said, "Life is a transparent envelope." Does Mr Wittgenstein agree?'

Those expecting an explosion of contempt were surprised. Anscombe took up the question with the delight she had acquired from Wittgenstein in – as they saw it – the philosophical puzzlement of the untutored young. Yes, said Anscombe. Consciousness – which could have been what the questioner and Mrs Woolf meant by 'life' – can indeed be understood in terms of an analogy with a transparent medium. Wittgenstein continued the thread with what, everyone knew, was his general way with such questions, by turning the question of 'consciousness' – a dangerous noun – into a question about those less threatening things, verbs. 'Thinking', 'feeling', 'wanting', 'willing': there were a few in the room who could see affinities with the sort of thing Austin did on Saturdays, but this didn't *feel* like the same thing at all.

Anscombe turned up every now and then at an Austin class, but she seems to have conceived of her role there as a spy.[103] At one, grandly titled 'Things', the topic was Ayer and Russell's insistence that it was a mistake to think that we see, in their vernacular, 'material objects'; what we really see are 'sense data'. Was this really a mistake, wondered Austin with the deceptively open-minded manner that portended a demolition job. The presence of

Anscombe did little to unsettle Austin, a man not given to being unsettled by anything at all. But she was famously blunt on these occasions, talking at every opportunity and never agreeing with what Austin said. But others found it puzzling. From what little they knew of Wittgenstein, there was barely anything to distinguish Austin's method from Wittgenstein's. Returning words to their ordinary uses, the refusal of specialist terminology, the absence of any impulse to systematic theorising: that was only the beginning of the list. The focus on language, on particular examples, on when we say what, on what we should say when: surely this was part of the common ground between the two men. Both men had no time for the old-style idealist metaphysics. Nor were they tempted by the anti-metaphysical grandeur of the early analytic project, looking for the austere logical skeleton under the messy clothing of natural language. No, 'ordinary language is all right', Wittgenstein had said in one of his lectures in the 1930s.[104] Austin agreed.

'To think that Wittgenstein fathered that bastard,' Anscombe once fumed at another participant as she struggled with her bike lock. She was talking of Austin, of course, seeing him as a cut-price Wittgenstein. The recipient of this rant, previously called Mary Wilson, had already failed her by marrying a promising young philosopher called Geoffrey Warnock, very much an Austin acolyte. To Anscombe, he was always 'that shit Warnock', just as Austin was always 'that bastard'.[105] The accusation seemed not so much one of plagiarism – Anscombe was in a strong position to know that there was little room for any direct influence – but of distortion. Perhaps the problem was that the things in Wittgenstein she found resonant, beautiful, inspiring, therapeutic and profound, were transformed by Austin, as she believed, into something contemptibly little-English, petty and shallow.

Austin seemed to enjoy his academic position and the duties that came with it – the marking of exams, the drawing up of regulations, serving on committees of university proctors. His interest in language was frequently an interest in the English language, and it didn't seem to bother him if a distinction in English couldn't be translated. He was funny, in a dry, ironic and occasionally silly way, strikingly different from the Zen-like humour of Wittgenstein that didn't seem part of an attempt to elicit anything as base as laughter. For all that the notion had come under suspicion over the previous thirty years, Austin still seemed in his folly to think that philosophy might be a quest for *truths*, and to hope that he, with his colleagues, might discover some. He seemed to find philosophy – and this was really shocking – enjoyable. One imagined him in a sitting room with comfortable chairs and recently dusted, well-stocked bookshelves, each book thoroughly annotated yet retaining its unbroken spine. One could not imagine him lying awake in bed haunted by the spectre of a philosophical problem, or understanding why someone else might.

Anscombe could not emulate the sparseness of Wittgenstein's living quarters (the deckchairs, the single bed). She had a husband, with new children arriving regularly, and room had to be found for nappies, blankets and perambulators. Her way of showing her indifference to the ordinary conditions of bourgeois life consisted in a happy tolerance of dirt.[106] And surrounded by children and the accumulated dust of many weeks, she began her first great work. It did count as *her* great work, even if it was 'only' a translation. Wittgenstein would trust the task to no one else, and she took it as a solemn duty, working assiduously at her German and at mastering the idiosyncratic features of Wittgenstein's own prose, some of it the influence of his Viennese upbringing, some of it aspects of his own distinctive idiolect.

In one of her many conversations with him, he told her he was wondering whether he was a second-rate artist. He thought he had found, a second time around, a form adequate to the shape of his thought. The short, relentless declarative sentences of the *Tractatus* had been whittled down from a larger mass of similar sentences from his notebooks. But the more recent work needed something different, and his word for it was *Bemerkung* ('remark' is as good a translation as any). The *Bemerkungen* he was writing now could be as short as a Tractarian sentence, but they could equally be several paragraphs long, or go on for an undivided couple of pages. His anxiety now was not a cry for reassurance, nor an appeal for flattery. Anscombe, devoted but incapable of lying out of kindness or deference, was in any case the wrong person from whom to seek either. But she might understand why he feared that his discovery of his form, so exciting to him, could eventually be recognised as an embarrassment.

What Anscombe was given was a collection of these *Bemerkungen*. She knew from Wittgenstein that this hadn't been a cop-out on his part, an imposition on his executors and translators by a man who didn't know what to make of his material. The introduction he wrote to the book he wanted to make out of that material, the *Philosophical Investigations*, was apologetic: 'I should have liked to write a good book. This has not come about, but the time is past in which I could improve it.'[107] But he wasn't apologising for not having written a continuous essay – say, like what he had dictated to his classes in the 1930s. There was no question of his producing such a work, and not simply out of incapacity. The *Investigations* could sometimes seem like an unedited notebook, but Wittgenstein put an enormous amount of effort into arranging the materials within it. The point was not to cut a straight line across the terrain; it was to survey it. The nature of the investigation, he said, 'compels us to traverse a wide field of thought criss-cross in all directions'.[108]

The proper analogy, he said once, was a photograph album. The same place had been photographed from a range of different positions. From the initial profusion of photographs, a careful selection had been made, and – Anscombe later wrote – 'arrayed in such a way as to give a good idea of the whole landscape'.[109] The book came out in 1953: the original German on the left, and Anscombe's translation on the right. This was nothing like the *Tractatus*, a book that seemed to provide the conclusions without providing the arguments. The new book provided the arguments without ever spelling out their conclusions. His preface explained why: 'I should not like my writing to spare other people the trouble of thinking.'[110]

The *Investigations* left its readers with a great deal to think about. It returned to the basic concern of the *Tractatus*, the nature of language, but approached the question this time by asking how it is we learn language. (Wittgenstein's years in the 1920s as a schoolteacher in an Austrian village may have informed some of what he said in these sections.)[111] He discussed the difficulties of definition, and the folly of trying to define things like 'games' with a simple list of necessary and sufficient conditions. Perhaps it was better to think of the many things we call games in terms of the sorts of resemblances we find among members of a family. There was something that could have been an argument about the impossibility of a 'private language', a language that no one other than the speaker can possibly understand. There were paradoxes to do with the possibility of following a rule. There were discussions of what we mean when talking about our sensations.[112] There were instructions to the readers, rhetorical questions never answered. There were things that may have been jokes, or riddles. There was enough here to keep philosophers busy for decades (as indeed it has).

Of course, the voice of Wittgenstein that monolingual Anglophones got to hear was at least as much the voice of Anscombe. Her English translation achieved, from early on in the book's career, a canonical status few translations have, partly from Anscombe's having gone through substantial stretches of the book with Wittgenstein and hearing him attempt his own translations, and partly from the uncanny knack she had for recreating in English the cadence and texture of his German. It must have been a wrench for her to let the book out into the world. For evermore, Wittgenstein would be public property, any idiot on the street able to venture an opinion.

She coped with this fact well enough, but there were limits. As his executor, she was fiercely loyal, leaping in to defend his reputation whenever she thought it was threatened by some ill-advised new attempt at biography or commentary.[113] The few stories she shared of Wittgenstein were stripped down to their philosophically significant bare-bones. At every chance she stressed that 'he did not think out a total position ... he was constantly enquiring ... I therefore deprecate attempts to expound Wittgenstein's thought as a finished thing'.[114] And she retained the authority to scold any who purported to channel the spirit of the man. 'Predictions of "what Wittgenstein would say" about some question one thought of were never correct.'[115] One had to take her word for it; who could know better? Some years later, in conversation with a group of graduate students, one of them nervously admitted to working on 'Kantian themes in Wittgenstein'. 'How interesting,' she said. 'I once knew someone called Wittgenstein.'[116]

6

Corruption

Even before he became president, Senator Harry S. Truman was known for his ostentatiously plain-speaking ways. 'If you don't like the heat,' he had once told a fellow senator, 'get out of the kitchen.'[1] In April 1945, he succeeded Franklin D. Roosevelt – who had just suffered a cerebral haemorrhage – to the presidency. He announced VE Day on his sixty-first birthday, 8 May 1945. Nazi Germany had surrendered, and there was now only the war in the Pacific, the Emperor of Japan having decided to dig his heels in. A short time into his presidency, the Secretary of War informed Truman of the details of the new weapon of which he had only heard rumours before. He wrote in his diary, 'We have discovered the most terrible bomb in the history of the world. It may be the fire destruction prophesied in the Euphrates Valley Era, after Noah and his fabulous Ark.'[2] In early August, he took the fateful decision to use it.

'It was', he said during his campaign for re-election in 1948, 'the hardest decision I ever had to make. But the President cannot duck hard problems – he cannot pass the buck … I decided that the bomb should be used in order to end the war quickly and save countless lives – Japanese as well as American.'[3] He never stopped insisting that it was either the bomb or a prolonged land invasion of Japan, in which vastly more people would have died. His hands would be dirty with the dust of the mushroom clouds over Hiroshima and Nagasaki, but they would only have been dirtier if he had refrained. Some people thought him worthy at least of pity:

who among us would have acted differently in the circumstances? Some had even thought there had been a sort of courage in it.

In 1956, three years after the end of his second term, Truman took the boat to Europe. He met Churchill and the Queen and the Duke of Edinburgh at Buckingham Palace. Along the way, he was greeted by cheering crowds. 'Too bad he's not campaigning for anything in this country,' a spectator was heard saying while watching him board the boat train. He was, the *Daily Telegraph* said, a 'living and kicking symbol of everything that everyone likes best about the United States'.[4] Among his many engagements in the country was a brief trip to Oxford where he was to be awarded an honorary doctorate in civil law.

Like other such honorary degrees, it needed the approval of Congregation – effectively the university's parliament, consisting (among others) of its academic staff. The decision should have been simple. Such things were usually a formality; no one had been known to vote against an honorary doctorate. Then the senior proctor received a notice that it might be less simple this time around. A Miss Anscombe of Somerville intended to raise an objection. The senior proctor consulted the university's registrar and informed Miss Anscombe of the necessary procedure. Had she got up a 'party', he asked? She had not. Word went around, and the theatre was full when it was time for the vote. Some, it seemed, were there on principle: Truman was at worst pitiable for the choice with which he had been faced, at best admirable for the choice that he had made. Others were informed only that some pesky women were out to make trouble.

Anscombe addressed the house. She thought it was perfectly simple. The bombing of Hiroshima and Nagasaki was murder. That made Truman a murderer. The university should not be giving honorary doctorates to murderers. It may as well be honouring Nero, or Genghis Khan. Alan Bullock (b.1914) of St Catherine's, fresh from writing an authoritative biography of Hitler, defended Truman. He didn't have to try very hard; the audience didn't need much persuading. When it came to it and the question was put, Elizabeth Anscombe cried out, 'Non placet': it does not please. Joining her were her Somerville colleagues Margaret Hubbard (a young Australian classicist) and Philippa Foot, along with Foot's husband Michael. Truman was granted the degree. Asked what he made of the opposition, he told the press he knew nothing of it. His position was unchanged. The Allied Powers had decided on the terms of Japanese surrender at the Potsdam Conference; they had let the Japanese emperor know the terms. He would not accept them, and did not do so until after the bombing of Hiroshima and Nagasaki. He said of the decision, 'If I had to do it again I would do it all over again.'[5]

In 1957, Anscombe published a fourteen-page pamphlet, available for a shilling from her house on St John Street.[6] It was dedicated 'with respect, but without permission, to the others who said "non placet"'.[7] She told her version of the history: the years of propaganda before and during the war that insisted that modern war was 'indivisible'. Civilians were fair game, because even the growing of a potato or the purchase of a postage stamp were contributions to the war effort. Then there was the agreement among Allied statesmen on the '"general principle" – marvellous phrase! – of using the new type of weapon'.[8] The attempt to secure a Japanese surrender on terms that might be realistically acceptable to them was at best perfunctory. She wouldn't go so far as to say that 'there was an exultant itch to use the new weapons'.[9] But she certainly thought that the Americans' knowledge of their new weapon had made a difference to how keenly they sought a less violent surrender.

No, she wasn't trying to strike a high-minded attitude. She had never been a pacifist. Nor was she a purist. Nor was she trying to make a symbolic protest against nuclear weapons. She was defending a simple principle: 'Choosing to kill the innocent as a means to your ends is always murder.'[10] That is what Truman had done, even if his choice consisted not in dropping the bomb himself but in putting his signature to a piece of paper. It was too late to stop him, and not much point in condemning him. But there was a chance that the dons of Oxford might have refrained from 'offering Mr Truman honours, because one can share in the guilt of a bad action by praise and flattery, as also by defending it'.[11]

Whence the willingness of her fellow dons to honour such a man, and such a deed? Surely the moral philosophers among them would have compunctions. But this was also the time that Anscombe had begun to read some contemporary works of moral philosophy. She knew her Aristotle and her Aquinas well, but not so much her A. J. Ayer, nor that voguish work by a man called Hare at Balliol who thought he'd improved upon the details of Ayer's system while retaining something of its spirit. At Somerville, it was her colleague Philippa Foot who taught these subjects, while Anscombe stuck to the logic and metaphysics and historical texts she knew best. But once she did begin reading, she found herself first confused, then appalled.

The works of Oxford moral philosophy from before the war, Anscombe had found, adopted a tone of reasonable earnestness. Some of them seemed to be saying that the rightness of actions was a matter of the *motive* from which they were done (did that include the actions of Himmler and Eichmann too, who could hardly be accused of failing to act from the motive of *duty*?). Others were greatly concerned with the conflicts between our duties. More precisely, between what seemed to be our duties – what they liked to call our *prima facie* duties – as when my *prima facie* duty to keep a promise to see my friend for tea at four o'clock might be outweighed by my other *prima facie* duty to save a child from a hungry alligator, or when my *prima facie* duty not to kill the innocent might be outweighed by my *prima facie* duty to advance the general good. This was in the 1920s.[12]

At some point in the 1930s, it became rather less common – a generational shift perhaps – to go on about *duty* in the style of a solemn sailor out of Gilbert and Sullivan and to talk instead of the 'expressive' features of moral language. On the expressive view of moral language, of which A. J. Ayer's 'emotivism' was one clearly if crudely articulated form, words like 'good' *describe* nothing at all. The question is not what goodness is but what we do in calling things good – roughly, we commend them. Around the same time, though the logical connection was unclear, it became the done thing to insist that ethics allowed for few if any general principles, and therefore, no absolute prohibitions. It was this latter tendency that Anscombe, devout Catholic as she now was, found both shocking and historically unprecedented.

Rules of thumb there could certainly be – 'don't lie'; or 'don't commit sodomy' – but there were exceptions to everything. Experience was all; with enough of it, one would know when and which lies might be told, when and with whom sodomy committed. Aristotle was sometimes invoked in support of this denial of the value of general principles. And with the denial of absolute prohibitions on anything, Anscombe said, it was hardly puzzling that a whole generation of moral philosophers endorsed views that amounted to 'a repudiation of the idea that any class of actions, such as murder, may be absolutely excluded'. Were the philosophers influenced by the wider culture of the 1950s? Or were they influencing it? Either way, they made Congregation's decision if not more palatable to Anscombe, at least a little more intelligible. The rot, she decided, was deep.

*

Richard Mervyn Hare (b.1919) was born the same year as Elizabeth Anscombe. His first family home was grand, but prodigal. As the family's finances declined, the houses grew more modest. The Hares were mostly 'businessmen and small landowners', though it was rumoured that there had been a Reverend Hare who had lived in a tub in the fashion of Diogenes the Cynic.[13] Somewhere in the family tree there was even an abolitionist who had lived in Bristol (a city whose wealth had been built on the slave trade), which must have taken even more courage than living in a tub.

Hare's father was an Oxford graduate (third class) who, despite the smatterings of philosophy he got with his Classics degree, preferred the verse of minor poets (he was one, too), shooting, fly-fishing, dancing the old-fashioned waltz and tinkering with short-wave radios. His mother went on annual expeditions to the Mediterranean with her watercolours. Hare was ten when his father died of a heart attack that may have been brought on by the stresses of a failing business. When he was fifteen, he lost his mother too.[14]

His adolescence was spent between guardians (older siblings, uncles) and boarding school. The first of these was Copthorne in Sussex – brutal, but sound on the ancient languages. Copthorne was followed by Rugby, where he received a classical scholarship, and failed in succession at rugby, cricket and cross-country running. He did, however, became moderately good at carpentry and very good at Greek and Latin verse composition. A school prize took him on a Greek cruise, and the Public Schools Exploring Society on an expedition to Newfoundland. Eventually, he rose to the giddy heights of head boy. When it came time to think about university, he followed the money. He had hoped to go to New College like his father but had to settle for Balliol instead, being 'not bold enough to refuse' the scholarship they offered him.[15]

At Balliol, he tried rowing, but gave it up after being declared good enough only for the third college boat. But 1938 was no time to be moping about that. About the time Chamberlain returned from Munich in the early autumn of that year, Hare had to make up his mind about the vexed question of whether to be a pacifist. He was in Kirriemuir in Scotland, dragged along by his uncles on a shooting holiday, and heard the news on the radio. He gave himself – old Rugbeian that he was – twenty-four hours in which to settle the matter once and for all. Conscience without indecision would become a sort of motto with him. The nays had it; when term began, he joined the Oxford Officers' Training Corps.[16]

In the summer of 1939, he drove to Greece: driving had first been a struggle, then his greatest delight. He dropped the car off at Athens, then took the train to Paris. When he got off the train, he found the newspapers announcing that Germany had invaded Poland. When back in Oxford, there was no question of his seeking to defer his conscription. He failed his medical (it was his eyes), and was put down for sedentary service overseas, but managed to get this overridden. Active service was what he wanted. The winter of 1939 was spent training on Salisbury Plain. Then there were the months of uncertainty, where he was either on leave or cooling his heels while waiting to know if he had been assigned to a regiment. Thinking it likely he would be killed, he used the quiet of his uncle's billiards room to write out his 'philosophy' in twenty pages. And he had a sudden epiphany on what seemed an irrelevant subject: he didn't like Beethoven any more. Bach could be '*food*, musical food' in a moment like this, but not Beethoven. His chords ran, he later said, 'exceedingly hollow'.[17] After Dunkirk and the evacuation of the army from France, he was put on the P&O *Strathaird* to sail for Bombay.

On the ship, the short essay grew to twice its length. When he wasn't writing, he was in the quiet bows of the ship, where he and a friend read aloud to each other: Hare's choice was Robert Bridges' *The Testament of Beauty*, a long philosophical poem full of oracular remarks about reason, ethics and the nature of Christ. At Bombay, he was summoned for an interview with two aged colonels of the Indian Army with the power to assign man to regiment. The interview was short: 'Which school?' 'Can you ride?' Hare's first answer pleased them, his second less so. He was sent off to the Mountain Artillery Training Centre at Ambala in the Punjab, where he learnt a little Urdu and from where he managed to visit Delhi, Agra and Lahore, each within a day's journey. His ultimate destination for the war, however, was Singapore.[18]

In the winter of 1940, Hare of the 22nd Mountain Regiment arrived in Singapore, attached to the 4th (Hazara) Mountain Battery, Frontier Force. He would not be required to deal with horses, just motor vehicles and Indian soldiers who needed to be taught to drive. He took to the job: he had loved driving, and now discovered he loved teaching it. He formed close relationships with the Punjabi soldiers and got along easily with the Indian officers in the regiment, most of whom had come out of the Royal Prince of Wales Military College at Dehradun, designed to be run as a simulacrum of an English public school for promising Indian boys who might go on to the Royal Military College, Sandhurst.[19]

Singapore was no safe haven. The Japanese armed forces invaded Thailand and Malaya in the December of 1941 and Hare's regiment found themselves in action. The Japanese had the early victories; morale was poor. Hare was in hospital for a period with malaria. He recovered just in time for the Battle of Singapore in the early months of 1942. The Allied forces were small, poorly organised, and utterly unprepared for the scale and precision of the attack. Hare was part of their last gun position, next to an old people's home in Singapore city, while artillery fire and bombs rained from every side. The place stank of death: human corpses on the streets, and the carcasses of cows floating down the Singapore river on their backs, bloated and ghastly.

After the surrender, the Allied soldiers disabled their guns and were rounded up in Changi jail. Outside, large numbers of Chinese locals suspected by the occupiers of hostile intentions were roped to one another and marched into the sea to their deaths. Later, when he learnt of how other people were suffering then in Auschwitz or the Gulag, Hare decided that he had had it good. In a Singapore winter, there was no question of anyone freezing to death; rags would do as well as clothes if the point was to preserve decency rather than protect against the elements. No one was well fed, but no one had – yet – died of starvation.

The officers were kept in one place and were allowed each other's company, as well as some rudimentary recreations.

Escape was unlikely. They could hardly pass off as locals, and it was 1,500 miles to the nearest Allied territory. There was one attempt; it ended with the escapees facing an inept, but ultimately successful, firing squad. The corpulent Major General Fukuye – for some reason, the prisoners could never quite pronounce his name correctly – insisted that every soldier sign a document in which he promised not to escape, and to obey the orders of the Great Nipponese Army.[20] At first, they refused. Then they – around 15,000 of them – were marched into the Selarang Barracks square meant for a much smaller group and told they could leave if, but only if, they signed. For a time, they held out. Then men started to sicken, and the Major General threatened to bring out the men who were in hospital to join them. Eventually, the commanders gave in. Some of the forms survive, one of them – by a young artist – read 'Signed: Ronald Searle. Dated: September 5 1942. At: Selarang Barracks, Singapore. Nationality: British. Rank or Position: Sapper, Royal Engineers.' Hare appreciated the gallows humour of another prisoner: 'Signed: Rawle Knox ... At: Pistol Point.'[21]

There was time aplenty to be philosophical. Hare had reconciled himself to the necessity of killing in war. He couldn't quite take the attitude of the Indian soldiers in the regiment, that soldiering was neither ignoble nor glorious, just well-paid and often fun, though it did put his tortuous moral reflections in perspective. But a Rugby man must act on a *principle*, and 'King and Country' seemed to him a poor one. On the other hand, there was something to be said for the thought that what he was really fighting for was India: the Japanese record in China did not portend good things for a subcontinent subsumed into a Japanese empire. The principle seems to have been what his later nemesis Elizabeth Anscombe would have called 'consequentialist', motivated less by an opposition to empire, or even to its being a Japanese empire, but by the likely consequences of a Japanese victory in the war.[22]

Stories of Japanese attitudes to honour gave him something to think about. He heard tell of the two Japanese prisoners who, when released, returned to their regiments where they saluted their commanding officers and fell onto their swords. He thought of old Sir David Ross of Oriel College and his idea that all human beings could find their way to objective moral truth by applying a special faculty called 'intuition'. Probably not, Hare decided.[23]

There were things to do. Some enterprising inmates had started a magazine appropriately titled *The Survivor*. Five copies were made with carbon paper for circulation. A wall cavity in its editorial 'office' concealed a wireless set, where through a chain of memorised whispers, the men in Changi jail managed to keep themselves apprised of the news of the war. There was even a basic theatre – the 'Changi Palladium' – where the men put on revues. One revue was titled, no doubt with heavy irony, *Gentlemen Only*.[24]

Hare spent his days trying to keep a secret record of the names of the Indian soldiers who had not defected to the Indian National Army. The INA, born of a heterodox part of the Indian nationalist movement, saw India's best interests in supporting the Japanese. The question of which soldiers had stayed true might become important later. He played bridge when he could, worked on his Urdu (and later, his Italian and Persian), sang in the prison's church choir, and worked in the prison's vegetable garden.[25]

A little while later in his imprisonment, a few books started to arrive from nearby Raffles College and the Red Cross. Among them were Alfred North Whitehead's *Process and Reality* and the Australian-born philosopher Samuel Alexander's *Space, Time and Deity*.[26] From them, and other books – none of them exactly at the cutting edge of British philosophy – he managed to learn something about Bertrand Russell. Having left Oxford with his Classics degree uncompleted (he hadn't even got to Greats, where modern philosophy was part of the curriculum), the ideas were new. He did his best with them, without tutors to help him. The essay on his personal philosophy that he had begun in England was turning into a monograph that he had titled – modestly and grandly – *An Essay in Monism*.[27] It was unlike anything then being written at Oxford, full of talk of 'rhythms' and 'factors' and 'prehension'. Even more eccentric was its talk of something he termed 'love': 'The meaning of love is that two persons "get inside" one another, so that the feelings of each become the feelings of both. By Love we see through another's eyes, hear through his ears, run with his feet, handle with his hands; and he does the same with ours.'[28]

In the spring of 1943, Hare was one of the officers sent to labour as 'coolies' on the railway the Japanese were building from Thailand into Burma: what would come to be called the 'Death Railway'. On the march up the River Kwai to the Three Pagodas Pass, he saw things he preferred not to mention in his autobiographical essay about his war: 'enough to say that, of the groups we were in, between 20 and 40 per cent died of various diseases and of malnutrition'.[29] And in all those eight months, he managed to keep hold of his secret list of Indian loyalists, and was never parted from *An Essay in Monism*. The popular 1957 film about the episode, *The Bridge on the River Kwai*, he insisted in later years, was 'a silly travesty', and the only thing to commend it was its evocative set design.

In his later years, he was not averse to bringing up his wartime experience. More than most moral philosophers, he could answer the charge that his ideas came of the limits of a cloistered experience. The POW camp was no cloister, and it was, in its way, a school of morals. Everyone, he told a journalist a couple of decades later, 'carried his moral luggage in his head; every man was born with his conscience, and this, rather than anything in society, he found, was the source of morality'.[30] There was no question of relying on such things as 'social' values. *That* was the cosy complacency of a really cloistered existence. Life on the Siam railway had involved a kind of society, but one which had 'to be formed, and constantly re-formed, out of nothing'. The usual moral principles came up against their limits; none of them could 'be applied without scrutiny to this very strange, constantly disintegrating situation'.[31]

The march nearly finished him. Eventually, he returned to Singapore, housed with his fellow officers in huts outside Changi jail. He spent most of his time in the vegetable garden, scribbling when he could in the ledger that contained *An Essay in Monism*. Then it ended: it was 1945 and he had spent most of the war in prison. The British officers were reunited with the Indians of all ranks, from whom they had been separated for most of the duration. Rations arrived – first beef, then pork, both gallantly refused by the Sikh and Muslim soldiers who wouldn't eat if they couldn't all eat. Eventually some mutton arrived, as well as various ardent spirits, not altogether licit, and everyone could be fed.

There was a parade, but a sorry one, with the soldiers all in rags. Lord Mountbatten arrived to address them. Then the SS *Tegelberg* appeared in Singapore harbour to take those British officers home who were not accompanying the Indian soldiers back to India. When Hare boarded, *An Essay in Monism* came with him. But when he read it, as the ship made its way through the Indian Ocean to the Suez Canal, he decided that the words in it were almost entirely worthless. The ledger, on the other hand, was a precious souvenir of his ordeal.[32]

*

Another war, and more casualties, though not all of them on the battlefield. When Hare returned to Oxford to finish his degree, looking forward to the philosophy component of Greats, he found that everything had changed. Old H. W. B. Joseph was gone. So was Collingwood, not nearly so old, and with whose son he had travelled to France before the war.[33] Men too young to remember much of the reign of Queen Victoria were occupying the venerable

Chairs: Gilbert Ryle had the Waynflete, Henry Price the Wykeham, Hamish Paton the White. The chairs came with power, and Ryle was the most willing to use it, wielding the letter of reference like a weapon with which to ensure that newly vacant positions in universities across the land would be occupied by people with the right ideas about the nature and purpose of philosophy, that is to say, with *his* ideas about the nature and purpose of philosophy.[34]

Younger men, who had been away doing something valiant or secret, began to return: J. L. Austin, A. J. Ayer, Isaiah Berlin, Stuart Hampshire. So did some of the promising young women, who had managed to finish their degrees: Philippa Foot, Elizabeth Anscombe and Iris Murdoch. Hare finally got to experience the delights of tutorials with Donald MacKinnon. Stylistically, there was never going to be a meeting of minds: MacKinnon's eccentricities, his sympathy for then-unpopular ideas and approaches placed him at the periphery of Oxford's intellectual life. Hare left his tutorials with no understanding of what MacKinnon had said but with deep gratitude for being pointed to what he always regarded as the right books, and a sense that they were saying important things about important things. He had the periodic relapse of malaria, which he treated with a form of quinine about as easy to get as gold dust (old Sandy Lindsay, still Master of Balliol, pulled a few strings). But he made it alive through his final exams with a first, and a temporary lecturership at his college, shortly to be made permanent.[35]

No one said anything of doctorates: a first in Greats was surely training enough for anything. 'DPhils' (which are in other places called 'PhDs') were generally agreed to be a sign of inferiority. Those who had earned one preferred to keep quiet about it. Hare allayed any prickings of conscience by writing a thesis of roughly doctoral length that was awarded a special prize named after the Victorian moralist T. H. Green. The set topic for the prize that year was Practical Reason. The examiners (among them, Ryle and Paton) persuaded him that while the first half showed promise, the second was best abandoned. Hare took the hint, and a few years into his fellowship, was ready with his first book, a development of the ideas that his examiners had found to be of greatest interest: *The Language of Morals* (1952).[36]

The title summed it up: the idea that philosophy could be (should be, would be) about language needn't mean it couldn't be about that traditional topic, morality. In fact, a way of doing philosophy that began and went through language, far from dismissing moral concerns to the margins of the subject, provided a new way of treating them. If the study of language could tell us something about the mind and about action, why on earth shouldn't it tell us something about the right and the good? Hare's way into the old questions that had occupied Aristotle and Hume and Kant and Mill – what are the ends of action? what makes for the best life? – was to set aside the right and the good and focus instead on 'right' and 'good'. Begin with the words and what we do with them; the rest will fall into place.

Hare began by asking what we *do* with our moral words. What are we doing when we disagree about what is right and wrong? What is it we disagree over, exactly? But equally, what makes something a case of disagreement, rather than of two people hurling expletives at each other? The pair crying, 'Banks are found on the High Street,' 'No, banks are found next to rivers,' aren't really disagreeing. Nor are those saying, 'Vanilla,' 'No, strawberry.' The first isn't a disagreement because the word 'bank' doesn't mean the same thing for the two speakers; the second isn't one either because expressions of likes and dislikes are not, at least directly, describing the world. So far, so relatively uncontroversial.

The question got interesting once the disagreement was more along the lines of, 'Truman was a murderer,' or, 'No, Truman was a saviour.' A. J. Ayer's provocation in the 1930s had been to insist that these sentences described no facts, and the function of such utterances was to manipulate the emotions of the hearer. Hare was both intrigued and unsatisfied. Manipulating the emotions of others was undoubtedly *one* of the things we did with our moral language, but it could hardly be the whole story.

Hare decided that Ayer was mixing up two questions, which a favourite distinction of Austin's would help him to keep apart. There were two ways in which we did things with words: there was what we did *by* saying something, and there was what we did *in* saying them. 'Open the door,' I say, thereby bringing it about that you, obediently, open the door. What I've done *by* saying those words is to bring it about that the door is opened. What I've done *in* saying them is to give you an order. Sometimes these things come together. But you could be slow, or deaf, or insubordinate. In which case I've still given an order, but the door remains resolutely shut. All our talk of right and good raises these separate questions: Ayer had been interested in the effects of our speaking this way, Hare in our intentions.

Ayer's interests in the effects of moral language had taken him to the position only half unfairly caricatured as the boo-hurrah theory of morals. Hare thought there were better models to be found for moral language than these exclamations: commands. The part of language that began to interest him was not interjections (yuck, yum, boo), but imperatives (be kind, don't kill). And this connected him to an extremely traditional philosopher of the canon: Kant. Kant's morality was, as he himself had described it, a morality of imperatives, and the most basic one of all, the categorical imperative. The *grammar* of imperative sentences hadn't been Kant's way to his conclusions, but Hare was a man of a different philosophical generation. The old German's views were sound enough, but they needed to be rescued from the elaborate metaphysics in which they lay entangled – the *transcendental* this and the *noumenal* that. There was no call for such extravagance. All we needed was a sensible combination of ideas: that imperative sentences didn't state facts, and that they could be rational or irrational. Putting these claims together was all the Kant we needed to get moral philosophy going again.

The positivists had been right to look for the nature of morality in its function. Yet he would go a step further: he had worked out what that function was. Simply enough, the point of morality – more specifically, the point of moral *language* – was to regulate and guide our conduct. Sentences purporting to guide our conduct couldn't be derived from statements that simply set out what the world was already like. The whole point, surely, was to *change* it. And with that idea, Hare thought, we could give up on old G. E. Moore's silly idea that the 'good' had to be a special 'non-natural' quality, real despite failing to show up under any microscope.[37] Hare's universe needed no non-natural qualities inaccessible to the senses; nor did it need a special faculty of intuition with which to detect it. All we needed was the faculty that everyone agreed we had: reason. The challenge was to articulate, in the right words, what reason demanded of us.

The consequences of that Kantian identification – of ethics with reason – would be developed later. But the immediate philosophical moral of the story was in one way optimistic. We now had a clear answer to the question of why moral philosophy was philosophy at all: imperative sentences had their own logic, and if logic was worth studying, so was the logic of imperatives. The philosophical question that earlier generations had put in such misleadingly metaphysical terms when they had spoken of the 'nature of rightness' could be put, as it deserved, into plainer words: moral philosophy, or ethics, was about the meaning of 'right' and 'wrong'.

This account of the proper place of moral philosophy came at a cost. The moral philosopher, to be an analyst, must stop being a moralist. Moralism was best left to the vicar. It had no place in a serious academic discipline. Philosophy could offer neither aid nor succour to the perplexed. One could hear, in that conclusion, a generation of philosophers relinquish the claims their predecessors had made to a special kind of cultural authority. But one could equally hear the cry of emancipation. As the rapturous review of Hare's book in the *New Statesman* had it, 'Morality is vindicated as a matter on which people must always decide for themselves and not superstitiously appeal to the philosopher for guidance.'[38] Our decisions had to be rational – as decisions, like other acts of mind, can be or fail to be – but they still had to be ours.

The strange impact of the book on its early readers had as much to do with its arguments – brisk, precise, often decisive – as with its tone. Even Richard Wollheim, the *New Statesman* reviewer, himself a recent graduate of Balliol and a former prisoner of war, baulked at 'the uniformly dismal character of the examples employed'.[39] The author of this manifesto of freedom and the supremacy of the individual conscience seemed almost perversely unwilling to find a prose register alive to its buried ethic. 'We move round and round in a charmless circle, looking in turn at the merits of motor cars, the merits of fire-extinguishers, the merits of sewage effluent.'[40] The workaday register that in Ryle had been charming (the clowns, the birthday parties, the silent performances of 'Lillibullero') and in Austin disorienting (the teapot catalogues, the hyena-impression gone too far) reappeared here as a laconic crispness. The magic really was gone.

*

Early in 1957, fresh from her defeat at Congregation, Elizabeth Anscombe briefly took to broadcasting.[41] Her remit from the BBC was to respond to the charge laid at the feet of her Oxford colleagues that their kind of ('linguistic') philosophy was 'corrupting the youth'. The brief may have been half-ironic: corrupting the youth was after all the charge for which Socrates himself was tried and convicted. But of course, the traditional idea was not that Socrates was *innocent* of that specific charge but rather that the ideas of his fellow Athenians about what counted as corruption were in need of a second look. Whatever it was Socrates had been guilty of, nothing followed directly from it about what was going on at Oxford.

Anscombe began reassuringly: no, she said, she did not think Oxford philosophy corrupted youth. But the tone was sarcastic, and the story was clearly going to be more complicated than that. She noted that a reviewer in *Mind* – reviewing, as it happens, Hare's *The Language of Morals* – had mentioned the charge only to acquit Hare of it immediately.[42] Hare was far too *earnest* to be a corrupter. Anscombe thought that a bit of a non sequitur. If one would be a corrupter, one had better be earnest: the young were hardly going to be taken in by a shyster.

So, the obvious earnestness of the Oxford moralists was neither here nor there. Nor did they wear their corruptions on their sleeves. Their manner was calculatedly innocuous: the emphasis on logic and language, the repeated insistence on the irrelevance of observable facts (after all, had not Hume shown one cannot derive an ought from an is?) and the general style of their illustrative examples lurched from the utterly banal ('Shall I return this library book?') to the ludicrous ('What should I do if stepping with my right foot will cause the death of twenty-five young men while stepping with my left will finish off fifty drooling old ones?') Who could be corrupted by this sort of thing?[43]

No one, Anscombe decided. But that hardly meant all was well. After all, people can be corrupted by teaching only if 'they have (or would have come to have) better ideas without this teach-ing'.[44] But nothing about the culture of Britain, c.1957, suggested that the plain man in his double-decker omnibus to Clapham would be getting better ideas from other places. It wasn't only at Oxford that people deferred moral decisions to tribunals or committees. It wasn't only at Oxford that people were arguing for the rehabilitation of violent criminals because one mustn't punish the poor creatures for things over which they had no control. And who were we to judge anyway – weren't they all just 'ways of life', with nothing to mandate a preference for one over another?

And – and perhaps this was the example she really cared about – it wasn't only at Oxford that Harry Truman had been greeted by cheering crowds, who seemed to agree that 'it was right to massacre the Japanese because it was … productive of a better total state of affairs than not doing so would have been'.[45] No, she concluded: the idea that good enough ends can justify any means wasn't only a philosopher's heresy; this kind of 'consequentialism' was everywhere. 'Oxford moral philosophy is perfectly in tune with the highest and best ideals of the country at large.'[46] It was innocent of corrupting the youth, but that charge was missing the point entirely. 'This philosophy is conceived perfectly in the spirit of the time and might be called the philosophy of the flattery of that spirit.'[47]

The point was sufficiently subtle that at least some listeners must have gone to bed puzzled about what had actually been said. Was Oxford philosophy a bad thing or not? When a transcript of the talk was published in the BBC organ the *Listener*, Anscombe's Oxford colleagues – now no longer in any doubt about what she had said in tones of such heavy irony – wrote in with protests. Hare professed to be puzzled. What exactly was Miss Anscombe saying? That 'I need not consider what the Gestapo will do to my friend when I have told them where he is'?[48] Or that 'the person who ordered the atom bomb to be dropped on Hiroshima had no duty to consider whether anybody would be killed by the explosion'?[49] Surely not: it was well known that Miss Anscombe had publicly called Harry Truman a murderer. In which case she, like all sensible people, agreed that the consequences of an action were directly relevant to the question of its morality.

Perhaps Miss Anscombe took what was reputed to be the Catholic view of lying: only a direct lie was sinful; '*suggestiones falsi*, however effective, may escape hell fire'.[50] Hence the alacrity with which she has issued her misleading jeremiad: her free-associative picture of an irredeemably corrupted generation had no basis in fact. Listeners anxious at the state of the world should take heart; Miss Anscombe was not representative of the Oxford way. She was 'unique, and those who come here are much more likely to meet plain, ordinary enquirers into the nature of morality, whose hope is to teach them by example and precept to think and speak about it clearly'.[51]

Hare's vindication of his, and Oxford's, honour was backed up by his colleague at Trinity College next door. Patrick Nowell-Smith (b.1914), a few years older than Hare and the author of a bestselling Penguin paperback guide to ethics (in later years, he was notorious for arguing, only half-ironically, that he had not just a right but a moral duty to sleep with other men's wives as a way of increasing the amount of happiness in the world),[52] took issue with Anscombe's talk on other grounds. How exactly did Miss Anscombe propose to draw 'a distinction between an act and its consequences'?[53] He addressed her example directly: 'Was Mr Truman's "act" the signing of an order, the killing of a number of Japanese, or the saving of a number of Japanese and other lives?'[54] Assuming it wasn't just the former, she was evidently willing to take the consequences into account in her moral assessment of actions. But if she was willing, as she should be, to take the consequences into account, why not take the saving of lives into account as well as the killing? Yes, these questions weren't easy, but Anscombe didn't help matters by pretending that they were. 'It is', he said grandly, 'with the elucidation of just such difficulties that moral philosophy is concerned.'[55]

Anscombe replied in the same tone of exaggerated politeness. She was grateful to Messrs Hare and Nowell-Smith for confirming her worst suspicions. Mr Hare was 'openly a consequentialist'.[56] That is, he didn't believe that there was *any* sort of action that one might simply exclude from consideration as wrong, or wicked, or evil. Mr Nowell-Smith was to be thanked for pointing out 'the colossal difficulty of making out the character of an act which is at once (a) sending chocolates through the post, (b) poisoning your aunt, (c) securing a legacy'.[57] These distinctions could be *so* subtle.

It is safe to say that Anscombe was never on friendly terms with Hare. And just in case her main point had been lost in the heavy-handed ironies of the exchange in the *Listener*, she made the point again, in prose no less vigorous but with the argumentative steps made a little bit more explicit. This time the venue was the journal *Philosophy*, but the tone of polemic was only dialled down the merest notch.[58] Helpfully, the paper began with an announcement of its theses. First, there ought to be a moratorium on moral philosophy while we worked out an adequate philosophical psychology. Secondly, that the concept of the 'moral', as it figured in our talk of moral obligations, moral rightness, moral goodness and so forth, was best dispensed with; it no longer made any sense. Thirdly, that from the late Victorian period onwards, pretty much every moral philosopher, despite the appearance of deep disagreement, was in fact of one mind – and, in fact, wrong – on all the basic questions.

The second thesis, almost perverse in its air of paradox, was the central one. Many readers, since the publication of the paper – 'Modern Moral Philosophy' – have been puzzled by it. Could Anscombe – already famous as a Catholic moralist – really be saying what she seemed to be saying? What was wrong with the category of the moral? And what had changed about the world that made it dubious? And what would be left if we did dispense with the concept? Was it to be self-interest and cynicism all the way down? To those who worried that this was the alternative, Anscombe might have said: the idea that the only alternative to the 'morality' of the philosophers is naked self-interest is itself a sign of just how confused we are.

Her first reason was historical. There is no mention of the 'moral' or anything directly equivalent in the ancient Greek philosophers; Aristotle, the most influential of them, in all his copious writings on ethics did entirely without the concept. What he did have was the concept of virtue and vice (not, take note, *moral* virtue and vice). He provided not just a concept but a complex psychological theory, more elaborate, subtle and explicit than anything from earlier in his tradition. Aristotle's theory of virtue belonged to a more ambitious picture, which contained in addition a theory of action, voluntariness, desire, emotion and belief, and how they all hang together. The *Nicomachean Ethics*, the messy compilation of what must have been Aristotle's notes for his lectures delivered to students at his Lyceum, has many perceptive things to say about happiness, courage, temperance, justice, judgement, friendship and contemplation, but nothing about morality. Why then were his expositors so anxious, in their translations and commentaries, to put the word in his mouth?

The explanation, Anscombe suggested, was unobvious and went deep. Something had happened in the course of the centuries in which the medieval world turned into the modern, something represented in its most abstract form by the philosophies of David Hume and Immanuel Kant. The first, a Scot and an unbeliever, proposed a definition of truth from which it followed that a statement like 'One oughtn't to lie' can't, despite appearances, really be true or false, and there is no way to deduce such a statement from facts about any bit of observable reality.[59] The latter, German and Christian, proposed that 'One oughtn't to lie' was really a law one made for oneself, constrained only by certain formal demands on what one can rationally legislate.[60] Anscombe thought both ideas silly.

The first she attacked in a paper, written around the same time as 'Modern Moral Philosophy' and published in *Analysis*.[61] Suppose she were to say to her grocer – 'Yes, I have asked you for a quarter of potatoes and you have delivered me a quarter of potatoes and sent me a bill, but it doesn't logically follow that I *owe* you any money, or that I *ought* to pay you. One cannot legitimately make inferences from claims about what is to claims about what ought to be.' Of course, this was very silly: what more is there to my owing you ten shillings than that I asked for the potatoes and you supplied them to me at the going rate? What great logical mystery is there about the transition from 'is' to 'ought'?

Ah, the Humean might say, it only follows that you owe the grocer because of the institutions in the background of the transactions. Well, indeed, Anscombe replied. Our talk about any number of things presupposes some institutions in the background, and 'ought' has nothing to do with it. To say that I give you a shilling requires the institution of money – or else what I give you is a worthless piece of nickel with the vacant face of George VI on it. The institution is what makes it a shilling in the first place. The same is true of my saying that what you did was *supply* me with potatoes or *sell* me some potatoes, rather than swap them in the hope of some worthless pieces of nickel. Or to say that I'm solvent, or that I broke a promise, or that Mr Geach is my husband. The fact that so much of our talk *presupposes* institutions – economic, legal, social – doesn't make our talk of shillings and promises and husbands into talk about institutions. Hume was on to something. Not because he'd got anything right, but because his silliness – Anscombe called it his 'sophistry' – made us *notice* something we'd taken for granted. But of course, like other philosophers' sophisms, it wouldn't stand a chance in a conversation with a doughty greengrocer, and that should tell us something.

The moral earnestness of an R. M. Hare seemed to be achieved at the cost of forgetting some extremely elementary truths of human life: for instance, that people were commanded to do horrible things by their conscience.[62] If one's theory didn't tie the supposed truths of morality back to one's relationships with other people and our shared institutions (marriage, promising, money and countless others), then in what sense was one's theory a theory of morality? What was the point in calling something a morality if it had so distant a connection with most of human life? What had gone wrong?

Between Aristotle and the modern age, Anscombe observed, came Stoicism and Christianity, both in their different ways wedded to seeing morality on the lines of an analogy with law.

In Christianity and in the Stoics, the law conception made good sense; after all, the law came with – indeed, *from* – a lawgiver. And with that conception came the whole family of legalistic terms: obligation, right, requirement, permission, blame, innocence, guilt. The 'juridical' terms went with the rest of the world picture, of God as judge and human life as a long wait for the last judgement. But at some stage – the Protestant reformation? the Enlightenment? – the metaphor lost its grounding, and the concept lost 'the framework of thought that made it a really intelligible one'. That earnest Protestant Kant, with his talk of self-legislation – and the obsession of his contemporaries with the structure of human contracts – was a way of squaring the moral circle: a law without a lawgiver, or rather, without any *external* lawgiver. It was, Anscombe said, rather like a voting procedure where I, being the only voter, always had it my way.

A world in which the lawgiver was gone but the laws retained was like a world in which there were no criminal courts but we still spoke of criminals, and philosophers worried their heads about what strange metaphysical entity a criminal was. The moral philosophy of the previous two centuries was a peculiar thing as a result. The law-like language continued, but with nothing to back it. And from the time of John Stuart Mill, that language was wheeled in to express a kind of ethic that was nothing like the law. Its great virtue was supposed to consist in its openness to the exceptional case, the flexibility in the face of complexity. After all, Anscombe said, it was hard to find a philosopher among her colleagues who was willing to say what nearly every philosopher of the ancient and medieval world had thought, that some things were just ruled out. Treachery? Torture? The judicial execution of the innocent?

The most that an honest consequentialist could say is that these things were generally wrong, but who could say in advance what unprecedented circumstances might come up? If the circumstances were bizarre enough, then the judicial execution of the innocent would be exactly the right – 'morally right' – thing to do, and only a perverse fetishism could get in the way of the tough-minded acknowledgement that this was so. If someone should say such a thing, wrote Anscombe in the most memorable of her rhetorical flourishes in the essay, 'I do not want to argue with him; he shows a corrupt mind.'[63]

She concluded that there wasn't much point in continuing the debate at this level. The partisans were doomed to talk at cross purposes. Instead, she said, it would be a better use of everyone's time to take a step back from moral philosophy and instead talk about such things as 'action', 'intention', 'pleasure', 'wanting'. Once we got clear enough in our minds about these things, it would be time to consider the case of 'virtue': again, there was no call to bring 'moral' into it. We could start with that basic sense of the word 'virtue', in which being good at mental arithmetic was as much of a virtue as, say, being courageous. Then maybe we could get around to 'norm' – not 'moral norm' but things like 'human beings have thirty-two teeth' – then to 'ought', and then to 'good'. Then, but only then, did we need to talk about the 'moral'. That is, of course, if there was still anything left for that concept to add. Anscombe presented the challenge as if to propose a laboratory where such inquiries were to be undertaken, but the invitation to co-operative inquiry was unlikely with her to take so Austinian a form. She was too much her own woman, now slowly shedding the stylistic influence even of Wittgenstein, to answer to the demands of literal teamwork.

Anscombe had allies. There was her husband Peter Geach, already the author of several well-regarded papers on logic and the philosophy of mind. After several years a househusband, he was now a lecturer at Birmingham, commuting almost daily. But there was also Iris Murdoch, now a fellow at St Anne's, a women's institution newly raised to the status of college, one of the few people thanked for her contributions to Anscombe's translation of Wittgenstein's *Investigations*. Philippa Foot was her colleague at Somerville, another lonely voice joining her in her opposition to Harry Truman's honorary degree. Mary Scrutton – now Midgley, after her marriage to Geoffrey Midgley, a young philosopher she met at the Joint Sessions – was teaching in Newcastle, but kept up a correspondence with her old college friends. The grouping was loose, but the women had enough in common to justify talk of an emerging resistance to the orthodoxy. Their work was, in many ways, entirely of a piece with what was now a flourishing tradition of 'analytic' philosophy, but in other respects, they were quite out of sympathy with its dominant currents.

Shortly after the war, the four women had found themselves in the same house in Park Town, a leafy terrace of Victorian houses in North Oxford. They were applying themselves to philosophy again, and, freed from the demands of imminent exams, were finally acquainting themselves with the contemporary philosophy that their tutelage during the war – with Wittgenstein or with Donald MacKinnon – had kept from them. Only Anscombe among them was a Christian. Still, they found something they had in common. Hume – the glib, reductive, sophistical Hume, or at any rate a useful caricature to which they gave his name – represented what they all rejected. The separation of fact and value, the idea that truth didn't belong in ethics or that our reasons (including our 'moral' reasons) depended ultimately on our desires: these were among the ideas they saw carried on in a linguistic register by their contemporaries.

A. J. Ayer would serve well for the very model of an analytic Humean: his dismissal of anything 'metaphysical', the obsequious deference to a narrow set of scientific ideals, the interest in language separated from much interest in the ends for which human beings used it, made for just the kind of opponent that was bound to generate a committed opposition. And now there was Hare, insisting that Hume had been basically right, but for new-fangled logical reasons to do with the nature of imperative sentences. The idea that ethics was, deep down, anything other than a matter of individual choice remained anathema. Midgley would, in a future memoir, describe the mood in Foot's Park Town kitchen, and the atavistic creed to which they were signing up, as a big, joint, 'No!'[64]

＊

Now that the old 'emotivism' of A. J. Ayer was *passé* (and Ayer, with his usual gunslinger attitude, hadn't bothered with revisiting the subject of ethics), it was Hare's 'prescriptivism' that offered the best target for new heterodoxies to reject. In Anscombe, the tone was righteous, enraged, the moral atmosphere distinctly redolent of brimstone. But, there being more than one way to skin a hare, other styles of response emerged. These were gentler, but for precisely that reason, likelier to hit on something that stuck in Hare's craw. In the same years of the late 1950s that Anscombe was writing her red-hot polemics, her Somerville colleague Philippa Foot, sense to the other's sensibility, was putting the same point in a tone of wounded reasonableness.

With her as with Anscombe, the chief difficulty with the views of Ayer and Hare was their denial that ethical judgements could be true, a linguistic point that went with a more general outlook in which morality was deeply tied to *choosing*, and not to seeing, learning or discovering. In Hare's theory, what one did in making a moral judgement was *prescribe* some course of action. Like expressions of emotion, they were not true or false in the same straightforward way as common or garden empirical statements. But this didn't mean that one could simply make up any ethical principles one pleased.

Other logical constraints could apply to prescriptions: they had to be rational, and that meant they had to be 'universalisable'. In choosing a moral principle, one chose not just for oneself but for everybody. But they were still things we choose, not things that we discover. With Hare, the point was not merely technical.

He seemed to find it repugnant that one could disclaim responsibility for what one did by protesting that one had only been following orders. 'There is a point', he said in a broadcast on the BBC, 'beyond which we cannot get rid of our own moral responsibilities by laying them on the shoulders of a superior, whether he be general, priest or politician, human or divine.'[65] Certainly there was the 'phenomenology' of moral thought to contend with. Much moral thinking *feels* like it is aspiring to get something right, something constrained by things beyond us, not some freewheeling creative act of invention. (Pick any moral judgement you take seriously and try to will yourself to believe the opposite.) But to Hare, this was simply another attempt to pass the moral buck on to the universe.[66]

These were the years when the full extent of the Holocaust had just become known, and those who had engineered it – the full order-following bureaucratic apparatus of the death machine – were on trial. Could someone looking at photographs of the death camps at Bergen-Belsen and Auschwitz-Birkenau continue to maintain that ethical judgements were ultimately not the sort of thing to be true or false? If some judgements couldn't be true and other ones false, what was there to be said about the Adolf Eichmanns of this world? Merely that he had his attitudes ('Hurrah genocide!') and we had ours ('Boo!')? Or that he had chosen his 'ultimate principle' and we had chosen ours? Combine that with the further view that there is nothing to make one set of attitudes any better than any other, and one had a position that, Foot later recalled thinking, just '*had* to be bad philosophy'.[67]

Foot's philosophical manner – unruffled, quiet, commonsensical – might be thought a variant on the dry and even manner that had been *de rigueur* since the 1930s. As Stuart Hampshire would put it, discussion of the most serious of matters had to be 'disinfected' by adopting a 'committee-man's tone of voice in speaking about them'.[68] Perhaps this was itself a response to the darkness, a quiet acknowledgement that the conventional ways of flaunting one's moral seriousness – grandstanding, portentousness – were not themselves morally neutral. Perhaps, indeed, this was *the* lesson of the war. Theodor Adorno, who had by then returned to Frankfurt after decades spent in Oxford, New York and Los Angeles, had put it to any would-be poet that it could only be barbaric to write poetry after Auschwitz.[69] Did the point not apply with equal force to philosophy? Part of the difficulty was finding a tone adequate to writing about it, even to writing about other things in awareness of its enormity. To say one was *angry* about the Holocaust was to sound ridiculous. Mere anger was hardly enough, and irony positively offensive. Of those subjects for which no suitable register could be found, perhaps it was best not to speak at all. The Wittgensteinian injunction to silence in the face of the unspeakable came to have a different resonance in these years.

But ethics was still being done, and theories of ethical language devised. If there was something wrong with those theories, one had to do more than accuse them of triviality. In their technicality, their grasp of modern logic, the mechanics of step-by-step argument, they were formidably well-armoured. A chink had to be found: Anscombe's vehemence played well to crowds who were already on her side. Something more Socratic would be called for if the clever young men were to be beaten at their own game. Foot's voice was ideally suited to this subtler game.

In three papers of the 1950s, Foot took on Hare with not a polemical aside in sight. Her general method was the *reductio ad absurdum*: a claim of Hare's would be taken up, its merits conceded, its implications explored. Then the puzzled face: surely this cannot be so. The strange implications, the counterintuitive consequences would be listed, their costs reckoned up. Example by wily example, the clever young men would be shown to have forgotten some very obvious facts about human life.

No empirical facts could determine, or indeed even constrain, what evaluative attitudes one could take to some behaviour. That was Hare: facts were facts, values values. What then, said Foot, of 'rudeness'? It is an evaluative term if anything is; after all, we standardly use it to condemn behaviour. But could anything be rude? Even if it didn't cause offence? Could one really judge some person to have been rude and behave accordingly towards him without also judging him to have done something of a certain sort? What about 'injury'? Or 'dangerous'? Could anything at all be an injury, anything be dangerous? Or were there constraints, based on empirical facts about human beings, on what could count as such? The same for 'pride': can I be proud about anything at all? Or must it involve some thought about my or someone else's achievements? And 'dismay': are there limits to what things I can regard with dismay? In each case, Foot was pointing out what seemed to her exceedingly obvious. What Hare wished to make a matter purely of choice and attitudes, she insisted involved a judgement – something that could be true or false.

Hare seemed to think that all there was to something being a moral thought was that one had adopted rules for oneself that one also prescribed to others. Their content was immaterial, their 'universal' form was everything. In which case, Foot pointed out, a moral principle could be entirely pointless as long as it had the right form. 'If people happened to insist that no one should run round trees left handed, or look at hedgehogs in the light of the moon, this might count as a basic moral principle about which nothing more need be said.'[70]

These criticisms were part of a positive project, one she shared with Anscombe. The first part of the project was to bring back 'naturalism' as a viable view of ethics. Naturalism had rather fallen into disfavour by then. G. E. Moore's arguments at the very start of the century had powerfully made the case against the naturalism of the nineteenth-century utilitarians. One of the attractions of the old utilitarianism was the fact that it turned that mysterious thing, 'rightness', into that unmysterious thing, pleasure. Pleasure was one more natural phenomenon among others, perfectly amenable to study by the natural scientist.[71] Moore, however, thought that the equation led to absurdity. We can ask, with a perfectly open mind, whether something that is conducive to pleasure is in fact good. In his phrase, 'This is pleasant, but is it good?' is an *open* question. And the same can be said for any other natural property one might care to substitute for 'pleasant'. What followed? Moore thought his argument showed that the good could not be reduced to any natural property. He went further: the good couldn't be reduced to anything. It was *sui generis*, a thing in its own right, outside or beyond nature.[72]

The positivists had agreed that Moore was on to something, but denied that his conclusion followed. True, good wasn't a natural thing; but what followed was not that it was a non-natural thing but that it wasn't a *thing* at all. Foot was reacting to both these rejections of naturalism.

No, the good needn't be the spectral unobservable entity of G. E. Moore's notorious arguments. Nor need it be a matter of choice. It could be yet another part of the world of nature, where human goods and bads weren't fundamentally different from the goods and bads of other living beings. The second part was to lay the foundations of an ethics in which virtue and vice were the central notions, not 'pro-attitude' and 'choice'. And the virtues, Foot suggested, could hardly be constituted by human choices, or any quality at all might be 'chosen' to be in one's personal pantheon of virtues. On the contrary, 'virtues must be connected with human good and harm, and ... it is quite impossible to call anything [whatsoever] good or harm'.[73]

Hare seemed to think it a merit of his position that there was nothing in it to rule out various forms of moral eccentricity: 'a man might say he had been harmed because a bucket of water had been taken out of the sea' or that 'harm had been done to him because the hairs of his head had been reduced to an even number'.[74] With enough imagination, enough contextual detail, some sense might be made of such claims. But Foot's point was that without such detail, they were ridiculous. We can't simply decide that something was a case of harm; some such claims are just false, even if they are made in earnest.

Hare's ideas about goodness were at their most peculiar when he tried to get his theory to fit biological evaluations. What, he asked, did we mean by calling something a 'good cactus'? He proposed that we think about it from the eyes of the first importer of a cactus to the country setting down standards for the goodness of cacti. But there can be other standards, other criteria for good cacti. No doubt, said Foot, there can. But shouldn't there be some room in all this for the fact that the cactus is a living thing, not an entrant in a beauty pageant? 'There is no reference to the fact that a cactus is a living organism, which can therefore be called healthy or unhealthy, and a good or bad specimen of its kind.'[75] Odd ideas about breed conformations can result in awards at dog-shows going to dogs that either show no special distinction, or look positively deformed: they simply happen to have a tail just a half-inch longer than average. But then we are no longer talking about 'good dogs', just the kind of dog that wins at dog-shows – hardly the same thing.

If the goodness of particular biological species is not merely a matter of what we choose, then why should human goodness be that? Why should the word 'good' change its meaning depending on whether it was being attributed to a knife, a cactus, a mother, or to a human being generally? Surely in each case the natural thing is to think of what a knife (or a mother, or a human being) is, in relation to the standards implicit in the kind of thing or creature concerned. Take that idea seriously, and we have simply returned to the ethical vision of Aristotle: we regard as human virtues those dispositions that, when exercised, make up what we judge to be a good human life. And what we judge to be a good human life is not simply a matter of our choices. As if we could arbitrarily choose to regard as good a human life without friendship, courage or justice. This was atavistic indeed, but the arguments did not have, in their style and tone, anything that Austin could have reproved: Hare's theory, in all its neatness, needed to be confronted with a little human reality.

7

Swimming

Exposing the mistakes of cocky young Englishmen could hardly be the stuff of an entire philosophy. Those errors could be put down to the faults of the individuals concerned, or of their youth, or the malformations of the Oxford syllabus. The sensible-to-a-fault manner of Foot's writings rather tended to encourage this: the methods were fine – they were just being misapplied. In Anscombe, rather more seemed to be at stake than in some parish council squabble, but it was too easy to see her thunderous cadences as merely churchy, just what the cocky young men expected from a Catholic who didn't see that the whole thing was nonsense, really. If one didn't believe in hell, how easy it was to think Anscombe had nothing to tell one.

Iris Murdoch, who returned to Oxford in 1948 a fellow of St Anne's College, made disengagement harder. Like George Eliot before her, she unsettled the usual triad of 'God, immortality, duty'. As Eliot had famously put it, 'how inconceivable the first, how unbelievable the second, how peremptory and absolute the third'.[1] Which was one way of saying at least that duty *seemed* no less absolute for no longer having God for its sanction and immortality for its reward. But 'duty' was not Murdoch's word; it belonged too much to a picture she ultimately wanted to reject, of ethics as action, decision, choice, will. In some form, the association of ethics with action went back to Aristotle; but go back one generation more, and the analogies were different. In Plato, action was the merest icing; the real ethical moment came when one *saw* aright, saw oneself, saw other people, saw the natural world in the light of the sun and not of the flickering fires of the cave in which we are captive. And the sun was a symbol not of God – 'inconceivable' – but of the *good*: peremptory and absolute.

This was a real turn. The undergraduate Murdoch had thought Plato an old reactionary, with nothing to say that Marx (or Freud or Sartre or some other trendy creature from the Continent) had not long superseded. She was unusual among her Oxford contemporaries in having actually read 'the continentals', the long tomes and the novellas.[2] Her attachment to the Continent was the first of many things to distinguish her from her colleagues.

Throughout the war, Murdoch had longed to be elsewhere than in the civil service. After the war, whenever that would be, she hoped to teach philosophy and to write novels. She had rued, even at Oxford, the 'second-handness' of her knowledge of much of life.[3] She was, in her clumsy way, being useful in London, but if she was going to be bored, she would rather have been bored doing menial things somewhere more dangerous. When she learnt of the existence of the United Nations Relief and Rehabilitation Administration (UNRRA),[4] she immediately wanted to work there instead.

She was listening, like everybody else, to live radio broadcasts of reports of the Normandy landings in the June of 1944, overwhelmed and thrilled, and two months later, of the liberation of occupied Paris. She applied to join the UNRRA that summer, hoping against hope to be posted to Europe working on 'relief' (rather than on 'rehabilitation', which meant staying in London). Her hopes were dashed. She was forced to spend the next fifteen months in London working in offices run by men from 'Milwaukee & Cincinnati & New Haven' – caricatures of American bureaucrats from some Frank Capra film from the 1930s.[5] Murdoch eventually got used to the ineptitude of her colleagues – she was not much better – and the chaos of the daily routine. She worked long days, her spirits kept up by the company of the

Czechs she encountered in her work 'getting supplies out to Displaced Persons', and by the earnestness and noble intentions of her incompetent colleagues.[6]

In the evenings of the cold winter of early 1945, she read Dostoevsky again, and Rilke. Then Arthur Koestler: after reading his account of the extent of Stalin's authoritarianism, she gave up her Communist Party card.[7] In the early summer of that year, a little while after VE Day – the Allied acceptance of Germany's official surrender – she found to her delight that the National Gallery – for much of the duration of the war displaying only one painting a month – had retrieved *fifty* from the Welsh mine where they had spent the war. This really was peace, she thought, as she looked at the Rembrandt self-portraits, the paintings by Van Eyck, Bellini and Mantegna.[8] Looking at a piece of art would be one of her models for the kind of shedding of ego she thought equally essential to ethics. She settled, politically, on the Labour Party. For the moment, that was as left-wing as she needed to be. When Clement Attlee was elected, she was jubilant: 'Oh wonderful people of Britain!'[9]

The long-sought-after foreign posting eventually arrived: she would be going to Brussels. She loved the sound of French mingled with Flemish, the cafés where they served cognac into the small hours. 'I get a frisson of joy', she told a correspondent, 'to think that I am of this age, this Europe – saved or damned with it.'[10] Her office in Brussels was decorated with a large reproduction of Bruegel's *Fall of Icarus* – an appropriate enough painting for 1945. As Auden's poem about the painting had put it, Bruegel had known, as so few artists who painted grand events did, the 'human position' of all suffering: the fact that other people's lives continue, barely touched by it all. Francophilia was abroad even in London: there were tricolours on the street, and the Free French seemed already to be figures of legend.

In her letters of these years, French things loomed large: the people (so beautiful, so beleaguered), the songs and films (so chic), the intellectuals (so dangerous, so bold, so intellectual). And then there was the philosophy, so utterly unlike anything that went by that name in Britain, so tantalisingly close to imaginative literature.[11] The philosophers had in common with their English counterparts an aversion to metaphysics, but where systematic theory had been replaced at Oxford with an attention to language, the French had turned instead to 'the concrete puzzle of personal existence'.[12] The flavour, she said, was 'phenomenalist' – but this had nothing in common, tonally, with the pre-war 'sense data' phenomenalisms of Moore and Russell. Both traditions took a keen interest in what was available to the senses, but where the one took this to consist in attention to the grammar of 'I see a patch of yellow' or 'this is a hand before me', the other took it to consist in something more detailed, more striking, more particular. In the British case, the banality was not accidental. What was banal could be generalised; the interesting was just too particular to be – well – philosophical.

What is negation, asks the British philosopher, reaching about for an example. How about 'The shoes are not under the bed'? What is negation, asks the French philosopher? And out comes a story: I go to the café expecting to meet Pierre. But Pierre is not there: I look from table to table, scan the features of patron after patron, but find a succession of non-Pierres. Well, many things are not in the café: Pierre, but also (say) a certain hippopotamus. But the absent hippo doesn't 'haunt' the café as the absent Pierre does. I experience a 'nothingness' where I had hoped to find my friend Pierre. Why can't this sort of thing figure in our accounts of negation? Why must it always be those now well-worn shoes missing from under my battered bed?[13]

The Pierre-haunted philosopher in the café was Jean-Paul Sartre (b.1905). In the middle of the German occupation, he had managed to publish *Being and Nothingness: An Essay on Phenomenological Ontology* (1943), where the missing Pierre is the hero of an early section about 'nothingness'. Murdoch met Sartre in Brussels, where he was mobbed on the streets by crowds as enthusiastic as those greeting the singer Charles Trenet. Murdoch was surprised to find the man so small. 'Simple in manner, squints alarmingly.'[14] She began to read him obsessively. He wrote, and spoke, with an arresting lucidity, with a dismaying, and compelling, obsession with violent sex.

The papers accused him of corrupting the youth, but what philosopher can treat that as anything other than a badge of the highest honour? Murdoch decided he was 'the real thing'.[15] Maybe that would be her calling: to bring these exotic creatures – Sartre, Albert Camus, Simone de Beauvoir – to England and to be their interpreter for curious English audiences.

From Brussels, she was sent on to Austria. She spent the December of 1945 in Salzburg, but the streets she walked were not the prosperous, tense, jackboot-scarred streets that Isaiah Berlin had known in the 1930s. Her Salzburg was 'bedraggled & poor & dirty', the most striking nearby landmark Hitler's house at Berchtesgaden on the other side of the German border. She continued to Innsbruck where she spent Christmas. Early in the new year, she met the novelist Raymond Queneau, whose novel *Pierrot mon ami* (1942) she had eagerly urged to Philippa Foot's attention while they were living together in Seaforth Place. He was there for an unlikely literary conference. They spoke in French, hers fluent and idiomatic from years of decent schooling, though her accent was poor. She found him 'a natural, absolute, philosopher'.[16] He in his turn thought her 'Big. Blonde. Common-sensical.'[17]

It would become a persistent pattern in her life that she acquired every few years a new older male mentor. Donald MacKinnon by now had broken off his friendship with her (she thought his wife was suspicious – though there was nothing to be suspicious of).[18] But he had written a reference for her when she was applying for the UN job and did so again when she applied for postgraduate courses (Newnham College, Cambridge; Vassar College in upstate New York); Eduard Fraenkel, who might write well of her work during the *Agamemnon* seminar, was far away. Queneau would do very well: the combination of solemnity and playfulness, of reticence and unguarded loquacity, the extensive knowledge of both philosophy and literature, were exactly what she wanted in a mentor.

At work, she was confronted with a city much more seriously wounded than London. The rations were small, and there was little to eat other than bread and potatoes. Large parts of the city seemed to be filled with consumptives. Most shops were boarded shut; no one had money to spend in them. Informal systems of barter developed; people were swapping cigarettes for fuel, or food.

She was transferred shortly to Puch, in the American zone, where life was not much better, and where the shortages were beginning to inspire outbreaks of violence in the refugee camp. As the snow began to thaw, she arrived in Vienna. This was no longer the city where Ayer and Quine might have sat around a table with Moritz Schlick (murdered in Vienna), Otto Neurath (dead in Oxford), Rudolf Carnap (escaped to Chicago), and not even the city her Somerville friend Mary Scrutton had visited on the eve of the *Anschluss*. This was the world of *The Third Man*, Harry Lime's Vienna, all racketeers and moonshine. Like Ayer and Scrutton before her, she managed a visit to the Kunsthistorisches Museum where she stared at length at the Rembrandt self-portrait in their collection.

From Vienna, she was transferred again to Graz. The population was starving: loaves of bread shared among dozens, straggly morsels of macaroni, coffee that looked and tasted like gutter-water. She did her best, acquiring a reputation for bohemianism and receiving the odd wolf whistle from any refugees who had the energy to spare. She got her place at Vassar College, but in a moment of imprudent integrity, scuppered her chances of being granted a visa by answering truthfully when the application form asked if she had ever been a member of the Communist Party.

When she resigned from the UNRRA, she had a long year of unemployment and penury ahead of her, a year spent reading Heidegger and more Sartre and learning that such interests were frowned on even more sharply in the Oxford of Ryle and Austin ('"romantic" & ergo unsound') than they were in the 1930s, and being rejected for lecturing positions.[19] Eventually, she won a Sarah Smithson studentship, which had previously been held by Elizabeth Anscombe, and was able (with a small additional Ministry of Education grant) to take up a place at Newnham College, Cambridge.

Her year in Cambridge brought her close, but not nearly close enough for her liking, to the world of Wittgenstein, whom she met twice. On neither occasion did the conversation go deep. It was in any case too late for her to be admitted to his circle, on the verge of being dissolved while he spent his retirement from his professorship away from Cambridge. She found him good-looking, small like Sartre, and 'with a very, very intelligent, shortish face and piercing eyes'.[20] Everything about him was unnerving: the 'trampish' appearance, the empty bookless room with no furniture but a camp-bed and two deckchairs, the confrontational, conventionless way in which he approached people and required them to relate to him. 'What's the good of having one philosophical discussion?' he told her once. 'It's like having one piano lesson.' In other words, it was too late. She always thought of him, she would later recall, 'with awe and alarm'.[21]

Wittgenstein she couldn't have, but she threw herself into the company of Wittgensteinians: Kanti Shah and Wasfi Hijab, students of Wittgenstein from India and Palestine respectively, let her read their notes of his lectures and were more than willing to talk about him (what other subject was there?). She, for her part, cooked for them in the rooms they shared at Trinity College, conscientious about not using animal fats for the vegetarian Shah. She was assigned that odd half-Wittgensteinian half-acolyte John Wisdom as a supervisor. And Elizabeth Anscombe, arriving regularly from Oxford, was a sort of conscience-keeper: her 'ruthless authenticity' made Murdoch deeply conscious of the self-indulgence of her own approach to philosophy.[22] She was steeped in sources both eclectic and promising, but it seemed beyond her to get her thoughts to coalesce into something that was both clear and true. Addressing the Moral Sciences Club in 1948 in rooms belonging to the early stalwart among the *Analysis* crowd, Richard Braithwaite, she was deeply embarrassed when Hijab simply walked out: there was, he said with a casual brutality he seemed to have learnt from his master, nothing to be said about her talk.

She was living another life in all this time. After all, she had met Sartre, knew Queneau, read all those exciting books in French. Who better to explain them to the British public? She was constantly being asked to address people about French existentialism, and dutifully did so, speaking one week at a bombed-out church in Soho, another at the BBC studios. With each attempt at conveying the interest of French ideas, she found her initial excitement beginning to ebb, then being replaced with a hard critical edge. The French were getting something right: yes, this is how philosophy should be, alive and provoking and engaging our passions as well as our intellect. But the substance was all wrong. She was out of sympathy with it for reasons not far from her reasons for being sceptical of Wittgenstein. In Wittgenstein, she found a marked tendency to play down the existence, the reality and complexity of what to her was everything: the 'inner life'. In the French writers, the inner life was neither denied nor belittled; it was simply misdescribed.

In the early stages of the Oxford fellowship she received the next year, she began to put her disparate observations and insights together into a short monograph on Sartre, *Romantic Rationalist*. When it was published in 1953, it was the first comprehensive work in English on his philosophy. While it sought to introduce British readers to the appeal of his work, it ended up sharply critical. Sartre's wartime lecture, 'Existentialism Is a Humanism', had come as close as anything he had written to boil his philosophy down to a slogan: 'existence precedes essence'. As he put it elsewhere, human beings do not have an essence – a basic nature – that determines how they must choose: 'Man is nothing else but that which he makes of himself.'[23] Murdoch ended up bridling at the false heroics of such statements, and their hint of solipsism. Why valorise the Sartrean hero, alone, 'free' and sexually voracious but incapable of loving?

Sartre wrote novels, which could be vehicles for the truthful depiction of human beings: that they are, as he himself often implied, 'precious and unique; but we seem unable to set it forth except in terms of ideology and abstraction'.[24] Sartre and most other existentialist novelists were impatient 'with the stuff of human life'.[25] It offered a picture of people as either totally determined or totally free, and both pictures were pernicious distortions.

Murdoch was writing this book while also working on several others, among them a never-published novel called *Our Lady of the Bosky Gates*, featuring as characters the Dalai Lama and the goddess Aphrodite.[26] But writing had to be consigned to the evenings, after the teaching and administration of the fellow's working day was done.

*

St Anne's was a new college, or more precisely, new as a college. It was a Victorian institution in its origins, founded not, in the usual way of such things, on a charter and an endowment but on a wish and a dream. The Society of Home-Students was set up to allow young women to attend lectures and have tutorials while living in family homes and lodgings across the city; it was nothing like a conventional collegiate existence, but it had the enormous advantage of being much cheaper. In 1942, it became 'St Anne's

Society'; ten years later, within a few years of Murdoch joining, it received the Royal Charter that made it a full-fledged college.[27]

Something survived in these early decades of its initial dream of access to an Oxford education for a woman of talent and spirit whatever her means. Soon, buildings were acquired on Bevington Road in North Oxford and turned into hostels for students who wanted to be in residence. The fellows, as they became with the granting of the Royal Charter, were willing to take risks in their decisions of whom to admit. The student body was, as a result, extremely mixed in abilities and temperaments. The senior common room had an air of bohemianism and sexual non-conformity. There was the economist Peter Ady (b.1914), and Jenifer Hart (b.1914), a historian and political scientist, both of whom rose to eminence and notoriety, the latter (probably falsely) accused of being a Soviet spy.[28] In the beginning, the place was run by the terrifying Eleanor Plumer (b.1885), a woman of enormous organisational nous but apparently devoid of human tenderness. When she retired in 1953, Lady Ogilvie (b.1900) was elected to be principal, similarly vigilant – as any woman in 1950s Oxford had to be of infractions that might undermine the cause – but a good deal more liberal. She was less likely than her predecessor to tell the students and staff to plan their pregnancies so they had their babies in the vacations.[29]

Murdoch acquired a mixed reputation. She hated lecturing; she was an inspiring lecturer. She was a superb tutor, thoughtful, kind and attentive; she was an incompetent organiser, forever sending off students for tutorials in logic with some inexperienced postgraduate but forgetting to check up on them. She was conscientious; she was bohemian, as likely as one of her wilder students to violate the curfew rules, attending the same parties, unashamed to be found lying in the nearby University Parks with her most recent lover. The disregard for clothes or personal hygiene turned her into a figure alternately mocked and revered. 'Did you hear ...', the stories would go around the undergraduate body – small enough, and enough like an English village, for gossip about the fellows to be the standard currency of everyday conversation. Did you hear that Miss Murdoch's hair was still wet at today's tutorial? Or that she had forgotten her stockings, or walked out in sandals, or gone to the shops without any money?

The Oxford of the 1950s seemed to be trying to compensate for all the parties they hadn't had during the war. There were parties in house basements, countryside parties in stables, boathouse parties along the river. Murdoch seemed to be at all of them, dancing to music playing from a nearby gramophone record, kissing the other guests, and the other fellows, and throwing herself into the river (outdoor swimming – a stately breaststroke, 'the most natural as well as the most comfortable way to enjoy the water' – was her greatest joy).[30] And every Monday, the weekly grind again: there was Plato to read, in Greek with the classicists and in translation with the ones reading PPE, and Aristotle (ditto), then Kant and Descartes (translations would do for both), then Berkeley and Hume (who made things easier on both tutor and student by having written in English).

So much was set centrally, and the students at all the colleges would be examined on their knowledge of the same texts in their university exams. But Murdoch would occasionally push at the boundaries of the approved syllabus. Lenin's *State and Revolution* would appear on the occasional reading list, or Sartre's 'Existentialism Is a Humanism', or something by Kierkegaard, or – in line with her emerging sympathies with mystical traditions – the French mystic and writer Simone Weil (b.1909), who had starved herself to death during the war. Even the standard topics of political theory did not look the same when she taught it. To talk about the liberal defence of democracy or free speech was usually a straightforward enough affair – one threw some Mill at one set of students and waited for them to produce an adequate discussion of the 'harm principle'. In Murdoch's tutorials, however, one's essay titles were rarely so standard. 'Liberalism', went one such essay prompt, 'cannot succeed as a creed until it purges itself of its romantic elements.'[31]

Because her interests were so varied, her opinions so protean, and her moods always shifting, a tutorial with her was not – as so often at Oxford – a matter of learning what she liked so one could reliably serve it up to her in essay after formulaic weekly essay. It seemed that there was no fact of the matter about what she liked. From the precise but dry writer, she demanded imagination; from the imaginative but woolly writer, precision. 'What is the cash-value of that?' she liked to ask – echoing a phrase of the American pragmatist William James. Translation: that's all very fine stuff, no doubt, but what does it mean?[32]

*

The metaphor of 'cash-value' was probably among those Murdoch had picked up from J. L. Austin, who liked to employ it at his lectures. Austin was then lecturing on the philosophy of perception and had started running his Saturday morning meetings. The lectures were coming to be known as the 'Sense and Sensibilia' series – how to resist that name, when a Mr J. Austin was talking about the meaning of our statements about supposed 'sense data'?[33] They were Austin's most systematic attempt yet to take down, once and for all, what he thought the theoretical excesses of the logical positivists. His stalking horse remained his old nemesis from the late 1930s, A. J. Ayer.

The idea of sense data was rather older than Ayer, going back to books on logic from the nineteenth century. It had been given a famously, and comically, unintelligible definition by G. E. Moore. 'Things of *the sort* ... which he sees in looking at his hand, and with regard to which he can understand how some philosophers should have supposed it to be the part of the surface of his hand which he is seeing, while others have supposed that it can't be, are what I mean by "sense-data".'[34]

In the rather friendlier formulation by Ryle's old friend Henry Price, one could instead start from an everyday experience of doubt about what one is really seeing. 'When I see a tomato', Price started unassumingly, 'there is much that I can doubt.' Can I be sure that this is in fact a tomato and not a piece of wax? Or a reflection? Or a part of an elaborate hallucination? Of one thing, however, one could be entirely sure: 'there exists a red patch of a round and somewhat bulgy shape, standing out from a background of other colour-patches, and having a certain visual depth, and that this whole field of colour is directly present to my consciousness'.[35]

The commonsense view was supposed to be this: when I see a tomato, what I see is a tomato. The tomato is the object of our perception. We might call that view 'direct realism', the view that we directly perceive 'material objects' (such as tomatoes). Ayer, by contrast, held that the objects of perception were not material objects but sense data, out of which we logically 'constructed' our more familiar world of tables, chairs and tomatoes. Ayer's most powerful argument for this position came from the familiar experience of optical illusions: when one sees, say, a mirage in the desert, it is of course false to say that one sees an oasis. After all, there is no oasis there *to* see. But one evidently sees something. What could that something be if not sense data?

Austin was infuriated by this argument, with its deceptive simplicity. He started by unsettling the dichotomy on which it was based: either we saw 'material objects' or we saw 'sense data'. Sometimes – as in mirages – we don't see 'material objects'. So in those cases, we must see 'sense data'. And so, it must be the case that we never see anything but sense data.

Did that really follow? Austin doubted it. Even if one was willing to grant that faced with a mirage, what we see is sense data and not an oasis, why would it follow that even when one was in front of a real oasis, what one saw was still sense data? True, one couldn't tell the difference. But – to use an example he didn't – sometimes one cannot tell the difference between identical twins. So I might think I am looking at Saul when in fact I am looking at Paul. Does that mean that the next time I'm looking Paul, I'm really looking at Saul? (Obviously not.) Does that mean that every time I am in the presence of either Saul or Paul, I am really looking at some third thing that is neither Saul nor Paul? The fact that we're *sometimes* wrong about what we see hardly means we are *always* wrong about what we see.

Austin's aim in his lectures was to show that the sense data theorist made assumptions that were not simply implausible but false. If we attended closely to the terms in which those views were expressed, he proposed, we would see that they were utterly confused. And that would bring us back to our commonsense 'realism', not as some grand philosophical theory but as our everyday practice before it was unsettled by misplaced philosophical anxieties.

The problem, as Austin diagnosed it, was the disjunction on which the sense data theorist's whole project rested: either we see 'material objects' or we see 'sense data'. Austin thought the concept of a 'material object' no more innocent than that of sense data. As he put it, 'what is spurious is not one term of the pair, but the antithesis itself'.[36] The point wasn't to deny that the 'immediate' objects of perception were not sense data but material objects, and thus, to replace 'phenomenalism' with 'realism'. The trouble with both -isms was that they made an absurd assumption, that the question, 'What kind of thing do we perceive?' had a single answer, which was either, 'Material objects,' or, 'Sense data.'

Why, urged Austin, should we think that question had a single answer? Why can't there be different sorts of things we perceive, in different situations? Why think that the concept of a 'material object' can include a range of things as wide as 'people, people's voices, rivers, mountains, flames, rainbows, shadows, pictures on the screen at the cinema, pictures in books or hung on walls, vapours, gases'. They were all things people claimed to see or hear or smell – that is, 'perceive'. But were they all 'material things'?

The problem, as he saw it, was how to get us to abandon that very tempting assumption, that 'illusion'? The way to this emancipation would be long and hard: 'there is no simple "argument". It is a matter of unpicking, one by one, a mass of seductive (mainly verbal) fallacies, of exposing a wide variety of concealed motives – an operation which leaves us, in a sense, just where we began.'[37]

That passage points to at least one of the ways in which Austin is thought to be like Wittgenstein, who famously remarked of philosophy that it 'leaves everything as it is'.[38] But crucially, the point of Austin's lectures wasn't to return us to the realism with which we had started. Rather, his point was that any -ism, even so-called 'commonsense' doctrines, were already departures from a pre-theoretical innocence free of all -isms. It was too late now to get back to that original innocence, so what one sought was what a later commentator called a 'second naïveté'. The project was conceived, like Ryle's exorcism of the 'ghost in the machine', as therapeutic: it was a cure for philosophical disease. The cure shouldn't involve contracting a new disease, or relapsing into an old one, but restoring the body to the healthy state it was in before it got sick in the first place.[39]

*

Murdoch thought Austin's work on perception 'detailed and brilliant', but there were limits to her sympathy. Yes, that nonsense about 'sense data' had to go, but to be replaced by what? 'Ordinary language'? There was certainly something to be said for that proposition. A philosophy holding itself constantly accountable to ordinary language – so messy, so variegated – would not fall prey to the usual philosophical temptation to seek, and to pretend to have found, unity. Most such vaunted achievements were really discoveries of a merely 'spurious' form of unity. 'It is the traditional inspiration of the philosopher,' she said, 'but also his traditional vice, to believe that all is one.' By contrast, she continued, the ordinary language philosopher simply says: 'Let's see.'[40]

Indeed, 'let's see' is sensible advice for most things. But Murdoch saw a flipside to Austin's commitment to the everyday. Applied to ethics, her own area of interest, philosophy in Austin's style produced work that was, to her mind, 'both unambitious and optimistic'. When we turned to ethical concepts, not all of which were tied to the ordinary uses of ordinary words, ordinary language was no longer a reliable guide. 'Good', 'right', 'obligation' could well turn out to be simple enough (though that should not be assumed). But 'rude' was harder (as Foot had shown), as was 'just' (as Anscombe had). And what about 'treacherous', or 'chaste', or 'proletarian' or 'Oedipal'? Murdoch concluded that the method could no longer be as neutral and modest as it claimed. 'It is useless to ask "ordinary language" for a judgment [when] we are dealing with concepts which are not ... unambiguously tied up to ordinary words. Ordinary language is not a philosopher.'[41] Murdoch, unlike Foot, was never invited to Austin's Saturday mornings.

She soon came to think that the downbeat, quotidian quality of the Oxford style represented by Austin and his colleagues risked turning British philosophy into a simple mirror image of its French and German counterparts. This was not simply a matter of method but a matter of tone and style. Murdoch liked Ryle, whose pipe-chewing, no-nonsense manner made him the occasional recipient of her confidences; he even lent her his copy of Heidegger's *Being and Time* – the book that he had once reviewed favourably for *Mind* – 'with a nice note'.[42] Ryle seems to have liked her; he too had spent his youth seeking after Continental oddballs.

When Murdoch's book on Sartre was published, a barbed line of hers comparing Sartre's world to Ryle's became justly famous. *The Concept of Mind*, she said, evoked a picture of a world 'in which people play cricket, cook cakes, make simple decisions, remember their childhood and go to the circus; not the world in which they commit sins, fall in love, say prayers or join the Communist Party'.[43] At the time, it seemed like a comparison much to Ryle's disfavour; but the statement is in fact distinctly ambivalent. If something was missing from Ryle's world, perhaps something was missing from Sartre's, too. What sort of life would it be where we lurched from a meeting of the Free French to a secret transaction with a backstreet abortionist to violent sex in a seedy hotel but never baked a cake, looked back to a childhood birthday party or went to the circus?

Something better than either was called for, neither an 'analysis of ordinary mediocre conduct' nor depictions of radical freedom in extraordinary situations. As if it could only be the one or the other. There really was something to Austin's question – 'what we should say when, what words we should use in what situation' – and in his justification of it. Austin's justification of his method was simple: 'We are using a sharpened awareness of the words to sharpen our perception of ... the phenomena.'[44] The point of looking at words is to let them help us to see the world.

In his more conservative, 'Burkean' moods, Austin seemed decidedly wary of any linguistic innovation: 'Our common stock of words embodies all the distinctions men have found worth drawing ... in the lifetimes of many generations: these surely are likely to be more numerous, more sound ... and more subtle ... than any that you or I are likely to think up in our armchairs of an afternoon.' In other moods, he disclaimed such Burkeanism. He, like Murdoch, had after all once admired the USSR and later cheered at the election of Clement Attlee, and indeed, coined a good few and often unlovely technical terms of his own: 'illocutionary', 'infelicity', 'constative'.

As Murdoch put it, the study of moral language was certainly part of the task of philosophers, but when it was done properly, our results would look nothing like they did in Ayer. Such a theory looked like the result of getting things exactly the wrong way around: not so much a theory derived from 'a patient scrutiny of ethical propositions' as Austin might have recommended, but rather 'as the by-product of a theory of meaning whose most proper application was in other fields'.[45] As Donald MacKinnon had once put it, 'The elimination of metaphysics is before all else an assault on man in the interests of a method.'[46]

Her colleagues were trying to improve on Ayer's efforts, but they were still getting it wrong to the extent that they were striving for a neutral – uncommitted, disengaged – analysis. No such neutrality, no such analysis, could be found. How were we to understand what 'ought' might mean without beginning with some judgements using the word – 'one ought to return one's borrowed library book', 'one oughtn't to tell lies', 'one ought not to drop nuclear bombs on civilian populations'. But to treat these examples as helping to reveal the meaning of the word risked importing into a 'neutral' account of the meaning of words what were quite substantial moral judgements. If the judgements were not neutral, then why shouldn't our analyses of meaning be equally compromised? Murdoch proposed instead that 'in so far as ethics sets out to be analysis rather than exploration it can attain only a precarious neutrality, like that of history, and not the pure neutrality of logic'.[47]

An exploratory rather than merely analytic ethics would be freer in its conceptual innovations: 'Great philosophers coin new moral concepts and communicate new moral visions and modes of understanding.'[48] Sartre did this, as did his Catholic counterpart, the reluctant existentialist Gabriel Marcel (b.1889). If we were honest, we would see that we had always been moralising – Moore had done it, as had H. W. B. Joseph, as had Kant and indeed Plato. Ayer too was a moralist, for an ethic of toleration and pluralism. So too was Hare, for an ethic of voluntariness and freedom. Any attempt to present one's ideals as if they were neutral analyses of the logical structure of moral language produced an essentially deceitful, or perhaps simply deluded, philosophy where the moralising was done 'unconsciously instead of consciously'.[49]

If we were always already moralists, why not come clean about the extent of our commitment? Or as Murdoch succinctly put it in a diary entry in 1951, 'Good = saintly?'[50] To reflect on the workings of a saint's mind could be a sort of analysis, perhaps, but it was hardly going to be linguistic, and it wouldn't stop at giving a 'relaxed picture of mediocre achievements'. And the best mode of such exploration might need recourse to something other than the relentlessly discursive forms available to the philosopher of the 1950s: statement, evidence, inference, conclusion.

*

Exploration could happen in a philosophical paper, and Murdoch tried to bring to her philosophical writings some existentialist *éclat*, as when she told the audience at the Aristotelian Society, in a critique of Ryle and Ayer's views on the nature of thought, how difficult it was to 'describe the smell of the Paris metro or what it is like to hold a mouse in one's hand'. The paper – the marvellously titled 'Nostalgia for the Particular' – was likely to have been greeted with some combination of puzzlement and delight. Here was a philosopher ostensibly in a dialectical exchange with Ryle and Ayer, but able to sneak in references to the smile of the *Mona Lisa* ('difficult to sum up'), quotations from the letters of Rilke ('Looking is such a marvellous thing'), and the experience of deciphering the language of a Persian rug (it called for not 'the thin light touch of recognition but a deep gazing').[51]

The point was that experience, and descriptions of experience, needn't be stripped of their complexity before they earned their right to figure in a piece of philosophy. For someone who had spent the previous few years among the philosopher-novelists of Paris, the natural form was obvious.

Murdoch's first published novel – several were abandoned

in the 1940s, their manuscripts destroyed – appeared in 1954. *Under the Net* was dedicated to Raymond Queneau, and had the picaresque structure of *Pierrot mon ami*. Her drifting hero Jake Donaghue – a translator of French novels when he's in work – owns a copy of Queneau's book, and indeed one of Beckett's *Murphy*, another novel about the entertaining travails of a 'seedy solipsist'. He makes philosophical jokes: 'Everywhere west of Earl's Court is contingent.'[52] He has philosopher friends, one of them an émigré linguistic analyst who is surrounded by an adoring band of 'beardless youths' – 'all natural metaphysicians'.[53] The only youths he can convert to the true faith, i.e. some idiosyncratic brand of linguistic analysis, immediately lose all interest in philosophy. 'His great aim is to dissuade the young from philosophy.'[54]

The title is a subtle reference to Wittgenstein: the 'net' is the net of theory (or perhaps of language, or logic, or concepts) and the titular phrase appears once, in a philosophical tract that Donaghue writes, based on the cod-Wittgensteinian utterances of his one-time friend, the film-maker Hugo Belfounder.[55]

That's the serious part; mostly the book operates as a system of moderately ordered chaos. There are various glamorous women with whom Jake gets entangled; there is an extremely intelligent and likeable dog called Mr Mars, and a complicated plotline involving the typescript of a translation of a French novel. One scene is set in a Hammersmith theatre where mimes perform Russian farces; another has characters eating foie gras out of cans after an impulsive decision to swim in the Thames at low tide; a long dreamy section follows Jake to Paris on Bastille Day.[56] Silliness and seriousness alternate, and it gets less and less clear which episodes are supposed to be the silly ones.

The novels to come immediately after were marked by different preoccupations, all clearly part of an attempt to work through, in her imagination, the figures of her Oxford education and wartime travels in Europe: the experience of displacement, usually embodied in the person of a refugee; swimming and water as symbols of emancipation from illusion and connection with reality; most of all, the central place of an 'enchanter' figure, who could both seduce and destroy (often with elements recognisable as borrowed from Wittgenstein or MacKinnon or Sartre or some other quasi-mentor). The novels were philosophical, even if she was occasionally disposed to deny it. The sense in which they were so was very different from anything a reader raised on Sartre's existentialist dramas might expect. The books, even when rife with symbolism, were not in the simple sense allegorical, with characters standing in for philosophical doctrines. And even though the characters occasionally expressed philosophical views, those views were more likely to be targets for the narrator's withering irony than a position advanced seriously for the reader's consideration.

The principal sense in which the novels were philosophical had something to do with the way in which they subverted the official philosophical line among her contemporaries. The idea of a positivist novel, or for that matter an anti-positivist one, is hard to credit. But could there not be something else, a novel that had the quality that has been detected in the early twentieth-century operas of Alban Berg, that of being able to 'express and mobilise for its dramatic purposes a picture of the self and of human life that bore a revealing relation to the picture of those things given or implied by positivism'?[57] If irony is, as one critic has defined it, 'the most general term that we have for the kind of qualification which the various elements in a context receive from the context', then Murdoch's novels created contexts within which philosophical positions, asserted in earnest in the seminar room, could be exposed to a critique that consisted simply in reminding the reader of what the philosophy leaves out. As it were, she refuted it *thus*.

The irony of the novels is the crucial second half of a project that always threatened to devolve into mawkishness, a surfeit of sincerity. Moral philosophy, as she conceived of it, was not what

R. M. Hare thought it was: 'the logical study of the language of morals'. The greatest challenge to understanding was not linguistic confusion but the lure of solipsism, the 'greedy ego'. The cure was not more analysis, but love. 'Love', she wrote in 1959, 'is the extremely difficult realisation that something other than oneself is real. Love, and so art and morals, is the discovery of reality.'[58] Love, art, morals: the combination was unusual among her philosophical contemporaries. But what was most unusual was the unabashed talk of 'the real': such abstractions were surely verboten after Austin's short way with them: 'The real what?'

It was not so much that Murdoch ignored his questions as that she thought she had answers to them. The real, she might have said in her usual quiet but decided way, as opposed to the illusory, the imaginary, the wishful, the deluded: these seemed to her the problems of life, and thus, of moral philosophy. The linguistic was only one of the many kinds of confusion by which we were beset. But to say that philosophy was other than – more than – the exposure of linguistic confusions was another way of saying that she was openly professing that loathed dogma of the interwar years, metaphysics. And so, indeed, in a perfectly respectable sense of that much-maligned word, she was.

Outside of the official settings of the Jowett Society and Austin's semi-official Saturday morning meetings, it was still possible to ask metaphysical questions. Murdoch was a member of the 'Metaphysicals' – mostly High Anglican men out of sympathy with the direction of Oxford philosophy – who met from 1948 in someone's college rooms for conversations at the boundaries between philosophy and theology. Occasionally R. M. Hare would turn up, but mostly it was the heterodox who felt at home here: the scholar of ancient Greek philosophy Ian Crombie of Wadham (b.1917), Michael Foster (who had stuck out as a sore thumb when he had had Ryle and Ayer for his colleagues), Austin Farrer (b.1904), Basil Mitchell (b.1917).

Oxford had, at least since mid-Victorian times, been a place where the previously godless caught faith and those of one faith caught another. But Murdoch didn't catch it herself.

The Metaphysicals were open to talking of love, and contemplation, and saw the unexpected convergences between positivism, linguistic analysis and French existentialism, as if Paris, Oxford and Vienna had all managed to get to the same pernicious falsehood. It is a sign of the temper of the times that one of the volumes to emerge from these discussions was titled *Faith and Logic*. The title suggested, boldly, that 'faith' was a legitimate subject of philosophical inquiry. But the title simultaneously registers the anxieties of the period, even among those least in sympathy with the spirit of the age: as if one could talk of such odd things as 'faith' just as one was allowed to talk of language and truth, only as long as the word was followed by that reassuring phrase '*and logic*'.

To name an Oxford club 'The Metaphysicals' was a bold thing indeed. The metaphysicians were the philosophical Mensheviks of Oxford. They had lost, but seemed unable to acknowledge their defeat. But in the usual way of such things, their presence itself marked a change in the air, and transformed everyone's sense of what was possible.

8

Thaw

Oxford philosophy made an unexpected television appearance in the May of 1968. Jonathan Miller (b.1934), the medical doctor turned comic actor and operatic director, had directed a feature for the BBC television series *Omnibus*, ordinarily a place for edifying documentaries. It was an adaptation of a classic ghost story by the medievalist M. R. James, 'Oh, Whistle, and I'll Come to You, My Lad'. The original story featured a historian, but Miller had decided to turn the protagonist into an Oxford philosopher. It is obvious what kind of philosopher Professor Parkins is when we see him in action at breakfast at the seaside bed and breakfast in Norfolk where he is spending his university vacation.

Old Parkins – a shambling Michael Hordern – is attacking his melon and kipper while an earnest military type asks him what he thinks are 'philosophical' questions. Does the old professor believe in ghosts, the colonel wonders. Parkins's face lights up, but he won't give a straight answer. What, he wants to know instead, does the question even mean? What exactly is it to believe in a ghost? It's straightforward enough if the question is whether one believes in *Australia*. One knows what procedures one might use to confirm its existence, or indeed to '*dis*confirm' it (Captain Cook, kangaroos, etc.). But do we agree on what a ghost is even supposed to be? So far, so positivist.

The colonel obligingly makes a suggestion: 'The survival of the human personality.' 'Ah,' says Parkins. Now we're talking.

Can the human personality survive death. That has at least the 'grammatical *appearance*' of a serious philosophical question. But does it really make sense? A man might 'survive a train crash', of course. But what would it mean to say that he had survived *death*? The 'grammar' of death is quite unlike the grammar of other catastrophic events in life. And that is why it makes only nonsense to say of a man that he had been 'very badly hurt' by his own death.

The colonel is only half-convinced, but is willing to let it pass. Parkins sits smugly, contemplating his victory. The question of ghosts has been not only solved, but *dis*solved, the question of their existence not so much settled as shown to be impossible even to ask.

But since this is a story by M. R. James, the complacent will be put firmly in their place. When Parkins insists, against all good sense, on picking up and blowing on a creepy 'whistle' he finds on a desolate East Anglian beach, he brings on himself a visitation from the supernatural realm. And now he has no more arguments, linguistic or otherwise. There it is, in the sheets of the empty twin bed rising up in the night, in defiance of all the decencies of logical grammar, and Professor Clever-Clogs is reduced to inarticulate non-linguistic burbles. And what, as someone had once asked Wittgenstein at breakfast, 'is the logical form of *that*?'[1]

This ghostly fantasia wasn't Jonathan Miller's first joke at the expense of Oxford philosophy. Eight years earlier, he was part of the iconic comedy revue *Beyond the Fringe* with Peter Cook, Dudley Moore and Alan Bennett, and appeared with Bennett for a sketch featuring curdled old creatures sipping sherry in a senior common room and whiling the hours away playing 'language games'. Such as, what is the correct analysis of 'There's too much Tuesday in my beetroot salad'? Or is that simply a 'pseudo-statement'? Could philosophy be of any relevance to Real Life? The title of the sketch provided a hint of the immediate provocation to take on this rarefied target: 'Words ... and things'.[2]

*

The first sign that there was the stuff here of a public controversy appeared in the letters pages of *The Times*. Bertrand Russell, now eighty-seven and the holder of a Nobel Prize in Literature, was kicking up a fuss. But this time his target wasn't the atom bomb, but the actions of one Gilbert Ryle, esq., editor of *Mind*. Ryle, it seemed, had written to the publishers Victor Gollancz to say that his journal would not be reviewing *Words and Things*, a book they had sent him, by a certain E. Gellner of the London School of Economics. 'I am returning it to you (separately) since I shall not have a review of the book in *Mind*. Abusiveness may make a book saleable, but it disqualifies it from being treated as a contribution to an academic subject.'[3]

Russell denied the charge on Gellner's behalf: 'Mr Gellner's book is not "abusive" except in the sense of not agreeing with the opinions which he discusses. If all books that do not endorse Professor Ryle's opinions are to be boycotted in the pages of *Mind*, that hitherto respected periodical will sink to the level of a mutual-admiration organ of a coterie.'[4] Ryle responded: the book in question contained 'about 100 imputations of disingenuousness ... against a number of identifiable teachers of philosophy'.[5] And what of it, other correspondents said. That was hardly good reason to deny it a review; surely a review was just the place to refute such spurious charges.[6]

The exchange in *The Times* brought Ernest Gellner (b.1925) just the kind of notoriety he liked. Gellner was the child of Austrian Jews from Bohemia, which had become only a few years before his birth part of Czechoslovakia. His childhood was spent in Prague – the Prague, as he later put it, of Kafka and Carnap[7] – where he learnt Czech, his parents' German, and English. His parents decided not to take their chances after the German occupation of Prague and moved to St Albans, north of London, in 1939. At seventeen, he received a scholarship to Oxford, an opportunity he credited to Sandy Lindsay, the Master of Balliol (and the failed parliamentary candidate in the 'Munich by-election' of 1938).[8] He was the beneficiary, he later said, of Lindsay's 'Portuguese colonial policy': 'keep the natives peaceful by getting able ones from below into Balliol'.[9]

He studied PPE but, midway through the war, was called upon to serve with the 1st Czechoslovak Armoured Brigade, and was involved in the Siege of Dunkirk.[10] Gellner could have returned to Prague after the war, but, already anti-Communist in his sympathies, he decided he was better off back in England.[11] He finished his interrupted Oxford degree, focusing on the philosophy papers even though his tutors tried to tell him he was only cut out for economics. His exams were a triumph: he took a first, and then was runner-up (*proxime accessit*) in the prestigious John Locke Prize awarded for performance in a special examination.[12] He got a job in Edinburgh teaching philosophy, then another at the LSE, but this time in the department of Sociology.

Gellner was falling out with what he saw as the pernicious orthodoxy of 1940s philosophy and the cult of Wittgenstein – or rather, the linguistic methods that Wittgenstein shared with Ryle, Austin and others. According to his interpretation, Wittgenstein was a sort of communitarian conservative, for whom 'there is no general solution to issues other than the custom of the community'.[13] There have been many who had held this idea before, and indeed since, but delivered in his oracular, charismatic way, the old idea seems to have been 'enthusiastically adopted as an unquestionable revelation … This was *the* Revelation. It wasn't doubted.'[14] Gellner, of course, rejected this picture. 'I explored it further and finally came to the conclusion that … it *was* rubbish.'[15]

'Rubbish' was a characteristically blunt Gellnerism. A decade on from that early encounter with linguistic philosophy, he was ready to pin his colours to the mast. *Words and Things* was not intended as a polite contribution to an ongoing discussion. It was a polemic; what it sought was the humiliation and destruction of the enemy. The strategy was two-pronged, part argument, part provocation. The dust-up in *The Times* meant that he had at least half succeeded.

Gellner's main charge against Oxford philosophy was that it was conservative, thanks to its deference to established linguistic usage.[16] Bertrand Russell's warm endorsement of the book came from his sympathy with this style of objection. Russell characterised Oxford philosophy as committed to the view that 'the language of daily life ... suffices for philosophy, which has no need of technical terms or of changes in the signification of common terms'.[17] He objected to this view because it was insincere, because it could be used to excuse ignorance of mathematics and the sciences by people whose education had been narrowly classical, because of its 'tone of unctuous rectitude', because it made philosophy trivial. Most of all he objected because it risked philosophers replicating 'the muddle-headedness they have taken over from common sense'.[18] These were fighting words, delivered in the elegant tones of the aged but unbowed Russell at his rhetorical best.

Gellner went further. Because Oxford philosophy was so committed to the linguistic status quo, it could say nothing that was not congenial to the social status quo. It was, he said, 'of its essence an ivory tower pursuit'.[19] Its conservatism didn't consist in any active espousal of conservative values. It came out, rather, in its repeated attempts at 'showing that the reasons underlying criticisms of accepted habits are in general mistaken'.[20] And it was no surprise to find the qualities of the philosophy embodied by the philosophers who perpetrated it.

It was, of course, difficult to find a clear statement of what Oxford philosophy was about. It was part of the movement's congenital evasiveness that no one ever came out and stated what they really believed. That left the task to the critic, and Gellner claimed to have identified several 'pillars' of Oxford philosophy that explained its conservatism. The first, and the target of his most withering put-downs, was the so-called 'paradigm case' argument.[21]

Roughly, the form of argument goes like this: words mean what they refer to when they are correctly applied; they are always and necessarily correctly applied in their 'paradigm' actual usages. But this means that language itself proves that, for instance, elephants exist. Because the word 'elephant' is often used successfully: and what could the word mean if not what it does mean when we use it to refer to an elephant? And in the same way, we can prove that we have free will. Clearly, the sentence, 'He did it of his own free will,' is both meaningful and often true, and so there must be such a thing as free will which we can in principle possess.[22] The same can be used to show that other people exist and therefore to refute solipsism, to show that knowledge exists and therefore to refute scepticism, and so forth.

Connected to this was a version of a principle that G. E. Moore had once accused of exemplifying the 'naturalistic fallacy', which was, on one of its formulations, the fallacy of deriving values (or 'norms') from facts. In the writings of Oxford philosophers, this took the form of holding that linguistic norms – what we ought to say – could be validly inferred from current usage – what we do or would say.[23] In short, how we currently use words is how they ought to be used. Linguistic innovation is therefore impossible, and the futile attempt to innovate undesirable.

It was important that the book at least seemed to contain arguments. Words and Things convicted Oxford philosophy for its absurd deference to the linguistic habits of the ordinary man. It convicted it for being an 'ivory tower pursuit', one that was 'unintelligible to anyone of a practical orientation'.[24] Its practitioners were, as one of his reviewers summarised Gellner's chargesheet, 'smug, unintelligent, upper class, superciliously apolitical, unhistorical and anti-scientific'.[25]

But Gellner's ability to provoke owed little to his criticisms. What won the book attention, and its author celebrity, was the lively tone, pitched at a high level of outrage and disdain. It was entertaining, especially if one had nothing at stake, and the chapter titles witty ('The Bait and the Trap', 'Philosophy by Filibuster', 'The Narodniks of North Oxford', etc.). A good old bang-about, as J. L. Austin might have said. Not the usual stuff of philosophy in Oxford, civil to the point of tedium.

Like other such provocations, Gellner's critique put the Oxford philosophers in a bind. If they ignored it as beneath contempt, they looked either cowardly or complacent. If, on the other hand, they took it seriously enough to merit rebuttals, they risked conceding that the accusers might have a case after all.

Gellner's book was reviewed widely enough and didn't suffer much for *Mind*'s neglect. The responses were divided, quite predictably, along party lines. Those who disliked Gellner's targets liked the book; those who didn't didn't. The friendly reviews expressed relief at someone finally taking on the whole squalid cult. The hostile reviews proposed that Gellner's polemic was, at best, an illuminating exaggeration, and at worst, a piece of incompetent hack-work, the product of ignorance and misunderstanding.[26] Even if Gellner occasionally had a point about some particular philosopher or argument, that left open the question of whether Oxford philosophy was *in general* guilty of these things. Was it that Oxford philosophy's standards themselves were faulty? Or was it just that its practitioners were failing to live up to the standards of their own practice?

Once the rubble had cleared, it was still unclear what had actually been shown. Had Gellner scored any palpable hits? Or were they all cheap shots, ad hominems directed at unrepresentative philosophers and arguments? To readers not steeped in the texts, it came to seem that the trouble with Oxford philosophers was that they spent their days thinking about 'words' when they should have been thinking about 'things'. But to the critique reduced to that crudity, one could simply reply: aren't words things too? Linguistic facts are, after all, one more set of facts in the world that can be studied like any other. Not all of them are interesting, but surely *some* of them are. And then, there's the fact that we can't talk about things except using words – what harm then in approaching things by looking, carefully, at the words we use to talk about them? As Austin had, in an unusual moment of explicitness about his methods, put it: 'We are using a sharpened awareness of words to sharpen our perception of … the phenomena.'[27]

Gellner, to be sure, seemed to think the whole show beyond salvage. Like Tertullian in the early Christian centuries, who, finding theology a disgrace to true faith, became a heretic, Gellner left the discipline for one he found more congenial: anthropology among the Berbers of Morocco.[28]

*

Ved Mehta (b.1934) had loved his time at Oxford. He arrived there in 1956, already something of a prodigy. He was born in Lahore, in India before the partition. He became blind in early childhood after an episode of meningitis, and was sent by his parents first to Bombay, then to a special school in Arkansas, then to college in California, where he was elected to Phi Beta Kappa – the honorary society of undergraduates whose name is formed of an acronym for the words of a Greek phrase that means 'philosophy is a guide to life'.[29] His original plan was to study philosophy at Balliol College. Two essays into his degree, he realised that what went on under that name at Oxford was not what he had expected,[30] and he was allowed to change to history, a more suitable subject for someone with his unsystematic, distractible intelligence. In 1959, he met William Shawn, the editor of the *New Yorker*, and published a few essays in the magazine. In 1961, Shawn offered him a position as a staff writer, where he remained for more than thirty years, writing an elegant, fluid and uncannily visual prose in which he made a point of never bringing up his own blindness.

Always on the lookout for a subject suited to his variety of roving narrative journalism, he thought there might be potential for a piece when he noticed the early rumblings of the Gellner affair in the letters pages of *The Times*. But by the time Mehta landed in Oxford, it seemed that Gellner, and indeed Gellner's targets, were yesterday's news. To get his bearings, he went to a friend – a pseudonymous 'John' – who had shown enormous philosophical promise as a student of Greats but had decided to stick with the non-philosophical parts of the degree: Greek and Latin literature, Greek and Roman history.

'John' took him through his exam scripts in the style of a seven-a-side goalkeeper reliving his finest hour for the nth time to an adoring audience. There was, 'Is my hearing a noise in my head as mechanical as the passing of a noise through a telephone?' Boring, because too obvious. Then there was the obscure, 'Who is Socrates?' (The question, being on the logic exam, was evidently not calling for historical knowledge.) And there was the ingenious: 'Could there be nothing between two stars?' Ingenious because there's peril in both: if no, then what is the something between them? A vacuum is surely nothing rather than something. On the other hand, to say yes would need an explanation of why the stars aren't all on top of each other. And finally, the old chestnut: 'If I know that Y is the case, is it possible for me not to know that I know it?'[31]

When Mehta met Gellner himself, the man was just as unbridled in person. He let rip about Austin, whose technique ('a creeping barrage') was really an attempt at browbeating. Austin, he said, was '*very* strongly obsessed with never being wrong'. Worse, he was cagey: 'he never stated the doctrines he was trying to get across'.[32] Worst of all, Austin wasn't as funny as he thought himself: 'the terrible playful girls-school wit', Gellner had termed it, 'a coy don's old-womanish humour', rather spectacularly mixing his sexist metaphors.[33]

Gellner mentioned C. P. Snow, whose pamphlet *The Two*

Cultures and the Scientific Revolution was still the flavour of the intellectual season, as a kindred spirit: the philosophical, like the literary, world was nervous about the ground it was losing to the sciences, with all their many technological successes to show for their efforts.[34] It was ridiculous, he said, that the Greats degree had the prestige it did. That prestige was owed to 'the social snobbery of Oxford and her self-perpetuating philosophers'. The whole thing was 'a defense mechanism of gentleman intellectuals, which they use to conceal the fact that they have nothing left to do'.[35]

'About the turn of the century,' said Gellner, 'Oxford was a nursery for running an empire; now it is a nursery for leaving the world exactly as it is. The linguistic philosophers have their job cut out for them – to rationalize the loss of English power.'[36] The critique was anti-establishment, certainly, but it wasn't exactly left-wing. 'Philosophers in the past', Gellner said – approvingly – 'were proud of changing the world and providing a guide to political life.'[37] It seemed to him obvious that providing 'a guide to political life' was indeed an honourable thing.

Mehta had found the controversy he was looking for. But the ultimate message of his reportage was that the dislike of Austin had itself become *passé*. Those without a bee in their bonnets about Austin and his influence took the sensible view that the man was dead now, unable to do any harm. It was true that to some outsiders, his death in 1960 – at only forty-eight – seemed a cataclysm: was he not to Oxford what Wittgenstein had been to Cambridge? But on the inside, for all his suave air of command around the younger fellows, he had never had – and to his credit, not really sought – Wittgenstein's mage-like mastery.[38] Oxford was a bigger place, and there were people waiting in the wings to take up the space he had once occupied.

*

Even in the 1950s there had been cracks, hints of Austin's falli-
bility. At least twice, it was agreed, he had been shown not to be
invincible in debate, both during symposia at the Joint Sessions.
On one occasion, in 1958, his opponent was Elizabeth Anscombe,
eight years his junior but accustomed to dealing with even more
difficult men and animated by the curdled loathing of many years.
Their topic was 'pretending', a subject that both agreed admitted
of a 'linguistic' treatment, and one that clearly spoke to some of
the deep concerns of both Oxford and Cambridge philosophy.[39]

With their shared anti-Cartesian temper, both traditions
were suspicious of the idea of 'introspection', in particular about
the thought that introspection guaranteed us infallible knowledge about ourselves. Against this, Ryle and Wittgenstein had
already been mounting a pincer attack from two sides. In Ryle,
the mood was decidedly sceptical and sometimes tended towards
a kind of 'behaviourism': our everyday psychological statements
('I am getting angry') don't refer to some kind of inner mental
state so much as they describe a complex kind of in-principle-
observable behaviour (teeth gritted, cheeks reddened, back sweaty,
heart pounding). But one *could* fake such things, and if one were
a gifted enough actor, there would surely be no observable difference between the real thing and the pretence.[40] The difference
between the pretence and reality consisted not in the fact that the
pretender's mind was in a different 'inner state', but rather that
the pretender was engaged in quite different behaviour. Someone
playing dead, or pretending to be a bear, didn't simply do what
bears or corpses did while thinking different thoughts; they did
different things. 'Pretending to growl like a bear, or lie still like a
corpse, is a sophisticated performance, where the bear's growling
and the corpse's immobility are naive.'[41]

Austin went about the discussion with his customary elan.[42]
The subtle distinctions were out in force, as were the bizarre questions. What is the difference between my *pretending to bite* your
calf and my *pretending to be biting* it? Between *pretending that*

and *pretending to*? Between pretending to bite and pretending to believe? What is going on where a man pretends to be cleaning windows, but is really trying to spy on the people in the house? (And what if he does, in fact, clean the windows while he's spying?)[43] The one answer that no one wanted to entertain was the tempting Cartesian one, that what distinguished the reality from the pretence was that in one of them was a special kind of 'mental occurrence' completely removed from behaviour.[44]

Where Austin was arch and funny, Anscombe was plodding, careful and relentlessly serious. But she could play his game perfectly well: she took up his ingenious example of the spy pretending to be cleaning the windows, a case where there was a real, if subtle, difference between the phrases 'pretending to be cleaning the windows' and 'pretending to clean the windows' (the former, but not the latter, was consistent with the windows actually getting cleaned). But she did not stop at noting such subtle differences in meaning. Her interest was in the context of the spy's behaviour: despite actually cleaning the windows, he was presenting the false appearance that 'in cleaning the windows, he is doing something in some ordinary proper course of things'.[45]

Anscombe's examples went further: 'Why cannot a baby six months old pretend to be in pain?'[46] (She must have been thinking of Wittgenstein's profound joke: 'Why can't a dog simulate pain? Is he too honest?') Wittgenstein's answer had been that 'the surroundings which are necessary for this behaviour to be real simulation are missing'.[47] Anscombe sought to provide what seemed to have been left out of Austin's version of the linguistic method: an account of the difference that the 'surroundings' of our language games make to what game we are playing.

The exchange was riveting, and examples flowed in profusion. Partisans disagreed, but it was clear that Austin was not by any means the *clear* victor. For a man who liked his victories clear, this would not have been a happy result.

*

Anscombe's moment of victory wasn't even the first time Austin had been bested at his game, and by someone of Anscombe's generation. An even younger challenger was Peter Frederick Strawson (b.1919). When Mehta arrived in Oxford, all roads seemed to point to him; his friend and informant 'John' declared Strawson 'now far and away the most original thinker of ... Oxford philosophy'.[48] Austin didn't yet have an acknowledged successor, but Strawson was perhaps the most plausible of the pretenders to the vacant throne. In 1950, at their symposium at the Joint Sessions, the subject of the debate was *truth*.

Then too the struggle was partly intergenerational; Strawson had just turned thirty, while Austin was just shy of forty. The substance of the debate was whether truth could be understood as a *property*, a *feature* of something. Is truth a real feature of a true sentence – as my height or weight is a real feature of me? The Cambridge philosopher and mathematician Frank Ramsey had suggested that this was a mistake.[49] To say that a sentence 'is true' doesn't really add any new content to that sentence. It could of course serve other functions to say it (manifesting belief, expressing agreement, showing a willingness to assert, and so forth) but as far as its content goes, 'it is true that the grass is green' says nothing that 'the grass is green' doesn't. Truth is, in other words, 'redundant', and if that's right, it could hardly be a genuine property of sentences. And since there was nothing else it could be a property of, it followed that it wasn't a property at all.[50]

Austin thought that went too far: perhaps truth wasn't a property of sentences, but it might still be a property of utterances; not of a set of words *as such*, but of those words as said by someone, somewhere, somewhen. The details of this theory involved a complex distinction between two sets of linguistic conventions, 'descriptive' and 'demonstrative'.

Descriptive conventions connect words with *types* of situation;

demonstrative conventions connect them with specific situations, depending on the context in which they're used. Someone says, for instance, 'It's raining.' Demonstrative conventions make this utterance point to a specific situation – what the weather is like where the speaker is standing. Descriptive conventions make the utterance indicate a *type* of situation – say, rainy weather. The speaker's utterance is true if the specific situation it points to is the type of situation it indicates: if, in other words, the weather around the speaker is rainy. Truth, then, isn't redundant. Something is being matched up with something else – words with the world.

Strawson disagreed. What was this but the old 'correspondence' theory of truth – dressed up, certainly, but still vulnerable to objections. The theory was at the heart of early analytic philosophy, the project shared, more or less, by Frege and Russell and the early Wittgenstein.

If truth is about sentences 'corresponding with' something that is not itself a sentence, we should be able to say what that something is. 'Rex barks' corresponds with – what? Rex? Not quite: better to say it corresponds with Rex's barking. Or, one might equally say, the *fact* that Rex barks. But what is a fact? Where do I find them? I can see Rex and hear him barking. But where do I see or hear the fact that Rex barks? What does it take for that fact to exist? Surely it takes nothing more and nothing less than this: that Rex barks. But to say that is simply to repeat the original sentence.[51]

To say that something is a fact is another, strained, way to say that a certain sentence is true. But that was precisely what we were trying to explain in the first place. And no, it wouldn't do to replace 'fact' with 'state of affairs', as Austin proposed. A 'state of affairs' is mysterious in precisely the same way. To the extent that we understand what states of affairs are, we're thinking of them simply as collections of facts.[52]

What, then, is truth? It would be better, Strawson proposed, to ask what we're saying when we *call something true*. Indeed, it would be even better to ask what we're *doing* in saying it. This distinction between saying and doing was already a hobbyhorse of Austin's; Strawson was using the enemy's main point against him. In one way, we're adding nothing to 'Snow is white' when we say, '"Snow is white" is true,' or, 'It is true that snow is white.' As Ramsey had said a long time before, it was like ascending the rungs of a ladder laid flat on the ground.[53] Strawson thought Ramsey had got that much right. But of course, there were things one could do with the phrase 'is true' that it's hard to do without it. I can use it to express agreement. 'Snow is white,' you say. 'That's true,' I say, nodding. 'Is it true that your daughter was ill yesterday?' the headmaster asks the mother. 'It's true,' the mother says, confirming her daughter's story.[54]

The point was made with a similar profusion of examples. Why can't we describe a map as true? What can we learn from the fact that both 'true' and 'fact' are often followed by 'that': 'it's true that', 'it's a fact that'? But the *coup de grâce* came in the concluding summary: Austin's mistakes could be 'shown by the detailed examination of the behaviour of such words as "statement", "fact", etc., and of "true" itself'.[55] In other words, the trouble with Austin was that he hadn't learnt to attend to the many uses of English words.[56]

*

Peter Strawson grew up in the London suburb of Finchley, one of four children of schoolteacher parents. He went to a state school, Christ's College, for secondary school, where he did his 'Higher Certificate' in English, French, Latin and history. He enjoyed grammar and poetry, and learnt to speak a confident and unaccented French.[57] He wrote poetry too, impressive efforts for a 15-year-old in a style somewhere between Matthew Arnold and T. S. Eliot, that was published in successive volumes of *The*

Threshold: An Anthology of Verse and Prose from the Schools of England ('We are the slaves of sorrow and regret; / There is no meaning in this life whose breath / We rate so high; there is no truth but death.')[58]

When he was admitted to Oxford in 1937, it was to study English. But he changed his mind before he arrived. In a burst of priggishness, he decided he ought to study something more suited to the times, which were so evidently in need of those who understood politics and economics. So it was PPE that he studied. But it became clear to him from early on that economics was dull, and politics only interesting when it was treated historically. That left him with philosophy, where he was set to study the standard papers: logic (in fact a messy combination of metaphysics, epistemology and philosophy of language) and Kant. He had John Mabbott of St John's for his principal tutor, and for one term was sent to a certain Paul Grice (b.1913), not much older than he was.[59] In 1937, Oxford was still coping with the publication of *Language, Truth, and Logic* and Strawson was one of the many undergraduates to be found lolling in the gardens of St John's with a copy, as enthralled as if he were reading *The Thirty-Nine Steps*.[60]

Strawson showed enormous promise as an undergraduate and came soon to think that what he wanted more than anything else in the world was to teach philosophy as, and where, he had been taught it. But an Oxford fellowship was not to be his; not yet. His exams were a disappointment: a mere 'second'. Respectable, but enough to scupper any chance of a fellowship.[61] The story went around that Isaiah Berlin, one of his examiners, failed to convince his co-examiner Sandy Lindsay that this brash, combative candidate deserved a first, despite his obvious lack of sympathy with idealism.[62] And there was also that other annoyance, the war.

It was the summer of 1940, and young men were needed for other things. He was sent for training with his regiment, the Royal Artillery, to Sussex. In the evenings he watched the RAF and Luftwaffe battle in the night sky; in the day, he was tasked with mastering 'the mysteries of radar'. He was briefly commander of a small radar station on the south coast and, in 1942, commissioned in a newly formed corps: the Royal Electrical and Mechanical Engineers.[63]

Strawson's career in the army was not distinguished (his brother, however, would rise to the rank of general), but to his old age, he enjoyed playing complex games of military strategy involving toy soldiers.[64] He was, however, proud of his work defending soldiers accused of delinquency at the courts martial, where he was defending officer.[65] The last year of the war he spent first in Italy, part of the occupying army, and then in Austria. When the war ended, he was offered further military promotion; he declined. The old dream persisted despite the poor exam result. There was no question of his getting anything in Oxford with a second-class degree. But his old tutor John Mabbott pointed him to an advertisement for a lectureship in philosophy at the University College of North Wales in Bangor, where he had himself spent a year before he got his Oxford position. Strawson was appointed, and found that there was a good deal to bone up on before he started lecturing: the usual suspects (Russell, Moore, Ramsey) and the helpful introduction to logic by Susan Stebbing.[66]

While in Bangor, he began to write, and published two papers, one on the logic of entailment that Ryle agreed to publish in *Mind* and one on ethics, published in *Philosophy*.[67] In 1947, he returned briefly to Oxford to take the competitive exam for the John Locke Prize: it was the second chance he must long have wished for, and he was determined not to muck it up.

This time he was luckier in his examiners: Ryle awarded him the handsome prize of £80 and recommended him to University College, which was then looking for a second lecturer. He got the job, which came with rooms where he could move in with his wife, Ann, who was starting an undergraduate degree at St Anne's as a mature student. And then began the usual grind: student after student arriving dutifully in line with his weekly essay.[68]

At University College, Strawson established a reputation for a kind of elegance that seemed to permeate everything he said and did. His sentences, his dress, his personal manner all gave the sense of being just so. His lectures, his students found, had the quality of some classical building: every pillar there for a reason, not a stone (or preposition) out of place. He spoke in complete paragraphs, every comma, every semicolon perfectly articulated. In tutorials, he was one of those immensely talented teachers (Ryle and Austin too shared this quality) of having something to offer every student, not just the clever ones. He was one of the few tutors to institute what was, at Oxford, the novel practice of expecting the essays to be handed in beforehand. Most tutors had the students read them out – a convenient way of catching up on sleep for the first fifteen minutes of the designated hour followed by a mini-lecture on the tutor's own current hobbyhorse, untethered from anything the student had said. Instead, Strawson would read the essay with care beforehand, then attempt to restate its central arguments in his own (usually much more eloquent) words to the somewhat overawed student, unused to being subject to such intense scrutiny. For a practice sometimes accused of arrogance, its practitioners often showed a humility rare among academics – the most muddled undergraduate essay deserves no less care and attention than the most tangled passage of Kant.

He would uncover difficulties, problems that actually made a difference to the student's argument. He would invite the student to think of other ways in which the essay could have been constructed, the argument sustained: finding links between the narrow question set and larger questions that turned on it. Then he would present his own answer to the question – not as the final word on the matter, but rather, as an example of what it might be to think through the question from scratch. All this would be spoken in sentences, indeed in paragraphs, that could be transcribed and published pretty much as spoken.[69] Oxford philosophy was full of famous talkers, but even among those colleagues (Ryle:

smug, hearty; Austin: dry, caustic; Berlin: allusive, incontinent; Murdoch: tentative, unexpected; Anscombe: oracular, sweary), Strawson held his own.

In the senior common room, Strawson was immediately distinguished by his urbanity and courtesy; his eyes seemed always to be smiling, as if at some private joke. In philosophy, as in everything else, he valued the conversation above all things: the chase, never the catch; methods, never doctrines. He made it clear at the dinner table that he expected the conversation to be intelligent, and his colleagues – in later years, much younger than him – generally lived up to the standards he set.[70]

The response to Austin won him the sort of respect owed to a recognised dragon-slayer. At the same time, Strawson was also beginning his attack on an older, but even more formidable, dragon, Bertrand Russell. In this, he was very much an Austinian. Now it would be Russell's logic that would get the ordinary language treatment. 'On Denoting', Russell's old paper on the logic of 'the', a classic nearly from the time it had been published, was ripe for a revaluation.[71]

One of the vaunted advantages of Russell's theory of 'definite descriptions' – phrases such as 'the present king of France' – was its ability to explain how such phrases could be meaningful even when there was nothing for them to be about (France is a republic). How is it that we can so much as understand what it means to say that 'the present king of France is bald'? Russell had proposed that the sentence could be decomposed into two simpler statements, one making a claim about something existing, namely, a king of France, the other making a claim about his baldness. The first was false, and so, for that reason, was the whole sentence.[72]

Strawson disagreed; the sentence wasn't, or wasn't best described as, false. It was better to say that it was an inappropriate thing to say, neither true nor false. The snappy term for the general phenomenon later to become popular was 'presupposition failure': it's not so much that the sentence states that there is a current king of France; it simply *presupposes* it. In the way that the sentence, 'He is rich, but kind,' presupposes, without quite stating, that rich people aren't usually kind. Or that 'Even Churchill could win this election' presupposes that Churchill's victory would in other circumstances be unlikely. And when one's listener doesn't share one's presupposition, a simple disagreement – expressed by a 'No', or 'That's not true' – will hardly be enough.[73]

What one needs is something '*meta*linguistic', something that calls the presuppositions into question: 'But there *isn't* a current king of France,' or, 'Why *but*?' or, 'What do you mean *even*?' The testing of the theory in the context of a realistic conversational exchange was exactly what Oxford was urging against the older Cambridge orthodoxy. To the extent that formal logic was supposed to be an attempt to model the underlying structure of ordinary language, Russell's theory failed. It was an honourable failure, but a deep one. His theory owed its neatness to its clumsy way with the realities of language use. Even with words such as 'the', there's no easy way to separate questions of meaning (semantics) from questions of practice, context and communication (pragmatics).[74]

Russell read, and disapproved of, Strawson's essay. It confirmed all his prejudices: they knew nothing of logic at Oxford.[75] Worse, they thought that logic should have to answer to the prejudices of the peasant. Oxford, it used to be said, was the home of lost causes; to Russell, it was the final repository of the 'metaphysics of the stone age'.[76]

Spurred by these early dialectical victories, Strawson turned his undergraduate lectures on logic into his first book, *An Introduction to Logical Theory*,[77] in which the general anti-Russellian point was put with even greater force. Formal logic, he said, was 'perspicuous, powerful, and elegant', certainly. It was 'an idealized abstraction of great power and beauty, an indispensable tool for clarifying much of our thought'. But it was 'not an adequate instrument for revealing clearly all the structural features of our language as we use it'.[78]

Gilbert Ryle, with his editor's hat on, entrusted Strawson with the solemn task of reviewing Wittgenstein's *Philosophical Investigations* for *Mind*, effectively making him the spokesman for the 'Oxford' view of the book. Strawson obliged, with a detailed, respectful, and wholly open-minded essay studded with perceptive remarks, and the occasional criticism. Wittgenstein's 'general aim', he wrote, 'is clear enough: ... to make us look at the speaking and writing of language as one human activity among others, interacting with others; and so to make us notice the different parts that words and sentences play in this activity'.[79]

There was one mention of the sceptical idea that so exalted a work should not be subjected to anything so cuass as a reviewer's attentions. But this was quietly, and politely, dismissed. True, Wittgenstein's book was no conventional philosophical essay; its structure and style were too deeply idiosyncratic. But the work clearly did possess a sort of unity. While any attempt to 'present his views in a more conventional form' came with the risk of distortion, there was good reason to take the risk. Strawson would try to 'trace and connect the main lines of his thought'.[80]

Strawson's review set the tone for Wittgenstein's reception in Oxford. There was nothing of Austin's snideness, nor anything of Anscombe's sense of being in the presence of a candidate for canonisation. Wittgenstein was a philosopher of genius, but hardly a god. And if he would take it ill that his 'remarks' were being plundered by those seeking to construct 'theories', well, he was dead now, and his wishes no longer mattered. He, and his book, were public property, and readers would make of him what they would.

*

Freed from the burden of the first-year lectures, Strawson's mind turned to other things. In the beginning, the word for his interests was 'logic', the word used in its expansive, forgiving, unmathematical Oxonian sense of 'the bit of philosophy that isn't ethics'.[81] He sometimes put it by saying there were two distinct but connected activities that could, quite legitimately, go on under the name of logic. There was the formal logic of 'entailments' (the kind of thing Russell's 'On Denoting' was about), and there were the 'referring rules' of ordinary language. Both were necessary in communication, and there were simply no good grounds for the formal logician's claim to sovereignty over the linguistic domain.[82]

Strawson's own definition of logic was deliberately catholic: 'the general theory of the proposition', where a 'proposition' is just the sort of thing that can be true or false.[83] This allowed room for everything from the ambitious symbolism of Whitehead and Russell's *Principia Mathematica* to the excursions of R. M. Hare into the 'logic' of imperatives: even if imperative sentences didn't express propositions, they could nevertheless stand in the sorts of relations that real propositions stood to each other. One could, for instance, infer 'Socrates is mortal' from 'Socrates is a man' and 'All men are mortal', and one could also infer 'Close the window' from 'It's raining' and 'If it's raining, close the window'. Every philosopher at Oxford was, *ipso facto*, a logician now, even if he could barely recite his thirteen times table.

In time, Strawson began to cast about for another label for his activities. He was teaching Kant and discovering the full extent of his sympathy with Kant's project. Kant's own word for the method of his philosophy was 'critique', a word that did not mean, in the now common sense, a 'criticism'. A 'critique', as Kant used the word, was an examination of the authority and limits of a rational faculty.[84] What can reason do, and what are its limits? Can it, for instance, acquire a priori knowledge? That is to say, how, if at all, can we ever know anything not given to us in experience? And how, come to that, can we know what is given to us *in* experience? What must things be like if knowledge of them is to be so much as possible? And what must *we* be like if we are to have such knowledge?[85]

To Strawson, Kant seemed to be asking exactly the right question. But being an Englishman of the 1950s rather than a Prussian of the eighteenth century, his methods, and his sense of the stakes, were different. Not for him the old anxieties about God and immortality, nor could he abide the tendencies that led Kant to a special kind of ('transcendental') idealism. Kant thought, obscurely, that human beings experience only appearances, not 'things in themselves'. In Strawson, this wasn't the really valuable insight of the *Critique of Pure Reason*.[86] And his methods were, unlike Kant's, linguistic.

How, Strawson asked, are we able to refer to individuals and particulars? How does 'Gilbert' refer to Gilbert, 'this wine glass' to this wine glass, 'the Second World War' to the Second World War? Equally, how does 'dog' refer to all dogs, 'three' to the number three, etc. In the background of these questions about language were questions of what might be called 'ontology', the study of being. What is there? Or – which may well be the same question – *what must we say* there is?

The book in which he pursued these inquiries appeared in 1959 with the unassuming title *Individuals*.[87] The attention to language was still there, but the level of abstraction was unusual: it was the work of someone who had spent the previous many years immersed in Kant rather than in Austin. The question he asked himself at the beginning went: is there a sort of thing we can think about, without our thoughts depending on thoughts about other sorts of thing?

But the route to thinking about thought had to go, inevitably, through a digression: thinking about language. Specifically, Strawson returned to the notion he'd used in his criticism of Russell. The usual word was 'reference', but Strawson, with the traditional English preference for verbs over abstract nouns, went instead for 'referring'. The use of the verb rather than the noun had a point:

words don't refer (though they 'have a reference'), people do. But what do we do when we refer to something, that is to say, to some particular thing? Strawson proposed that our ability to refer had something to do with our ability to place what we're referring to in a 'spatio-temporal' framework.

When I think of, say, Strawson's *Individuals*, I need to be able to think of it as a book published in 1959, with me in 2023. If I think about it next year, I need to be able to 'update' this framework, or else I wouldn't be thinking about the same thing as I did the previous year; in Strawson's terms, I wouldn't be able to 'reidentify' the same particular. The point went further. How can I think of Strawson's headache? I could hardly think of the ache, without there being a head for it to be 'in'.[88] That makes bodies referentially 'basic': I can refer to them without needing to refer to anything else, but I can't refer to other things without ultimately referring to ('material') bodies.[89]

Is that true? And must it be true? Could there be a way of thinking – a 'conceptual scheme' – such that we could think about particular things, but where the most basic particulars *weren't* material bodies?[90] Here, Strawson's methods began to look quite unlike anything in Ryle or Austin. They had some of the imaginative audacity of Wittgenstein's sudden question to the reader ('Why can't a dog simulate pain?'), but strung out into a whole chapter. To work out just how basic to our thought material bodies located in space are, we should try a kind of imaginative experiment: imagine *a world without space*.[91] Whatever would that be?

One way to imagine a world without space would be to think of which of our *senses* would make no sense in such a world. Sight would have to go: to see is to see objects in space. So would touch, for the same reason. But what about hearing? Auditory experience, Strawson was assuming, doesn't *as such* presuppose space in the way that sight does. Couldn't there be a world, and a way of thinking about a world, in which there were people who couldn't see or feel, but could hear? What if sounds were one's only sensory experiences? Without touch or vision to give them the idea of spatial location, could such creatures still think of particular things when they were unable to conceive of them as located in space? Couldn't they say, for instance, that 'this chord I heard on Monday is the same as the chord I heard played on Tuesday'? If they could, perhaps it would tell us that space isn't in fact basic to our thinking about particulars, because we can conceive of ways of thinking where space isn't basic in the way that it is to creatures like us.[92]

Strawson's arguments were, as he freely admitted, inconclusive. But the imaginative experiment was only ever meant to be exploratory. In its grandeur and its sustained strangeness, it looked like nothing else in the philosophy of his contemporaries. From thinking about 'bodies', in the widest possible sense, it continued to thinking about *persons*: what are they? How must we think about them? Must persons have bodies? Must they *be* their bodies?[93] In the background of all this were the same questions that had animated both Wittgenstein and Ryle: was there a way beyond Descartes's 'dualism' of mind and body? Was there a way out of the solipsism to which Descartes had seemed to doom us, creatures whose only certain knowledge was of the contents of their minds, never of anything out in the world?

Strawson was teasing out another way of answering this question: it was barely coherent to think of ourselves as disembodied minds, and therefore, barely coherent to account for our knowledge of the world by beginning with our knowledge of our minds. If we can think of ourselves as beings who can see, sense, feel, grieve, rage, Strawson thought, it's only because we already think of ourselves as embodied: one body among others, all located in space and time. To understand ourselves, there was no point working, in Cartesian style, from the inside out. Self-understanding had to come, paradoxically, from the outside in. The bodiless person, he said, 'is strictly solitary'; his 'idea of himself as an individual' requires him to 'think of himself as *dis*embodied', that is to say, 'a *former* person'.

What sort of thing was this? One could sense the ghost of Descartes contending with the methods of Kant, run through the machinery of Ryle and Wittgenstein and stamped with an Austinian attention to our ordinary ways of speaking about such things. 'Logic', even in its most catholic sense, could hardly be the right word. Putting the question to himself when writing his preface, Strawson settled on a bold choice, but an inevitable one. This was metaphysics. What else could it be? But this wasn't the sort of thing that Russell and Moore had rejected, nor the kind of thing the positivists had found meaningless. It had a speculative boldness, yes, but constrained by an acute awareness of the gap between what the premises actually entailed and what one wanted to say. Strawson didn't insist that this is how things were, but he did insist that this is how we had to think. And to bring out the necessity that governed our thoughts was itself a bulwark against the darkest philosophical threat of all: scepticism. If the sceptic's claims can't so much as be *stated* without undermining themselves, then there is no case to answer. Strawson had rediscovered the form and power of Kant's 'transcendental arguments'.[94]

To put it another way, if these were truths, they were as much truths about *us* as they were truths about the world. Strawson was content, he said, to give an 'account of the actual structure of the world of *our* experience' (emphasis added). Some features of human thinking change with history and culture, but some things *must* stay constant for us to be able to make sense of something changing in the first place, as opposed to one set of creatures going extinct and some new creatures taking their place. 'There is a massive central core of human thinking', Strawson said, 'which has no history ...; there are categories and concepts which, in their most fundamental character, change not at all ... They are ... the indispensable core of the conceptual equipment' of all human beings, the most sophisticated and the least.[95] Perhaps this sort of thing was metaphysics too, but of a new kind. *Individuals* was published with the half-audacious, half-apologetic subtitle, *An Essay in Descriptive Metaphysics*.

*

Strawson had applied the previous year, a little optimistically, to the Wykeham Chair in Logic vacated by Henry Price, but was pipped to it by A. J. Ayer – despite Ayer's lacking the support of the two other professors, Ryle and Austin. Austin had favoured Strawson; Ryle a third candidate, the long-serving William Kneale.[96] But Ayer had the support of his old mentor, Maurice Bowra of the pre-war 'immoral front' – now Sir Maurice Bowra and the vice-chancellor of the university, the external member of the panel, John Wisdom of Cambridge, and two representatives from New College, who may have liked the idea of having a celebrity don in the fellowship.

Ayer had spent the previous decade and a half enjoying the high life of a metropolitan intellectual, appearing on the radio as the voice of an assured, suave secular liberalism, mixing on equal terms with poets and novelists at louche parties before disappearing on international lecture tours where he was granted audiences with foreign leaders.[97] Driven from London to his new home, he went gloomy at the Headington roundabout north-east of the city where the carved wooden sign marked the limits of the 'City of Oxford'. 'My heart sinks,' he said to his companion. 'It always has at the sight of Oxford.'[98]

Initially, he might have consoled himself with the thought that Austin had spent the previous fifteen years attacking him, and now he would be there to reply, continuing the weekly sparring the war had interrupted. But then Austin died young, not yet fifty, of cancer, with little warning, leaving Ayer – who thrived on the provocations of a worthy opponent – with no one to be provoked by. There was much else to be gloomy about. The old All

Souls group could not be resurrected: Austin was dead, Donald MacKinnon had taken up a position in Aberdeen where his burr and piety had found a more natural home, and Tony Woozley had moved to St Andrew's.[99]

*

Isaiah Berlin, the other prominent member of the All Souls group, could scarcely be conceived of in any other place, any more than a polar bear can be conceived of in a desert. But he had, during the war, decided to make a different kind of lateral move: not between universities, but disciplines.

Berlin had spent the war years writing characteristically eloquent dispatches from Washington, impressing Churchill with the style and insight of his cables.[100] Towards the end of the war, he met a certain Professor Henry Sheffer (b.1882) of Harvard who persuaded him that the only parts of philosophy worth doing, because the only parts where there was real, exact knowledge to be had, were logic and psychology. It made sense to speak of *progress* in both, but it was absurd to think of progress – an advance of learning – in ethics or epistemology. Neither, he said, was 'that kind of study'.[101]

Berlin put the question to himself: did he wish to spend the remainder of his days on 'a study, however fascinating and important in itself, which, transforming as its achievements undoubtedly were, would not, any more than criticism or poetry, add to the store of positive human knowledge'? He decided that he didn't. He 'should prefer a field in which one could hope to know more at the end of one's life than when one had begun; and so I left philosophy for the field of history of ideas'.[102]

Sheffer's distinction was tendentious, to say the least, but the move might have been justified on other grounds, namely that Berlin was never entirely at home in the sorts of things Oxford philosophy was increasingly about, but very much at home in what he called 'the history of ideas'. Even there, his methods were homespun, the product of wide reading and genuinely inspired guesswork rather than careful, plodding scholarship.[103] But he flourished in his *sui generis* discipline, applying to it his magpie intellect and capacity for ingenious juxtapositions of thinkers and ideas, all the while making the case for the kind of liberalism he had slowly been evolving from his undergraduate years. The simplest statement of it appeared in the lecture he gave in Oxford in the Michaelmas term of 1958 when he ascended to the Chichele Chair in Social and Political Theory. He was succeeding G. D. H. Cole, once of the 1930s Pink Lunch Club where the anti-appeasers of Oxford heard from union radicals, Spanish Republicans and Continental refugees about the state of the world over bread, cheese and cheap beer.

His title, 'Two Concepts of Liberty', showed the influence of his years spent among the philosophers: one talked of liberty by talking of the *concept* of liberty. But of course, a careful examination of the history of modern Western thought on liberty revealed that there were in fact *two* distinct concepts of liberty implicit in it. His labels for the concepts were 'negative' and 'positive' liberty. At points, he suggested that the distinction could be captured with a simple linguistic device: negative liberty was freedom *from*, positive liberty freedom *to*. But his main point was neither conceptual nor linguistic but unabashedly political – as he later put it, 'anti-Marxist, quite deliberately'.[104]

A refugee from Bolshevism, Berlin was never going to be a Marxist, but his previous writings on Marx had at least striven for a judicious impartiality. This lecture was different, with a moral and political urgency that had been seeded by a fortuitous formative encounter he had had in 1945 with the Russian poet Anna Akhmatova, in Leningrad. From her he had learnt much of what it was like to live in Leningrad during the war, to live and write in the USSR under Stalin. From her he also acquired a sense of what political courage and truthfulness might be, of the impossible demands on the integrity of the individual placed by living in an authoritarian society.[105] He also gained a powerful sense of the dependence of such societies on lies and delusions, among them their Orwellian insistence that the freedoms of capitalist societies were somehow unreal. 'I was maddened', he later said, 'by all the Marxist cheating which went on, all the ... Stalinist and Communist patter about "true freedom".' Such talk, he said bluntly, 'cost innocent lives'.[106]

Following the strictures of Robin Collingwood, Ryle's idealist predecessor in the Waynflete Chair in Metaphysics, Berlin made the distinction between the concepts in terms of the two questions they were there to answer. Negative liberty, he said, corresponded to the question, 'How much am I governed?' Or, in more homely terms, 'How many doors are open?'[107] Positive liberty, by contrast, corresponded to the question, 'By whom am I governed?' That distinction divided the history of political thought into two camps. On one side, what Berlin evidently regarded as the sensible one, stood such figures as Benjamin Constant and John Stuart Mill, urging that the only freedom that mattered was freedom *from* something, for instance the meddlings of states, however well-intentioned. On the other and more sinister side stood a certain kind of positive liberty theorist – Rousseau, Hegel, Stalin – who insisted that liberty was self-realisation. That view was in itself unobjectionable until it was combined with a further pair of ideas: that society or the state was in a better position than the individual to determine what somebody's self-realisation consisted in, and that there could never be a conflict between distinct values.

On both counts, that approach was untruthful to human psychology and the nature of the world. Today they tell you that we may need to sacrifice some of our freedom in the name of some other value: equality, for instance, or security, or public health. Tomorrow they insist, in the face of everything we know, that the apparent sacrifice is no sacrifice at all: the sort of freedom we lose when the state expropriates my land, or plants listening devices into my bedroom ceiling (as they did with Anna Akhmatova) is not a freedom deserving the name. Berlin baulked at the mutilation of language. If we have, as Rousseau notoriously said, to be 'forced to be free',[108] then we had better ask some hard questions about the 'inflated' way in which the word 'free' is being used here.[109] Today they tell you that they only want to help you realise your best interests; tomorrow that they know your true interests better than you – beset with what Friedrich Engels notoriously called 'false consciousness' – can know them yourself; and now we're in the Gulag.[110]

The 'freedom from'/'freedom to' formulation was a mistake. As many would later point out, all claims about freedom necessarily involve references to both an obstacle to be free from, and an end to be free to do or realise.[111] We are always free *from* something *to* do something. But Berlin did nevertheless seem to have identified an important distinction in the history of ideas, even if he was still reaching for language to do justice to his insight. There was certainly something that distinguished Mill from Stalin in how they saw the state's relation to liberty – roughly, foe or friend – but that distinction had nothing to do with prepositions. Stalin could claim, quite grammatically, to be trying to free his people *from* capitalist ideology, as Mill might claim to want freedom *to* be eccentrically ourselves.

In any case, the lecture was a masterpiece of Cold War rhetoric: resonant, zealous, yet also reasoned. Everything is what it is and not another thing, he declared.[112] Not all good things come together. Mix up your values, pretend there's no conflict, and you mix up your politics, and try to claim there are no hard choices. But there are. We might have to compromise on our freedom to have more equality or security or something else we value, but let us be honest that a compromise is what it is. It is, moreover, dangerous to pretend that 'real' freedom requires some superior power to tell us how best to live. Politics had better be aware of both the hard choices we must face, and the pitfalls we can fall into if we make the wrong one.[113]

*

The tone was resolutely Oxonian, if only because Berlin had no other tone. But this was bold, speculative, and in its way *engagé*, in striking contrast to anything that happened at Austin's Saturdays. And the moment was ripe for ambitious programmatic statements. Berlin was talking about liberty, Strawson about individuals and bodies. In North Oxford, Anscombe, as one member of her audience put it, 'wrestled with the concept of a want week after week': the grand proclamation that there was no point doing ethics until we had an adequate philosophy of psychology was being followed up with some of the necessary hard labour.[114]

Anscombe's monograph *Intention* was published in 1957, a short, dense exploration of what it is for an action to be intentional. Wittgenstein's way into the question was to ask another: 'What is left over if I subtract the fact that my arm goes up from the fact that I raise my arm?'[115] Anscombe set out not so much to answer the question as to make it clear why Wittgenstein had asked it. Wittgenstein was hoping to expose the absurdity of a certain way of understanding an intention: as a 'private' entity in the mind that accompanies some actions but not others.

But what, after all, is an 'intention'? How exactly are we to isolate it 'in the mind'? If 'intention' doesn't refer to anything 'internal', was the only option to think of it as something essentially external – manifested in behaviour? Gilbert Ryle had sometimes indicated that looking to behaviour was a preferable strategy. But that was unsatisfactory in its own way. We know all too well that we sometimes intend to do things but forget or otherwise fail to do them. An unrealised intention could hardly be manifested in behaviour. Are we to deny that such things exist?

Anscombe had no wish to deny the obvious. An intention was

not a spectral mental entity; nor was it simply an aspect of behaviour. The trick was to give up on trying to theorise the notion of an 'intention' in isolation. The place to start was within the contexts of human life in which our concepts of intention have a use. We had to ask, as Austin might equally have recommended, what we are doing when we ascribe intentions to agents. As Richard Wollheim nicely summarised it in his short review for the *New Statesman*, what Anscombe urged us to do was to attend to the 'the whole context – particularly, as it turns out, the verbal context – in which we ascribe intention to an agent and his action'.[116]

Stylistically, the book had a strangeness and intensity it inherited from Anscombe's tutelage under Wittgenstein. It was divided into fifty-two short sections, the whole thing adding up to barely a hundred pages. There was little signposting, and the book, while largely free of jargon, had an aura of mystery about it. The American philosopher Judith Jarvis (*mariée* Thomson), reviewing the book in the *Journal of Philosophy*, warned that 'the reader must carry along the thread of the argument by himself'; Wollheim in the *New Statesman* that 'the reader should be careful to take up [Miss Anscombe's] book at what he finds to be his most attentive hour'.[117] What the attentive reader would find, Jarvis wrote, was a work 'rich in suggestion and example that ... amply repays careful study'.[118]

Attending to the wider linguistic context in which we ascribe intentions, Anscombe proposed, would reveal two central insights. First, to call some action intentional is to say that we can ask the question 'Why?' about it. Secondly, actions aren't really intentional or unintentional except *under some description* (the book's greatest influence on the discipline may be its popularising of that phrase). Some action on my part could simultaneously be described as my intentionally eating soup, unintentionally eating it with a fork, intentionally eating it fast, unintentionally ruining my white shirt.

In its method, *Intention* had something of Austin's ear for the subtle distinction and Ryle's eye for the category mistake. But Anscombe distinguished herself from her Oxford colleagues by asking what she thought a further set of questions they neglected: How do very young children acquire such a concept, or learn to use words in this way? She, like Wittgenstein, also found value in frequently posing the counterfactual question: 'What might we have said if ... ?' What would our language be like if the world were quite different? The task was not just to analyse our actual use of language, but to press the question of what it meant that we used words the way we did.[119] But it had also an eye to a larger point that went well beyond the dialectics of academic philosophy.

In her debate with her Oxford colleagues a few years previously about whether Harry Truman should be awarded an honorary doctorate, part of what had been in question was the precise nature of what Truman had done. Couldn't someone say that while he had intentionally signed a piece of paper – or even more generously, that he had signed a piece of paper *with the intention of* ending the war – his action had the consequence, not itself intended, of killing a great many Japanese civilians? One could say it, but would it be true? The question was complex and deep, and Anscombe was laying the foundations for a theory that would answer it to Truman's discredit. Part of what was disreputable in the Cartesian idea of intention was how easy it made it for Truman to put himself in the moral clear – as if he could simply make a little speech to himself as he signed, 'All I mean to be doing is ...' But one cannot simply determine for oneself what descriptions one's actions fall under; nor can one simply determine for oneself what one is doing intentionally.

Another question that *Intention* made inescapable was how to classify this sort of work. In its approach, it was impeccably Wittgensteinian, and therefore, linguistic. But in its ambitions, its aspirations to system and coherence, it looked like a piece of old-fashioned metaphysics. So, was it or was it not metaphysics?

Anscombe, like Strawson writing at the same time, left one wondering why it mattered what one called it.

*

The *Times Literary Supplement* in 1960 ran an anonymous essay titled 'The Post-Linguistic Thaw'. The author was widely known to be Strawson, writing shortly after the death of Austin.[120] He deplored the editor's title: he was far from wanting to suggest that the heyday of 'linguistic' philosophy had been a long Narnian winter.[121] He quoted an unnamed Australian philosopher of his acquaintance, returning to Oxford having last been there in the late 1940s, who rued the loss of the old revolutionary quality, 'in which every new move was delightfully subversive and liberating'.[122] But such things never did survive long. At some point, the revolutionaries had to leave the barricades to return to the desks vacated by the clerks of the *ancien régime*. What had the excitement been about, among men and women returning to the discipline after a world war spent thinking about other things? Strawson thought it had something to do with the unexpected combination this philosophy offered, of 'magnitude of claim with modesty of pretension'.[123]

The big claims were about the imminence of a final dissolution: ancient knots would be cut, the old metaphysical doctrines hunted to extinction. Once the old detritus was cleared, then the *revelation*, 'of a whole world of infinite subtlety and diversity with its own fine and complex structure, a world which had always lain about us to be observed as soon as we ceased straining our eyes towards imaginary grandeurs and simplicities'.[124] That world would reveal itself once we ceased straining our eyes and tried instead to *listen*, not least to ourselves.

Wasn't this the oldest back-and-forth of all, the same one captured in Raphael's *School of Athens*? Up points Plato's hand, to the heavenly heights of abstraction; down faces Aristotle's extended palm, to the earthly depths of human life. Listen hard enough, attentively enough, to what we say and do with our words, and we are freed 'from the philosophical fantasies or perplexities engendered by a reflection which was incomplete, uncontrolled or obsessive'.[125] There was this to hope for, and also, somewhat more perversely, the further hope of self-annihilation: the point of philosophy, done in this style, was to finish off philosophy once and for all. This had been a positivist hope too, but positivism too would have to fall to the linguistic sword.

All the while, the revolutionaries were mocked and resisted. The mockery was often ten years out of date. Long after anyone in Oxford would admit to being a positivist, the attack was based on a picture of philosophy as technical and science-worshipping. And by the time the attackers cottoned on to the new mood and revised their accusations (Strawson's essay provided a useful list: 'dullness, triviality, pedantry, abdication, evasion, frivolity, complacency, conservatism and obscurity'), Oxford had moved on yet again. And the whole time, the place – to the dismay and consternation of its critics – seemed not to be losing its attractions for foreigners: Americans, Australians, Indians, were curious and fascinated. They wanted to study with those dull, trivial dons, and paid for the tickets and hotels that would bring such figures to their own countries and campuses.[126]

Strawson didn't yield an inch to the accusers. Instead, he went on a counterattack: 'What was clear seemed obscure to those whose unconscious demand was for obscurity, and the study of the familiar seemed contemptuously esoteric in a region where everything was expected to be strange.'[127] Was it so incredible that the movement might attract adherents among the young? Was it so odd that they saw the excitement of consorting with philosophers who – however regrettable their disdain for the late and great – hadn't been silenced by the weight of giants standing atop their shoulders? Was it so unfortunate that the young should be seduced by the promise of truths and facts, established in co-operative conversation, over theories that had all been shown to be so many castles of sand? Was this not what Ernest Nagel, travelling across Europe in the thirties, had conjectured about the intellectual excitement of Vienna? That such a style of philosophy could feel to the young almost a kind of *adventure*?

Then came the concessions. Philosophy in the Saturday-morning style could not, 'by itself, satisfy the persistent philosophical craving for generality, for the discovery of unifying pattern or structure in our conception of the world'.[128] And here we needed more than 'reminders assembled for a particular purpose', if only because sometimes our purposes themselves were not particular but general.[129] Wittgenstein had not managed to convince everyone that the craving was itself part of the problem, needing the interventions of the philosophical therapist rather than the reassurance of being treated as a serious philosophical question. And once the craving for system was understood to be a respectable motivation to thought – rather than the symptom of some psychically disfiguring disease – the history of philosophy could be returned to its place of honour. If the dead philosophers were wrong, they were wrong in their particular claims and their arguments for them, not for seeking systematic answers to general questions.

Even Austin had, before his untimely death, made some movements in the direction of the system that had, surely, been what gave his co-operative idea of philosophy its ultimate point. In the lectures he had given at Harvard in the late 1950s while contemplating a move from Oxford to California, the hotchpotch of illuminating examples was replaced by something more unified: a 'general classificatory theory of acts of linguistic communication'.[130] Stuart Hampshire, of both the inter-war All Souls group and the post-war Saturday club, had just published a systematic work (*Thought and Action*) connecting an anti-Cartesian philosophy of mind with questions in both epistemology and ethics.[131] Iris Murdoch was lecturing, unabashedly, on the relevance of metaphysics to ethics.[132] Herbert Hart (b.1907), a former Chancery barrister who had returned to academia after the war, was applying Austin's methods to jurisprudence, a subject that had previously been left to the theoretically minded lawyer, and a promisingly titled book – *The Concept of Law* – was due to be published.[133]

And for those willing to read these (and other) writers, the general charge of boringness was decisively refuted by the direct and fluent English of the actual books. Strawson put it to his readers that philosophers writing in English in the 1950s lived up to the high standards of Locke, Berkeley and Hume, their prose styles running the gamut: 'Augustan elegance' (Ayer), 'sharp lucidity' (Austin), 'strange, persuasive cadence' (Wisdom), and the 'wide-ranging vocabulary', the 'taut and balanced sentence structure' of Ryle, who was, in this matter as in so many others, everybody's teacher.[134]

What was this thaw? The end of Oxford philosophy? But why identify a tradition with its most ossified phase? Why not see the history instead as a story of oscillation – between the looseness of late-Victorian idealism and the too-stern strictures of the positivist high noon? If that was the right way to think about the 'thaw', then perhaps the thaw was not the end of anything, but a slow coming into itself of the real potential of the tradition, freed from its misunderstandings – its underestimation – of its own power and promise.

9

Donkeys

The revolutionary energies of the late 1940s appeared to be on the wane a decade later. The surest sign was the appearance in 1956 and 1958 of two books taking stock of the putative revolution. 'When a revolutionary movement begins to write its own history,' wrote Peter Strawson in the *Times Literary Supplement*, 'something at least of its revolutionary impetus has been lost'.[1] The first of these histories was a collection of transcripts of talks originally delivered on the BBC's Third Programme (what would later become Radio 3), with an introduction from Ryle, bearing the bold title *The Revolution in Philosophy*. The second, a slim monograph by Geoffrey Warnock, told a brisk, and extremely partial (in both senses of the word), history of philosophy in England since 1900.[2] 'The wise rambler', said Ryle, introducing *The Revolution in Philosophy* with a characteristically English analogy, 'looks back over his shoulder in order to link up the place he has got to with the country through which he has recently passed.'[3]

Both volumes were reviewed in *Philosophy* by a young philosopher then in the early years of a fellowship at New College.[4] Both reviews were sympathetic, but only to a point; they were evidently a work of someone in the know, but not in any further sense the work of an insider. What the radio talks left unsaid, Bernard Williams (b.1929) complained in a review, was what, if anything, this so-called revolution amounted to: what unified all the many things that had happened under its banner?[5]

He proposed his own answer. The philosophy of the previous

259

sixty years had been preoccupied with one thing: limits. The limits of language, of meaning, of thought, of the sayable: these were, in a way, old concerns. But stating the limits of thought turned out to be impossible, for a quite simple reason. To draw the limits of something, we must be able to think what lies on both sides of the limit. But we can't: what's beyond the limits of the thinkable is – literally – unthinkable. But if we can't think it, perhaps there are other things we might do: approach it, come as close to it as we can, and then stop. Beyond that, there is nothing to think, nothing to say, no words – or none that are meaningful. There is silence, or there is nonsense.[6]

Of course this hadn't been Kant's way of putting it, but Wittgenstein's in his *Tractatus*, and some people in Vienna had taken the view that what he had meant to say was the same thing they wanted to say: that the limits of sense were to be drawn 'positivistically round the propositions of natural science'.[7] However, Williams continued, Wittgenstein had also been happy to say there that all the propositions of 'our colloquial language are actually, just as they are, logically completely in order'.[8] In his later work, he returned to his earlier sentiment, endorsing one part of it, rejecting another. Yes, he seemed to be saying now, everything in our colloquial – everyday, ordinary – language is indeed in order. But that doesn't mean, as Williams summarised it, that 'there must therefore be an order in which everything is'.[9] We must make, Wittgenstein now said, 'a radical break with the idea that language always functions in one way'.[10]

Williams was unsure just how sharp a break there had been between the early work of Wittgenstein and the late.[11] But there were lines of continuity: 'casually [in the *Tractatus*] he remarks "in philosophy the question 'Why do we really use that word, that proposition?' constantly leads to valuable results", and in the *Investigations* we find the results of asking just this sort of question'.[12] The great lesson of the *Tractatus* seemed to be this: 'philosophy cannot go beyond language as it humanly is … we are committed to the language of human life, and no amount of speculative investment is going to buy a passage to outer space, the space outside language'.[13]

What is outside language is unstateable; 'the *Investigations* takes its unstateability for granted, and works patiently in the world it is given, the world of human language'.[14] Philosophers could forswear nonsense now, precisely because they were better placed to know just how much sense there still was for them to speak. We could speak sense with our words, about our words, and that still left us with enough to do: we knew how much more there was left to do, and had an incitement to get started doing it. What more could a revolution ask for?

The second book in the same, taking-stock kind of vein, by Geoffrey Warnock, was a unified work by a single mind rather than an anthology, and it raised different questions. Warnock's *English Philosophy since 1900*, wrote Williams, was spare, elegant, 'admirably clear and very well written', but these qualities came in part from its having 'the basic straightforwardness of a moral tale', a historical fable about philosophers.[15] Things start with 'the macabre picture of British Idealism': but Idealism is a corrupt doctrine, delusional and dangerously foreign, really a sort of occupying army. G. E. Moore appears in the story as the native hero to drive out the fell invader. In this, he has his somewhat shaky allies: 'Russell, brave but unsteady; Positivism, secretly in love with the metaphysical enemy.' Warnock cannot leave out Wittgenstein, but the story is told with 'a slight sense of strain at having to take so extravagant a figure so seriously'. But the story has a happy ending: 'with Ryle, victorious peace is almost achieved; and the story ends with Common Sense again on the throne, and the citizens of Oxford, calm but not idle, earning the unambitious rewards of honest toil'.[16]

Williams was untempted by the story. It could doubtless be seen as the expression of an entirely predictable Oxford parochialism and complacency. But this story of English philosophy as a journey from common sense to common sense – just the long way around – mirrored other such stories: Christianity as the long path from paganism to paganism? or, a few decades later, the Eastern Bloc as the long path from capitalism to capitalism?[17] This idea of a 'Common Sense view of the world' Williams found deeply suspect, especially if it was supposed to be, as Moore had thought, 'perfectly unsurprising, undistressing, quite certainly true'.[18] Again, this had the flavour of another kind of fable, one found for instance in Rousseau: 'the natural man corrupted by the machinations of priests and kings'.[19]

But what about the fact that some metaphysical questions seem to arise anyway? That our ordinary ways of speaking and thinking about the mind, to pick an obvious example in this connection, are closer to those of Descartes than they are to those of Wittgenstein? As Stuart Hampshire had pointed out in his *Mind* review of Ryle's book, the ghost was haunting the machine long before any philosophers had detected it there. Philosophical problems, Williams proposed, are not aberrations put into the minds of stout yeomen by priests and kings, any more than it is only the dark murmurings of hairy older boys that get the younger ones wondering how babies are born. The questions are natural, and the questioning can even be healthy.[20]

*

Williams came to philosophy, like most of his Oxford colleagues, from an undergraduate degree in Classics. He grew up in Essex and went to Chigwell, a 'minor public school', where a headmaster with an obsession with Oxbridge gave him an excellent training in the ancient languages. He was a schoolboy at the eastern edge of London during the war; for a time after the war, he flew Spitfires for the RAF during his period of National Service. His schooldays were spent talking philosophy with friends: the USA or the USSR, artistic freedom or moral responsibility. He was introduced to the writings of D. H. Lawrence and F. R. Leavis by a dubious gambling addict of a Classics teacher, once a student of A. E. Housman's, who left Williams with one conviction: 'what matters above all, in intellectual matters as everywhere else, is the difference between the living and the dead, and … the mark of the living is to be found in the complexity of its detailed structures, together with the fact that you cannot predict what form it will insist on taking'.[21] This combination – *Women in Love* as well as Housmanesque textual criticism – left him with another, and for him unusually optimistic, conviction: 'that getting it right need not mean killing it off'.[22]

Williams arrived at Balliol College to find that his degree would involve a substantial amount of philosophy. He had, for his principal tutor, a young R. M. Hare, still bruised from his war, but indefatigable and a formidable arguer. Williams cut his teeth arguing with Hare every week, trying but failing to change the older philosopher's opinions. He was a member of a talented set of undergraduates who worked together on their essays, devising arguments of mounting complexity against Hare that each would deliver in his weekly tutorial. Williams was always the last one in, and to him was given the task of administering what they hoped would be the *coup de grâce*. Hare never changed his mind.[23]

Hare's effects on Williams were primarily negative: they had a grudging respect for each other's talents, but Williams was temperamentally opposed to virtually everything Hare stood for. A generation after Murdoch and Midgley, he too was a participant at Eduard Fraenkel's endless seminar on the *Agamemnon*, where he was the rare undergraduate the magus thought destined for scholarly greatness.[24] (There is no evidence that the accolade came for Williams at the cost as it had for Fraenkel's female students.) When he graduated with the congratulatory first everyone had predicted, he was elected to an All Souls fellowship, a couple of decades after Berlin, Austin and Hampshire had been.[25] When he returned as a college fellow after his National Service, there was no expectation that he would do any further degrees.

Williams threw himself into the life of Oxford philosophy in the fifties. He went to Ryle for informal supervision and came to like him very much. Ryle never convinced him of his more distinctive positions, but gave what Williams later recognised to be good advice: keep away from -isms; it's 'better to write a short good book later than a bad long book earlier'.[26] Austin, on the other hand, he gave a wide berth: he had seen too clearly the numbing effect he could have on the young. Having by that stage a thriving social circle of his own – he was married to Shirley Williams (née Catlin), a Labour MP whom some were beginning to see as a future prime minister – Williams never went to Austin's Saturday mornings.[27] Austin, dangerously charismatic, was liable to clip the wings of the young before they'd had the chance to work out what they wanted to say. But Williams resented Austin's absurd terror of metaphysical excess: to fear metaphysics in the Oxford of the 1950s was more paranoid than prudent. 'He always seemed to me', Williams later said, 'like a Treasury official who thought that the British economy needed deflating, when there were already three million unemployed.'[28]

Iris Murdoch and Philippa Foot gave him a vision of what ethics might look like once freed from the strictures of Ayer and Hare on what was and wasn't meaningful. He never quite adopted Murdoch's Platonism, which he thought veered into the merely cosy, or Foot's naturalism, which seemed to him to dodge difficult questions about the diversity of human values.[29] But he was always grateful for their having pointed him to what would become one of his basic ideas: that the persistent focus on the 'right' and 'good' took our attention away from the concepts that really mattered in life – the honourable, the shameful, the treacherous, the truthful, the authentic.[30] An atheist, though an unpushy one, and a committed liberal, he could only agree so much with Elizabeth Anscombe.[31] But he did learn from her just how little mere cleverness counted for in philosophy.

Oxford philosophy, he later recalled, 'was very eristic: there was a lot of competitive dialectical exchange, and showing that other people were wrong'. 'Eristic' was a term familiar from the dialogues of Plato, often used by Socrates to refer to the cheap rhetorical ploys of the notorious sophists, aiming at victory and humiliation rather than truth. Williams was particularly at risk of falling for this vision of philosophy, being clever, quick, articulate, and rather good at the cut-and-thrust. But it was hard to keep that up with Anscombe in the room, conveying in her manner and person 'a strong sense of the seriousness of the subject'.[32] Cleverness, she persuaded him, would never be enough.

In time, Williams found his way to an appreciation of Wittgenstein, and the qualities of his that his more admirable students embodied: 'appreciation of what is not there in the argument or on the page'.[33] Most of all, he showed what it was like to have one's eye always on the big picture, how all the little things hung together. He craved the sort of philosophy that helped itself to the resources of imaginative literature: emotion beyond the expressions of boo and hurrah; imagination that went beyond the ability to devise a good counterexample; and that other, undefinable, thing, *depth*.[34] Wittgenstein had it, as did Nietzsche; Russell didn't, nor did Carnap: an ability to see past the obvious, to uncover things about human life that call on qualities of mind that go beyond cleverness.[35]

Some of this he got from another of his colleagues, David Pears (b.1921), one of the models for the Wittgensteinian figure in Iris Murdoch's *Under the Net*. Pears was also a stylistic model for some of Williams's own work in this period, in particular his 'ironic taste for formulae which offer the tone or register of rigorous analysis but actually deliver a condition which is deliberately, and realistically, vague'.[36] Where the phenomena were themselves vague, an analysis that replaced the vagueness with precision was itself a falsification. What was needed, Williams found, was a prose style that combined 'the more conversational and the more formal aspects of analytic philosophy' – rather as, say, Debussy combined these elements in his music. Williams teamed up with Pears to offer a class on the topic of personal identity.

Questions about personhood – what is a person, must a person have a body, what makes it true that this child, this adolescent, this senile old man could all be the same person – had been entertained since the 1930s. Austin's All Souls group had been much exercised about what one should say about the character of Gregor Samsa in Kafka's 'The Metamorphosis'. Does it make sense to think he could be transformed into a large insect *and still be Gregor Samsa*?[37] But with the publication of Strawson's *Individuals*, there was finally room for a really ambitious treatment of the subject, without the old anxieties that one's colleagues would accuse one of metaphysics.

Williams gave Strawson's book a detailed, admiring but also deeply critical review. He was puzzled and unconvinced by Strawson's arguments about the possibility of a disembodied individual still being able to perceive from a particular point of view. Strawson had claimed, with an ingenious and complex argument to support it, that the connection between perception and the body was a contingent one. One could conceive of a sort of being with three bodies, but sharing a unified 'perceptual experience' – because one of the three bodies had its eyes open and the others had them shut. Williams was unconvinced.

His objection involved trying to imagine what it might be like to be such a being, with three bodies that might well be in different places. Say I am 'S', the unified perceiver, and my bodies are Andy, Bob and Charlie. Andy is in Ankara, Bob in Bombay, Charlie in Chicago. You, in Chicago, try to punch Charlie. I, S, see you coming. If I were a single body, I could both turn my head aside to avoid the blow and look around for somewhere to run to. But since I am not, it seems like I, S, could turn Charlie's head aside to escape the blow, and turn Bob's head to look for an escape route. But Bob is in Bombay, and his perceptions can hardly help.

It can't then be a merely 'contingent fact that we perceive, move and act from the same place'.[38] The idea that these things could be separated was another lingering element of the Cartesian ideology that Strawson claimed to have abandoned.

The lingering Cartesian dogma made it hard for Strawson to sustain his other intriguing claim: that there could not be a being who had only ever existed in a disembodied state. If Strawson thought it was a contingent fact that a subject of perception used only one body, why shouldn't it be equally contingent that he had a body at all? Why not, then, a wholly and eternally disembodied perceiver? The answer must presumably be that there is no perception except from a point of view, and a point of view needs a body. Strawson could not have it both ways.

Most of Williams's early papers were about – as the title of his first collection had it – 'problems of the self'.[39] There was a long history of suspicion about that category in British philosophy. In its most recent form, that scepticism was articulated in terms familiar from the writings of Bertrand Russell and A. J. Ayer, that the self is really just a series of experiences. But Russell and Ayer would have found a surprising ally in that doughty old idealist, F. H. Bradley, who took roughly the same view. What Russell would have called a 'construct', Bradley had called an 'abstraction'. Against these worthy opponents, Williams wanted to assert something bold: that the self is no mere interpretation, but a feature of human experience that cannot be eliminated. And the link between the self and the body, far from being a contingent matter, may be the deepest fact about it.

In its crudest form, Williams's thesis was this: persons are material bodies. It isn't enough to say I *have* a body (who exactly is the body's owner, or possessor?). Better to say I *am* a body. In several subtle, searching essays, Williams mounted arguments to the effect that this view of persons was the only way to understand the special sense we have of being *the same person*, across the many changes that take place over time. In this, he was arguing against a powerful tradition that saw the body as strictly superfluous: what makes me me, what makes me the same person I was last week, is some kind of continuity in psychology.

On any account, this was metaphysics. No self-respecting positivist could have any truck with this kind of inquiry. But his argumentative strategy commanded attention. His most remarkable stylistic innovation – since much imitated – was the use of ingenious 'thought experiments' – wacky imaginary scenarios against which we can test our concepts and self-conceptions. In 'The Self and the Future', he discovered numerous tensions lurking in the old fantasy of a body-swap: what would happen if a prince and a pauper swapped not only clothes but bodies? What should we make of someone who claimed to remember being Napoleon at the Battle of Waterloo?[40] Would I fear torture any less if I were told that just before the torture started, my memories would be removed and replaced with those of someone else? Would that mean that it was someone other than me who was being tortured? Suppose one still felt anxious for one's body – one might well say, for oneself. What did that tell us about what we really thought we were?

And yet, the anti-metaphysical stances of positivism and ordinary language had left their mark. Williams's concerns were at a remove from the old questions about mind and body. The point of the science-fictional parables was not simply to refute the Cartesian picture but to show it up as inadequate to the complexity of our experience of being persons, with bodies as well as psychologies. Every now and then, one could see a glint of something Austinian and linguistic in his methods: what does it mean, he once asked, that we say at a funeral both, 'That is Auntie's body in the coffin,' and, 'We buried Auntie'?[41] As Austin had said of a different problem, the philosopher's task was that of 'unpicking, one by one, a mass of seductive (mainly verbal) fallacies'. But Williams did not agree that the procedure must leave us 'just where we began'.[42]

Another target for his powerful critical mind was the 'prescriptivism' of his old Balliol tutor, R. M. Hare. Hare had hoped to make a real advance on the 'emotive' theory of ethics that Ayer had proposed in the 1930s. Ethical judgements were better seen as akin to commands than to expressions of emotion. Commands, and other imperatives, had a sort of logic of their own, which meant that the kind of rational discussion of ethical judgements that Ayer's view ruled out turned out to be respectable after all. But Williams found Hare's view not much of an improvement, urging against it an objection similar to one that had been thought devastating for the emotivist. If 'murder is wrong' was equivalent to an expression of disapproval of murder, then many perfectly innocuous forms of ethical thinking would turn out to be deeply confused. 'Murder is wrong' is a thought one might entertain by itself; but the thought might equally appear 'embedded' in a more complex sentence. Say, the negation: 'Murder is not wrong.' Or the interrogative: 'Is murder wrong?' Or the simple conditional: 'If murder is wrong, then I oughtn't to hire a hitman.' But can the emotive interpretation of the sentence make the slightest sense of those utterances? What could 'if boo murder' even mean? Conditionals require their elements to be either true or false, but what Ayer denied was precisely the possibility that an ethical judgement might be either. The argument was powerfully made in a paper by Peter Geach, 'Assertion'.

Williams was suspicious along similar lines about the idea of an 'imperative inference', a notion central to Hare's whole project. Inferences – the idea of one thought being concluded from another – are easy enough to understand when the sentences involved are simple indicative ones. 'Either it's raining or it's sunny. It's not raining. So it's sunny.' Hare proposed that the same idea could be extended to imperatives. 'Either drink coffee or smoke a cigar. Don't smoke a cigar. Therefore, drink coffee.' Williams could not see that this was an inference in the same sense as the earlier indicative one. For one thing, imperatives aren't always commands: they might be requests or pieces of counsel. And the expectation that orders are to be obeyed can hardly extend to those softer imperatives. It simply isn't true that 'we wish our advice to be taken' in the same way that we expect our commands to be obeyed. As Williams gently put it, 'Don't we leave that to the person we are advising?'[43]

No, what appeared at first blush to be an imperative inference was really better described in other terms. I do not literally address a command to myself: 'Drink coffee!' At most, I might think, 'I should drink coffee' or, 'I shouldn't smoke a cigar.' But sentences with 'shoulds' in them were what Hare, like Ayer before him, had found to be suspect. Williams was joining in a project that Philippa Foot before him had pioneered: the positivists and their predecessors had forced themselves into a dialectical corner, where they found themselves bound to deny the extremely obvious.

So much was Williams at his logical best. In other moods, he showed what he had learnt from Wittgenstein and his acolytes about depth. An opera by the Czech composer Leoš Janácek, *The Makropulos Case*, provoked a tense, troubling article about the human desire for immortality. Could immortality – as distinct from an unusually long life – be anything other than tedious?[44] Language, ordinary or otherwise, was not the main concern: what had to be engaged, as Richard Wollheim, writing in the *Listener* put it, were the reader's 'deepest beliefs and feelings'. In Williams's prose, abstract yet urgent, they were indeed engaged: 'engaged and adjusted under the influence of reason'.[45]

And the ghost of Eduard Fraenkel cropped up every now and then, as when a paper ('Ethical Consistency') that started with a logical puzzle about the nature of logical consistency as applied to ethical judgements took an unexpected turn into Greek tragedy. How, asked Williams, should we understand the position of Agamemnon at Aulis, asked by the goddess to sacrifice his daughter Iphigenia as a condition of a military victory? He is a commander and has a commander's obligations to his cause and his soldiers; he is also a father. Say he obeys the goddess and averts a military catastrophe. He is guilty of no purely logical fault. Would it be simply irrational for him to lie awake at night, thinking of the daughter he killed? If not, then ethical judgements are not straightforwardly like other judgements: the existence of tragic choice is a fact of life, not a puzzle in logic.

*

Herbert Marcuse (b.1898) had a most illustrious academic parentage: he had both Edmund Husserl and Martin Heidegger as his teachers. Being Jewish, he saw soon enough that Heidegger would be no help, and an academic career in the Germany of the 1930s was unlikely to be in the offing. Like many prudent academic Jews in that decade, he emigrated. After a war spent working in American intelligence, he returned to academia in the 1950s: at Columbia, then Harvard, then Brandeis in Massachusetts. In his time at Brandeis, he published a pioneering synthesis of the work of Marx and Freud – *Eros and Civilization*. In the early 1960s, he turned his attention to the task of producing a Freudian–Marxist critique of the industrial society of post-war America. Among the many targets of the 1964 book in which he delivered his conclusions, *One-Dimensional Man*, was Oxford philosophy.

No enemy of analysis in its Freudian or Marxian forms, Marcuse found himself immediately disappointed with the impotence of the Oxford variety: 'The therapeutic treatment of thought remains academic,' he complained.[46] He abhorred its self-denying, self-abasing quality: 'The philosophers themselves proclaim the modesty and inefficacy of philosophy. It leaves the established reality untouched; it abhors transgression.'[47]

Austin and Ryle were picked out for condemnation. Why the 'chumminess of speech', the allergy to 'metaphysics'? The Oxford attitude, Marcuse wrote, 'militates against intelligent non-conformity; it ridicules the egghead'.[48] The language of analysis, he continued, doubtless choosing the chilling adjective with care, was a 'purged' one – purged of radicalism, purged of critique. 'Linguistic analysis abstracts from what ordinary language reveals in speaking as it does – the mutilation of man and nature.'[49]

There was nothing to fault in the 'exactness and clarity' of this philosophy. Yet it was 'destructive of philosophic thought, and of critical thought as such'.[50] Marcuse was appalled at Wittgenstein's suggestion that every sentence in our language 'is in order as it is'. No Marxist could accept that; 'every sentence', he said, 'is as little in order as the world is which this language communicates'.[51]

Some linguistic analysts saw their aims as therapeutic. And so they should be, wrote Marcuse. But in a world where totalitarianism was a real and concrete threat, 'the therapeutic task of philosophy would be a political task'. But linguistic analysis was able to incorporate politics only as one object of analysis among others – the state or the law might be analysed as we analyse 'bachelor' or 'knowledge'. But what if one wanted to take the analysis one step further: why does bachelorhood have the meaning that it does? Why is it that some people are likelier to be counted as knowers than others? To do that was to bring in politics in a quite different way. At its worst, Oxford philosophy was 'an escape into the non-controversial, the unreal, into that which is only academically controversial'.[52]

A few years before Marcuse, in the November of 1957, the Oxford student magazine the *Isis* published an eloquent, well-informed and acerbic broadside about Oxford philosophy that anticipated a surprising number of his objections. The author, Perry Anderson (b. 1928), was an undergraduate at Worcester College. A history student with Marxist commitments, he would graduate the next year to become one of the central intellectual figures of the British New Left and an editor of the *New Left Review*, a journal founded by the Marxist sociologist Stuart Hall (b. 1932). The main lines of critique also anticipated some of those shortly to come in Ernest Gellner's book. Oxford philosophy was rebarbative in its

Englishness, its bourgeois-ness, its imbrication in 'the ideology of the welfare state', its whole social world (public schools, common rooms), but worst of all, its xenophobia (generally manifested in its suspicion of anything coming out of France or Germany).[53]

It was precocious stuff, extremely well written, but also part of a pattern that would soon become familiar. Oxford philosophy was middle class, conventional, cosy; old maids cycling through autumn mists to Holy Communion and Home County hobbit holes full of pipe smoke. Real philosophers were in the *épater les bourgeois* business; they wrote to shock the middle classes, and conventionality was the enemy. Real philosophers, in other words, were French at heart.[54]

It was Williams who took to the letters pages of the *Isis* to salvage something of the honour of Oxford philosophy.[55] In a way, he was uniquely well positioned to do it; in another, he could only do it out of loyalty. On most points, his own interests and emerging vision of the subject were much closer to Anderson's, his critiques of Austin sharing something of Marcuse's sense that something important and deep was being left out. A person of wide-ranging interests in philosophy, music and public life, he was, even at that age, clearly bound for a career quite different from that of his tutors. Not for him the years spent at one college, fighting the good fight on the wine committee and making witty speeches at the annual boat club dinner. He was attracted to a more Continental vision of the academic life, where the life of the philosopher had room in it for a passionate interest in modernist opera and political activism (albeit of the social democratic rather than revolutionary Marxist sort).

Still, Williams put up a defence of his colleagues: yes, 'some academic philosophers are smug', he admitted, '(particularly in England, where smugness is the peculiar corruption of the national virtue)' but this showed 'little about their type of philosophy as such. *Every* philosophy has its hollow men; only, the more obscure the philosophy, the harder it is to tell which they are.'[56]

Anderson, he said, seemed to have a number of distinct targets. Smugness (all could agree this was bad); academicism (this was less clear: Austin and Hegel were after all both university professors); Englishness (this was hardly a vice in itself). In the background of Anderson's criticism was a picture, basically Marxist in inspiration, of what kinds of philosophy were worth reading. And when Marx had spoken of the 'poverty of philosophy', what he was attacking – as Williams put it – was 'philosophy ... whose *first* aim is to understand the world rather than to change it'. Oxford philosophy, it is quite true, did hold to that view. As such, it rejected a crucial tenet of the Marxist worldview. But in retaining that unMarxist commitment, it too was an enemy of smugness in its own way. The whole point of a close attention to words was surely that our words were not innocent, that they came with presuppositions and histories attached. And the idea that one must understand the world as a *condition* of changing it is itself a tenet of political responsibility: what could be smugger than the idea that one knows the world well enough to set about changing it with revolutionary violence?

That was where the anti-smugness of the Oxford philosophers put them at odds with the Marxist enemies of smugness. Oxford philosophy, Williams said loyally, was just as opposed to the smugness of 'the revolutionary ideologue, the justified sinner, assured of history on his side'. There was, quite rightly, no room in Oxford philosophy for the mere smugness of hatred, the feeling that 'as long as the springs of indignation freely bubble, I am all right, a free man, assured arbiter of whether what I say is true or false, coherent or incoherent, sense or nonsense'.[57]

These were fighting words, but to most of Anderson's actual criticisms they had little relevance. Anderson's reply to Williams made this amply clear. The linguistic philosophy of the fifties, he said (this was not long after the British humiliation at Suez in 1956), was the product of a risible class, one 'which has won a provisional victory at home, but faces complete defeat abroad'. No doubt important discoveries were being made at Oxford; but in Paris and Frankfurt, and indeed Moscow and Beijing, those philosophers – Ryle, Austin, Hare – were being seen 'from a superior point of reference. Marx understands Austin who understands words.'[58] What did Williams really make of the fact that one could take a philosophy degree without having been required 'to read a line of: Plato, Aquinas, Spinoza, Pascal, Leibniz, Comte, Hegel, Schelling, Fichte, Schopenhauer, Marx, Nietzsche and Kierkegaard, among others?' And finally, a little dig at Gilbert Ryle, whom Anderson had gone to hear on the subject of 'Forgetting the Difference between Right and Wrong'.

> After the talk he was asked by someone: 'Do you think Nietzsche's book *Beyond Good and Evil* contains a logical fallacy within the title? Or do you think you can discard the difference, while still remembering it?' He puffed on his pipe in one of those inimitable ways they cultivate here, and said: 'Never read the book. Of course, I expect Nietzsche just wanted a good title for it.' Funny? These are the people who are supposed to be teaching philosophy, not learning it. And with this sort of porcine insensitivity and ignorance, their activity comes very near impertinence.[59]

Williams didn't reply, and there was nothing for a loyal defender to say to these things beyond: yes, these things are true. And – but? – so are the following: that there is no *defence* for ignorance and porcine insensitivity, except those things can be, unwittingly, agents of intellectual emancipation from the weight of tradition.[60] It was perhaps a shame that Oxford undergraduates weren't required to read the philosophers Anderson named. But how much of a shame it was depended on the value of what they were reading instead and, more generally, what they were doing other than reading.

And here, something further was called for. No canon could

ever satisfy everybody. Could one be sure that a syllabus that met the Marxist's requirements would not fall short of someone else's?[61] Anderson's call was not simply one to 'diversify' a narrow homogeneous curriculum. He was presenting a particular ideologically inspired picture of what a philosophy course should look like as a simple demand of intellectual responsibility. Of course, he would have said that the fact that Oxford philosophy, invested in a naïve picture of itself as ideologically neutral, was no less ideological. It could only sustain that image of itself because the unreflective conservative liberalism of the bourgeois is the ideology that dares not speak its name. Or thus Marxists have always claimed. But whether that criticism should be accepted was, and remains, an entirely open question.[62]

*

Some critics of Oxford philosophy – Ernest Gellner, Perry Anderson and Herbert Marcuse among them – wrote in anger. But their discontents were felt by others too, and would be expressed in a different emotional register. In fact, it happens every year at the beginning of the autumn: a long sigh of disappointment rises from undergraduates across the land. Wooed to philosophy by the promise of long smoky inquiries into the good, the true and the beautiful, they find themselves confronted instead by truth tables and the ugly symbols of the predicate calculus. Some learn to cope with the absence of 'the meaning of life' on the syllabus, and the presence instead of 'The Meaning of Meaning' – though the disappointment lingers. Others consider dropping out and suing for false advertising.

Gillian Rose (b.1947) was one such student: in later life, she would ignore the conventional divisions between philosophy and theology. Arriving at St Hilda's College 'in love with Socrates', she found that she had instead to settle for Jean Austin. Rose's memoirs of her time there contain an unforgettable – and unfair

– portrait of her teacher, by then several years into her widowhood and deeply invested in protecting her late husband's philosophical legacy. She had, Rose writes, an 'aura of tense dejection, chain-smoking with shaky hands, her nails stained orange with nicotine'. She would herd her first-year students into her sitting room with a view of the Isis and the Oxford Botanical Gardens. 'Remember, girls, all the philosophers you will read are much more intelligent than you are' – that was one of her precepts. Another was, 'You do understand, philosophy has absolutely no use at all.' Without her more catholic interests to keep up morale, Rose said, that experience of philosophy 'would have induced a life-long alienation from it'.[63]

That, at any rate, is one view of the matter. Another view is this: a woman of no small talent, with four small children to bring up alone, acquired a smoking habit. Finding her students altogether too quick to dismiss the philosophers they read as stupid, she enjoins humility and generosity: read them charitably, don't overestimate your own ability to refute what you're only beginning to understand. Finding her students seduced by inflated conceptions of the rewards of philosophy, she made sure to remind them that it might be a mistake to look for utilitarian justifications of philosophy, and irresponsible to make promises on its behalf that may be impossible to keep (for instance, that it will make you happier, wiser, more virtuous). That is, as I say, another possible view of the matter.

Oxford philosophy, Rose complained elsewhere, teaches young people 'to be clever, destructive, supercilious and ignorant. It doesn't teach you what's important. It doesn't feed the soul.'[64] And here, she may have been on to something. The case for the defence is not helped by the existence of those who cheerfully plead guilty to all charges. Colin McGinn (b.1950), who studied for the BPhil a few years after Rose graduated, found the atmosphere of Oxford philosophy 'intimidating and thrilling at the same time'. But it seems to have pleased him, on the whole, to find that philosophical debate was not 'the sonorous recitation of vague profundities but a clashing of analytically honed intellects, with pulsing egos attached to them'. And McGinn, for one, thought it none the worse for these features.[65] Given how he sets up the choice – between vague profundities and macho posturing – one might well come out on the side of the chest-thumpers: an honest fight has its own integrity. It was brutal, but at least it wasn't bogus.

Yet to say only so much is to give faint praise. There is another way to respond to the charge that Oxford philosophy had nothing in it to 'feed the soul'. This is to say that Rose could speak only for herself. Other people have been through the same apprenticeship and come out of it feeling differently, and not because they embraced the cult of cleverness, ignorance and disdain.

*

The best witness for the defence is Stanley Cavell (b.1926), an American philosopher of great range and humanity, who could not be further from the butch style represented by McGinn. Cavell encountered J. L. Austin in 1955 when he was giving the William James lecture at Harvard, where he unveiled his evolving theory of 'speech acts' to an audience outside Oxford – later to be published as *How to Do Things with Words*.[66]

The lectures were part of a project that had been implicit in much of what Austin had been saying for some time. The central idea in them was a simple one: saying is a kind of doing. This is true in two ways, both obvious, though one is more obvious than the other. One can of course do things – specifically, make things happen – with one's words. I tell you to open the window; you do; the window is now open. I have, as it were, opened the window with mere words.[67]

There is also a subtler way in which one does things with words. 'I promise you I'll return the money,' I tell you, thereby bringing two new things into the world: an obligation and a right. I have an obligation to give you the money, you a right to have it back. 'I do,' I say in church, and thereby transform myself into a married man. 'I hereby name this ship …' and *voilà* – the ship now has a name it didn't have a moment ago. Promising, marrying, naming – and for that matter, betting, warning, informing, consenting – are all things we do *in* saying something. The saying 'I promise' and the promising aren't two separate things; they are one and the same thing. There is, as Hume had once noted, a sort of magic in that.[68]

Some readers of Austin haven't seen the magic and found Austin's point to be banal: well, of course we sometimes do things with words.[69] But the significance of the point lay in its rejoinder to a style of philosophy that treated language as primarily in the business of doing one thing: describing. Of course, some language describes. But describing is only one of the things we do with our words. That means that the standards by which we assess our uses of words can't only be the ones appropriate to description. Our descriptions can be true or false. But can an order be true or false? Try it: 'It is true that open the door?' A request? And what about a warning? 'The bull is about to charge' can, of course, be true or false. But those words aren't always a warning – say, if I'm safely behind high walls, or if I'm watching a matador on television. But sometimes they do express a warning, and when they do, it's not enough to assess them simply as true or false. Warnings can be assessed in other ways: some are unnecessary or superfluous, and they may or may not be heeded.

The obviousness of the central thesis, once pointed out, didn't stop the lectures being the inauguration of an exciting new project. The project of the philosophy of language, at the heart of the 'analytic' tradition since its founding with Frege, was to understand language in relation to such notions as meaning, reference and truth. But many things can be true but in some other way suspect. 'A. J. Ayer does not beat his children.' 'A. J. Ayer is either a philosopher or a highwayman.' 'The present king of France is not bald.' A good case can be made that these sentences are all true. But aren't there other complaints one might have against someone who asserted them? By the same token, consider the following questions. What if I say the wrong name while reciting my wedding vows? If someone not an ordained minister performs a marriage ceremony? Or if a dubious character picks up a bottle and 'names' the ship the *Generalissimo Stalin*?

Austin was, at the least, opening up the field to a more diverse range of inquiries: into the many 'misfires' and 'abuses' of language that cannot be understood simply in terms of falsehood. The philosophy of language turns out to be part of the philosophy of action. And though he did little to make this fact explicit, it means that the philosophy of language was at once aesthetics, ethics and politics. Like the positivists, Austin saw that it was an interesting question to ask what ethics *did*. But why does the fact that ethical sentences express emotion and function as devices of persuasion mean that they can't also be *true*?

In the style of other works of the period, Austin didn't only report on his 'results': he dramatised the process by which he reached them. The lectures began with a dummy distinction: between two kinds of statement or 'locution' that he called 'constatives' and 'performatives'. But in the course of the lectures, the initial distinction started to look flimsier and flimsier. Are there really things we say that don't involve our doing anything at all? And can't we do some things just by stating something? 'There is a bull in that field': in one context, those words would be no more than a neutral description of the scenery. In another, it would be an urgent warning. From which it follows that there cannot be anything simply *in the words themselves* that allows us to tell a 'constative' apart from a 'performative'.[70]

If he had done nothing else while at Harvard, Austin's trip would have been consequential indeed for the immediate future of the discipline. But he also laid the foundations for a different set of influences on the direction of philosophy at another, less formal venue. While at Harvard, he offered – as the terms of the William James bequest required – a graduate seminar on the somewhat unpromising topic of 'Excuses'. No doubt some people laughed derisively: so that's what the great Austin had come all the way from Oxford to sell them. Others were intrigued. 'We saw before us', wrote George Pitcher (b.1925), then also a graduate student at Harvard, 'the possibility of adventure.'[71]

The room in Emerson Hall, far too tiny given the speaker's intellectual stature, was packed. Austin appeared, his usual blue suit not in the best of wear. To some he evoked their idea of a family lawyer, trustworthy but underpaid.[72] Or perhaps he was more like a Latin teacher at a well-regarded boys' school: very sound on grammar, but inclined to expect far too much from the boys, who'd much rather be playing rugby than reciting their conjugations. The voice was measured, eerily calm; every syllable was articulated, the delivery surprisingly pleasant. There was no further striving after effect.

Austin announced, without excitement, that he would be putting into practice some of his general views on how progress might be made in philosophy: they would be looking closely at some features of ordinary language, in particular the part of language that consisted in giving and receiving excuses. If they liked their philosophy to come with abstract nouns, they were free to think of themselves as engaged in an inquiry into 'the philosophy of extenuation'. Some of this, he promised, would be philosophically rewarding. It might even, he added implausibly, afford them some fun: 'the fun of discovery, the pleasures of co-operation, and the satisfaction of reaching agreement'.[73] So much the audience had probably heard from the transatlantic academic grapevine. Indeed, so far, so tame.

Then came the general picture: when do we usually give excuses, and what are they? Typically, when we're accused. Of what? Well, doing something bad, or wrong, or inept, or unwelcome or in some other way 'untoward'.[74] We're expected to defend ourselves. How do we do that? Sometimes we admit the fact: yes, I did what I am accused of, but what of it? In the circumstances, who wouldn't? That is to say, we *justify* ourselves. At other times, we protest: yes, I suppose there's a sense in which I did that. But it wasn't really *me* who did it (I was nudged, threatened, misled!). Or perhaps, I didn't really *do* that (it was an accident, a slip!). Or perhaps I didn't do *just* that (I was trying to do something else, and this just happened!). No more need be said about justifications: philosophers had been all over that for a while now. Excuses, on the other hand, even if they raised exactly the same questions from a new angle, seemed virgin territory.

Austin liked to begin with what looked like a case of linguistic superfluity: a distinction without a difference. Is there a difference between doing something 'attentively' and 'doing it with care'? No, the Harvard students would say. Well, then, consider this: an old man is driving his car, very slowly, his eyes locked onto the street. But he's driving right in the middle of the road, and other motorists are swerving to avoid him. Surely he's driving attentively, but hardly with care; we can pay attention at the right time without paying attention to the right things. What about the difference between an intention and a purpose? No difference, one was tempted to say. Why then would it sound strange if a girl's father were to ask her suitor, 'Young man, what are your purposes?' rather than, as he surely should, 'What, young man, are your intentions?'

Then there were sudden flashes of linguistic insight: when can we excuse our behaviour by appealing to 'force of habit'? Only, Austin proposed, when the habit is not in itself particularly objectionable. A smoker is forgiven for lighting up in a non-smoking carriage 'by force of habit' (this was the fifties, after all). A killer on a rampage? Less so. Sometimes, the examples came from the law courts – in Oxford, he had been cultivating the company of Herbert Hart, who had returned to academia after many years as a successful Chancery barrister in London, well stocked with legal examples of just the kind to intrigue Austin. But Austin was never one to defer to anything, not even something as congenial to his tastes as the English common law.

Suppose a man is found hacking away at a pile of logs under the bedclothes, wrongly believing it to be his enemy in the bed. The courts would not, he said, deem this attempted murder. But surely it is: he is attempting to murder his enemy. Sometimes, the example felt like the plot of an unwritten and somewhat trashy novel: Jones is preparing for a long march through the desert. One of his enemies poisons his water flask. Another, knowing nothing of the poisoning, drains its contents. Jones dies of thirst on the walk. Who killed Jones?

Then there were adverbs, indispensable when giving excuses. 'I did it involuntarily,' we sometimes say – referring perhaps to a twitch, or a case of the fidgets. But this tends to encourage the unfortunate notion that all actions can be either voluntary or involuntary. But then what is a yawn? (Try both: 'I yawned voluntarily'; 'I yawned involuntarily.' And finally, there was the immortal parable of the two donkeys. 'I did it by mistake'; 'I did it by accident.' Surely synonymous? Never. Consider this:

You have a donkey, so have I, and they graze in the same field. The day comes when I conceive a dislike for mine. I go to shoot it, draw a bead on it, fire: the brute falls in its tracks. I inspect the victim, and find to my horror that it is *your* donkey. I appear on your doorstep with the remains and say – what? 'I say, old sport, I'm awfully sorry, etc., I've shot your donkey *by accident*'? Or '*by mistake*'? Then again, I go to shoot my donkey as before, draw a bead on it, fire – but as I do so, the beasts move, and to my horror yours falls. Again the scene on the doorstep – what do I say? 'By mistake'? Or 'by accident'?[75]

There was the necessary moment of silence while the students thought through the two cases, with Austin's old question ('what should we say when … ?') hanging over them. And there it was, unmistakeable, virtually an epiphany. How could they *ever* have thought the phrases interchangeable? And onward went the Harvard soldiers: 'deliberately', 'intentionally', 'on purpose'? What about 'recklessly', 'heedlessly', 'thoughtlessly'? And 'absent-mindedly', 'inadvertently', 'unwittingly'? No one was so reckless as to assume those distinctions were there for no reason. Suddenly, the atmosphere changed. They could join in too. They became, George Pitcher later recalled, 'like children at a party'.[76] Hands were raised, more examples proposed, differences denied and exposed, distinctions made and unmade.

What got them going was the fun of it. What kept them at it was the gradual dawning of the point of it all. What they were investigating, Pitcher said, 'was far from trivial, for it was nothing less, at bottom, than the concept of human action itself'.[77] And behind the mayhem, was a method, and one methodical man making sure that progress was being made. Of course, Austin would not have claimed to be proposing anything so grand as a theory of human action. He was quite content to describe their immediate task as being that of listing 'the kinds of fool you make of yourself'.[78]

'The material,' Stanley Cavell wrote later, 'together with the procedures inspiring them … knocked me off my horse'. Writing a few years after Austin's death, Cavell cautioned readers of his posthumous publications against 'too hasty or simple a description' of Austin's methods. What his methods were: that was itself a philosophical problem, 'as outstanding a philosophical problem as any to be ventured from within those procedures'. Austin didn't himself seem to treat his methods as intrinsically deep: in his compulsively English way, he was allergic to anything that smacked of an attempt at profundity. 'The rapture of the deep' was the great enemy of good philosophy. When he did give himself a grand-sounding label – 'linguistic phenomenology' – he was positively chagrined: 'that is rather a mouthful'.[79]

But Cavell felt no need to defer to Austin's own modest claims for himself, or even to his occasional hints that his style of philosophy was no more than descriptive linguistics done in the slightly amateur manner of a science in its infancy. For one thing, Austin was rarely interested in self-analysis: his few concessions to his listeners' demands for a 'methodological statement' consisted in some homespun bits of advice, which is rather different. The context for such advice was also, frequently, polemical: there was always some positivist or Cartesian or existentialist to be put in his place, and the demands of one-upmanship hardly encouraged candid self-assessment.

Cavell proposed three things that distinguished what Austin was doing from common or garden descriptive linguistics. First, what Austin encouraged was a sensitivity that consisted as much in being attentive to words as in being attentive to the world. Secondly, he was never satisfied with a mere description of what people say; he looked for an answer to the question of *why* they said what they said (why is a mistake not always an accident and an accident not always a mistake?). And finally, there was a way of applying Austin's method where one could safely, and unguiltily, ignore anything anybody else said: one could ask the question simply of oneself, 'What should *I* say when … ?' What was I asking? Was I trying to characterise my linguistic habits? Or my linguistic morals? Or something else, for which there may be no more explicit word than the delightfully ambiguous 'should'?

The 'tracing of the shudder of an exquisite distinction', Bernard Williams once called it. As Cavell painted it, Austin's 'linguistic phenomenology' was done with two aims, one destructive and one constructive. The destructive aim was to rid philosophy of its stupid distinctions, when there were better ones to hand. The constructive aim was to improve our perception, and as such, not a long way off the comparisons made by a discerning art critic.

'In this crosslight', Cavell said, 'the capacities and salience of an individual object in question are brought to attention and focus.' The distinction between 'mistake' and 'accident' is a distinction between ways in which actions can go awry; between 'sure' and 'certain' ways in which mind can relate to world; between 'I believe' and 'I know' ways in which we express our limits, and our responsibilities to each other.

Austin's methods seemed to Cavell of profound – and profoundly moral – significance, in the sense they exuded of 'the human voice ... being returned to moral assessments of itself'.[80] Even while the parable of the donkey had nothing to say of the *morality* of shooting an innocent donkey, the amorality of its presentation concealed a deeper concern with the concepts basic to any morality. The human voice, as Cavell conceived it, was not just that of the philosopher, but the voice of all humanity in its native tongue. To understand 'ordinary language' was to understand ourselves, and everything about ourselves that is manifested in our use of language, including our morals.

Austin's language was English, and some of his distinctions were untranslatable. But the *activity* itself could in principle be done anywhere and by anyone: no doubt different distinctions would be unearthed in French and Swahili and Mandarin.[81] But the real point wasn't the particular distinctions so much as the attention, and attentiveness, it engendered to what we were saying.

Austin's Englishness was the only way he had of being; but it was also, Cavell suggested, a mask, all the more effective for being identical with his face. He was, in a sense, pulling off the ultimate pretence: not of being an English professor (because he *was*, after all, English and a professor) but – to draw a subtle linguistic distinction he would have relished – of being *merely* an English professor. That made the novelty of his proposals hard to recognise; one did not expect novelty from such a man, with that bank manager's face, in that crumpled blue suit.

The traditional mask of the Knower, Nietzsche had notoriously said, was that of the sage and the ascetic. Wittgenstein, with his aphorisms and his deckchairs and his hard single bed, played up to the stereotype. Austin, by contrast, sought new ones: the Englishness of his pose 'made it unnoticeable as a pose'. He sought, from his audience, 'patience and co-operation, not depth and upheaval'. All this made it all too easy to adopt the cynical tones of Ernest Gellner. Austin could be dismissed as a creature of the tutorial system, the senior common room, the Greats degree, of the mock Tudor cottage in the provincial suburb. But what of that? That was, Cavell said, no more than an exposure of the 'conditions ... within which this work was produced or initiated'. It wasn't by itself an exposé, an unmasking, of a kind that casts doubt on the thing exposed.

Why should the bourgeois decorum that surrounded the Austinian project settle the question of its value? 'To touch the question of its value, the value of those conventions themselves, as they enter the texture of the work, would have to be established.'[82] For those who sought radicalism, Cavell proposed, Austin had more to offer than was evident at first blush. What was essential to his project was the ideal of careful attentiveness to the sound of the human voice; as the lectures at Harvard had shown, it was not just an interest in language as an inert phenomenon of description, but an interest in language as a vehicle of human agency. We do things with words. And so, the traditional concepts of philosophy, denoted by such words as 'knowledge', 'reality', 'justice', 'beauty', are not labels tacked onto bits of the world. They are among a set of tools we use for conducting ourselves within the world. The question 'what is knowledge?' was transmuted by Austin into a different question: What am I doing when I claim to know something? How is it different from what I do when I only claim to believe it? In more abstract terms, then, what is the relationship between what I claim to know and what I am willing to take responsibility for?

Is it really hard to believe that so demanding a philosophy

could have been produced in such homely, such cosy conditions, rather than on a picket line, or a smoky Left Bank café in occupied Paris? Didn't even La Rochefoucauld himself – that provocateur-moralist of seventeenth-century France – manage, despite his outrageous remarks, to get himself repeat invitations to polite salons run by respectable society ladies? Perhaps that tells us less about his aphorisms, and more about the inattention of his fellow saloniers. On this view of Austin, even a philosophy with a focus on language turned out to be a humanistic project through and through. Language, as Austin conceived of it, was action, an exercise of human agency, and an occasion for the taking of responsibility. The philosophy of language, far from being a technical, technocratic exercise to be left to people with a talent for the manipulation of symbols, had been transformed into another way of reflecting on the human condition itself.

No one whose chief complaint with linguistic philosophy is its supposed anti-scientific philistinism or essentially bourgeois character will be much persuaded by this sort of thing, but it never was meant for their ears. Cavell, a bourgeois and unrepentant humanist, was speaking to a different constituency, with other concerns: for those disappointed in the failure of something calling itself 'philosophy' to provide a 'philosophy of life'. In Cavell, it all came down to a single word in a single phrase of Austin's: 'What should we say when … ?' 'Should' is ambiguous, but that's the point: does Austin mean 'ought to'? Or just 'would'? Or something else altogether, reducible to neither? To every one of the traditional questions of philosophy bequeathed him, Austin's skill was in devising examples about which he could then ask: what should we say now? Sometimes, we know what we should say, but not why we should say it. Sometimes, we don't even know what we should say: words fail us.

The question of what we *would*, as a matter of fact, say, is not a simple matter of empirical investigation. Once we come down to it, when the example is devised with sufficient imagination, the question of what we would say is simply another way of turning our minds to the question of what we *ought* to say, and to the question of when our words simply fail us and we need new ones.

Austin, Cavell suspected, really was inimitable; and subsequent history has so far borne him out: no one has in fact succeeded in imitating him. For a time, it was suspected that this was because no one thought so nondescript a character, and so unremarkable an achievement, worth emulating. Wittgenstein had his imitators: young men from across the oceans, born decades after he died, have been observed clutching their skulls in poses of agony, combing the vintage shops for open-necked shirts in just the right 1940s style, and cultivating the slightest hint of a Viennese cadence.

No one, by contrast, has found much inspiration in Austin's 'liking for sound preparation and [his] disapproval for sloppy work and lazy efforts'. In a way, he died with his life's work incomplete; in another, he didn't. As Cavell put it, 'In example and precept, his work is complete, in a measure hard to imagine matched. I do not see that it is anywhere being followed with the completeness it describes and exemplifies.'[83]

He had wanted a *phrontisterion*, a crack team of linguistic investigators to be led, naturally, by him.[84] (Is it to be doubted, his great acolyte Geoffrey Warnock asked, 'that he would have done such work extraordinarily well?')[85] For a time, he considered accepting an offer of a professorship from the University of Berkeley. America was so large, so populous, so open to immigrants and their novelties, its students so guileless and without pretence that one could, for once, let down one's guard without fear that some googly-bowler of a colleague would see that as a chance to make his long-planned attack. Oxford, with its eight-week terms and ossified syllabi, made brisk reform next to impossible, even for so assured an administrative hand. But what might not be possible under the blue skies of California?

He returned to England having resolved not to accept the job:

he was not the sort to confide in colleagues, and we may never know what decided the matter. Over the next few years, others remarked that he looked somewhat worn, but he was not the sort of person one asked about his health. When he died, of cancer, it came as a surprise to those who thought they knew him well. What were they to do on Saturday mornings now?

Austin had lived long enough to acquire a kind of immortality. For decades afterwards, the intellectual consciences of an entire generation of philosophers spoke in his voice, reading their latest sloppy sentence back to them in that famous voice: 'dry and slow, very clear and with all edges, as it were, very sharply defined'.[86] In moments of forgetfulness, heads would turn at some imprudent remark to see how Austin was reacting, then turn back sheepishly, their owners reconciled to having to make up their own mind for a change. 'It was his opinion', said Warnock, 'that one instinctively waited to hear. His, one might almost say, were the standards that had to be satisfied.'[87] There was life, of a kind, in Oxford philosophy after he died. But it might be better to say that it was another Oxford, and another philosophy – in some ways better and freer, because less harried, in some ways worse, because sloppier – without him.

10

Ghosts

The life and death of J. L. Austin coincided with the rise and fall of the thing variously called 'Oxford philosophy', 'linguistic philosophy' and 'ordinary language philosophy'. There was still philosophy at Oxford after Austin; some of it was about language, and much of it drew on the resources of ordinary language in one way or another. But there was no keeping up the pretence of unity any more – not, of course, that there had ever much been pretending. Yet, the question remains: what should we make of this much-maligned tradition today? There is no need for a single, final judgement. I prefer to ask the question that the Italian philosopher Benedetto Croce once asked in a different connection: what is living and what is dead of Oxford philosophy? I don't mean simply to ask what vestiges of the 1950s have survived and made it to a new age. I mean to ask if there was ever anything *vital* in the 1950s way of doing philosophy. In other words, is there anything from that era that *deserved* to survive?

I have already identified, over the last few chapters, a few things that are dead and should not be resurrected. The first of these is the over-ambitious scope of the aspiration for dissolving philosophical problems by the simple device of showing them to arise from the misuse of language. We know now that there are simply too many questions that will not yield to such methods. That does not tell us the methods are no good. But they do tell us that no one had any business restricting philosophy to those methods alone.

Problems can be soluble without being dissoluble; it's just that solving them takes more work, and work of a different and more 'theoretical' kind. Why shouldn't our many piecemeal observations about meaning or goodness or justice hang together in something like a theoretical structure? And if they do, what dishonour in seeking such a theory? Michael Dummett, one of the philosophers to begin his career during the post-linguistic 'thaw', once remarked, 'Philosophy would interest me much less if I did not think it possible for us eventually to attain generally agreed answers to the great metaphysical questions.'[1] In his earliest youth, he might have been laughed at by no less than A. J. Ayer for such a remark. By the time he wrote those words, he was occupying the very Chair in Logic that had once been Ayer's.

The second dead feature of some Oxford philosophy is its paranoid preoccupation with the avoidance of nonsense, as defined according to strictures that disallowed far too much that patently *did* make sense. Even Gilbert Ryle came to the view that the old 'Viennese dichotomy "Either Science or Nonsense" had too few "ors" in it'.[2] Philosophy since the 1960s has learnt that some kinds of metaphysics may belong within the realm of sense. It may be that we are still learning just how many 'ors' there are.

The third dead feature of Oxford philosophy is its entanglement with the least appealing features of its place of origin: the suspicion of the foreign and the exotic. In its most obviously rebarbative form, this suspicion manifested itself as simple intellectual xenophobia. In its most rarefied articulations, that suspicion was directed towards the aspiration to depth itself – for which J. L. Austin pointedly used a French phrase, *ivresse des grandes profondeurs*. That aspiration was seen not simply as risky and vulnerable to humiliating failure but as somehow compromised from the start, a sort of affectation. But the rapture of the deep is a real phenomenon; the fact that some people mistakenly fancy that they are feeling it while wading in the shallows is not in itself a point against it. If my story is right, then the fear of depth produced a culpable failure to appreciate what was deep in the Oxford tradition itself.

The fourth dead feature of the Oxford tradition is the strain in it of (especially linguistic) conservatism. The resistance to jargon was capable, when embodied by talented stylists, of producing writing of great elegance and accessibility. In the hands of the less able, it conveyed only the misleading impression that ordinary words, unimaginatively deployed, would suffice to articulate all truths of importance. Iris Murdoch's dictum – 'Ordinary language is not a philosopher' – should have been taken more fully to heart by her targets, along with Williams's reminder to the conservative anxious to preserve old things that 'the old is only what used to be new'.[3]

So much, then, is dead. Is there much point prodding the corpse for signs of life? We might turn to Iris Murdoch again for help. As part of her quixotic attempt to get her anti-Cartesian genera- tion of philosophers to look again at the notion of the 'inner life', she devised what may be her most famous philosophical parable. A certain woman, call her 'M', dislikes her daughter-in-law, 'D'. Good-hearted though the younger woman is, D is 'inclined to be pert and familiar, insufficiently ceremonious, brusque, sometimes positively rude, always tiresomely juvenile. M does not like D's accent or the way D dresses. M feels that her son has married beneath him.' Her poor son, she keeps telling herself, 'has married a silly vulgar girl'.

But that isn't the end of the story. M is reflective and self-criti- cal. Perhaps, she wonders, her judgements of her daughter-in-law come of prejudice, snobbery and maternal jealousy. 'Let me look again.' When she does, she finds that other epithets are available to describe D. She finds that D may be 'not vulgar but refresh- ingly simple, not undignified but spontaneous, not noisy but gay, not tiresomely juvenile but delightfully youthful'. Is M deluding herself? Perhaps. But the example is fictional and we are free to imagine the case as one where M is not so much deluded as 'moved by love or justice'.[4]

What is still living in Oxford philosophy, I asked. We cannot begin to answer that question until we, like M, are willing to ask the question in that spirit. My question is not what defences of Oxford philosophy are available, but rather, what would be a just, a loving, view of it? I am not just inviting us, boringly, to see the good in all things. I am, rather, raising the question, in all earnestness, of whether the charitable picture might not in fact be the true one.

*

In 1960, the year of Austin's death, R. M. Hare published an essay based on a lecture that he had given at various German universities in the late 1950s. The lecture had been titled 'The Study of Philosophy in Great Britain'. The published version was titled, significantly, 'A School for Philosophers'. Hare made it clear that he wrote advisedly: 'for' and not 'of'. The idea that there was an Oxford school *of* philosophy was the unfortunate effect of seeing what was done at Oxford through a lens that only made sense in Germany. There was no Oxford school of thought; no one at Oxford wanted there to be.

Hare set out the features of Oxford philosophy to his German audiences. First, he said, Oxford philosophers saw themselves primarily as teachers, not as writers. With secure jobs from which only the most grotesque wickedness could get them sacked, they didn't need to write (or 'publish') unless they felt they had something to say. 'In some other places the staff are in danger of spoiling their chances of promotion, or even further employment, unless they keep up a constant output of published writing.'[5] Well, Oxford was not like that. (This is no longer true.)

The one thing an Oxford philosopher couldn't get away with was a neglect of teaching. How much of it there was, and how intense! There was no question of an Oxford philosopher doing to a student what Husserl was once rumoured to have done

– 'produced about six bound volumes and said: "Here are my books; come back in a year's time."'[6] Instead, the Oxford philosopher would spend his days giving 'tutorials' to students the majority of whom had no intention of becoming academics, but were rather likely to be 'businessmen, politicians, schoolmasters, clergymen, lawyers, journalists, civil servants, and, indeed, almost anything but philosophers'.[7]

Once a week, these students would go their tutors, sometimes alone and sometimes with another student, for what they would probably call a 'tute'. They would have been told to read a few books or articles and to write an essay answering a question the tutor had previously set. The tutorial would typically begin with one of the students reading the essay out. The rest of the hour would be spent discussing the essay. The tutor's week consisted mostly of this activity, about ten to twenty hours of it.

How did this system of teaching affect the student? By most accounts, profoundly. Everything in an essay would be subjected to the critique of a 'highly skilled and usually merciless critic, not only in respect of its truth, but also in respect of relevance, accuracy, significance and clarity'.[8] Ambiguity, vagueness, pretentiousness: all such sins would be exposed. There was no question of the tutors expecting their students to parrot their own views back to them. If they did, those views would be subjected to the same withering critique. The point was not to tell them what to think, but how. The student had to learn 'to express his thought clearly to himself and to others; to make distinctions where there are distinctions to be made, and thus avoid unnecessary confusion – and not to use long words (or short ones) without being able to explain what they mean'.[9] In all this, style was as highly esteemed as argumentative substance. Style, 'in the sense of an effective, unambiguous, clear and ordered expression of one's thought, which cannot be achieved unless the thought itself has the same qualities'.[10]

The tutor too was deeply marked by these encounters. For one thing, the tutor had to *embody* – rather than simply preach – the principles enjoined on the students. Week after week, problem after problem would have to be stated and raised from first principles. There was no question of the Oxford philosopher taking delight in the construction of 'imposing edifices'. At no point could he stop asking himself the question, 'How can philosophy begin?' How to avoid it, when every day he had to get people to philosophise, young people who had never done it before?[11]

In conversations with colleagues, too, the same principles applied. It was not as it was in Germany: a paper, followed by a speech from the floor, and another speech, and another, with some kind of formal reply by the speaker. 'There has seldom, in my experience, been any dialogue or argument – just a succession of different views, none of which, not even the principal speaker's, is subjected to any elenchus.'[12] *Elenchus* was of course the term used to describe the methods of Socrates, as depicted in the dialogues of Plato: short, punchy interrogations that aim to clarify positions, pose objections and expose inconsistencies. At Oxford, Hare said, 'Speeches of more than a few sentences are rare; if anybody says more than about five sentences in succession, people begin to look embarrassed.'[13] It was like a game, not in the sense that it was frivolous, but in that the rules were well understood by all the players.

The whole point of the philosopher's training, from the structure of the undergraduate tutorial onwards, was to 'teach us to put our theses in a form in which they can be submitted to this test. Ambiguities and evasions and rhetoric, however uplifting, are regarded as the mark of a philosopher who has not learnt his craft; we prefer professional competence to a superficial brilliance.'[14] Did that not rob philosophy of its mystique? Well, quite. Philosophers at Oxford didn't have 'philosophies' that they declaimed to each other, having already assumed that agreement was out of the question. (Nothing quite riled the Oxford philosopher like the innocent question, 'What's your philosophy?') On the contrary: while they disagreed, they did so on the assumption that agreement was in principle possible, and if not agreement, then at least mutual understanding. What, then, was this thing called 'Oxford philosophy'? What did Oxford philosophers all have in common? Hare proposed this answer: 'what we share are not tenets but standards (which we may or may not live up to, but go on trying); Oxford, that is to say, is not so much a school of philosophy as a school for philosophers'.[15]

If Hare was right, then the question of whether Oxford philosophy died in 1960 is not a matter of whether faith in certain tenets survived Austin. It is rather a matter of whether a style and an aspiration survived the man who had most influentially embodied them, and there, the answer can only be that they did. No lover of Murdoch or the inner life, Hare nevertheless pointed the way to a loving reappraisal of the Oxford tradition.

*

J. L. Austin inspired several philosophical projects whose enthusiasts regarded him as their St Peter. There were of course the therapeutic Austinians, who saw him – as Stanley Cavell had done – as no less concerned with the salvation of our souls than Wittgenstein had been.[16] The attention to ordinary language had been a kind of spiritual exercise, an attempt at self-knowledge. Then there were those, mostly at American universities, who saw him as a proto-linguist whose speculations could now be turned into rigorous theories. There were others who thought the real task was to separate two sets of questions that Austin had seemed to run together, the 'semantic' and the 'pragmatic'. What words meant was one question; what we did with them was quite another.[17] Both were interesting, but could be pursued independently. In the 1960s, Austin's theory of 'speech acts' – in his excellently titled *How to Do Things with Words* – inspired a style of intellectual history that overturned the conventional (indeed, Oxford) style in which such histories had previously been written.

Austin had urged us to distinguish between merely saying something, doing something in saying it, and bringing something about by saying it. The Cambridge historian Quentin Skinner (b.1940) put the distinction to use as a principle of historiography. Where the Oxford tradition had historians of philosophy treat texts from past centuries as though they had been published 'in last month's issue of *Mind*',[18] Skinner and his Cambridge colleagues suggested that it might make better sense to begin in the knowledge that they had not. An author from the sixteenth century was not simply making an 'argument' that could be extracted without distortion from its original context and held up for philosophical scrutiny in the twentieth. The point of intellectual history was not just to report what the great dead philosophers had said, and what their words meant, but what they had been *doing* with their words. Sometimes, they were simply arguing, but they might also be concealing, provoking or subverting. To understand what those other 'illocutions' might be, one needed knowledge of the history of more than philosophy.[19]

More recently, Austin has inspired a large tranche of feminist theory. Feminist writers have found that his ideas can illuminate everything from sexual consent (what goes wrong when a woman's 'no' is not understood as a real refusal of consent?) to heterosexual marriage (what more is needed to make something a real marriage than people saying the words 'I do'?). It isn't so much that Austin's theory had some well-hidden feminist core as that the framework of concepts and terminology he introduced made it possible to raise, in a joined-up way, political questions that had previously been seen as quite separate.[20]

But philosophy had acquired other preoccupations and new centres. The centre of gravity of international philosophy was moving westward, from the Old World to the New. Rudolf Carnap had made it through the war and was keeping the old Viennese spirit alive in America. Even more influentially, W. V. O. Quine at Harvard, a youngish visitor to Vienna when A. J. Ayer had first been there, was now at the centre of a new project, a descendant of the old Viennese positivism, that kept science at the centre of philosophy. Philosophy, as he conceived of it, was about 'what science could get along with'. Problems that arose from ordinary language were not real problems if it turned out that they did not 'arise in science as reconstituted with the help of formal logic'. To reconstitute science in that way simply *was* to solve the philosophical problem. In the slogan Quine made famous, 'philosophy of science is philosophy enough'.[21]

Another Harvard philosopher, John Rawls (b.1921), returned from the Pacific Front and spent a year at Oxford in the early 1950s trying his hand at the kind of thing that people at Oxford seemed to think impossible: an ambitious, systematic theory of justice that would set out principles to govern the distribution of benefits and burdens by the institutions of a well-regulated society.[22] *A Theory of Justice* was published in 1971 to wide acclaim, including from Oxford philosophers pleased that the dire prognoses for political philosophy in the 1950s had been so magnificently disconfirmed.[23] Part of what made Rawls's theory new was simply the fact that it was a *theory* at all. When he was writing, the idea of philosophers developing a substantial political theory was seen as the merest folly. And like other theories that have reshaped their disciplines – ambitiously, one might name Darwin and Einstein, and riskily, Freud – Rawls had limited respect for the way in which language was used. Rawls's theory made conceptual room for itself by cutting through the thickets of previous linguistic practice. When Rawls declared that 'it is obviously impossible to develop a substantive theory of justice founded solely on truths of logic and definition', he was doing two things at once: he was affirming the limits of logic and affirming that the limits of philosophy did not stop with the limits of logic.[24]

By the late 1970s, philosophers were even beginning to do metaphysics again. Not just metaphysics of the modest 'descriptive' sort that Peter Strawson had inaugurated, but the sort of metaphysics that claimed to describe how things were out in the world. A logical prodigy called Saul Kripke (b.1940) claimed that we could talk of metaphysical necessity, of how the world must be, and not just of how we must think, or what sentences must mean, and no one laughed, as they would surely have done even twenty years previously.[25] A bearded savant called David Lewis (b.1941) claimed that the 'possible worlds' that Leibniz had described a few centuries previously were entirely real: worlds in which Hubert Humphrey and not Richard Nixon had won the 1968 US presidential election, worlds where the moon was really made of blue cheese. The difference between how things are and how things might have been was just a difference of perspective. From the perspective of people in other possible worlds, how things might have been (for us) was just how things *were* (for them). By anyone's reckoning, metaphysics was back.[26]

All this was, of course, a far cry from anything that would have been thought respectable at Oxford in the 1950s. But in time, these figures and their ideas made their way there. Students who had once been made to write essays on verificationism and imperatives were now encouraged to apply the same methods to the questions of whether Rawls was right about the extent of inequality compatible with justice, how literally we should take talk of 'possible worlds', or whether it was a scientific embarrassment to hold that numbers existed.[27] Items of jargon that would once have been thought vulgar beyond endurance – 'anomalous monism', 'rigid designator' – were now permitted, and even, in moderation, encouraged: but the demand that these terms be 'given a sense' was still rigorously observed. It had always been an essential principle of Oxford philosophy that philosophy was allowed to be complex: after all, thought and life and reality are complex. Technicality that reflected and allowed us to get a grasp on this complexity was only to be welcomed. What philosophy still abhors is obscurity, the jargon that has not been 'given a sense', the -ism that cannot be stated.

If 'Oxford philosophy' was identified in terms of the questions it permitted and those it regarded as empty, by the end of the century it was a different beast altogether. But an observer looking to the form rather than the content would not easily perceive the difference. If Oxford had ever been a school *of* philosophy, it was certainly no longer that. But a school *for* philosophers it certainly remained; indeed, it remained the same school, and in shaping how an academic question in philosophy should be discussed, its influence is as powerful as it ever was.

A reanimated Ryle or Hare might rue the near-nonsense (as they would surely regard it) being talked at seminars, but they would have no trouble understanding it, nor indeed any trouble being understood when they rose to make an objection. Their objections might not be well received, but they would still be of interest.[28] Whatever the new philosophy was about, the way in which it was being done showed the lasting effects of standards they had done so much to enforce. Murdoch's just gaze must find something to love in the democratic ideal of the seminar conceived as a Socratic enterprise: one tests the speaker's claims precisely because one goes into the conversation open, in principle, to having one's mind changed. The prohibition on declamatory addresses follows from a more basic ethical principle that was at work even in the 1950s: let no one join this conversation who is unwilling to be vulnerable.

*

The point can be put in more value-laden terms. From its earliest origins in ancient Greece, Western philosophy has gained its identity through a contrast with sophistry. If sophistry is non-rational, cynical, manipulative, then philosophy represents a rejection of it, by committing itself to rational, disinterested persuasion.[29] Philosophy has, to that extent, always been a matter of style, but style understood in the sense that Hare proposed: 'an effective, unambiguous, clear and ordered expression of one's thought' achievable only if 'the thought itself has the same qualities'. To put it another way, philosophy since Socrates might be seen as a tradition of *responsible* speech. It is responsible by making itself accountable: to language, to logic, to reality itself.

Oxford philosophy was one form that impulse for accountability took. It took from the Viennese positivists the suspicion of speculation ungirded to observation. From the science that inspired them, it took its suspicion of great men and their theories, putting in their place an ideal of collegial, co-operative inquiry that makes progress, however slowly and collectively. From both, it took the idea, which has since become an entirely familiar feature of philosophy and other humanities disciplines, that it is good for knowledge to be shared – in journals and at conferences – and for there to be shared conventions (for instance, those governing 'peer review') for distinguishing a real breakthrough from the outpourings of a crank.[30] Mid-century philosophers took seriously the idea that philosophy, like science, was something that could be got right, and devised institutions in which people could work together to get it right. At their best, those institutions managed to help people to get things right without killing off what was alive in the targets of their analysis.

Many years later, Hare's student Bernard Williams put up a defence of his tradition of philosophy not in terms of its doctrines or methods but simply in terms of the 'virtues' that it embodied. Oxford philosophy, and the phase of the 'analytic' movement descended from it, believed, and was right to believe, that what it offered embodied 'certain virtues of civilized thought'. What virtues were these? Principally, the fact that philosophy in this style 'gives reasons and sets out arguments in a way that can be explicitly followed and considered; and because it makes questions clearer and sorts out what is muddled'. Oxford philosophers were not unique in doing this, but what of that?

The point can be extended into a description of philosophy

more loving and attentive than the one that Oxford philosophers gave of themselves. Philosophy in that tradition, Williams wrote, 'asserts important freedoms, both to pursue the argument and, in its more imaginative reaches, to develop alternative pictures of the world and of human life'.[31] Some of those pictures – such as the one offered by logical positivism – were neither especially appealing nor usually presented as the worldviews they were. Nevertheless, one could not deny that positivism *was* a worldview, revisionary and radical, with something to say (and to deny) about human beings and their place in the universe.

Philosophy remained, on the Oxford conception, 'both a creative activity and an activity pursued under constraints – constraints experienced as, among others, those of rational consistency'. It has something in common with the sciences in how it experiences these constraints, and 'the terms in which it approves those who most imaginatively work within them'. What it has most in common with the sciences is its commitment to 'the old Socratic ideal that mere rhetoric and the power of words will not prevail'.[32] If it didn't always satisfy its own ideals, it nevertheless committed itself, in the open, to the ideals against which it was found wanting.

Murdoch herself had a few things to say about the tradition of which she was a dissident member. 'It is certainly a great merit of this tradition', she said, 'that it attacks every form of spurious unity. It is the traditional inspiration of the philosopher, but also his traditional vice, to believe that all is one. Wittgenstein says, "Let's see."'[33] As Wittgenstein had elsewhere parenthetically put it, 'We want to replace wild conjectures and explanations by quiet weighing of linguistic facts.'[34]

The most noteworthy thing about Wittgenstein's slogan is not the statement of method suggested by the emphasis on linguistic facts, but the pair of moral adjectives it contrasts: the 'wild' on the one side and the 'quiet' on the other. Something of this spirit was also present in Murdoch's remarks about philosophical style.

In an interview with the broadcaster Bryan Magee (b.1930), she described what she was 'tempted to say' was the 'ideal philosophical style'. That style would be marked by 'a special unambiguous plainness and hardness ... an austere unselfish candid style. A philosopher must try to explain exactly what he means and avoid rhetoric and idle decoration.'[35]

Philosophy, she said, 'is not self-expression; it involves a disciplined removal of the personal voice'. The personal voice – what in her ethical writings she would call the 'greedy ego' – was the great enemy of good philosophy. 'Bad writing', she said, 'is almost always full of the fumes of personality.' Of course, philosophical writers could hardly help revealing something of themselves in the writing. But the first question raised about the writing was not a personal one. One asked, simply, 'Is the conclusion true, is the argument valid?'[36]

The jokiness and ironic detachment of much Oxford philosophy, the feature so many of its critics found rebarbative, turns out in this light to be something deeper. Jokiness stands in one sense against seriousness; in another, it represents only a rejection of the characteristic *postures* of seriousness, of which humourlessness is surely the most obvious. The American writer and critic Susan Sontag (b.1933), who spent a fruitful but ambivalent term at Oxford studying under J. L. Austin, wrote famously in 1964 of a sensibility she called Camp, that its whole point was to 'dethrone the serious. Camp is playful, anti-serious. More precisely, Camp involves a new, more complex relation to "the serious". One can be serious about the frivolous, frivolous about the serious.'[37] It's not that Oxford philosophy *was* Camp – though some of it was – but that some of it was interesting for the same reasons that Camp art is interesting: it subverts some of the traditional rhetoric of seriousness in the inherited tradition to find room for another, more playful, more ambiguous, vision of what philosophy might be.

Like Murdoch's M, then, we can go through an exercise in

imaginative charity. Where we are minded to call Oxford philosophy pedantic, consider calling it, instead, 'vigilant'. For
'mundane', say that it had 'a lively appreciation of the value of
the ordinary'. In its very anti-romanticism, its disclaiming of
rhetoric, it embodied a counter-romance and a counter-rhetoric:
the rhetoric of plain-speaking, the romance of the ascetic. And
consider, above all, that even at its most frivolous and whimsical,
it was never unserious.

All things, can of course, be redescribed in more generous
terms – even slavery and genocide. Not all things should be. The
purpose of the redescription of Oxford philosophy isn't simply
to bring out the obvious fact that there were good and bad things
about it. The point is to bring out the fact that the matter of what
counts as a good thing and what counts as a bad remains an open
question. One might say that everything about it, the good and
the bad, was what is good or bad about philosophy. And that
follows from the fact that Oxford philosophy was, whatever its
critics have thought, a kind of philosophy.

*

There were already signs, even before the death of Austin, that
'Oxford philosophy' was on its way out. But as with Nietzsche's
death of God, the news would take a while to reach everyone. And
like with God, the power of its methods, the increased sensitivity
to language that it engendered in those who did it, the powerful
sense of accountability to the ordinary, would continue to be felt
long after anyone was willing to make large claims on its behalf.

In time, it would be regarded as one more oddity of the 1950s
that grown men and women sat about fusty common rooms
intoning those old phrases. What *on earth* do you mean by. I
should like to make a distinction. Common sense. Nonsense.
'Metaphysical'. Nothing can be blue and green all over. Not interested in -isms. We haven't given a sense to the notion. Category

mistake. Pseudo-proposition. Language game. Logical grammar. Boo murder. Meaning is use. Why do we say. What we should say when. Thereof we must be silent.

Few people alive today sound like that. We have new clichés now. But the old clichés, when one encounters them in the dusty pages of an old journal, have the same power to puzzle and to challenge – much like an old church puzzles and challenges a passing heathen cyclist. That family of things – variously called 'Oxford philosophy', 'ordinary language philosophy', 'linguistic philosophy' – is dead. But its descendants still live; and it was once alive. And while it was alive, many saw it – as Philip Larkin saw an empty church – as a 'serious house on serious earth'. And that, Larkin thought, 'never can be obsolete'.[38]

The hunger to be more serious can take many forms, and not all of them need look the same. People have been thought pedantic because they cared about small things as well as big, frivolous because they dared laugh at the portentous, and ignorant because they didn't defer to the great and glorious dead. But there *was* good in them, and the good lay in their special way of being serious, their special way of taking responsibility. Not everyone enjoyed it. But it *was* an adventure. And while it lasted, it felt a terribly serious one.

11

Epilogue

A. J. Ayer survived into the new age, a professor at Oxford in the Wykeham Chair in Logic that had once been held by that old realist, John Cook Wilson. New developments in philosophy gave him no pleasure. But then, he had never been short of pleasures. There was football: he supported Tottenham Hotspur, a loyalty chosen because he liked their name.[1] People who didn't read philosophy knew him from his appearances on the BBC's *The Brains Trust*, obligingly representing most people's idea of the philosopher: flamboyantly rational, the public slayer of sacred cows. In the 1950s and 1960s, he announced publicly – as few of his fellow liberals dared – that he was in favour of the decriminalisation of homosexual behaviour. After all, he remarked, 'as a notorious heterosexual I could never be accused of feathering my own nest'.[2] He was married four times, to three women (he remarried his second wife after the death of his third).[3] Some thought his ways a betrayal of philosophy's ancient promise of seriousness. The *Daily Telegraph*'s obituary was titled 'The Man Who Hated Wisdom'.[4]

It was said that he died twice, declaring after the first near-death experience that he had seen nothing to merit a late-life conversion. Two years before his death, in 1989, he managed – in an encounter that made for a much-repeated anecdote – to rescue the supermodel Naomi Campbell from the unwanted attentions of Mike Tyson. Tyson informed Ayer, in rather strong words, that he was the world heavyweight champion. Ayer replied: 'And I am the former Wykeham Professor of Logic. We are both pre-eminent in our field; I suggest that we talk about this like rational men.'[5]

*

Elizabeth Anscombe held her fellowship at Oxford until 1969, after which she moved to Cambridge to occupy the professorial chair that had previously been Wittgenstein's. In many ways, she remained a Wittgensteinian. But she departed radically from Wittgenstein's example in the way she wrote and thought about ethics. Her early paper on how to get from an 'ought' to an 'is' had already pointed towards a way in which one might refute Wittgenstein's notorious contention that there couldn't be any meaningful ethical talk, because there were no ethical propositions and no ethical facts. Ethics was, in his view, ineffable.[6] In contrast, she had proposed that 'You owe me five pounds' most certainly stated a fact, and if statements about what you owe could be meaningful, so could statements about what you ought (and oughtn't) to do.[7] And there were a great many things Anscombe believed we ought not to do. She was a vocal critic of contraception and an active campaigner against abortion, and defended both in ways that suggested that she thought ethics entirely effable.[8]

In 1997, Anscombe was seriously injured in a car accident, which followed an earlier riding injury. Blood clots had to be removed from her brain. She survived, but with her faculties severely undermined. She died of kidney failure in Addenbrooke's Hospital in Cambridge in 2001, the place where she had delivered all her seven children, shocking the nurses by insisting that she was *Miss* Anscombe. She was buried in St Giles's graveyard in north-west Cambridge. Twelve years later, her husband Peter Geach was buried next to her, both their graves a few inches from Wittgenstein's.[9]

In the years after her death, *Intention* has become the focus of a passionate interpretative debate. The early view of it as a rough outline or promissory note for a theory she never went on to deliver has been replaced with a revisionary view of it as quite complete on its own terms, both a vindication of a promise in the work of Wittgenstein and the product of an independent intelligence.[10] One hears tell of bearded men walking the streets of Pittsburgh declaring themselves proud 'Anscombeans'.

*

Iris Murdoch gave up her philosophy fellowship at St Anne's in 1963, only fifteen years into her academic career. She wrote fiction prolifically into the 1990s and the publication of the 'new Iris Murdoch novel' became a sort of annual ritual. *The Sea, the Sea* won the Booker Prize in 1978. She published one substantial work of philosophy in later life, a demanding and still poorly understood tome titled *Metaphysics as a Guide to Morals*, published in 1992. The prose and plot of her twenty-fifth novel, *Jackson's Dilemma* (1995), had readers writing in to point out errors and inconsistencies.[11] Audiences at her public appearances noted that she often looked bewildered.[12] Shortly afterwards, she was diagnosed with Alzheimer's disease, and it was this experience that formed the basis of a popular film about her life – *Iris* (2001) – where she was played, as a young woman, by Kate Winslet and, in her final years, by Judi Dench. One could watch the film without learning that she had ever been much of a philosopher. Dismissed as woolly-headed and merely 'intuitive', it has taken a while for her philosophical corpus to be picked up again by hard-headed philosophers surprised to find in it a coherent, systematic and serious body of proposals ripe for reappraisal.[13]

*

Philippa Foot published her first and only book that wasn't a collection of papers in 2001. *Natural Goodness* was a distillation of the main work of her life: to show that ethics was objective, and that ethical facts were part of nature. 'Good' was as much part of the natural world as, say, 'healthy'.[14] 'I'm a dreadfully slow thinker, really,' she once told an interviewer. 'But I do have a good nose for what is important. And even though the best philosophers combine cleverness and depth, I'd prefer a good nose over cleverness any day!'[15] She followed her nose at her own pace, taking seriously one of her favourite dictums from Wittgenstein: that it's hard in philosophy to be *slow* enough.[16]

*

Mary Midgley left Oxford for Newcastle in 1950. Her husband Geoffrey Midgley was a lecturer at what was to become the University of Newcastle. For a time, it looked like she had abandoned academia entirely, instead fashioning herself as an intellectual journalist, publishing reviews and essays for *New Statesman*. But the wide reading of those decades eventually found expression in a book of philosophy, *Beast and Man*. Out of sympathy with both the scientific and linguistic pretensions of Oxford philosophy, and even more with what she saw as a veneration of competitiveness, she had produced something that showed its respect for science by taking its findings seriously, yet not deferring to it as the final standard of meaningful speech. The book was about the significance of evolutionary theory for the understanding of human behaviour, an attempt to find a position that neither treated human beings as wholly determined by their biology nor as entirely free, in the style of the French existentialists. She took up a position in the Philosophy department at Newcastle in 1965 and taught there until 1980, when she took early retirement to give herself more time to write and travel. She died in 2018, a few months after the publication of her final book, *What is Philosophy For?* She made it amply clear in the pronouncements of her final years what she thought philosophy was not: 'a form of highbrow chess for graduate students'.[17]

*

R. M. Hare changed his mind about few things, but his early views on the logic of moral language slowly evolved towards an articulation of a substantive moral theory: simply by reflecting on the nature of the moral 'ought', we would be led to the philosophy that best reflected the basic demand that we 'universalise' our maxims. Surprisingly, this turned out to be a kind of utilitarianism.[18] When he was not trying to explain his theory to colleagues whom he accused of misunderstanding it, he liked to run convivial reading parties for his undergraduates from Balliol College at a house he had on the Welsh island of Anglesey. He became a vegetarian, more or less, but it was gardening that had converted him, not an argument. When Ved Mehta met Hare in Oxford, he was struck most of all by his understated eccentricity: writing in a caravan in his garden, sockless. He was disappointed when his publisher didn't allow the editors of his Festschrift to title it, as he had proposed, *Hare and Hounds*.[19] Hare died in 2002, having managed to revise a set of lectures given in Sweden into a volume with a title characteristic of him, *Sorting Out Ethics*. Convinced that he had in fact sorted out ethics, even if colleagues persisted in misunderstanding him, he died of complications from pneumonia in hospital, after he had suffered a series of strokes.[20]

*

If Oxford philosophy could be embodied in one person, that person was Peter Strawson. His measured, elegant sentences were the rest of the world's idea of how an Oxford philosopher ought to look and sound. Once when lecturing in Communist-era Yugoslavia, Strawson was accused of having 'a bourgeois outlook'. He owned up immediately: 'But I *am* bourgeois, an elitist liberal bourgeois.'[21]

Over the years, Strawson moved away from his early interests in logic and 'descriptive' metaphysics and ranged across philosophy. An iconic paper, 'Freedom and Resentment', presented a possible solution – or dissolution – of the problem of free will that is still seriously debated.[22] Strawson never sought, as Ayer had done, the place of a public intellectual. He was happy with his private passions: 'philosophy, friends and family apart, my life has been enriched by the enjoyment of literature, landscape, architecture, and the company of clever and beautiful women'.[23] He died in 2006 at the John Radcliffe Hospital in Oxford.[24]

*

And with that, we return to the philosopher with whom we started. No doubt there were those who worried that Gilbert Ryle would die unhappy. He had never married, nor for all that anyone knew had he wanted to. Asked if he read novels, he replied, 'All six of them, once a year.' 'Novel' for him meant one written by Jane Austen: no other woman seems to have commanded his loyalties.[25]

In an essay Ryle wrote about Austen's novels, he credited her with bringing the sensibly pagan views of Aristotle into the wretched Protestant air of the Regency. She didn't divide the world, as 'Calvinists' are said to do, into the 'Saved or Damned'.[26] She knew that things were complicated, and had the language – the 'ample, variegated and many-dimensional vocabulary' – to match the complexity of her sensibility.[27]

Austen captured her characters by describing 'their tempers, habits, dispositions, moods, inclinations, impulses, sentiments, feelings, affections, thoughts, reflections, opinions, principles, prejudices, imaginations and fancies'.[28] Which was another way of saying, she described their minds with no need for ghosts to animate the machines.

In September 1958, Ryle had driven his old student Freddie Ayer to Venice for a meeting of the World Congress of Philosophy as, a few decades before, he had taken him to see Wittgenstein.

They had been talking philosophy for nearly thirty years, and there wasn't a great deal left to say. And Ryle did not share Ayer's greatest non-philosophical interest, that is, women. Curious, perhaps, Ayer asked him if he was a virgin. Ryle said he was. But if that were to change, Ayer went on (his reputation as a talker was not for tact), would it be boy or girl, did he think? 'Boy, I suppose,' said Ryle, hands still on the steering wheel; they continued, silent, across the flatlands of France.[29]

The hint of uncertainty ('I suppose') was entirely of a piece with the philosophy he had spent much of his life defending. There was nothing special about the 'inner' life, he had always held, preferring to look to the 'overt intelligent performances' of the body. Old Boswell, Ryle had once written, 'described Johnson's mind when he described how he wrote, talked, ate, fidgeted and fumed. His description was, of course, incomplete, since there were notoriously some thoughts which Johnson kept carefully to himself and there must have been many dreams, daydreams and silent babblings which only Johnson could have recorded and only a James Joyce would wish him to have recorded.'[30]

On the dreams and silent babblings of Gilbert Ryle, the historical record is silent. Of his writings, talkings, eatings, fidgetings and fumings, on the other hand, recollections abound. The most eloquent by far is the account left by Robert Craft, secretary to and later collaborator with Igor Stravinsky, when he brought the old composer and his wife, Vera, to Oxford for lunch with Isaiah Berlin in the spring of 1963. Ryle played his usual Bulldog Drummond character: 'parka, tweeds, specs, pipe', a stubborn refusal to yield his bread plate, and a round of epigrammatic dismissals of suspicious foreigners. John Dewey and William James? 'Great American Bores.' What about the French Jesuit Teilhard de Chardin? 'Old teleological pancake.' The French phenomenologist Maurice Merleau-Ponty? 'French *clarté*, indeed!'

Craft was not convinced that Ryle's best aperçu of the afternoon was entirely spontaneous: 'Every generation or so philosophical progress is set back by the appearance of a "genius".' When he left – the conversation was veering perilously close to the subject of music and Ryle was known to confess to having 'no ear for tunes' – Stravinsky felt he had been in the company of 'a very brilliant schoolboy who, without meaning to, has made us feel like very dull schoolboys'.[31]

During their awkward lunch, the one moment of convergence between Ryle and Vera Stravinsky's interests came when the latter made a useful suggestion on how to stop the birds getting at his cherry tree. The beleaguered cherry tree was in Ryle's garden in the little village of Islip, where he moved after he retired. The village being a half-day's walk or ten minutes' train journey north from Oxford station, there was little risk of his being isolated from college life. He reappeared in Magdalen to be filmed in the early 1970s, in conversation with his old colleague Jim Urmson (b.1915), by Michael Chanan, a student of Isaiah Berlin's who was making a series of films featuring Oxford philosophers in conversation. The conversation turned to that old chestnut: the purpose of philosophy. 'I'm asking', said Chanan, 'about – about whether you think philosophy can actually be of benefit in some … moral sense.' 'Well,' said Ryle, 'the answer that you would like me to give is "yes", so I'm going to give the answer "no".' He continued:

> you really want to say there's no point in studying philosophy unless you can point to some dividends of a non-philosophic sort – not of course *cash* dividends, but dividends in the way of becoming more virtuous, or becoming more happy, or becoming more inspired to write poems, or plays, or something of the sort; but I don't want to say that the point of studying philosophy is to get dividends.[32]

But what about getting *clear*? 'Ah,' said Ryle, 'getting clear, certainly!' But what was the value of that? 'What's the value of getting truth?' Ryle snapped. 'Well,' said Chanan, 'you're the philosopher, I'm asking you.' Ryle laughed. 'Well, I'd say the value of getting clear is the same as the value of getting truth, as opposed to remaining in error or darkness.'

And they left it at that. He could have done better, but he could have done much worse.

No one thought him lonely in his retirement. For company, he had his twin sister Mary, housebound owing to a hip condition, and her daughter Janet, and the presence in the village (should he crave further philosophical stimulation) of John Mabbott, of the now finally disbanded Wee Teas.[33] Mary was busy enough, brailling textbooks for use by blind students. Mabbott had dedicated his own retirement to the Council for the Protection of Rural England, and took responsibility for keeping open the forty or so public rights of way in his and some nearby parishes. Ryle joined him on these walks, four to six miles in the morning several times a week. Other walkers in the Oxfordshire countryside who appeared at The Swan shortly after noon were likely to find there, holding court, 'a man of genially military appearance, with a knobbly, cubic head ... rather soldierly in speech and manner'.[34] He could easily be taken for a retired major, which (after a fashion) he was. The recipe for his preferred mixture, the Prof's Special, was a secret between him and the landlord.

A few years into his rural retirement, he suffered a stroke, but a minor one from which he recovered in ten minutes, no symptoms recurring for a happy year in which he continued the cycle of walks. In the early autumn of 1976, he attempted something more ambitious, driving up with Mabbott to the village of Goathland on the eastern edge of the North York Moors, where the pair spent an unseasonably sunny fortnight, doing ten-mile walks every day. Some of the conversation was philosophical: Ryle was exercised about the lengths of certain Platonic dialogues, which posed difficulties for an eccentric view that he had formed about their having been composed for public performance, with Plato reading the part of Socrates until, in his old age, his health declined – which would explain why his later dialogues give the character of 'Socrates' less and less to say.[35]

On their way back to the inn after two weeks' walking, Ryle had a second stroke; his left side was paralysed. Again, he recovered soon enough. By the time they got to Whitby hospital, he seemed fine. He could talk and explained the situation to the doctors himself, but they thought he should be admitted under observation. The next day, the hospital rang Mary Ryle in Islip to tell her that Gilbert had suffered another stroke, this time a serious one. He died later that evening, 6 October – 'swiftly and cleanly as would be expected of him', his obituarist wrote.[36]

On Mabbott fell the responsibility of conveying the news. Letters had to go out to his numerous academic correspondents across the world, many no doubt anxiously awaiting the grand old man's judgements upon their manuscripts. Mabbott had to find postage for letters to France, Germany and Italy, the USA and Canada, Australia and Israel, but also to Mexico, Pakistan and Soviet Armenia, conveying what comments Ryle had left, and an explanation of their incompleteness.[37] Ryle had always been an assiduous and generous correspondent. The little-Englishness of his personal style was only one half of his character. This was a man who boasted (though he did not brag about) friends and colleagues in countries in four continents; someone who had, as a young man, taught himself Italian to read Croce and German to read Husserl. However disparagingly he spoke of 'Continentals', he could hardly be accused of ignorance.

As the editor of *Mind*, his in-tray can't ever have been empty, but he dealt with the administrative burden briskly, and somewhat brusquely. 'Dear Mr Feldman,' went one rejection letter written shortly after Christmas 1967, 'I am returning your paper. There may be a little bit in it, but it doesn't seem to cut enough ice. Yours sincerely, G. Ryle'.[38] 'Is it true, Professor Ryle,' he was once asked by an American visitor, 'that you accept or reject an article on the basis of reading just the first paragraph?' 'That used to be true at one time,' Ryle is supposed to have replied. 'I had a lot more time in those days.'[39]

Students did impressions of the half-cough with which he punctuated his sentences, the characteristic elongation of the vowel at the end of each sentence. Others appreciated, though they did not always take, the advice that he had given them. Better to place one's trust in 'particular inquiries ... than in global positions' – or as he would more bluntly have said, 'Not interested in isms.'[40]

Ryle was, in both the good and the bad sense of the word, collegial. 'Claims to Führership vanish when postprandial joking begins,' he once said, with a characteristic lack of tact, at a conference in Royaumont, France, where British philosophers were to mingle with their French coevals. 'Husserl wrote as if he had never met a scientist – or a joke.'[41] He was funny, and suspicious of the unfunny. He thought a sense of humour and the regular company of non-philosophers could be a prophylactic against many of the vices to which philosophers are prone.

Führership of the doctrinal sort held no attractions for him, but he showed leadership on things other philosophers of his seniority considered distractions. Philosophy at Oxford had no lending library until he started one from the books he was sent for review in *Mind*. He left a good deal of money, and most of his books, to a young college, Linacre, rather than to one he had been at. His colleges, old and rich, were less likely to need the gift. By the time he died, he had succeeded in persuading the university that – as he punningly put it – 'Philosophy needs premises of its own'. He duly secured some, in a small building in the cobbled quaintness of Merton Street, a dozen or so paces away from the aptly named Logic Lane. When Philosophy finally got 10 Merton Street all to itself, there was no question of the old Powicke Room being allowed to keep its name, nor any question of what was top of the list of alternative names.

'Dear Ryle,' wrote the Curator of the Management Committee,

The Management Committee has been discussing names of rooms in the new building ... As you have had so much to do with getting the Graduate Library and the associated B.Phil. on their feet, it was felt that it would be a good idea that a Philosophy seminar room should be called the Ryle Room. I have been asked to discover whether you have any reasonable objection? If not, we shall go ahead; if so we might of course still use that name, despite the accidental resemblance to your own, but also might not.

The reply came with its usual promptness:

I'm delighted with the idea. I shall always be showing visitors over our new home & pausing for long enough for them to ask 'And what is this room called?'[42]

This was two weeks before the final Yorkshire holiday. A year or two later, Mabbott appeared with a photograph for the wall of the Ryle Room: the man himself, sinking into a lawn chair in his Islip garden, looking up from *The Diary of Samuel Pepys*.

Acknowledgements

The debts I have accumulated in writing this book are numerous, and it is only by restricting myself to those who made the most direct contributions to it that I am able to draw up a list. To many family, friends, teachers and colleagues not named below, I owe more than I can capture in a mere acknowledgement.

I am, most of all, grateful to Jack Wearing for his exemplary research assistance at various stages of this project, which saved me a good deal of labour and stopped me making many an error. For their help with my notes, references and appendices during my periods of illness and indisposition, I am grateful to Alex Bonham, Matt Dougherty, Alex Fisher, Kieran Lee Marshall, Peter McLaughlin and Alex Murphy.

For their comments on the text and/or arguments of this book, I am grateful to Paolo Babbiotti, Pascal Brixel, Tim Button, Roger Crisp, Matthew Dougherty, Cora Diamond, David Egan, Alex Fisher, Monty Fynn, Anil Gomes, Nat Hansen, Ella Hopcroft, Joel Isaac, Claire Kirwin, Michael Kremer, Cathy Mason, Peter McLaughlin, A. W. Moore, Stephen Mulhall, Alex Murphy, Makan Nojoumian, Martha Nussbaum, Matthieu Queloz, Paul Sagar, Matthew Simpson, Robert Simpson, Edward Skidelsky, Maarten Steenhagen, Michael Tanner, Zoe Walker, Robert Watt, Jack Wearing, Tommy Wide and Samuel Williams. I also benefited from the questions of audiences at seminars in Oxford, Cambridge, London, Southampton, Manchester, Milton Keynes, Turin and Chicago. These discussions saved me, as one says, from many embarrassing errors; responsibility for any errors that remain rests, of course, entirely with me.

The research that went into this book could not have been carried out without the assistance and advice of a great many archivists and librarians, at the Bodleian Library, Oxford, the Casimir Lewy Library and the University Library, Cambridge. I relied a good deal on the efficiency and generosity of the administrative staff at the Faculty of Philosophy, Cambridge – Heather Sanderson, Charlie Evans, Clare Dickinson and Anna Simpson – for making my experience of working there so pleasant. I am similarly grateful to Robinson College for providing me with the office space in which I wrote this book, and for the warm food and fellowship that sustained me through the process.

I am grateful to my agents, Sophie Scard, Caroline Dawnay and Kat Aitken, for being such committed champions of this book. Its text has been transformed by countless contributions from my editors Ed Lake, Nick Humphrey, Clio Seraphim and Sam Matthews.

I owe a great deal to my teachers, but it was in tutorials with Lesley Brown and Roger Crisp that I got my abiding sense of the *affect* of Oxford philosophy. To Ben Morison, I am grateful for exemplifying the closest thing in the sublunary realm to the Platonic ideal of the tutorial. It was he who first urged me to read J. L. Austin's 'A Plea for Excuses'. 'I think you'll enjoy it,' he said; I did.

Glossary

Analysis: Breaking down a concept into simpler parts. For example, a 'bachelor' may be analysed into 'unmarried man'.

Behaviourism: The view that describing someone's states of mind involves no more than describing the various dispositions to behaviour that the person possesses. For example, to say that someone fears spiders is just to say that he tends to avoid being near them.

Cartesian: Pertaining to the philosophical views of the seventeenth-century French mathematician and philosopher René Descartes, in particular, his 'dualism' of mind and body.

Dialectic: The process of reasoning and debate, often conducted by means of question and answer designed to uncover assumptions and hidden contradictions among our beliefs.

Empiricism: A tradition of philosophy claiming that there is no knowledge except what is obtained from experience.

Ethics: The study of right and wrong, good and bad, virtue and vice.

Idealism: The belief that reality is fundamentally mental in nature, that reality depends in some important way on our minds, concepts and perceptions.

Logic: The science of inference; the study of (valid) arguments.

Logical positivism: A philosophical movement that emerged in Vienna, committed to the view that the meaning of a statement is its method of verification, and consequently suspicious of 'metaphysical' statements that could not be verified directly or indirectly by the evidence of our senses.

Metaphysics: The branch of philosophy concerned with questions about the nature of reality that cannot be answered by the application of scientific methods.

Phenomenology: The study of structures of consciousness as experienced from the first-person point of view. Associated in the twentieth century with philosophers such as Edmund Husserl, Martin Heidegger and Jean-Paul Sartre.

Realism: The belief that the world, or some part of it, exist independently of our minds, concepts and perceptions.

Solipsism: The belief that only oneself and one's (current) experience exists.

Stoicism: A philosophical tradition influential in the Greek and Roman world. Its most prominent aspect is its promotion of a picture of virtue that makes the virtuous person indifferent to worldly suffering.

Appendix of Names

Brief biographies of canonical philosophers mentioned in this book

Socrates (c.470–399 BCE): Ancient Greek philosopher, known for his novel style of conducting philosophical discussions in public spaces by a method of questioning that revealed his interlocutors to have contradictory beliefs. He was condemned by an Athenian jury to death for the crimes of impiety and corrupting youth. He is not known to have written any books.

Plato (c.429–347 BCE): Ancient Greek philosopher, a student of Socrates, known for his body of dialogues, most of which depict Socrates carrying on philosophical conversations with young Athenian men on subjects such as love, beauty and justice. Major works: *Apology, Republic, Theaetetus.*

Aristotle (384–22 BCE): Ancient Greek philosopher, a student of Plato, known for his treatises on philosophical and scientific subjects. Major works: *Metaphysics, Nicomachean Ethics, Poetics.*

Thomas Aquinas (1225–74): Italian philosopher and theologian who attempted to synthesise Aristotelian philosophy with the principles of Christianity. Major work: *Summa Theologica* (1485).

René Descartes (1596–1650): French mathematician and philosopher best known for his attempt to place the natural sciences on a firm philosophical footing by demonstrating the possibility of knowledge about the external world. Major works: *Discourse on the Method* (1637), *Meditations on First Philosophy* (1641).

John Locke (1632–1704): English philosopher often credited as the first empiricist as well as a pioneering theorist of liberalism. Major works: *Essay Concerning Human Understanding* (1689), *Two Treatises of Government* (1689).

Gottfried Wilhelm Leibniz (1646–1716): German mathematician and philosopher who made pioneering contributions to metaphysics. Major work: *The Monadology* (1714).

George Berkeley (1685–1753): Anglo-Irish philosopher best known for his 'immaterialist' theory of reality, a form of idealism that denies the existence of material substances and holds that objects only exist insofar as they are perceived. Major works: *A Treatise Concerning the Principles of Human Knowledge* (1710), *Three Dialogues Between Hylas and Philonous* (1713).

David Hume (1711–76): Scottish philosopher who made influential contributions to epistemology and moral philosophy, aiming to develop a psychological basis for a theory of human nature. Major works: *A Treatise of Human Nature* (1740), *An Enquiry Concerning the Principles of Morals* (1751).

Immanuel Kant (1724–1804): German philosopher of the Enlightenment who made seminal contributions to metaphysics, epistemology, ethics and aesthetics. Major works: *Critique of Pure Reason* (1781), *Groundwork of the Metaphysics of Morals* (1785).

Georg Wilhelm Friedrich Hegel (1770–1831): German philosopher who made seminal contributions to metaphysics, ethics, political philosophy and the philosophy of history. Major works: *The Phenomenology of Spirit* (1807), *Elements of the Philosophy of Right* (1820).

John Stuart Mill (1806–73): English philosopher and campaigner, associated with a defence of empiricist views in epistemology, utilitarian theories in ethics, and with liberal and feminist positions in politics. Major works: *System of Logic* (1843), *On Liberty* (1859), *Utilitarianism* (1863).

Karl Marx (1818–83): German philosopher and political economist, an important theorist of revolutionary socialism. Major works: *Communist Manifesto* (1848), *Capital* (four volumes, 1867–83).

Friedrich Engels (1820–95): German philosopher and political economist, best

Appendix of Names

known for his works co-authored with Karl Marx. Major works: *Communist Manifesto* (1848), *The Condition of the Working Class in England* (1845).

Thomas Hill Green (1836–82): English philosopher best known as the central figure in the tradition of British idealism. Major work: *Prolegomena to Ethics* (1883).

Henry Sidgwick (1838–1900): English philosopher best known for his work in ethics, much of which aimed to defend a form of utilitarianism. He was also active in educational reform and a campaigner for women's education at Cambridge. Major work: *The Methods of Ethics* (1874).

William James (1842–1910): American philosopher and psychologist. A founding member, with Charles Sanders Peirce, of the school of American pragmatism. Major works: *The Will to Believe* (1897), *The Varieties of Religious Experience* (1902).

Friedrich Nietzsche (1844–1900): German classical scholar and philosopher best known for his critiques of the institutions of morality and religion. Major works: *The Birth of Tragedy* (1872), *Beyond Good and Evil* (1886), *On the Genealogy of Morality* (1887).

Francis Herbert Bradley (1846–1924): Central figure in the tradition of British idealism. Major works: *Ethical Studies* (1876), *Appearance and Reality* (1893).

Gottlob Frege (1848–1925): German logician, mathematician and philosopher, generally regarded as the founder of the tradition of 'analytic' philosophy. Major works: *The Foundations of Arithmetic* (1884), 'On Sense and Reference' (1892).

Bertrand Russell (1872–1970): British philosopher and activist central to the tradition of 'analytic' philosophy in virtue of his contributions to mathematics, logic and the philosophy of language. Major works: *The Principles of Mathematics* (1903), *The Problems of Philosophy* (1912), *Sceptical Essays* (1928).

Ludwig Wittgenstein (1889–1951): Austrian philosopher known for his contributions to logic and the philosophy of language. His later work was foundational to the development of the tradition of 'ordinary language philosophy', aiming to show philosophical problems to arise from the misuse of language, thus allowing problems to be not so much solved as 'dissolved'. Major works: *Tractatus Logico-Philosophicus* (1921), *Philosophical Investigations* (1953).

Martin Heidegger (1889–1976): German philosopher best known for his contributions to the traditions of phenomenology and existentialism. Achieved notoriety for his support of the Nazi Party. Major work: *Being and Time* (1927).

Jean-Paul Sartre (1905–80): French philosopher central to the traditions of phenomenology and existentialism, the latter captured roughly in his slogan, 'Existence precedes essence'. Major works: *Being and Nothingness* (1943), *Existentialism Is a Humanism* (1946).

Notes

Epigraphs

1. Nietzsche, *The Gay Science*, §173; Bergson, 'La Philosophie française', p. 254.

0. Giddiness

1. Plato, *Theaetetus*, 148e.
2. Plato, *Theaetetus*, 155c.
3. Plato, *Theaetetus*, 155cd.
4. Dummett, *Frege: Philosophy of Language*, p. ix.
5. Murdoch, 'The Idea of Perfection', in *Existentialists and Mystics*, p. 299.
6. I particularly regret how little I say about the work of Stuart Hampshire, a philosopher of great imagination and insight. The scope of the book – I end the story, more or less, in 1960 – means that I have virtually nothing to say about such figures as Michael Dummett, H. L. A. Hart and Richard Wollheim, and only a little to say about Bernard Williams, as their most important work was done after that date. For different reasons, I have carefully rationed my discussions of Wittgenstein: so vast and imposing a figure threatens to dominate the scene if he is allowed anything more substantial than a couple of teasing cameos.
7. e.g. G. J. Warnock, *English Philosophy since 1900*; Urmson, *Philosophical Analysis: Its Development Between the Two World Wars*; Passmore, *A Hundred Years of Philosophy*; Soames, *Philosophical Analysis in the Twentieth Century, 1: The Dawn of Analysis*; and *2: The Age of Meaning*; Glock, *What Is Analytic Philosophy?*; Dummett, *Origins of Analytical Philosophy*; Hacker, *Wittgenstein's Place in Twentieth-Century Analytic Philosophy*; Akehurst, *The Cultural Politics of Analytic Philosophy: Britishness and the Spectre of Europe*.

8. Borges, 'The Argentine Writer and Tradition', in *Labyrinths*, p. 164.
9. Sontag, 'Notes on Camp', in *Against Interpretation*, p. 276.
10. A fine example is Uschanov, 'The Strange Death of Ordinary Language Philosophy'; others include Baz, *When Words Are Called For* and Laugier, *Why We Need Ordinary Language Philosophy*.
11. See, e.g. Lanchester, 'The Case of Agatha Christie'.
12. Shulman, *Spring, Heat, Rains: A South Indian Diary*, p. 111.
13. The authors are, respectively, Gilbert Ryle, J. L. Austin, Elizabeth Anscombe and P. F. Strawson. If I were to make a fuller list of the canonical works of this tradition, I would add the following: A. J. Ayer, *Language, Truth, and Logic*; R. M. Hare, *The Language of Morals*; the essays in Philippa Foot, *Virtues and Vices* and Iris Murdoch, *The Sovereignty of Good*; Stuart Hampshire, *Thought and Action*; and (at the tail end of the tradition) Bernard Williams, *Morality*.
14. Bourdieu, *Outline of a Theory of Practice*.

1. Fog

1. Gilbert Ryle, 'Autobiographical', p. 1.
2. Bernard Williams (b.1929), twenty-nine years his junior, called him Gilbert; Anthony Kenny (b.1931) was asked to call him Ryle. See Kenny, *Brief Encounters*, p. 81.
3. John Charles Ryle, *Knots Untied*, p. 420.
4. Ryle, *Knots Untied*, p. 1.
5. An Old Brightonian, Second Lieutenant Vincent Waterfall of Hampden House/Chichester House was one of the first two soldiers to be killed in the war. A list of old Brightonians who died in the First World War is available here: www.brightoncollegeremembers.com/the-roll-of-honour.
6. Pevsner and Sherwood, *Oxfordshire*, p. 187.
7. Chanan, 'You Might as Well Say "I See What I Eat" Is the Same Thing as "I Eat What I See"'; Ryle, 'Autobiographical', pp. 1–2.
8. Ryle, 'Autobiographical', p. 2.
9. Ryle, 'Autobiographical', p. 2. See also Ryle's warm reception of Karl Popper's *The Open Society and Its Enemies*, much of it a blistering attack on Plato's supposed totalitarianism: Ryle, review of K. R. Popper, *The Open Society and Its Enemies*.
10. Ryle, 'Autobiographical', p. 2.
11. Croce, *What Is Living and What Is Dead of the Philosophy of Hegel*, p. 6.

12. Ryle, 'Autobiographical', p. 2.
13. Ryle, 'Autobiographical', p. 2.
14. Paton, 'Fifty Years of Philosophy', p. 337.
15. Paton, 'Fifty Years of Philosophy', p. 337.
16. Ryle, 'The Genesis of "Oxford" Philosophy', p. 109.
17. Ryle, 'Autobiographical', p. 4.
18. S. C. Carpenter, *Church and People*, p. 483.
19. Bradley, *Appearance and Reality*, pp. 128–9.
20. Wollheim, *F. H. Bradley*, p. 15.
21. Collingwood, *An Autobiography*, p. 16; Ryle, 'Fifty Years of Philosophy and Philosophers', p. 381.
22. Collingwood, *An Autobiography*, p. 18.
23. Collingwood, *An Autobiography*, p. 19.
24. Cook Wilson, *Statement and Inference*, p. 74.
25. Prichard, *Kant's Theory of Knowledge*, p. 118.
26. Ryle, 'Autobiographical', p. 4.
27. Ryle, 'Genesis', p. 114.
28. Ryle, 'Fifty Years of Philosophy and Philosophers', p. 385.
29. Ryle, 'Genesis', p. 113.
30. Chanan, 'You Might as Well Say "I See What I Eat" Is the Same Thing as "I Eat What I See"'.
31. Ryle, 'Fifty Years of Philosophy and Philosophers', p. 383.
32. Ryle, 'Genesis', p. 110.
33. Ryle, 'Fifty Years of Philosophy and Philosophers', p. 383.
34. Quoted in Prichard, 'H. W. B. Joseph', p. 191. Joseph was another of the 'Oxford realists'; the quotation is attributed to 'Mr J. Sparrow', a student of Joseph's. To be exact, the tradition did not die with the early realists and was not restricted to philosophy. J. L. Austin (b.1911) appears to have taken a similar view of publication and his volume of *Collected Papers* is a slim one indeed. Ryle himself was known to advise students not to do a PhD if they could help it (for a time, they could help it): 'Better to write a short good book later than a bad long book earlier.' (Williams, *Essays and Reviews*, p. 153.)
35. Plato, *Phaedrus*, 275e–276a.
36. Sidgwick, 'A Lecture Against Lecturing', p. 349.
37. Sidgwick, 'A Lecture Against Lecturing', p. 350.
38. Plato, *Theaetetus*, 151e.
39. Paton, 'Fifty Years of Philosophy', p. 344.
40. Paton, 'Fifty Years of Philosophy', p. 344.

41. Paton, 'Fifty Years of Philosophy', p. 344.
42. Paton, 'Fifty Years of Philosophy', p. 344.
43. *Wanted!*, p. 3.
44. *Wanted!*, pp. 3–4.
45. *Wanted!*, p. 4.
46. *Wanted!*, p. 8.
47. Currie, 'The Arts and Social Studies', p. 112.
48. Ryle, 'Autobiographical', pp. 5–6; Mabbott, *Oxford Memories*, p. 76.
49. Magee, 'Conversation with Gilbert Ryle', p. 110.
50. Ryle, 'Autobiographical', p. 6.
51. Danchev, 'Franks, Oliver Shewell, Baron Franks'.
52. Sidgwick and Sidgwick, *Henry Sidgwick: A Memoir*, p. 34; quoted in Woolf, *Sowing*, pp. 129–30.
53. Ryle, 'Autobiographical', p. 6.
54. C. S. Lewis, *The Four Loves*, p. 65.
55. Ryle, 'Autobiographical', p. 6.
56. Mabbott, *Oxford Memories*, p. 78.
57. Waugh, *Brideshead Revisited*, p. 20.
58. Ryle, 'Introduction', pp. 2–3.
59. This is not to say that philosophy was, as such, atheistic: Lewis was a few years away from his conversion from agnosticism; Ryle's colleague at Christ Church was Michael Foster, who wrote extensively on creation and theological mystery.
60. Ryle, 'Introduction', p. 4.
61. Ryle, 'G. E. Moore', p. 271.
62. Woolf, *Sowing*, pp. 136–7.
63. Paul, 'G. E. Moore', p. 69.
64. Paul, 'G. E. Moore', p. 69.
65. Woolf, *Sowing*, p. 137.
66. Woolf, *Sowing*, p. 137.
67. Woolf, *Sowing*, p. 134.
68. Geach, *Truth, Love and Immortality*, p. 10.
69. Moore, 'An Autobiography', p. 21.
70. Moore, 'An Autobiography', p. 18.
71. Moore, 'An Autobiography', p. 19.
72. Broad, 'John McTaggart Ellis McTaggart', p. 13.
73. Williams, 'Limpidity and Impudence'.
74. Woolf, *Sowing*, p. 135.
75. McTaggart, 'The Unreality of Time'.

76. Moore, *Philosophical Studies*, p. 210.
77. This is Iris Murdoch's pithy summary of Moore's strategy (Murdoch, *The Sovereignty of Good*, p. 1).
78. Moore, *Philosophical Studies*, p. 208.
79. Moore, 'A Defence of Common Sense', pp. 127–8; see also DeRose, 'Introduction: Responding to Skepticism', pp. 1–27 for a useful critical discussion of Moorean arguments against the sceptic.
80. Ryle, 'G. E. Moore', p. 270.
81. Quoted in Woolf, *Sowing*, p. 139.
82. Woolf, *Sowing*, p. 139.
83. Ryle, 'G. E. Moore', p. 270.
84. Nagel, 'Impressions and Appraisals I', p. 10 n. 2.
85. Sidgwick and Sidgwick, *Henry Sidgwick: A Memoir*, p. 395.
86. Sidgwick and Sidgwick, *Henry Sidgwick: A Memoir*, p. 396.
87. Broad, *Five Types of Ethical Theory*, p. 144.
88. Quoted in Woolf, *Sowing*, p. 146.
89. Woolf, *Sowing*, p. 147.
90. Woolf, *Sowing*, p. 147.
91. Woolf, *Sowing*, p. 148.
92. Ryle, 'Autobiographical', p. 7.
93. Ryle, 'Autobiographical', p. 4.
94. Ryle, 'Autobiographical', p. 3.
95. Quoted in Woolf, *Sowing*, p. 133.
96. Russell, 'Knowledge by Acquaintance and Knowledge by Description'.
97. Russell, *The Problems of Philosophy*, p. 32.
98. Russell, *Introduction to Mathematical Philosophy*, p. 167.
99. Russell first develops this kind of analysis in his 'On Denoting'.
100. Russell, *My Philosophical Development*, p. 99.
101. Ryle, 'Autobiographical', p. 7: 'Having no mathematical ability, equipment, or interest, I did not make myself even competent in the algebra of logic.'
102. Ryle, 'Autobiographical', p. 8.
103. Ryle, 'Autobiographical', p. 6.
104. Ryle, 'Autobiographical', pp. 6–7.
105. Ryle, 'Systematically Misleading Expressions', p. 139.
106. Ryle, 'Systematically Misleading Expressions', p. 143.
107. Ryle, 'Systematically Misleading Expressions', pp. 144–6.
108. Ryle, 'Systematically Misleading Expressions', p. 161.
109. Ryle, 'Systematically Misleading Expressions', pp. 169–70.

110. Berlin in Chanan, 'I'm Going to Tamper With Your Beliefs a Little'.

2. Nonsense

1. This was the title of a review by Hilary Spurling of Ben Rogers' biography of Ayer, published in 2000 in *The New York Times*. Spurling attributes the phrase to a schoolmaster at Winchester College.
2. Rogers, *A. J. Ayer: A Life*, p. 52.
3. Auden's college room is described in detail in Humphrey Carpenter, *W. H. Auden: A Biography*, p. 79.
4. Rogers, *A. J. Ayer: A Life*, p. 53. Also, Ayer, *Part of My Life*, p. 75.
5. Spender, *World Within World*, p. 33.
6. Rogers, *A. J. Ayer: A Life*, pp. 30–32.
7. The quotation is from Russell, *Sceptical Essays*, p. 1. Ayer mentions his childhood reading of it in Ayer, *Part of My Life*, pp. 53–4.
8. Ayer, *Part of My Life*, p. 54.
9. Ayer, *Part of My Life*, p. 76.
10. Ayer, *Part of My Life*, pp. 76–7; see also the description of Ryle in Williams, *Essays and Reviews*, pp. 152–3.
11. Oxford in the 1920s is the subject of many a reverent memoir. A succinct account appears in Berlin, *Letters 1928–1946*, p. 17. But see also Spender, *World Within World*. And for an account of a slightly earlier period, see the essays in Hollis, *Oxford in the Twenties*.
12. Waugh, *Brideshead Revisited*, p. 45.
13. Berlin, *Letters 1928–1946*, p. 17.
14. Spender, *World Within World*, p. 38.
15. Ayer, *Part of My Life*, p. 80.
16. Ryle, 'Autobiographical', p. 5.
17. Quoted in, e.g. Jaakko Hintikka, 'Ernst Mach at the Crossroads of Twentieth-Century Philosophy', p. 89.
18. Ryle, review of Martin Heidegger, *Sein und Zeit*, p. 370.
19. See, for instance, Adorno, *The Jargon of Authenticity* and Wolin, *The Heidegger Controversy*. For a more accessible discussion of the interpretative controversies around Heidegger's politics, see also Bakewell, *At the Existentialist Café*, ch. 34.
20. Ryle, review of Martin Heidegger, *Sein und Zeit*, p. 364.
21. G. A. Cohen, *Finding Oneself in the Other*, p. 104 n. 22.
22. Auden and Garrett, *The Poet's Tongue*, p. viii.
23. Ayer, *Part of My Life*, p. 94.

24. Rogers, *A. J. Ayer: A Life*, p. 57.
25. Mitchell, *Maurice Bowra: A Life*, p. 245.
26. Collini, 'Delighted to See Himself'.
27. Ayer, *Part of My Life*, p. 99.
28. Wilson, letter to the *London Review of Books*.
29. Rogers, *A. J. Ayer: A Life*, p. 58.
30. Rogers, *A. J. Ayer: A Life*, p. 65.
31. Rogers, *A. J. Ayer: A Life*, p. 69.
32. Spender, *World Within World*, p. 40.
33. See Monk, *The Duty of Genius*, pp. 205–7 for an account of Ogden and Ramsey's translation of the *Tractatus*.
34. Wittgenstein, *Tractatus*, §1.
35. Quoted in Rogers, *A. J. Ayer: A Life*, p. 73.
36. Quoted in Rogers, *A. J. Ayer: A Life*, p. 73.
37. See Monk, *The Duty of Genius*, pp. 38–42 for Russell's early impressions of Wittgenstein.
38. Ayer, *Part of My Life*, p. 121; Rogers, *A. J. Ayer: A Life*, p. 79.
39. Ayer, *Part of My Life*, p. 113.
40. Rogers, *A. J. Ayer: A Life*, p. 73; see also Mabbott, *Oxford Memories*, p. 72.
41. Blumberg and Feigl, 'Logical Positivism', p. 282.
42. Blumberg and Feigl, 'Logical Positivism', p. 282.
43. Blumberg and Feigl, 'Logical Positivism', p. 296.
44. Ayer, *Part of My Life*, pp. 120–21.
45. Wittgenstein, *Tractatus*, §7.
46. Ayer, *Part of My Life*, pp. 115–16.
47. Ayer attributes this phrase to one of the examiners, John Sparrow (hearsay); see Ayer, *Part of My Life*, p. 125.
48. Ayer, *Part of My Life*, p. 128.
49. Ayer, *Part of My Life*, p. 135.
50. Ayer, *Part of My Life*, p. 133.
51. Quine, *The Time of My Life*, p. 94.
52. A few years later, two other women would be part of the group: the mathematician Olga Taussky-Todd (b.1906) and the psychologist Else Frenkel-Brunswik (b.1908). See Janssen-Lauret, 'Women in Logical Empiricism', for a discussion of the contributions to logical empiricism from women within the Vienna Circle and related movements. After Wittgenstein's return to Cambridge, a surprising number of the students who attended his lectures were women, despite his

purported 'general dislike of academic women and especially of female philosophers' (Monk, *The Duty of Genius*, p. 498); among them were Alice Ambrose (b.1906), Margaret MacDonald (b.1907), Margaret Masterman (b.1910) and G. E. M. Anscombe (b.1919). But see Connell, 'Alice Ambrose and Early Analytic Philosophy', for a critical discussion of Wittgenstein's dismissive attitude towards Ambrose and the serious impact his treatment of her had on her career and the subsequent reception of her work.

53. See Schlick, *Problems of Ethics*.

54. Nagel, 'Impressions and Appraisals I', p. 8.

55. Ayer, *Part of My Life*, pp. 134–5.

56. For general discussions of the intellectual climate in early twentieth-century Vienna, see Schorske, *Fin-de-siècle Vienna: Politics and Culture*, and Janik and Toulmin, *Wittgenstein's Vienna*.

57. Nagel, 'Impressions and Appraisals I', p. 9.

58. Nagel, 'Impressions and Appraisals I', p. 9.

59. Ayer, *Part of My Life*, p. 121.

60. Ayer, *Part of My Life*, p. 157.

61. For a discussion of Stebbing's attitude to Moore and his influence on her, see Stebbing, 'Moore's Influence', p. 530.

62. Stebbing, 'Logical Positivism and Analysis', p. 36.

63. Stebbing, 'Logical Positivism and Analysis', p. 36.

64. Ayer, *Part of My Life*, p. 157.

65. Ayer, *Part of My Life*, p. 151.

66. *Analysis*, 'Statement of Policy', pp. 1–2.

67. For accounts of Ryle's drinking records, see Trevor-Roper, *The Wartime Journals*, p. 155.

68. Trevor-Roper, *The Wartime Journals*, p. 127.

69. Ayer, *Part of My Life*, p. 152. See Cassirer, *Mein Leben mit Ernst Cassirer*, pp. 211–25 for Ernst's wife Toni's account of the Cassirers' time in Oxford.

70. Ayer, *Part of My Life*, p. 152.

71. Ayer, *Part of My Life*, pp. 144–5.

72. Ayer, *Part of My Life*, p. 153.

73. Cornforth was one of a handful of students who joined the Cambridge University branch of the Communist Party after a session of the Moral Sciences Club at which David Guest, a student of Wittgenstein's, excitedly read out passages from Lenin; see Rée, *Proletarian Philosophers*, p. 161 n. 33.

74. Black, Wisdom and Cornforth, 'Symposium: Is Analysis a Useful Method in Philosophy?', p. 118.
75. Ayer, *Part of My Life*, p. 156.
76. Ayer, *Part of My Life*, pp. 164–5.
77. Ayer, *Part of My Life*, p. 140.
78. Ayer, *Part of My Life*, p. 140.
79. Ayer, *Part of My Life*, pp. 153–4.
80. Ayer, *Part of My Life*, p. 154.
81. Carnap lectured at the Bauhaus in 1929, announcing to his audience, 'I work in science, and you in visible forms; the two are only different sides of a single life.' Quoted in Galison, 'Aufbau/Bauhaus: Logical Positivism and Architectural Modernism', p. 710.
82. Ayer, *Part of My Life*, p. 166.

3. Argy-Bargy

1. Woolf, *The Sickle Side of the Moon*, p. 255.
2. Ignatieff, *Isaiah Berlin: A Life*, p. 40.
3. Ignatieff, *Isaiah Berlin: A Life*, p. 49.
4. Ignatieff, *Isaiah Berlin: A Life*, p. 49.
5. Ignatieff, *Isaiah Berlin: A Life*, p. 51.
6. Ignatieff, *Isaiah Berlin: A Life*, pp. 54–5.
7. Ignatieff, *Isaiah Berlin: A Life*, pp. 53–4.
8. Ignatieff, *Isaiah Berlin: A Life*, p. 53. See also Spender, *World Within World*, pp. 71–2.
9. Ignatieff, *Isaiah Berlin: A Life*, p. 61.
10. Ignatieff, *Isaiah Berlin: A Life*, p. 59.
11. Ignatieff, *Isaiah Berlin: A Life*, p. 61.
12. Ignatieff, *Isaiah Berlin: A Life*, p. 61.
13. Pevsner and Sherwood, *Oxfordshire*, p. 92.
14. Pevsner and Sherwood, *Oxfordshire*, pp. 94–5.
15. See the Library History page on the All Souls College website: www.asc.ox.ac.uk/library-history.
16. Berlin, *Letters 1928–1946*, p. 152.
17. Ignatieff, *Isaiah Berlin: A Life*, p. 64.
18. Ignatieff, *Isaiah Berlin: A Life*, p. 66.
19. Ignatieff, *Isaiah Berlin: A Life*, pp. 69–70.
20. Ignatieff, *Isaiah Berlin: A Life*, p. 71.
21. Ignatieff, *Isaiah Berlin: A Life*, p. 71.

22. Ignatieff, *Isaiah Berlin: A Life*, p. 75. I have corrected the German grammar slightly – *anderen* for *andere* – on the assumption that the error was either Ignatieff's or Berlin's, not Namier's.

23. Ignatieff, *Isaiah Berlin: A Life*, p. 70.

24. Quoted in Warnock, 'John Langshaw Austin, A Biographical Sketch', p. 3.

25. Warnock, 'A Biographical Sketch', pp. 5–6.

26. Stone, *The Social Contract of the Universe*, p. 37.

27. Laird, review of C. G. Stone, *The Social Contract of the Universe*, p. 138.

28. Longworth, 'John Langshaw Austin'.

29. 'Michael Ignatieff's Biographical Interviews', MI Tape 5, p. 18.

30. Berlin in Chanan, 'I'm Going to Tamper With Your Beliefs a Little'.

31. Michael Ignatieff writes, 'Thinking, for him, was always a dialogue either with a friend or with a book. A blank sheet of paper aroused dread.' Ignatieff, *Isaiah Berlin: A Life*, p. 244.

32. Berlin, 'Austin and the Early Beginnings of Oxford Philosophy', p. 5.

33. Berlin, 'Austin and the Early Beginnings of Oxford Philosophy', p. 5.

34. Ayer, *Part of My Life*, p. 161.

35. Berlin in Chanan, 'I'm Going to Tamper With Your Beliefs a Little'.

36. Berlin, 'Austin and the Early Beginnings of Oxford Philosophy', p. 15.

37. Berlin in Chanan, 'I'm Going to Tamper With Your Beliefs a Little'.

38. Berlin in 'Michael Ignatieff's Biographical Interviews', MI Tape 6, p. 26.

39. Warnock, 'A Biographical Sketch', p. 11 n. 1.

40. Warnock, 'A Biographical Sketch', p. 4.

41. Housman, 'The Application of Thought to Textual Criticism', p. 68.

42. Housman, 'The Application of Thought', p. 69.

43. Housman, 'The Application of Thought', p. 73.

44. Stadler, 'Documentation: The Murder of Moritz Schlick', in Stadler (ed.), *The Vienna Circle: Studies in the Origins, Development, and Influence of Logical Empiricism*, p. 906.

45. Berlin, *Letters 1928–1946*, p. 179. See also Skidelsky, *Oswald Mosley* and Copsey, *Anti-Fascism in Britain*, p. 42.

46. Berlin, *Letters 1928–1946*, p. 179. But see Copsey, *Anti-Fascism*, pp. 39–40 for other views about the left and the police.

47. Berlin, 'Austin and the Early Beginnings of Oxford Philosophy', p. 7.

48. Berlin, 'Austin and the Early Beginnings of Oxford Philosophy', pp. 7–8.

49. Berlin, 'Austin and the Early Beginnings of Oxford Philosophy', p. 8.

50. Berlin, 'Austin and the Early Beginnings of Oxford Philosophy', p. 8.

51. Hampshire in Chanan, 'I'm Going to Tamper With Your Beliefs a Little'.
52. Ignatieff, *Isaiah Berlin: A Life*, p. 86.
53. Ayer, *Part of My Life*, p. 161; cf. Pitcher, 'Austin: A Personal Memoir', p. 30.
54. Berlin, 'Austin and the Early Beginnings of Oxford Philosophy', pp. 9–11.
55. Hampshire in Chanan, 'I'm Going to Tamper With Your Beliefs a Little'.
56. Berlin, 'Austin and the Early Beginnings of Oxford Philosophy', p. 12 n. 3.
57. Warnock, 'A Biographical Sketch', p. 6.
58. Franklin, 'Ludicrous, but Interesting'.
59. Warnock, 'A Biographical Sketch', p. 7.
60. Bradley, *Appearance and Reality*, p. 1.
61. Berlin, 'Austin and the Early Beginnings of Oxford Philosophy', pp. 9–10; cf. p. 16.
62. Berlin, 'Austin and the Early Beginnings of Oxford Philosophy', pp. 10–11.
63. In Chanan, 'I'm Going to Tamper With Your Beliefs a Little'.
64. Stebbing, 'Logical Positivism and Analysis', p. 36.
65. Warnock, 'A Biographical Sketch', p. 7.
66. Berlin in Chanan, 'I'm Going to Tamper With Your Beliefs a Little'.
67. Berlin, 'Austin and the Early Beginnings of Oxford Philosophy', p. 10 n. 2.
68. Berlin, 'Austin and the Early Beginnings of Oxford Philosophy', p. 10.
69. Berlin, 'Austin and the Early Beginnings of Oxford Philosophy', p. 10.
70. Hampshire in Chanan, 'I'm Going to Tamper With Your Beliefs a Little'.
71. Berlin, 'Austin and the Early Beginnings of Oxford Philosophy', p. 1.
72. Stebbing, *Thinking to Some Purpose*, p. 5.

4. Blood

1. Midgley, *The Owl of Minerva*, p. 23.
2. Midgley, *The Owl of Minerva*, p. 25.
3. Midgley, *The Owl of Minerva*, p. 3.
4. Midgley, *The Owl of Minerva*, p. 58
5. Midgley, *The Owl of Minerva*, p. 62.

6. Midgley, *The Owl of Minerva*, p. 62.
7. Midgley, *The Owl of Minerva*, p. 66.
8. Midgley, *The Owl of Minerva*, p. 76.
9. Pevsner and Sherwood, *Oxfordshire*, p. 187.
10. Midgley, *The Owl of Minerva*, p. 87.
11. Midgley, *The Owl of Minerva*, p. 86.
12. Berlin, *Letters 1928–1946*, p. 179.
13. Healey, *The Time of My Life*, p. 29.
14. Julian Amery is also sometimes credited with the coinage. See Happold and Conway, 'Healey on Healey'.
15. MacNeice, *Autumn Journal*, §xiv.
16. Quoted in Inglis, *History Man*, p. 249.
17. Campbell, *Roy Jenkins*, p. 29.
18. Conradi, *Iris Murdoch*, p. 90.
19. MacNeice, *Autumn Journal*, §xiv.
20. Conradi, *A Very English Hero*, p. 114.
21. Davenport-Hines, 'Introduction', in Trevor-Roper, *The Wartime Journals*, p. 7.
22. Mitchell, *Maurice Bowra*, p. 241.
23. Mitchell, *Maurice Bowra*, p. 241.
24. Midgley, *The Owl of Minerva*, p. 86.
25. Midgley, *The Owl of Minerva*, p. 86.
26. Midgley, 'The Golden Age of Female Philosophy'.
27. Ayer, *Part of My Life*, p. 224.
28. Diamond, 'Obituary for Anthony Woozley', p. 215.
29. Ryan, 'Stuart Newton Hampshire', p. 110.
30. Conradi, *Iris Murdoch*, p. 124.
31. This was the experience of Dennis Nineham, reported in Conradi, *Iris Murdoch*, p. 125 n.
32. Midgley, *The Owl of Minerva*, p. 116.
33. Conradi, *Iris Murdoch*, p. 123.
34. Midgley, *The Owl of Minerva*, p. 125.
35. Conradi and Lawrence, 'Professor Philippa Foot'. I have written of Bosanquet (*mariée*, Foot) in Krishnan, 'Is Goodness Natural?'
36. Mary Warnock, *A Memoir*, p. 75.
37. Teichman, 'Anscombe, (Gertrude) Elizabeth Margaret', p. 33.
38. Kenny, 'Peter Thomas Geach', p. 187.
39. Kenny, 'Peter Thomas Geach', p. 187. It is more than possible that this

story was, as Mac Cumhaill and Wiseman suggest, an in-joke between the couple (*Metaphysical Animals*, p. 30).

40. Wilamowitz-Moellendorff, *Greek Historical Writing and Apollo*, p. 25.
41. Wilamowitz-Moellendorff, *History of Classical Scholarship*, p. 1.
42. Stray, 'Eduard Fraenkel', p. 124.
43. Mary Warnock, *A Memoir*, pp. 82–3.
44. Rowse, 'Oxford in War-time', p. 262.
45. Nicholas, 'German Refugees in Oxford: Some Personal Recollections', pp. 743–4.
46. Midgley, *The Owl of Minerva*, p. 97.
47. Murdoch, quoted in Conradi, *Iris Murdoch*, p. 116.
48. Attributed to an unnamed scholar in Stray, 'Eduard Fraenkel', p. 143.
49. Conradi, *Iris Murdoch*, p. 495.
50. Williams, *Shame and Necessity*, pp. x–xi.
51. Scottish classical scholar Colin Macleod, quoted in Stray, 'Eduard Fraenkel', p. 144.
52. Murdoch, quoted in Stray, 'Eduard Fraenkel', p. 143.
53. Auden, 'September 1, 1939', in *Another Time*.
54. Mary Warnock, *A Memoir*, p. 84.
55. Mary Warnock, *A Memoir*, p. 84.
56. Murdoch, 'The Agamemnon Class, 1939', quoted in Conradi, *Iris Murdoch*, p. 122.
57. See, e.g. Mitchell, *Maurice Bowra*, p. 174.
58. Midgley, *The Owl of Minerva*, p. 126.
59. Quoted in Conradi, *Iris Murdoch*, p. 135.
60. Quoted in Conradi, *Iris Murdoch*, pp. 136–7.
61. Conradi, *Iris Murdoch*, p. 137.
62. Conradi, *Iris Murdoch*, p. 155.
63. Teichman, 'Anscombe, (Gertrude) Elizabeth Margaret', p. 48.
64. Kenny, 'Peter Thomas Geach', p. 188.
65. The word is mentioned in Teichman, 'Anscombe, (Gertrude) Elizabeth Margaret', p. 34; Lipscomb (*The Women Are Up to Something*, p. 294 n. 47) suggests, on the testimony of Anscombe and Geach's daughter, that the phrase was in fact used of the marriage of Bernard and Shirley Williams, the former teaching at Cambridge while the latter divided her time between the House of Commons and her constituency.
66. Teichman, 'Anscombe, (Gertrude) Elizabeth Margaret', p. 38.

5. Saturdays

1. Noted in a letter to Ryle, printed in Collingwood, *An Essay on Philosophical Method*, p. 256.
2. Inglis, *History Man*, p. 194.
3. Collingwood, *An Autobiography*, p. 52.
4. Collingwood, *An Autobiography*, p. 29.
5. Inglis, *History Man*, p. 125.
6. Collingwood, *Religion and Philosophy*.
7. Collingwood, *Essay*, pp. 141–2.
8. *Analysis*, 'Statement of Policy', pp. 1–2.
9. For an accessible discussion of Hegel's conception of philosophy, see §3.1.1 of Redding, 'Georg Wilhelm Friedrich Hegel'.
10. Williams, 'An Essay on Collingwood', p. 352.
11. Collingwood, *An Autobiography*, p. 122; see also Williams, 'An Essay on Collingwood', pp. 351–2.
12. Inglis, *History Man*, p. 45.
13. Inglis, *History Man*, p. 199.
14. Inglis, *History Man*, p. 18.
15. Collingwood, *An Autobiography*, Preface.
16. Collingwood, *An Autobiography*, p. 167.
17. Inglis, *History Man*, p. 249.
18. Collingwood, *An Autobiography*, p. 167.
19. Inglis, *History Man*, p. 305.
20. Strawson, 'Ryle, Gilbert'.
21. Lord Dacre [Trevor-Roper], 'My War', p. 31. Quoted in Winter, 'A Higher Form of Intelligence', p. 853.
22. Mabbott, *Oxford Memories*, p. 107.
23. Mabbott, *Oxford Memories*, p. 107.
24. Mabbott, *Oxford Memories*, p. 108.
25. Mabbott, *Oxford Memories*, p. 108.
26. Mabbott, *Oxford Memories*, p. 108.
27. Quoted in Uschanov, 'The Strange Death of Ordinary Language Philosophy'.
28. Strawson, 'Ryle, Gilbert'.
29. Ryle, 'Autobiographical', p. 12.
30. Ryle, 'Autobiographical', p. 10.
31. A still vexed question about the interpretation of the *Tractatus*: see the papers in Crary and Read (eds), *The New Wittgenstein*, including the useful dissent from P. M. S. Hacker.

32. Ryle, 'Autobiographical', p. 10.
33. Ryle, 'Autobiographical', p. 12.
34. For a sophisticated account of the history of these problems and their transformation in Descartes's work, see Williams, *Descartes: The Project of Pure Enquiry.*
35. Ryle, *The Concept of Mind.*
36. Ryle, *The Concept of Mind*, p. 5.
37. Ryle, *The Concept of Mind*, p. lx.
38. The metaphor of 'guerrilla warfare' is in Dennett, 'Re-introducing *The Concept of Mind*, a Foreword', pp. viii–xix, xiii, xii; the reference to an exorcism appears in Ayer, 'An Honest Ghost', p. 74.
39. Hampshire, review of Gilbert Ryle, *The Concept of Mind.*
40. Ryle, *The Concept of Mind*, p. lxi.
41. Ryle, *The Concept of Mind*, p. 47.
42. Ryle, *The Concept of Mind*, p. 15.
43. Ryle, *The Concept of Mind*, p. 22.
44. Ryle, *The Concept of Mind*, p. 43.
45. Ryle, *The Concept of Mind*, p. 56.
46. Ryle, *The Concept of Mind*, p. 23.
47. Ryle, *The Concept of Mind*, p. 12.
48. Ryle, *The Concept of Mind*, p. 27.
49. Ryle, *The Concept of Mind*, p. lxi.
50. Williams, *Essays and Reviews*, p. 153.
51. For a history of the emergence of silent reading, see Manguel, *A History of Reading.*
52. Ryle, *The Concept of Mind*, p. 16.
53. Jonathan Rée compares Ryle's 'knowing naivety of language' to a feature of the style of such earlier English writers as 'Lewis Carroll, Edward Lear, A. A. Milne and John Betjeman' ('English Philosophy in the Fifties').
54. Austin, 'Intelligent Behaviour'.
55. Hampshire, 'Critical Review', p. 20.
56. For an example of philosophical scepticism about psychological forms of behaviourism, see Williams's review of B. F. Skinner's *Beyond Freedom and Dignity* (*Essays and Reviews*, pp. 87–9). See also George, 'Behaviorism'.
57. Hampshire, 'Critical Review', p. 44.
58. Austin, 'Intelligent Behaviour'.
59. Hampshire, 'Critical Review', p. 44.

60. Hampshire, 'Critical Review', p. 17
61. Hampshire, 'Critical Review', p. 18.
62. Austin, 'Intelligent Behaviour'.
63. The account to follow is based primarily on the memoir by G. J. Warnock, 'Saturday Mornings', and G. J. Warnock's more impersonal essay, 'John Langshaw Austin, A Biographical Sketch'.
64. Warnock, 'A Biographical Sketch', p. 9.
65. Warnock, 'A Biographical Sketch', p. 9.
66. Warnock, 'A Biographical Sketch', p. 11.
67. See Camus, *The Fall*, pp. 10–11.
68. Warnock, 'A Biographical Sketch', p. 13.
69. Warnock, 'A Biographical Sketch', p. 14 n. 1.
70. Wittgenstein, *Philosophical Investigations*, §66.
71. Warnock, 'A Biographical Sketch', pp. 14–15 n. 3.
72. Warnock, 'A Biographical Sketch', p. 4.
73. Warnock, 'Saturday Mornings', p. 31.
74. Austin and Anscombe, 'Pretending', p. 264.
75. Warnock, 'Saturday Mornings', pp. 32–3.
76. Pitcher, 'Austin: A Personal Memoir', pp. 25–6.
77. White, *A Philosopher's Story*, p. 211.
78. Warnock, 'Saturday Mornings', p. 35.
79. Warnock, 'Saturday Mornings', p. 40.
80. Warnock, 'Saturday Mornings', p. 40 n. 6.
81. Warnock, 'Saturday Mornings', p. 37.
82. Hare, *The Language of Morals*, p. 152.
83. Williams, *Shame and Necessity*, p. 23 n. 6.
84. Wisdom, 'Philosophical Perplexity', p. 72 n. 1.
85. Wisdom, 'Philosophical Perplexity', p. 83.
86. Wisdom, 'Philosophical Perplexity', p. 76.
87. Wisdom, 'Philosophical Perplexity', p. 77.
88. Wisdom, 'Philosophical Perplexity', p. 77.
89. The quotations are from Ryle, *The Concept of Mind*, p. 15; Austin, *How to Do Things with Words*, p. i; Wisdom, 'Philosophical Perplexity', p. 88.
90. Wisdom, 'Philosophical Perplexity', p. 88.
91. I am echoing the insightful remarks by Bernard Williams about Wisdom's style in Williams, *Essays and Reviews*, p. 101: 'If one is forced to a comparison of these two ways of writing philosophy in a style without exposition or the apparatus of proof, Wisdom's jokiness

runs the risk of coming out of it as English things do from some other comparisons with Viennese things (music, for instance).'

92. Monk, *The Duty of Genius*, p. 433.
93. Wittgenstein to R. Rhees, 28 November 1944, in McGuinness (ed.), *Wittgenstein in Cambridge*, p. 371.
94. Wittgenstein to Miss Curtis, 18 May 1945, in McGuinness (ed.), *Wittgenstein in Cambridge*, p. 374.
95. Wittgenstein, 'Reference for Elizabeth Anscombe', quoted in Mac Cumhaill and Wiseman, *Metaphysical Animals*, p. 321.
96. Kenny, 'Peter Thomas Geach', p. 188.
97. Monk, *The Duty of Genius*, p. 577.
98. Quoted in Blackburn, *Truth: A Guide for the Perplexed*, p. 57.
99. I follow here the account given by Mary Warnock, who knew her in these years: *A Memoir*, p. 60.
100. The quoted phrase is from Mary Warnock, 'A Tremendous Coup', p. 395, and is consistent with the account in Midgley, *The Owl of Minerva*, p. 159.
101. Quoted, though acquired at third hand (from P. M. S. Hacker via J. O. Urmson and H. L. A. Hart), in Dancy, 'Harold Arthur Prichard'. Memories of the event slightly differ on exactly what Prichard said, but it came to roughly the same thing.
102. Via Philippa Foot, quoted in McGuinness, 'Two Cheers for the "New" Wittgenstein', p. 266.
103. Mary Warnock, *A Memoir*, p. 69.
104. Wittgenstein, *Blue and Brown Books*, p. 28.
105. Mary Warnock, *A Memoir*, pp. 72, 69.
106. Asked by a *Guardian* journalist interviewing her for a feature on career women, 'How do you manage a household with a husband and six children while carrying on your full-time career?', she is supposed to have answered, 'You just have to realise that dirt doesn't matter.' (The story is told in Searle, 'Oxford Philosophy in the 1950s', p. 180, on the whole a tasteless and prurient memoir; this anecdote, however, rings true.)
107. Wittgenstein, *Philosophical Investigations*, p. viii.
108. Wittgenstein, *Philosophical Investigations*, p. vii.
109. Anscombe, 'On the Form of Wittgenstein's Writing', p. 210.
110. Wittgenstein, *Philosophical Investigations*, p. viii.
111. Bartley, *Wittgenstein*, ch. 3.
112. These discussions have spawned a large philosophical literature, e.g.

Baker and Hacker, *Wittgenstein: Meaning and Understanding*; and Hintikka and Hintikka, *Investigating Wittgenstein*.

113. Her response to W. W. Bartley's psychosexual biography of Wittgenstein is representative (see her letter to the *Times Literary Supplement* of 16 November 1973). But she was also capable of receiving warmly works that she thought embodied the spirit of his thought – see her review of Kripke, *Wittgenstein on Rules and Private Language*.

114. Anscombe, 'Ludwig Wittgenstein', p. 187.

115. Anscombe, 'Ludwig Wittgenstein', p. 188.

116. This story is told by A. W. Moore, who was the graduate student in it, at www.whatisitliketobeaphilosopher.com/#/adrian-moore/.

6. Corruption

1. Knowles, 'Harry S. Truman'.
2. Axelrod, *The Real History of the Cold War*, p. 56.
3. Truman, *1948: Containing the Public Messages, Speeches, and Statements of the President, January 1 to December 31, 1948*, p. 239.
4. McCullough, *Truman*, p. 1134.
5. 'Oxford Don Fights Honor for Truman', p. 3.
6. Anscombe, 'Mr Truman's Degree', pp. 62–71.
7. Kenny, 'Elizabeth Anscombe at Oxford', p. 182.
8. Anscombe, 'Mr Truman's Degree', p. 63.
9. Anscombe, 'Mr Truman's Degree', p. 65.
10. Anscombe, 'Mr Truman's Degree', p. 66.
11. Anscombe, 'Mr Truman's Degree', p. 70.
12. Ross, *The Right and the Good*, p. 19.
13. Hare, 'A Philosophical Autobiography', p. 270.
14. Hare, 'Autobiography', pp. 269–71.
15. Hare, 'Autobiography', p. 273.
16. Hare, 'Autobiography', p. 276.
17. Mehta, *Fly and the Fly-Bottle*, p. 47.
18. Hare, 'Autobiography', pp. 276–7.
19. Hare, 'Autobiography', pp. 277–8.
20. Hare, 'Autobiography', p. 280.
21. Hare, 'Autobiography', p. 280. Searle's form is reproduced in Davies, *Ronald Searle*, p. 56 – the Searle in question the man behind *Molesworth* and *The Belles of St Trinian's*. The Knox behind the other form was, as it happens, the son of 'Evoe' Knox, editor of *Punch*, and

the brother of the (future) novelist Penelope Fitzgerald, then working for the BBC in London.

22. Hare, 'Autobiography', p. 281.
23. Hare, 'Autobiography', p. 281.
24. Davies, *Ronald Searle*, pp. 57–8.
25. Davies, *Ronald Searle*, p. 261.
26. Hare himself attributes this book to the physicist Arthur Eddington, but he was probably mixing up Alexander's book with Eddington's similarly titled *Space, Time and Gravitation*.
27. Hare, 'Autobiography', p. 282.
28. A. W. Price, 'Richard Mervyn Hare' (*Stanford Encyclopedia*).
29. Hare, 'Autobiography', p. 283.
30. Hare, 'Autobiography', p. 283.
31. Mehta, *Fly and the Fly-Bottle*, p. 30.
32. Hare, 'Autobiography', p. 283.
33. Hare, 'Autobiography', p. 273.
34. Ray Monk, for instance, writes that 'as the accepted leader of philosophy at Oxford, [Ryle] was able to exert a personal influence on a good proportion of the philosophers who staffed the philosophy departments in the fast-growing number of post-war universities. Most of these young philosophers had been graduate students at Oxford, many supervised by Ryle himself and then "placed" by him.' Monk describes a colleague at the University of Southampton being hired by a process that consisted simply of somebody 'call[ing] Gilbert and ask[ing] him who he could recommend' (Monk, 'How the Untimely Death of R. G. Collingwood Changed the Course of Philosophy Forever').
35. Hare, 'Autobiography', p. 285.
36. Hare, 'Autobiography', p. 286.
37. Moore, *Principia Ethica*, p. 55.
38. Wollheim, review of Hare, *The Language of Morals*, p. 762.
39. Wollheim, review of Hare, *The Language of Morals*, p. 762. For an account of Wollheim's time as a prisoner of war, see Wollheim, 'A Bed out of Leaves'.
40. Wollheim, review of Hare, *The Language of Morals*, p. 762.
41. Anscombe, 'Does Oxford Moral Philosophy Corrupt the Youth?'
42. Braithwaite, review of Hare, *The Language of Morals*, p. 249.
43. Anscombe, 'Oxford Moral Philosophy', p. 267.
44. Anscombe, 'Oxford Moral Philosophy', p. 267.

45. Anscombe, 'Oxford Moral Philosophy', p. 267.
46. Anscombe, 'Oxford Moral Philosophy', p. 267.
47. Anscombe, 'Oxford Moral Philosophy', p. 271.
48. Hare and Nowell-Smith, 'Oxford Moral Philosophy', p. 311.
49. Hare and Nowell-Smith, 'Oxford Moral Philosophy', p. 311.
50. Hare and Nowell-Smith, 'Oxford Moral Philosophy', p. 311.
51. Hare and Nowell-Smith, 'Oxford Moral Philosophy', p. 311.
52. Radford, 'Patrick Nowell-Smith obituary'.
53. Hare and Nowell-Smith, 'Oxford Moral Philosophy', p. 311.
54. Hare and Nowell-Smith, 'Oxford Moral Philosophy', p. 311.
55. Hare and Nowell-Smith, 'Oxford Moral Philosophy', p. 311.
56. Anscombe, 'Oxford Moral Philosophy', p. 349.
57. Anscombe, 'Oxford Moral Philosophy', p. 349.
58. Anscombe, 'Modern Moral Philosophy'.
59. Hume, *A Treatise of Human Nature*, Book 3, Part 1, §1.
60. Kant, *Groundwork of the Metaphysics of Morals*, §2.
61. Anscombe, 'On Brute Facts'.
62. Mehta, *Fly and the Fly-Bottle*, p. 50.
63. Anscombe, 'Modern Moral Philosophy', p. 17.
64. Midgley, 'Then and Now', §3. See also Midgley, *The Owl of Minerva*, p. 147. For a telling of the history of this period of philosophy from the point of view of this heterodox grouping, see Lipscomb, *The Women Are Up to Something*, and Mac Cumhaill and Wiseman, *Metaphysical Animals*.
65. Hare, 'Can I Be Blamed for Obeying Orders?', p. 8.
66. As Bernard Williams, responding to this debate in the early 1970s, would write: 'Moral thinking *feels* as though it mirrored something, as though it were constrained to follow, rather than be freely creative … The consciousness of a principle of action as freely decided upon is very unlike the consciousness of a moral principle, which is rather of something that has to be acknowledged' (*Morality*, p. 36).
67. Voorhoeve, *Conversations on Ethics*, p. 92.
68. Berlin in Chanan, 'I'm Going to Tamper With Your Beliefs a Little'.
69. Adorno, 'Cultural Criticism and Society', p. 34.
70. Foot, *Virtues and Vices*, p. 107.
71. For a reckoning with the attractions of utilitarianism in roughly these terms, see Williams, *Morality*, pp. 83–5.
72. Moore, *Principia Ethica*, pp. 62–72. For a detailed later discussion tracing the profound influence of Moore's critique of naturalism on

subsequent moral philosophy, see Darwall, Gibbard and Railton, 'Toward *Fin de Siècle* Ethics: Some Trends', esp. pp. 115–21 and pp. 164–74.

73. Foot, *Virtues and Vices*, p. 120.
74. Foot, *Virtues and Vices*, p. 120.
75. Foot, *Virtues and Vices*, p. 141. Foot's final word on this subject appeared in her elegant final book, *Natural Goodness*, esp. chs 2–3.

7. Swimming

1. The story is told in Myers, 'George Eliot'.
2. Hare is quoted as saying so in Mehta, *Fly and the Fly-Bottle*, p. 51.
3. Conradi, *Iris Murdoch*, p. 87.
4. It was the precursor to the Office of the UN's High Commissioner for Refugees.
5. Conradi, *Iris Murdoch*, p. 207.
6. Conradi, *Iris Murdoch*, p. 207.
7. Conradi, *Iris Murdoch*, p. 210.
8. Conradi, *Iris Murdoch*, p. 210.
9. Conradi, *Iris Murdoch*, p. 211.
10. Conradi, *Iris Murdoch*, p. 212.
11. Conradi, *Iris Murdoch*, p. 214.
12. Conradi, *Iris Murdoch*, p. 215.
13. Williams and Montefiore, Introduction to *British Analytical Philosophy*, p. 14. The reference to Pierre is of course roughly based on a famous passage in Sartre's *Being and Nothingness*.
14. Conradi, *Iris Murdoch*, p. 215.
15. Conradi, *Iris Murdoch*, p. 216.
16. Conradi, *Iris Murdoch*, p. 234.
17. Conradi, *Iris Murdoch*, p. 233.
18. Conradi, *Iris Murdoch*, pp. 255–8.
19. Conradi, *Iris Murdoch*, p. 253.
20. Mehta, *Fly and the Fly-Bottle*, p. 53.
21. Conradi, *Iris Murdoch*, p. 266.
22. Conradi, *Iris Murdoch*, p. 266.
23. Sartre, 'Existentialism Is a Humanism'.
24. Murdoch, *Sartre*, p. 148.
25. Murdoch, *Sartre*, p. 146.
26. Conradi, *Iris Murdoch*, p. 54.

27. 'History', St Anne's College, www.st-annes.ox.ac.uk/this-is-st-annes/history/.
28. Lacey, *A Life of H. L. A. Hart*, ch. 13 gives a full account of the charges and the grounds for thinking them false.
29. Conradi, *Iris Murdoch*, p. 292.
30. Murdoch, 'Taking the Plunge'.
31. Conradi, *Iris Murdoch*, p. 299.
32. Conradi, *Iris Murdoch*, p. 299.
33. For a general discussion of Austin's penchant for a good pun, see Ricks, 'Austin's Swink'.
34. Moore, 'A Defence of Common Sense', pp. 54–5.
35. H. H. Price, *Perception*, p. 3.
36. Austin, *Sense and Sensibilia*, p. 4.
37. Austin, *Sense and Sensibilia*, pp. 4–5.
38. Wittgenstein, *Philosophical Investigations*, §124.
39. For a reading of Austin along these lines, see Putnam, *The Threefold Cord*.
40. Murdoch, *Existentialists and Mystics*, p. 340.
41. Murdoch, *Existentialists and Mystics*, p. 346.
42. Conradi, *Iris Murdoch*, p. 303.
43. Murdoch, *Sartre*, pp. 78–9.
44. Austin, 'A Plea for Excuses', p. 130.
45. Murdoch, 'Metaphysics and Ethics', in *Existentialists and Mystics*, p. 61.
46. MacKinnon, 'And the Son of Man That Thou Visitest Him: Part 2', p. 269.
47. Murdoch, 'Vision and Choice in Morality', in *Existentialists and Mystics*, p. 98.
48. Murdoch, 'Vision and Choice in Morality', in *Existentialists and Mystics*, p. 83.
49. Murdoch, 'Metaphysics and Ethics', in *Existentialists and Mystics*, p. 74.
50. Conradi, *Iris Murdoch*, p. 305.
51. The quotations are, respectively, from Murdoch, 'Nostalgia for the Particular', in *Existentialists and Mystics*, pp. 48, 56, 54.
52. Murdoch, *Under the Net*, p. 26.
53. Murdoch, *Under the Net*, p. 27.
54. Murdoch, *Under the Net*, p. 28.
55. Murdoch, *Under the Net*, p. 91.

56. Murdoch, *Under the Net*, p. 188.
57. Williams, *On Opera*, p. 112.
58. Murdoch, 'The Sublime and the Good', in *Existentialists and Mystics*, p. 215.

8. Thaw

1. In some versions of the story, the exchange happened on a train; the person who said the words to Wittgenstein was the economist Piero Sraffa. Malcolm, *Ludwig Wittgenstein: A Memoir*, pp. 57–8.
2. Bennett, Cook, Miller and Moore, *The Complete Beyond the Fringe*, pp. 49–52.
3. Quoted in Slater and Köllner, 'General Headnote to Part XI', p. 607.
4. Mehta, *Fly and the Fly-Bottle*, p. 2.
5. Mehta, *Fly and the Fly-Bottle*, p. 3.
6. Mehta, *Fly and the Fly-Bottle*, pp. 3–4.
7. Davis, 'An Interview with Ernest Gellner', pp. 63–4.
8. See my account of the by-election campaign in Chapter 4 of this book.
9. Davis, 'An Interview with Ernest Gellner', p. 64.
10. Davis, 'An Interview with Ernest Gellner', p. 64.
11. Davis, 'An Interview with Ernest Gellner', pp. 64–5.
12. Hall, *Ernest Gellner: An Intellectual Biography*, p. 38.
13. Davis, 'An Interview with Ernest Gellner', p. 65.
14. Davis, 'An Interview with Ernest Gellner', p. 65.
15. Davis, 'An Interview with Ernest Gellner', p. 65.
16. Gellner, *Words and Things*, pp. 223–5.
17. Russell, 'The Cult of "Common Usage"', p. 303.
18. Russell, 'The Cult of "Common Usage"', p. 303.
19. Gellner, *Words and Things*, p. 235.
20. Gellner, *Words and Things*, pp. 224–5.
21. Gellner, *Words and Things*, pp. 30–37.
22. Gellner, *Words and Things*, p. 31.
23. Gellner, *Words and Things*, pp. 37–40.
24. Gellner, *Words and Things*, p. 246.
25. Marshall Cohen, 'The Angry Young Philosopher', p. 180.
26. Apart from Cohen, cited above, other hostile reviewers included G. J. Warnock, MacIntyre and Dummett. More sympathetic to Gellner were Acton and Crick. Despite A. J. Ayer's general antipathy to Austin and

ordinary language, he had a low opinion of Gellner's attack: see Ayer, 'Linguistic Philosophy'.

27. Austin, 'A Plea for Excuses', p. 130.
28. For judicious discussions of the 'Gellner affair' and its lasting effects on the discipline, such as they were, see Uschanov, 'Ernest Gellner's Criticisms of Wittgenstein and Ordinary Language Philosophy', and Tripodi, *Analytic Philosophy and the Later Wittgensteinian Tradition*, pp. 30–41.
29. Φιλοσοφία Βίου Κυβερνήτης, also translated 'love of learning is the guide to life'. See 'About Phi Beta Kappa', pbk.org/About.
30. Mehta, *Fly and the Fly-Bottle*, p. 3.
31. Mehta, *Fly and the Fly-Bottle*, p. 17.
32. Mehta, *Fly and the Fly-Bottle*, p. 35.
33. Gellner, 'Poker Player', p. 776.
34. Snow, *The Two Cultures*.
35. Mehta, *Fly and the Fly-Bottle*, p. 37.
36. Mehta, *Fly and the Fly-Bottle*, p. 37.
37. Mehta, *Fly and the Fly-Bottle*, p. 37.
38. For a dissenting voice, see Simpson, *Reflections on 'The Concept of Law'*, pp. 42–3.
39. Austin and Anscombe, 'Pretending'.
40. Ryle's discussion of pretending occurs in *The Concept of Mind*, pp. 234–40.
41. Ryle, *The Concept of Mind*, p. 236.
42. Austin's immediate target was not Ryle but a philosopher called Errol Bedford: see Bedford, 'Emotions'.
43. Austin and Anscombe, 'Pretending', pp. 263–7.
44. Austin and Anscombe, 'Pretending', pp. 290–91.
45. Austin and Anscombe, 'Pretending', p. 290.
46. Austin and Anscombe, 'Pretending', p. 290.
47. Wittgenstein, *Philosophical Investigations*, §250.
48. Mehta, *Fly and the Fly-Bottle*, p. 21.
49. Strawson, 'Intellectual Autobiography', p. 8.
50. Ramsey, 'The Nature of Truth', pp. 6–24.
51. Austin, Strawson, and Cousin, 'Truth', pp. 133–5.
52. Austin, Strawson, and Cousin, 'Truth', pp. 137–8.
53. Ramsey, 'The Nature of Truth', pp. 12–13.
54. Austin, Strawson, and Cousin, 'Truth', pp. 145–53.
55. Austin, Strawson, and Cousin, 'Truth', p. 156.

56. For a more detailed philosophical summary of the Strawson–Austin exchange, see Snowdon and Gomes, 'Peter Frederick Strawson', §3.
57. Strawson, 'Intellectual Autobiography', p. 3.
58. Strawson, '*Ecce Homo!* (Epstein)'. I am grateful to Galen Strawson for permission to quote these lines.
59. Strawson, 'Intellectual Autobiography', pp. 4–5.
60. Strawson, 'Intellectual Autobiography', p. 8.
61. Strawson, 'Intellectual Autobiography', p. 5.
62. Snowdon, 'Strawson, Sir Peter Frederick'.
63. Strawson, 'Intellectual Autobiography', p. 5.
64. O'Grady, 'Sir Peter Strawson obituary'.
65. Strawson, 'Intellectual Autobiography', p. 5.
66. Strawson, 'Intellectual Autobiography', p. 6.
67. Strawson, 'Necessary Propositions and Entailment-Statements', and Strawson, 'Ethical Intuitionism'.
68. Strawson, 'Intellectual Autobiography', pp. 6–7.
69. Snowdon, 'Strawson on the Concept of Perception', pp. 293–4.
70. Snowdon, 'Strawson, Sir Peter Frederick'.
71. See my discussion of Russell's theory of definite descriptions in Chapter 1 of this book.
72. Russell, 'On Denoting'.
73. Strawson, 'On Referring'.
74. Strawson, 'Intellectual Autobiography', p. 7.
75. Russell, 'Mr Strawson on Referring'.
76. The phrase is Austin's ('A Plea for Excuses', p. 11), used to describe an attitude towards Oxford philosophy that Russell certainly held. Austin was probably making reference to a common misquotation of Russell: 'common sense is the metaphysics of savages'. This phrase, not Russell's, originated in the discussion of Russell's views in MacIntosh, *The Problem of Knowledge*, p. 243; this discovery is due to Leach, 'Bertrand Russell and Common Sense for Savages'.
77. Strawson, *An Introduction to Logical Theory*.
78. Strawson, 'Intellectual Autobiography', pp. 8–9.
79. Strawson, review of *Philosophical Investigations*, p. 72.
80. Strawson, review of *Philosophical Investigations*, p. 70.
81. R. M. Hare wrote that Oxford philosophers used 'logic' in 'an eccentrically wide sense of the word': Hare, 'A School for Philosophers', p. 48.
82. Strawson, *An Introduction to Logical Theory*, pp. 211–13.

83. Strawson, 'Introduction', in *Philosophical Logic*, p. 1.

84. Kant, *The Critique of Pure Reason*; the clearest definition of 'critique' is at pp. 147–8.

85. A reliable introduction to the themes and arguments of Kant's *Critique of Pure Reason* is Buroker, *Kant's 'Critique of Pure Reason': An Introduction*.

86. Strawson, 'Intellectual Autobiography', pp. 12–13.

87. Strawson, *Individuals*.

88. Strawson, *Individuals*, pp. 15–30.

89. Strawson, *Individuals*, pp. 38–58.

90. Strawson, *Individuals*, pp. 59–62.

91. Strawson, *Individuals*, pp. 62–3.

92. Strawson, *Individuals*, pp. 63–86. For more discussion of Strawson's argument in this chapter, see Evans, 'Things Without the Mind'.

93. Strawson, *Individuals*, pp. 87–116.

94. For a critical discussion of Strawson and Kant, see Stroud, 'Transcendental Arguments'.

95. Strawson, *Individuals*, p. 10.

96. Strawson, 'Intellectual Autobiography', p. 11. See also Quinton, 'Alfred Jules Ayer' for an account of the controversy over the election.

97. Collini, 'No True Answers: A. J. Ayer', esp. pp. 401–2.

98. Wollheim, 'Ayer: The Man, the Philosopher, the Teacher', p. 30.

99. Fergusson, 'MacKinnon, Donald MacKenzie'; Diamond, 'Obituary for Anthony Woozley', p. 216.

100. On Berlin's residence in Washington, see Ignatieff, *Isaiah Berlin: A Life*, pp. 109–34; for Churchill's reaction to Berlin's cables, see p. 125.

101. Berlin, *Concepts and Categories*, p. xii.

102. Berlin, *Concepts and Categories*, p. xii.

103. For an illuminating account of the editorial interventions that transformed Berlin's occasional pieces into works of genuine scholarship, see Hardy, *In Search of Isaiah Berlin: A Literary Adventure*. For a representative critique of Berlin's scholarly methods, see Norton, 'The Myth of the Counter-Enlightenment'.

104. Berlin and Lukes, 'In Conversation', p. 92.

105. See the detailed and evocative account of this encounter in Ignatieff, *Isaiah Berlin: A Life*, pp. 148–69.

106. Berlin and Lukes, 'In Conversation', p. 92.

107. Berlin and Lukes, 'In Conversation', p. 93.

108. Rousseau, *On the Social Contract*, I.VII.8.

109. Berlin, 'Two Concepts of Liberty', pp. 171–2.
110. Berlin, 'Two Concepts of Liberty'. For Engels's use of 'false consciousness', see his letter to Franz Mehring 14 July 1893.
111. MacCallum, 'Negative and Positive Freedom', pp. 312–34.
112. Quoting Joseph Butler, preface to *Fifteen Sermons Preached at Rolls Chapel*, p. 13.
113. Berlin, 'Two Concepts of Liberty', pp. 212–17.
114. Barry, 'The Strange Death of Political Philosophy', p. 278.
115. Wittgenstein, *Philosophical Investigations*, §621.
116. Jarvis, review of G. E. M. Anscombe, *Intention*, p. 31; Wollheim, 'A Familiar Concept?', p. 671.
117. Wollheim, 'A Familiar Concept?', p. 672.
118. Jarvis, review of G. E. M. Anscombe, *Intention*, p. 31.
119. See the insightful discussion of these features of Wittgenstein's method in Wiseman, *Routledge Philosophy Guidebook to Anscombe's 'Intention'*, pp. 60–61. I shall be arguing in the next chapter that the contrast between Wittgenstein and Austin was seriously overdrawn in this respect.
120. Strawson, 'The Post-Linguistic Thaw', pp. 71–7.
121. The analogy might be pushed further. It was long rumoured that C. S. Lewis only began composing the Narnia books after a humiliating public argument with Elizabeth Anscombe persuaded him that he was no good at philosophy. He is supposed to have got his own back by having as his villainess a witch famously seductive in argument. Serious biographers agree that there was such an encounter, but no one has found any grounds for thinking the defeat did any more than inspire Lewis to tidy up his arguments a little. See Lipscomb, *The Women Are Up to Something*, pp. 145–8.
122. Strawson, 'Thaw', p. 71.
123. Strawson, 'Thaw', p. 71.
124. Strawson, 'Thaw', pp. 71–2.
125. Strawson, 'Thaw', p. 72.
126. To name only a few prominent philosophers to have studied for their BPhils and/or DPhils at Oxford: Thomas Nagel, Daniel Dennett, Cora Diamond and George Boolos (American), G. A. (Jerry) Cohen and Patricia Churchland (Canadian), Peter Singer and David Armstrong (Australian), Rosalind Hursthouse (New Zealander), Arindam Chakrabarti (Indian).
127. Strawson, 'Thaw', p. 74.

128. Strawson, 'Thaw', p. 74.

129. Wittgenstein, *Philosophical Investigations*, §127.

130. Strawson, 'Thaw', p. 75.

131. Hampshire, *Thought and Action*. For a thorough discussion of the book and its place in the intellectual context of the time, see Williams, review of Stuart Hampshire, *Thought and Action*, in *Essays and Reviews*, pp. 8–16.

132. Two of Murdoch's most important lectures on this topic ('The Idea of Perfection' and 'The Sovereignty of Good Over Other Concepts') were collected together with a paper on the same theme ('On "Good" and "God"') as Murdoch, *The Sovereignty of Good*.

133. Hart, *The Concept of Law*.

134. Strawson, 'Thaw', p. 77.

9. Donkeys

1. Strawson, 'Thaw', p. 75.

2. Ayer et al., *The Revolution in Philosophy*, and Warnock, *English Philosophy since 1900*. Strawson could also have mentioned Urmson, *Philosophical Analysis: Its Development Between the Two World Wars*.

3. Ayer et al., *Revolution*, p. 1.

4. Moore, 'Williams, Sir Arthur Owen Bernard'.

5. Williams, review of Ayer et al., *The Revolution in Philosophy*.

6. Williams, review of Ayer et al., *Revolution*, p. 67.

7. Williams, review of Ayer et al., *Revolution*, p. 66. See also Williams, 'Wittgenstein and Idealism'.

8. Wittgenstein, *Tractatus*, §5.5563.

9. Williams, review of Ayer et al., *Revolution*, p. 67.

10. Wittgenstein, *Philosophical Investigations*, §304.

11. A good introduction to the debate is Crary and Read, introduction to *The New Wittgenstein*, pp. 1–18; see also Hacker's opposed take in the same volume, 'Was He Trying to Whistle It?'.

12. Williams, review of Ayer et al., *Revolution*, p. 67.

13. Williams, review of Ayer et al., *Revolution*, p. 67.

14. Williams, review of Ayer et al., *Revolution*, p. 67.

15. Williams, review of Warnock, *English Philosophy since 1900*, p. 168.

16. Williams, review of Warnock, *English Philosophy*, p. 168.

17. See Williams, *Shame and Necessity*, p. 12 for an explicit use of this analogy.

18. Warnock, *English Philosophy*, p. 55.
19. Williams, review of Warnock, *English Philosophy*, p. 169.
20. Williams, review of Warnock, *English Philosophy*, pp. 169–70.
21. Williams, Untitled typescript on education, p. 3. I am grateful to Patricia Williams and A. W. Moore for permission to quote from this unpublished draft, of a never-published essay on the history and politics of British school education for *Granta*.
22. Williams, Untitled typescript on education, p. 3.
23. Lucas, 'Obituary of R. M. Hare'; see also A. W. Price, 'Richard Mervyn Hare' (*Stanford Encyclopedia*).
24. Williams, *Shame and Necessity*, pp. x–xi.
25. Moore, 'Williams, Sir Arthur Owen Bernard'.
26. Williams, review of Gilbert Ryle, *On Thinking*, in *Essays and Reviews*, pp. 152–6.
27. For an account of Shirley Williams's early political career, see Peel, *Shirley Williams: The Biography*, and her own memoirs, *Climbing the Bookshelves*.
28. *Cogito*, 'Bernard Williams', p. 143.
29. Williams, review of Iris Murdoch, *The Fire and the Sun*, in *Essays and Reviews*; Williams, *Ethics and the Limits of Philosophy*, ch. 3; Williams, *Morality*, pp. 74–81.
30. See Williams, *Ethics and the Limits of Philosophy*, pp. 129–31, 140–55; the debt to Foot and Murdoch is explicitly registered at p. 239 n. 7.
31. For an example of Williams's unpushy atheism, see his gentle but firm essay on Anglican theology, which he accused of having an 'eery compulsion' towards the 'scientifically refutable': Williams, 'The Theological Appearance of the Church of England', in *Essays and Reviews*, pp. 17–24. In 1972 Williams co-wrote, with his Cambridge colleague Michael Tanner, a critical reply to Anscombe's 'Contraception and Chastity' which they characterised as 'the reflections of two pagans': Williams and Tanner, 'Reply', in Bayles (ed.), *Ethics and Population*. In the later part of his life, Williams became increasingly influenced by Nietzsche, and came to be more and more concerned with the consequences of an atheistic worldview for philosophy: see Williams, *Shame and Necessity*, chs 1, 6.
32. Williams, 'A Mistrustful Animal', p. 81.
33. Williams, 'A Mistrustful Animal', p. 81. For Williams's opinion of Wittgenstein, see Williams, 'Nietzsche's Minimalist Moral Philosophy', p. 4.

34. See the discussion between Williams and Ayer on the 1972 television documentary *Logic Lane*: www.youtube.com/watch?v=UoeNO7-HyYE.

35. For a more detailed discussion of Wittgenstein's 'depth', see Krishnan, 'You're Talking Nonsense'.

36. Williams, foreword in Charles and Child (eds), *Wittgensteinian Themes*, p. xv.

37. Berlin, 'Austin and the Early Beginnings of Oxford Philosophy', p. 11.

38. Williams, 'Strawson on Individuals', in *Problems of the Self*, p. 125.

39. Williams, *Problems of the Self*.

40. Williams, *Problems of the Self*, pp. 11–12.

41. *Cogito*, 'Bernard Williams', p. 148.

42. Austin, *Sense and Sensibilia*, pp. 4–5. See my earlier discussion of Austin's remark in Chapter 7.

43. Williams, 'Imperative Inference', in *Problems of the Self*, p. 153 n. 1.

44. Williams, 'The Makropulos Case', in *Problems of the Self*.

45. Wollheim, review of Williams, *Problems of the Self*.

46. Marcuse, *One-Dimensional Man*, p. 175.

47. Marcuse, *One-Dimensional Man*, p. 177.

48. Marcuse, *One-Dimensional Man*, pp. 178–9.

49. Marcuse, *One-Dimensional Man*, p. 179.

50. Marcuse, *One-Dimensional Man*, p. 181.

51. Marcuse, *One-Dimensional Man*, p. 182.

52. Marcuse, *One-Dimensional Man*, p. 203.

53. Anderson, 'The Minstrels of MI5', p. 18.

54. Anderson, 'The Minstrels of MI5', p. 18.

55. Williams, 'The Hatred of Philosophy', p. 20.

56. Williams, 'The Hatred of Philosophy', p. 20.

57. Williams, 'The Hatred of Philosophy', p. 20.

58. Anderson, 'The Hatred of Philosophy', p. 31.

59. Anderson, 'The Hatred of Philosophy', p. 43.

60. For a development of this defence of analytic philosophy, see Crane, 'Philosophy, Logic, Science, History'.

61. To point out only the most obvious thing: Anderson's list, like that of most Marxists of the period, was, with the possible exception of Plato, composed entirely of straight white men.

62. Yet another broadly Marxist-inspired critique of Oxford philosophy and undergraduate curriculum was Trevor Pateman, 'The Poverty of Philosophy, Politics and Economics: A Critique of the Form and Content of the Oxford Honour School of P.P.E.'. Anderson himself

returned periodically to issue stern jeremiads at the intellectual state of the nation in the *New Left Review*, e.g. 'Components of the National Culture'.

63. Rose, *Love's Work*, pp. 129–30.
64. Lloyd, 'Interview with Gillian Rose', p. 207.
65. Quoted in Midgley, *The Owl of Minerva*, p. 163.
66. Cavell, *Little Did I Know: Excerpts from Memory*, p. 149.
67. Austin, *How to Do Things with Words*.
68. Hume, *A Treatise of Human Nature*, p. 524.
69. For a clear example of someone who had this reaction to Austin, see Simpson, *Reflections on 'The Concept of Law'*, p. 9: 'I was quite unable to see what was so path-breaking in J. L. Austin's work on performatives. What on earth was so innovatory about it? In what weird world did the Oxford philosophers live in, which pointing out the obvious ranked as some kind of intellectual breakthrough? What sort of hole had they dug themselves into, and why?'
70. The structure of Austin's lectures has long been misunderstood. Max Black wrote, in his review of the published version of these lectures, that they 'might well have borne the subtitle "In Pursuit of a Vanishing Distinction"' (Black, 'Austin on Performatives', p. 217). But as Marina Sbisà rightly notes, it is clear from the text that 'from the very start the performative/constative distinction plays an instrumental role ... Constatives are just a straw man, to be replaced with an analysis of assertion as an illocutionary act [i.e. actions performed *in* rather than *by* saying certain words].' The lectures 'make sense only in the light of the main thesis which will be revealed later in the book, i.e. that all speech should be considered as action' (Sbisà, 'How to Read Austin', p. 462). Some readers of Austin have taken him to be making a radical point here, indeed taken him to be questioning the very idea that a sentence has a 'literal meaning'. For a reading of Austin along these lines, see Crary, 'The Happy Truth: J. L. Austin's *How to Do Things with Words*'; for a challenge to Crary's reading, see Hansen, 'J. L. Austin and Literal Meaning'.
71. Pitcher, 'Austin: A Personal Memoir', p. 17.
72. Pitcher, 'Austin: A Personal Memoir', p. 17.
73. Austin, 'A Plea for Excuses', p. 1. I am assuming here that Austin used roughly the same words to his Harvard audience as he did to his audience in Bedford Square, London, a few months later.
74. Austin, 'A Plea for Excuses', p. 2.

75. Austin, 'A Plea for Excuses', p. 11 n. 4.
76. Pitcher, 'Austin: A Personal Memoir', p. 19.
77. Pitcher, 'Austin: A Personal Memoir', p. 19.
78. Austin, 'A Plea for Excuses', p. 12.
79. Austin, 'A Plea for Excuses', p. 8.
80. Cavell, *The Claim of Reason*, p. xvi.
81. Williams and Montefiore, *British Analytical Philosophy*, pp. 9–10.
82. Cavell, 'Austin at Criticism', pp. 74–5.
83. Cavell, 'Austin at Criticism', p. 75.
84. The Greek word is a coinage of Aristophanes', from his comedy *The Clouds*; it is sometimes rendered 'think-tank'.
85. Warnock, 'A Biographical Sketch', p. 13.
86. Warnock, 'A Biographical Sketch', p. 20.
87. Warnock, 'A Biographical Sketch', p. 21.

10. Ghosts

1. Dummett, *The Logical Basis of Metaphysics*, p. 19.
2. Ryle, 'Autobiographical', p. 10.
3. Murdoch, *The Sovereignty of Good*, p. 56; Williams, *Essays and Reviews*, p. 44. For a general discussion of why there are reasons for philosophers, even those moved by broadly Wittgensteinian considerations about the risks of being befuddled by language, to take seriously the possibility and desirability of linguistic innovation, see A. W. Moore, *The Evolution of Modern Metaphysics*, pp. 275–8.
4. Murdoch, *The Sovereignty of Good*, pp. 16–18.
5. Hare, 'A School for Philosophers', p. 40.
6. Hare, 'A School for Philosophers', p. 38.
7. Hare, 'A School for Philosophers', p. 39.
8. Hare, 'A School for Philosophers', pp. 40–41.
9. Hare, 'A School for Philosophers', p. 41.
10. Hare, 'A School for Philosophers', p. 41.
11. Hare, 'A School for Philosophers', p. 42.
12. Hare, 'A School for Philosophers', p. 43.
13. Hare, 'A School for Philosophers', pp. 43–4.
14. Hare, 'A School for Philosophers', p. 44.
15. Hare, 'A School for Philosophers', p. 53.
16. See, for instance, Cavell, 'Austin at Criticism' and 'Passionate and Performative Utterance' (among many other works of homage); for an

example of ordinary language philosophy invoked within recent literary studies, see Moi, *Revolution of the Ordinary: Literary Studies after Wittgenstein, Austin, and Cavell.*

17. These lines of critique appear in their most influential form in Geach, 'Assertion' and Grice, *Studies in the Way of Words.*

18. The principle is mentioned, though not endorsed, in Williams, *The Sense of the Past*, p. 258.

19. Skinner, *Visions of Politics, 1: Regarding Method*, pp. 82–3.

20. See, e.g. Langton, 'Speech Acts and Unspeakable Acts' and Butler, *Excitable Speech: A Politics of the Performative.*

21. Quine, 'Mr Strawson on Logical Theory', p. 446.

22. I have written in more detail about the Oxford reception of Rawls in Krishnan, 'John Rawls and Oxford Philosophy'.

23. Two enthusiastic Oxford readers of Rawls were Bernard Williams (see Williams, *Essays and Reviews*, pp. 82–7) and Stuart Hampshire (see Hampshire, 'A New Philosophy of the Just Society'). The one significant dissenting voice, who declared the Rawlsian project bankrupt for its failure to offer a thorough analysis of moral language, was R. M. Hare (see Hare, 'Rawls' *Theory of Justice* – I' and 'Rawls' *Theory of Justice* – II'). For a discussion of the 'dire prognoses' for political philosophy in the 1950s and 1960s, see Smith, 'Historicizing Rawls', and Bejan, 'Rawls's Teaching and the "Tradition" of Political Philosophy'.

24. Rawls, *A Theory of Justice*, p. 51.

25. To put it in more technical terms, the notions of 'necessity', 'analyticity' and 'a priority', treated as effectively equivalent in the work of the logical positivists, were wrenched apart as pertaining to quite different things: necessity and contingency were matters of metaphysics, analyticity and syntheticity matters of semantics, a priority and a posteriority matters of epistemology. A robust defence of Kripke's distinction and its significance in the history of twentieth-century philosophy may be found in Soames, *Philosophical Analysis in the Twentieth Century, 2: The Age of Meaning*, pp. 335–460.

26. The metaphysical tradition continues today in the influential work of the most recent person to hold the Wykeham Chair in Logic that was once A. J. Ayer's, Timothy Williamson. See, for instance, Williamson, *Vagueness*; Williamson, *Knowledge and Its Limits*; Williamson, *The Philosophy of Philosophy;* Williamson, *Modal Logic as Metaphysics.*

27. The reality of 'possible worlds' is defended in David Lewis, *On the Plurality of Worlds*, and an influential argument defending the existence

of numbers on the grounds of their indispensability is made in Quine, 'Existence and Quantification'.

28. For instances of philosophers influenced by Wittgenstein and Austin making critical interventions in recent philosophy, see Bauer, *How to Do Things with Pornography* and Hacker, 'A Philosopher of Philosophy'.

29. For a fuller and more generous account of the ancient Greek sophists, see Taylor and Lee, 'The Sophists'.

30. See the useful discussion of the very notion of a 'marketplace of ideas' in Williams, *Truth and Truthfulness*, pp. 216–17.

31. Williams, *Essays and Reviews*, p. 214.

32. Williams, *Essays and Reviews*, p. 214.

33. Murdoch, *Existentialists and Mystics*, p. 340.

34. Wittgenstein, *The Big Typescript*, p. 92.

35. Murdoch, *Existentialists and Mystics*, pp. 4–5.

36. Murdoch, *Existentialists and Mystics*, p. 5.

37. Sontag, *Against Interpretation*, p. 288.

38. Larkin, 'Church-Going', p. 59.

11. Epilogue

1. Ayer, *Part of My Life*, pp. 26–7.

2. Rogers, *A. J. Ayer: A Life*, p. 284.

3. Wollheim, 'Ayer, Sir Alfred Jules'.

4. Scruton, 'The Man Who Hated Wisdom'.

5. Rogers, *A. J. Ayer: A Life*, p. 344.

6. Wittgenstein, 'A Lecture on Ethics'.

7. Anscombe, 'On Brute Facts'. See also the helpful discussion of this paper in Wiseman, 'Anscombe on Brute Facts and Human Affairs'.

8. Anscombe, 'Contraception and Chastity'.

9. Teichman, 'Anscombe, (Gertrude) Elizabeth Margaret'.

10. For the early interpretation, see Davidson, *Essays on Actions and Events*. For a revisionary view, see Moran and Stone, 'Anscombe on Expression of Intention: An Exegesis'. Also see Wiseman, *Routledge Philosophy Guidebook to Anscombe's 'Intention'* and Schwenkler, *Anscombe's 'Intention': A Guide*.

11. Bayley, *Iris: A Memoir of Iris Murdoch*, p. 218.

12. Saunders, *Field Notes from My Dementia*.

13. To name a couple of valuable recent volumes, Broackes (ed.), *Iris*

Murdoch, Philosopher, esp. pp. 1–91; Caprioglio Panizza and Hopwood, *The Murdochian Mind*, and a valuable essay, Hopwood, 'The Extremely Difficult Realization That Something Other Than Oneself Is Real: Iris Murdoch on Love and Moral Agency'.

14. Foot, *Natural Goodness*, pp. 36–7.
15. Voorhoeve, *Conversations on Ethics*, p. 87.
16. Foot, *Natural Goodness*, p. 1.
17. Heal, 'Mary Midgley obituary'.
18. Hare, *Moral Thinking: Its Levels, Method, and Point*.
19. Seanor and Fotion (eds), *Hare and Critics: Essays on Moral Thinking*.
20. A. W. Price, 'Hare, Richard Mervyn' (*ODNB*).
21. O'Grady, 'Sir Peter Strawson obituary'.
22. Strawson, 'Freedom and Resentment'. For further discussion see Hieronymi, *Freedom, Resentment, and the Metaphysics of Morals*.
23. O'Grady, 'Sir Peter Strawson obituary'.
24. Snowdon, 'Strawson, Sir Peter Frederick'.
25. An often-quoted remark, e.g. Johnson, 'The Novel Jane Austen Wrote When She Was Twelve'.
26. Ryle, 'Jane Austen and the Moralists', p. 294.
27. Ryle, 'Jane Austen and the Moralists', p. 299.
28. Ryle, 'Jane Austen and the Moralists', pp. 299–300.
29. The anecdote is relayed in Rogers, *A. J. Ayer: A Life*, p. 252.
30. Ryle, *The Concept of Mind*, pp. 58–9.
31. The quotations are all from Craft, *Stravinsky: Chronicle of a Friendship*, pp. 223–5.
32. Chanan, 'You Might as Well Say "I See What I Eat" Is the Same Thing as "I Eat What I See"'.
33. The account here is drawn from Mabbott, *Oxford Memories*, pp. 142–4.
34. The description is from Williams, *Essays and Reviews*, p. 152.
35. Owen, 'Gilbert Ryle', p. 265. The book, entertaining and deeply eccentric, is Ryle, *Plato's Progress*.
36. Owen, 'Gilbert Ryle', p. 265.
37. Owen, 'Gilbert Ryle', p. 265.
38. I discovered this story on Twitter: Stephen Mumford, @SDMumford (13 April 2017).
39. Kenny, *Brief Encounters*, p. 82.
40. Williams, 'Replies', p. 186.
41. For a critical (in both senses) discussion of Ryle's conduct at the

Royaumont conference with extensive quotation, see Glendinning, *The Idea of Continental Philosophy*, p. 71 ff.

42. Both letters are quoted in Isaacson, 'Oxford Philosophy in 10 Merton Street, and Before and After', p. 2. I am grateful to Daniel Isaacson for correspondence about his article.

Bibliography

The corpus of books and papers that makes up 'Oxford philosophy' is enormous. As with any other intellectual tradition, a good deal of what came out of Oxford philosophy was dross – dull, derivative, wrong-headed and justly forgotten. But in case a reader persuaded by my arguments for the lasting worth of the best work in the tradition wishes to read the original works, I recommend the works in the bibliography marked with asterisks (books) or daggers (papers).

Acton, H. B., review of Ernest Gellner, *Words and Things*, in the *Listener* (10 December 1959).

Adorno, Theodor W., 'Cultural Criticism and Society', in *Prisms: Studies in Contemporary German Social Thought* (Cambridge, MA: MIT Press, 1981), pp. 17–34.

——, *The Jargon of Authenticity* (London: Routledge & Kegan Paul, 1973).

Akehurst, Thomas L., *The Cultural Politics of Analytic Philosophy: Britishness and the Spectre of Europe* (London: Continuum, 2010).

Analysis, 'Statement of Policy', vol. 1, no. 1 (November 1933), pp. 1–2.

Anderson, Perry, 'Components of the National Culture', *New Left Review*, vol. 1, no. 50 (1968), pp. 3–57.

——, 'The Hatred of Philosophy', *Isis* (4 December 1957).

——, 'The Minstrels of MI5', *Isis* (6 November 1957).

Anon., *Wanted! A New School at Oxford* (Oxford: Blackwell, 1909).

Anscombe, G. E. M., 'Contraception and Chastity', in *Faith in a Hard Ground: Essays on Religion, Philosophy and Ethics*, ed. Mary Geach and Luke Gormally (Exeter: Imprint Academic, 2008), pp. 205–31.

——, 'Does Oxford Moral Philosophy Corrupt the Youth?', *Listener* (14 February 1957).

——, *Intention* (Oxford: Basil Blackwell, 1957).*

————, letter to the *Times Literary Supplement* (16 November 1973).

————, 'Ludwig Wittgenstein', in *From Plato to Wittgenstein: Essays by G. E. M. Anscombe*, ed. Mary Geach and Luke Gormally (Exeter: Imprint Academic, 2011), pp. 173–88.

————, 'Modern Moral Philosophy', *Philosophy*, vol. 33, no. 124 (January 1958), pp. 1–19.†

————, 'Mr Truman's Degree', reprinted in *The Collected Philosophical Papers of G. E. M. Anscombe*, vol. 3 (Oxford: Blackwell, 1981), pp. 62–71.

————, 'On Brute Facts', *Analysis*, vol. 18, no. 3 (January 1958), pp. 69–72.

————, 'On the Form of Wittgenstein's Writing', in *From Plato to Wittgenstein: Essays by G. E. M. Anscombe*, ed. Mary Geach and Luke Gormally (Exeter: Imprint Academic, 2011), pp. 206–11.

————, review of Saul A. Kripke, *Wittgenstein on Rules and Private Language*, in *Ethics*, vol. 95, no. 2 (January 1985), pp. 342–52.

Auden, W. H., *Another Time* (London: Faber & Faber, 1940).

Auden, W. H., and John Garrett, *The Poet's Tongue* (London: G. Bell & Sons, 1935).

Austin, J. L., *How to Do Things with Words* (Oxford: Oxford University Press, 1962).

————, 'Intelligent Behaviour', *Times Literary Supplement* (7 April 1950).

————, 'A Plea for Excuses', *Proceedings of the Aristotelian Society*, vol. 57, no. 1 (1957), pp. 1–30; reprinted in J. L. Austin, *Philosophical Papers*, ed. J. O. Urmson and G. J. Warnock (Oxford: Oxford University Press, 1961), pp. 123–52.†

————, *Sense and Sensibilia*, ed. G. J. Warnock (Oxford: Oxford University Press, 1962).*

Austin, J. L., and G. E. M. Anscombe, 'Pretending', *Proceedings of the Aristotelian Society, Supplementary Volumes*, vol. 32, no. 1 (1958), pp. 261–94.

Austin, J. L., P. F. Strawson, and D. R. Cousin, 'Truth', *Proceedings of the Aristotelian Society, Supplementary Volumes*, vol. 24, no. 1 (1950), pp. 111–17.

Axelrod, Alan, *The Real History of the Cold War: A New Look at the Past* (New York: Sterling Publishing, 2009).

Ayer, A. J., 'An Honest Ghost', in Oscar P. Wood and George Pitcher (eds), *Ryle* (London: Macmillan, 1970), pp. 53–74.

————, *Language, Truth, and Logic* (London: Victor Gollancz, 1936).*

————, 'Linguistic Philosophy', *Spectator* (20 November 1959).

————, *Part of My Life* (2nd edn, Oxford: Oxford University Press, 1978).

Ayer, A. J., et al., *The Revolution in Philosophy* (London: Macmillan, 1956).

Baker, Gordon P., and P. M. S. Hacker, *Wittgenstein: Meaning and Understanding* (Oxford: Blackwell, 1983).

Bakewell, Sarah, *At the Existentialist Café* (London: Vintage, 2016).

Barry, Brian, 'The Strange Death of Political Philosophy', *Government and Opposition*, vol. 15, nos. 3/4 (1980), pp. 276–88.

Bartley III, W. W., *Wittgenstein* (Philadelphia and New York: J. B. Lippincott, 1973).

Bauer, Nancy, *How to Do Things with Pornography* (Cambridge, MA: Harvard University Press, 2015).

Bayley, John, *Iris: A Memoir of Iris Murdoch* (London: Duckworth, 1998).

Baz, Avner, *When Words Are Called For* (Cambridge, MA: Harvard University Press, 2008).

Bedford, Errol, 'Emotions', *Proceedings of the Aristotelian Society*, vol. 57, no. 1 (1957), pp. 281–304.

Bejan, Teresa, 'Rawls's Teaching and the "Tradition" of Political Philosophy', *Modern Intellectual History,* vol. 18, no. 4 (2021), pp. 1058–79.

Bennett, Alan, Peter Cook, Jonathan Miller, and Dudley Moore, *The Complete Beyond the Fringe* (London: Methuen, 1987).

Bergson, Henri, 'La Philosophie française', *Revue de Paris* (15 May 1915).

Berkeley, George, 'Alciphron, or the Minute Philosopher', in David Berman (ed.), *George Berkeley: 'Alciphron, or the Minute Philosopher' in Focus* (London: Routledge, 1993) pp. 17–161.

Berlin, Isaiah, 'Austin and the Early Beginnings of Oxford Philosophy', in Isaiah Berlin et al., *Essays on J. L. Austin* (Oxford: Clarendon Press, 1973), pp. 1–16.

————, *Concepts and Categories: Philosophical Essays* (London: Hogarth Press, 1978).

————, *Letters 1928–1946*, ed. Henry Hardy (New York: Cambridge University Press, 2004).

————, 'Two Concepts of Liberty', in *Liberty*, ed. Henry Hardy (Oxford: Oxford University Press, 2002), pp. 166–217.

Berlin, Isaiah, and Steven Lukes, 'In Conversation', *Salmagundi*, no. 120 (1998), pp. 52–134.

Black, Max, 'Austin on Performatives', *Philosophy*, vol. 38, no. 145 (July 1963), pp. 217–26.

Black, Max, John Wisdom and Maurice Cornforth, 'Symposium: Is Analysis a Useful Method in Philosophy?', *Proceedings of the Aristotelian Society, Supplementary Volumes*, vol. 13 (1934), pp. 53–118.

Blackburn, Simon, *Truth: A Guide for the Perplexed* (London: Penguin, 2005).

Blumberg, Albert E., and Herbert Feigl, 'Logical Positivism: A New Movement in European Philosophy', *Journal of Philosophy*, vol. 28, no. 11 (1931), pp. 281–96.

Bourdieu, Pierre, *Outline of a Theory of Practice*, tr. Richard Nice (Cambridge: Cambridge University Press, 1977).

Borges, Jorge Luis, 'The Argentine Writer and Tradition', in *Labyrinths: Selected Stories and Other Writings* (New York: New Directions, 1962).

Bradley, F. H., *Appearance and Reality* (9th impression, Oxford: Clarendon Press, 1930).

Braithwaite, R. B., review of R. M. Hare, *The Language of Morals*, in *Mind*, vol. 63, no. 250 (April 1954), pp. 249–62.

Broackes, Justin, 'Introduction', in *Iris Murdoch, Philosopher* (New York: Oxford University Press, 2012), pp. 1–91.

Broad, C. D., 'John McTaggart Ellis McTaggart, 1866–1925', *Proceedings of the British Academy*, vol. 13 (1927), reprinted as an Introduction to J. M. E. McTaggart, *Some Dogmas of Religion* (2nd edn, London: E. Arnold, 1930), pp. xxv–lii.

———, *Five Types of Ethical Theory* (London: Routledge & Kegan Paul, 1930).

Buroker, Jill Vance, *Kant's 'Critique of Pure Reason': An Introduction* (Cambridge: Cambridge University Press, 2006).

Butler, Joseph, preface to *Fifteen Sermons Preached at Rolls Chapel*, in David McNaughton (ed.), *'Fifteen Sermons' and Other Writings on Ethics* (Oxford: Oxford University Press, 2017), pp. 3–16.

Butler, Judith, *Excitable Speech: A Politics of the Performative* (Abingdon: Routledge, 1997).

Campbell, John, *Roy Jenkins: A Well-Rounded Life* (London: Jonathan Cape, 2014).

Camus, Albert, *The Fall*, tr. Justin O'Brien (New York: Vintage, 1956).

Caprioglio Panizza, Silvia, and Mark Hopwood, *The Murdochian Mind* (Abingdon: Routledge, 2022).

Carnap, Rudolf, *The Logical Structure of the World: Pseudoproblems in Philosophy*, tr. Rolf A. George (Berkeley: University of California Press, 1967).

Carpenter, Humphrey, *W. H. Auden: A Biography* (reissue, London: Faber & Faber, 2011).

Carpenter, S. C., *Church and People 1789–1889* (London: SPCK, 1959).

Cassirer, Toni, *Mein Leben mit Ernst Cassirer* (Hamburg: Felix Meiner Verlag, 2003).

Cavell, Stanley, 'Austin at Criticism', *Philosophical Review*, vol. 74, no. 2 (1965), pp. 204–19.

———, *The Claim of Reason: Wittgenstein, Skepticism, Morality, and Tragedy* (New York: Oxford University Press, 1979).

———, *Little Did I Know: Excerpts from Memory* (Palo Alto: Stanford University Press, 2010).

———, 'Passionate and Performative Utterance', in R. B. Goodman (ed.), *Contending with Stanley Cavell* (New York: Oxford University Press, 2005), pp. 177–98.

Chanan, Michael (dir.), 'Appearance and Reality' (ep. 6 of *Logic Lane*, Chanan Films, 1972).

———, 'I'm Going to Tamper With Your Beliefs a Little' (ep. 2 of *Logic Lane*, Chanan Films, 1972).

———, 'You Might as Well Say "I See What I Eat" Is the Same Thing as "I Eat What I See"' (ep. 6 of *Logic Lane*, Chanan Films, 1972).

Charles, David, and William Child (eds), *Wittgensteinian Themes: Essays in Honour of David Pears* (Oxford: Oxford University Press, 2001).

Cogito, 'Bernard Williams', [interview] in Andrew Pyle (ed.), *Key Philosophers in Conversation: The 'Cogito' Interviews* (London: Routledge, 1999), pp. 142–63.

Cohen, G. A., *Finding Oneself in the Other*, ed. Michael Otsuka (Princeton: Princeton University Press, 2012).

Cohen, Marshall, 'The Angry Young Philosopher', *Commentary*, vol. 30, no. 8 (1960), pp. 178–80.

Collingwood, R. G., *An Autobiography* (Oxford: Oxford University Press, 1939).

———, *An Autobiography and Other Writings*, ed. David Boucher and Teresa Smith (Oxford: Oxford University Press, 2017).

———, *An Essay on Philosophical Method* (Oxford: Clarendon Press, 2005).

———, *Religion and Philosophy* (London: Macmillan, 1916).

Collini, Stefan, 'Delighted to See Himself', review of Leslie Mitchell, *Maurice Bowra: A Life*, in *London Review of Books* (12 February 2009).

———, 'No True Answers: A. J. Ayer', in *Absent Minds: Intellectuals in Britain* (Oxford: Oxford University Press, 2006), pp. 393–409.

Connell, Sophia, 'Alice Ambrose and Early Analytic Philosophy', *British Journal for the History of Philosophy*, vol. 30, no. 2 (2022), pp. 312–35.

Conradi, Peter J., *A Very English Hero: The Making of Frank Thompson* (London: Bloomsbury, 2013).

———, *Iris Murdoch: A Life* (London: HarperCollins, 2002).

Conradi, Peter J., and Gavin Lawrence, 'Professor Philippa Foot', *Independent* (19 October 2010).

Cook Wilson, John, *Statement and Inference with Other Philosophical Papers* (Oxford: Clarendon Press, 1926), p. 74.

Copsey, Nigel, *Anti-Fascism in Britain* (New York: Routledge, 2016).

Craft, Robert, *Stravinsky: Chronicle of a Friendship, 1948–1971* (New York: Alfred A. Knopf, 1972).

Crane, Tim, 'Philosophy, Logic, Science, History', *Metaphilosophy*, vol. 43, nos. 1–2 (2012), pp. 20–37.

Crary, Alice, 'The Happy Truth: J. L. Austin's *How to Do Things with Words*', *Inquiry*, vol. 45, no. 1 (2002), pp. 59–80.

Crary, Alice, and Rupert Read (eds), *The New Wittgenstein* (New York: Routledge, 2000).

Crick, Bernard, review of Ernest Gellner, *Words and Things*, in *Political Quarterly*, vol. 31, no. 1 (1960), pp. 102–4.

Croce, Benedetto, *What Is Living and What Is Dead of the Philosophy of Hegel*, tr. Douglas Ainslie (London: Macmillan, 1915).

Currie, Robert, 'The Arts and Social Studies, 1914–1939', in B. Harrison (ed.), *The History of the University of Oxford, 8: The Twentieth Century* (Oxford: Clarendon Press, 1994), p. 112.

Danchev, Alex, 'Franks, Oliver Shewell, Baron Franks (1905–1992)', in the *Oxford Dictionary of National Biography*.

Dancy, Jonathan, 'Harold Arthur Prichard', in Edward N. Zalta (ed.), *The Stanford Encyclopedia of Philosophy* (Metaphysics Research Lab, Stanford University, Spring 2018).

Darwall, Stephen, Allan Gibbard, and Peter Railton, 'Toward *Fin de Siècle* Ethics: Some Trends', *Philosophical Review*, vol. 101, no. 1 (1992), pp. 115–89.

Davidson, Donald, *Essays on Actions and Events* (Oxford: Oxford University Press, 1980).

Davies, Russell, *Ronald Searle: A Biography* (London: Sinclair-Stevenson, 1990).

Davis, John, 'An Interview with Ernest Gellner', *Current Anthropology*, vol. 32, no. 1 (1991), pp. 63–72.

Dennett, Daniel C., 'Re-introducing *The Concept of Mind*, a Foreword', in Ryle, *The Concept of Mind* (New York: Penguin Classics, 2000), pp. viii–xix.

DeRose, Keith, 'Introduction: Responding to Skepticism', in Keith DeRose and T. A. Warfield (eds), *Skepticism: A Contemporary Reader* (Oxford: Oxford University Press, 1999), pp. 1–27.

Diamond, Cora, 'Obituary for Anthony Woozley', *Proceedings and Addresses of the American Philosophical Association*, vol. 83, no. 2 (2009), pp. 215–17.

Doney, Willis, review of Ernest Gellner, *Words and Things*, in *Philosophical Review*, vol. 71, no. 2 (1962), pp. 252–7.

Dummett, Michael, *Frege: Philosophy of Language* (Cambridge, MA: Harvard University Press, 1981).

———, *The Logical Basis of Metaphysics* (Cambridge, MA: Harvard University Press, 1991).

———, *Origins of Analytical Philosophy* (Cambridge, MA: Harvard University Press, 1996).

———, 'Oxford Philosophy', *Blackfriars*, vol. 41, no. 479 (1960), pp. 74–80.

Engels, Friedrich, letter to Franz Mehring 14 July 1893, tr. Donna Torr, in *Karl Marx and Friedrich Engels: Correspondence 1846–1895* (London: Lawrence and Wishart, 1936), pp. 510–12.

Evans, Gareth, 'Things Without the Mind: A Commentary upon Chapter Two of Strawson's Individuals', in *Philosophical Subjects*, ed. Z. Van Straaten (Oxford: Oxford University Press, 1980).

Fergusson, David, 'MacKinnon, Donald MacKenzie', in the *Oxford Dictionary of National Biography* (23 September 2004).

Findlay, John N., critical notice of *Words and Things*, by Ernest Gellner, *Indian Journal of Philosophy*, vol. 3, no. 2 (1961), pp. 130–38.

Foot, Philippa, 'Morality as a System of Hypothetical Imperatives', *Philosophical Review*, vol. 81, no. 3 (July 1972), pp. 305–16.†

———, *Natural Goodness* (Oxford: Oxford University Press, 2001).

———, *Virtues and Vices and Other Essays in Moral Philosophy* (Oxford: Clarendon Press, 1978).

Fowler, Robert L., 'Blood for the Ghosts: Wilamowitz in Oxford', *Syllecta Classica*, vol. 20 (2009), pp. 171–213.

Franklin, James, 'Ludicrous, but Interesting', review of Karl Sigmund, *Exact Thinking in Demented Times*, in *New Criterion* (December 2017).

Galison, Peter, 'Aufbau/Bauhaus: Logical Positivism and Architectural Modernism', *Critical Inquiry*, vol. 16, no. 4 (1990), pp. 709–52.

Geach, P. T., 'Assertion', *Philosophical Review,* vol. 74, no. 4 (1965), pp. 449–65.

———, *Truth, Love and Immortality: An Introduction to McTaggart's Philosophy* (London: Hutchinson, 1979).

Gellner, Ernest, 'Poker Player', *New Statesman* (28 November 1969).

———, *Words and Things: A Critical Account of Linguistic Philosophy and A Study in Ideology* (London: Victor Gollancz, 1959).

George, Graham, 'Behaviorism', in Edward N. Zalta (ed.), *The Stanford Encyclopedia of Philosophy* (Metaphysics Research Lab, Stanford University, Spring 2019).

Glendinning, Simon, *The Idea of Continental Philosophy* (Edinburgh: Edinburgh University Press, 2006).

Glock, Hans-Johann, *What Is Analytic Philosophy?* (Cambridge: Cambridge University Press, 2008).

Grice, H. P., *Studies in the Way of Words* (Cambridge, MA: Harvard University Press, 1991).

Hacker, P. M. S., 'A Philosopher of Philosophy', *Philosophical Quarterly,* vol. 59 (2009), pp. 337–48.

———, 'Was He Trying to Whistle It?', in Crary and Read (eds), *The New Wittgenstein,* pp. 353–88.

———, *Wittgenstein's Place in Twentieth-Century Analytic Philosophy* (London: John Wiley & Sons, 1996).

Hall, John A., *Ernest Gellner: An Intellectual Biography* (London: Verso, 2010).

Hampshire, Stuart, 'Critical Review of *The Concept of Mind*', in Oscar P. Wood and George Pitcher (eds), *Ryle* (London: Macmillan, 1970), pp. 17–44.

———, review of Gilbert Ryle, *The Concept of Mind,* in *Mind,* vol. 59, no. 234 (April 1950), pp. 237–55.

———, 'A New Philosophy of the Just Society', *New York Review of Books* (special supplement, 24 February 1972).

———, *Thought and Action* (London: Chatto & Windus, 1959).*

Hansen, Nat, 'J. L. Austin and Literal Meaning', *European Journal of Philosophy,* vol. 22, no. 4 (2014), pp. 617–32.

Happold, Tom, and Zoe Conway, 'Healey on Healey', *Anticipations* (Summer 1996).

Hardy, Henry, *In Search of Isaiah Berlin: A Literary Adventure* (London: I. B. Tauris, 2018).

Hare, R. M., 'Can I Be Blamed for Obeying Orders?', in *Applications of Moral Philosophy* (London: Macmillan, 1972), pp. 1–8.

——, *The Language of Morals* (Oxford: Oxford University Press, 1952).*

——, *Moral Thinking: Its Levels, Method, and Point* (New York: Oxford University Press, 1981).

——, 'A Philosophical Autobiography', *Utilitas*, vol. 14, no. 3 (November 2002), pp. 269–305.

——, 'Rawls' *Theory of Justice* – I', *Philosophical Quarterly*, vol. 23, no. 91 (April 1973), pp. 144–55.

——, 'Rawls' *Theory of Justice* – II', *Philosophical Quarterly*, vol. 23, no. 92 (July 1973), pp. 241–52.

——, 'A School for Philosophers', in *Essays on Philosophical Method* (London: Macmillan, 1971), pp. 38–50.

——, *Sorting Out Ethics* (Oxford: Clarendon Press, 1997).

Hare, R. M., and P. H. Nowell-Smith, 'Oxford Moral Philosophy', *Listener* (21 February 1957).

Hart, H. L. A., *The Concept of Law* (Oxford: Oxford University Press, 1961).

Heal, Jane, 'Mary Midgley obituary', *Guardian* (12 October 2018).

Healey, Denis, *The Time of My Life* (London: Michael Joseph, 1989).

Hepburn, R. W., and Iris Murdoch, 'Vision and Choice in Morality', *Proceedings of the Aristotelian Society*, Supplementary Volumes, vol. 30 (1956), pp. 14–58.†

Hieronymi, Pamela, *Freedom, Resentment, and the Metaphysics of Morals* (Princeton: Princeton University Press, 2020).

Hintikka, Jaakko, 'Ernst Mach at the Crossroads of Twentieth-Century Philosophy', in Juliet Floyd and Sanford Shieh (eds), *Future Pasts: The Analytic Tradition in Twentieth-Century Philosophy* (Oxford: Oxford University Press, 2001), pp. 81–100.

Hintikka, Merrill B. and Jaakko Hintikka, *Investigating Wittgenstein* (Oxford: Blackwell, 1986).

Housman, A. E., 'The Application of Thought to Textual Criticism', *Proceedings of the Classical Association*, vol. 18 (1921), pp. 67–84.

Hollis, Christopher, *Oxford in the Twenties: Recollections of Five Friends* (London: Heinemann, 1976).

Hopwood, Mark, 'The Extremely Difficult Realization That Something Other Than Oneself Is Real: Iris Murdoch on Love and Moral Agency', *European Journal of Philosophy*, vol. 26, no. 1 (2018), pp. 477–501.

Hume, David, *A Treatise of Human Nature: A Critical Edition*, ed. David Fate Norton and Mary J. Norton (Oxford: Clarendon Press, 2007).

Ignatieff, Michael, *Isaiah Berlin: A Life* (New York: Metropolitan Books, 1998).

———, 'Michael Ignatieff's Biographical Interviews' (IBVL, 2017: bit.ly/3qtaB6F).

Inglis, Fred, *History Man: The Life of R. G. Collingwood* (Princeton: Princeton University Press, 2009).

Isaacson, Daniel, 'Oxford Philosophy in 10 Merton Street, and Before and After' (September 2012), media.philosophy.ox.ac.uk/assets/pdf_file/0014/27230/Oxford_Philosophy_in_10_Merton_Street,_and_before_and_after.pdf.

James, M. R., 'Oh, Whistle, and I'll Come to You, My Lad', in *Ghost-Stories of an Antiquary* (London: Edward Arnold, 1905), pp. 181–226.

Janik, Allan, and Stephen Toulmin, *Wittgenstein's Vienna* (London: Weidenfeld and Nicolson, 1973).

Janssen-Lauret, Frederique, 'Women in Logical Empiricism', in Thomas Uebel and Christoph Limbeck-Lilienau (eds), *The Routledge Handbook of Logical Empiricism* (London: Routledge, 2021), pp. 127–35.

Jarvis, Judith, review of G. E. M. Anscombe, *Intention*, in *Journal of Philosophy*, vol. 56, no. 1 (1959), pp. 31–41.

Kant, Immanuel, *The Critique of Pure Reason*, ed. Paul Guyer and Allen W. Wood (Cambridge: Cambridge University Press, 1998).

———, *Groundwork of the Metaphysics of Morals*, ed. Mary Gregor (Cambridge: Cambridge University Press, 1998).

Kenny, Anthony, *Brief Encounters: Notes from a Philosopher's Diary* (London: SPCK, 2018).

———, 'Elizabeth Anscombe at Oxford', *American Catholic Philosophical Quarterly*, vol. 90, no. 2 (2016), pp. 181–9.

———, 'Peter Thomas Geach, 1916–2013', *Biographical Memoirs of Fellows of the British Academy*, vol. 14 (2015), pp. 185–203.

Knowles, Elizabeth (ed.), 'Harry S. Truman', *The Oxford Dictionary of Quotations* (8th edn, Oxford: Oxford University Press, 2014).

Kripke, Saul, *Naming and Necessity* (Cambridge, MA: Harvard University Press, 1980).

Krishnan, Nikhil, 'Is Goodness Natural?', *Aeon* (28 November 2017).

———, 'John Rawls and Oxford Philosophy', *Modern Intellectual History*, vol. 18, no. 4 (2021), pp. 940–59.

———, 'You're Talking Nonsense', *New Yorker* (16 May 2022).

Johnson, Claudia L., 'The Novel Jane Austen Wrote When She Was Twelve', *Paris Review* (14 September 2018), www.theparisreview.org/blog/2018/09/14/the-novel-jane-austen-wrote-when-she-was-twelve/.

Lacey, Nicola, *A Life of H. L. A. Hart: The Nightmare and the Noble Dream* (Oxford: Oxford University Press, 2006).

Laird, John, review of C. G. Stone, *The Social Contract of the Universe*, in *Philosophy*, vol. 6, no. 21 (1931), pp. 138–9.

Lanchester, John, 'The Case of Agatha Christie', *London Review of Books* (20 December 2018).

Langton, Rae, 'Speech Acts and Unspeakable Acts, *Philosophy & Public Affairs*, vol. 22, no. 4 (1993), pp. 293–330.

Larkin, Philip, 'Church-Going', in *Collected Poems* (London: Faber & Faber, 2003).

Laugier, Sandra, *Why We Need Ordinary Language Philosophy*, tr. Daniela Ginsberg (Chicago: Chicago University Press, 2013).

Leach, Stephen, 'Bertrand Russell and Common Sense for Savages', *Philosophy Now*, vol. 135 (2019), pp. 32–3.

Lewis, C. S., *The Four Loves* (New York: Harcourt, 1960).

Lewis, David, *On the Plurality of Worlds* (Oxford: Blackwell, 1986).

Lipscomb, Benjamin J. B., *The Women Are Up to Something: How Elizabeth Anscombe, Philippa Foot, Mary Midgley, and Iris Murdoch Revolutionized Ethics* (New York: Oxford University Press, 2021).

Lloyd, Vincent, 'Interview with Gillian Rose', *Theory, Culture and Society*, vol. 25, no. 7–8 (1 December 2008), pp. 201–18.

Longworth, Guy, 'John Langshaw Austin', in Edward N. Zalta (ed.), *The Stanford Encyclopedia of Philosophy* (Metaphysics Research Lab, Stanford University, Fall 2021).

Lucas, John, 'Obituary of R. M. Hare', *Balliol Annual Record*, pp. 30–32.

Mabbott, J. D., *Oxford Memories* (Oxford: Thornton's of Oxford, 1986).

MacCallum, Gerald, 'Negative and Positive Freedom', *Philosophical Review*, vol. 76, no. 3 (1967), pp. 312–34.

McCullough, David, *Truman* (New York: Simon and Schuster, 2003).

Mac Cumhaill, Clare and Rachael Wiseman, *Metaphysical Animals: How Four Women Brought Philosophy Back to Life* (London: Penguin, 2022).

McGuinness, Brian, 'Two Cheers for the "New" Wittgenstein', in José L. Zalabardo (ed.), *Wittgenstein's Early Philosophy* (Oxford: Oxford University Press, 2012).

—— (ed.), *Wittgenstein in Cambridge: Letters and Documents 1911–1951* (London: John Wiley & Sons, 2012).

MacIntosh, Douglas, *The Problem of Knowledge* (New York: Macmillan, 1915).

MacIntyre, Alasdair, 'The Hunt Is Up!', *New Statesman* (31 October 1959).

MacKinnon, Donald, 'And the Son of Man That Thou Visitest Him: Part 2', *Christendom* (1948), pp. 260–72.

Macleod, Colin, 'Eduard David Mortier Fraenkel', *Oxford Magazine* (13 March 1970).

MacNeice, Louis, *Autumn Journal* (London: Faber & Faber, 1939).

McTaggart, J. M. E., 'The Unreality of Time', *Mind*, vol. 17, no. 68 (1908), pp. 457–74.

Magee, Bryan, 'Conversation with Gilbert Ryle', in *Modern British Philosophy* (London: Secker & Warburg, 1971), pp. 100–114.

Malcolm, Norman, *Ludwig Wittgenstein: A Memoir* (2nd edn, Oxford: Oxford University Press, 1984).

Manguel, Alberto, *A History of Reading* (New York: Viking, 1996).

Marcuse, Herbert, 'The Triumph of Positive Thinking', in *One-Dimensional Man* (London: Routledge, 2006), pp. 174–203.

Mehta, Ved, *Fly and the Fly-Bottle: Encounters with Contemporary British Intellectuals* (London: Weidenfeld and Nicolson, 1963).

Meyerhoff, Hans, and Alvin N. Main, 'A Conservative Therapy', *Nation* (24 September 1960).

Midgley, Mary, 'The Golden Age of Female Philosophy', *Guardian* (28 November 2013).

———, *The Owl of Minerva: A Memoir* (Abingdon: Routledge, 2005).

———, 'Then and Now', *In Parenthesis*, www.womeninparenthesis.co.uk/then-and-now/.

Miller, Jonathan, *One Thing and Another: Selected Writings 1954–2016* (London: Bloomsbury, 2017).

Mitchell, Leslie, *Maurice Bowra: A Life* (Oxford: Oxford University Press, 2009).

Moi, Toril, *Revolution of the Ordinary: Literary Studies After Wittgenstein, Austin, and Cavell* (Chicago: Chicago University Press, 2017).

Monk, Ray, 'How the Untimely Death of R. G. Collingwood Changed the Course of Philosophy Forever', *Prospect* (5 September 2019).

———, *Ludwig Wittgenstein: The Duty of Genius* (London: Jonathan Cape, 1990).

Moore, A. W., 'The English Language and Philosophy', *Rue Descartes*, no. 26 (December 1999), pp. 73–80.

————, *The Evolution of Modern Metaphysics* (Cambridge: Cambridge University Press, 2012).

————, 'Williams, Sir Arthur Owen Bernard', in the *Oxford Dictionary of National Biography* (4 January 2007).

G. E. Moore, 'An Autobiography', in P. A. Schilpp (ed.), *The Philosophy of G. E. Moore* (Evanston: Northwestern University Press, 1942).

————, 'A Defence of Common Sense', in *Contemporary British Philosophy, Second Series*, ed. J. H. Muirhead (London: George Allen and Unwin, 1925), pp. 192–233.

————, *Philosophical Studies* (London: Routledge & Kegan Paul, 1922).

————, *Principia Ethica*, ed. T. Baldwin (Cambridge: Cambridge University Press, 1993).

Moran, Richard, and Martin J. Stone, 'Anscombe on Expression of Intention: An Exegesis', in Anton Ford et al. (eds), *Essays on Anscombe's 'Intention'* (Cambridge, MA: Harvard University Press, 2011), pp. 33–75.

Murdoch, Iris, *Existentialists and Mystics: Writings on Philosophy and Literature* (London: Penguin, 1999).

————, *Sartre: Romantic Rationalist* (London: Bowes & Bowes, 1953).

————, *The Sovereignty of Good* (London: Routledge, 1970).*

————, 'Taking the Plunge', *New York Review of Books* (4 March 1993).

————, *Under the Net* (London: Chatto & Windus, 1954).

Myers, F. W. H., 'George Eliot', in *Modern Essays* (London: Macmillan, 1885).

Nagel, Ernest, 'Impressions and Appraisals of Analytic Philosophy in Europe I', *Journal of Philosophy*, vol. 33, no. 1 (1936), pp. 5–24.

Nicholas, Barry, 'German Refugees in Oxford: Some Personal Recollections', in *Jurists Uprooted: German-Speaking Émigré Lawyers in Twentieth-Century Britain*, ed. Jack Beatson and Reinhard Zimmermann (Oxford: Oxford University Press, 2004), pp. 743–8.

Nietzsche, Friedrich, *The Gay Science: With a Prelude in German Rhymes and an Appendix of Songs*, ed. Bernard Williams (Cambridge: Cambridge University Press, 2001).

Norton, Robert Edward, 'The Myth of the Counter-Enlightenment', *Journal of the History of Ideas*, vol. 68, no. 4 (2007), pp. 635–58.

O'Grady, Jane, 'Sir Peter Strawson obituary', *Guardian* (15 February 2006).

Owen, G. E. L., 'Gilbert Ryle', *Proceedings of the Aristotelian Society*, n.s. vol. 77 (1976), pp. 265–70.

'Oxford Don Fights Honor for Truman', *The New York Times* (19 June 1956).

Passmore, John, *A Hundred Years of Philosophy* (New York: Basic Books, 1967).

Pateman, Trevor, 'The Poverty of Philosophy, Politics and Economics: A Critique of the Form and Content of the Oxford Honour School of P.P.E.' (Oxford, 1968).

Paton, H. J., 'Fifty Years of Philosophy', in H. D. Lewis (ed.), *Contemporary British Philosophy* (London: George Allen and Unwin, 1956), pp. 337–54.

Paul, G. A., 'G. E. Moore, Analysis, Common Usage, and Common Sense', in A. J. Ayer et al., *The Revolution in Philosophy* (New York: St. Martin's Press, 1956), pp. 56–69.

Peel, Mark, *Shirley Williams: The Biography* (London: Biteback Publishing, 2013).

Pevsner, Nikolaus, and Jennifer Sherwood, *Oxfordshire, The Buildings of England* (London: Yale University Press, 2002).

Philby, Kim, *My Silent War* (New York: Grove Press, 1968).

Pitcher, George, 'Austin: A Personal Memoir', in Berlin et al., *Essays on J. L. Austin* (Oxford: Clarendon Press, 1973), pp. 17–30.

Plato, *Complete Works*, ed. John M. Cooper and D. S. Hutchinson (Indianapolis: Hackett Publishing, 1997).

———, *Phaedrus*, tr. Alexander Nehamas and Paul Woodruff (Indianapolis: Hackett Publishing, 1995).

———, *The Theaetetus of Plato*, tr. Myles Burnyeat and M. J. Levett (Indianapolis: Hackett Publishing, 1990).

Price, A. W., 'Hare, Richard Mervyn (1919–2002), philosopher', in the *Oxford Dictionary of National Biography*.

———, 'Richard Mervyn Hare', in Edward N. Zalta (ed.), *The Stanford Encyclopedia of Philosophy* (Metaphysics Research Lab, Stanford University, Winter 2016).

Price, H. H., *Perception* (London: Methuen, 1932).

Prichard, H. A., 'Does Moral Philosophy Rest on a Mistake?', *Mind*, vol. 21, no. 81 (January 1912), pp. 21–37.

———, 'H. W. B. Joseph, 1867–1943', *Mind*, vol. 53, no. 210 (April 1944), pp. 189–91.

———, *Kant's Theory of Knowledge* (Oxford: Clarendon Press, 1909).

Putnam, Hilary, *The Threefold Cord: Mind, Body, and World* (New York: Columbia University Press, 2001).

Quine, W. V. O., 'Address: Existence and Quantification', in Joseph Margolis (ed.) *Fact and Existence* (Toronto: University of Toronto Press, 2019), pp. 1–17.

————, 'Mr Strawson on Logical Theory', *Mind*, vol. 62, no. 248 (1953), pp. 433–51.

————, *The Time of My Life* (Cambridge, MA: MIT Press, 1985).

Quinton, Anthony, 'Alfred Jules Ayer 1910–1989', *Proceedings of the British Academy*, vol. 94 (1997), pp. 255–82.

Radford, Colin, 'Patrick Nowell-Smith obituary', *Guardian* (22 February 2006).

Ramsey, Frank, 'The Nature of Truth', in *On Truth: Original Manuscript Materials (1927–1929) from the Ramsey Collection at the University of Pittsburgh*, ed. Nicholas Rescher and Ulrich Majer (Dordrecht: Kluwer Academic Publishers, 1991), pp. 6–24.

Rawls, John, *A Theory of Justice* (Cambridge, MA: Harvard University Press, 1971).

Redding, Paul, 'Georg Wilhelm Friedrich Hegel', in Edward N. Zalta (ed.), *The Stanford Encyclopedia of Philosophy* (Metaphysics Research Lab, Stanford University, Winter 2020).

Rée, Jonathan, 'English Philosophy in the Fifties', *Radical Philosophy*, no. 65 (Autumn 1993), pp. 3–21.

————, *Proletarian Philosophers: Problems in Socialist Culture in Britain, 1900–1940* (Oxford: Clarendon Press, 1984).

Ricks, Christopher, 'Austin's Swink', *University of Toronto Quarterly*, vol. 61, no. 3 (Spring 1992), pp. 297–315.

Rogers, Ben, *A. J. Ayer: A Life* (New York: Grove Press, 1999).

Rose, Gillian, *Love's Work* (London: Chatto & Windus, 1995).

Ross, W. D., *The Right and the Good*, ed. P. Stratton-Lake (Oxford: Oxford University Press, 2002).

Rousseau, Jean-Jacques, *On the Social Contract*, in *'The Social Contract' and Other Later Political Writings*, ed. Victor Gourevitch (2nd edn, Cambridge: Cambridge University Press, 2019).

Rowse, A. L., 'Oxford in War-time', in *The English Spirit: Essays in History and Literature* (London: Macmillan, 1944), pp. 260–65.

Russell, Bertrand, 'The Cult of "Common Usage"', *British Journal for the Philosophy of Science*, vol. 3, no. 12 (1953), pp. 303–7.

————, *Introduction to Mathematical Philosophy* (Nottingham: Spokesman, 2008).

————, 'Knowledge by Acquaintance and Knowledge by Description', *Proceedings of the Aristotelian Society*, vol. 11, no. 1 (1911), pp. 108–28.

————, *My Philosophical Development* (London: Routledge, 1995), p. 99.

————, 'On Denoting', *Mind*, vol. 14, no. 4 (1905), pp. 479–93.

————, *The Problems of Philosophy* (London: Williams and Norgate, 1912).

————, *Sceptical Essays* (London: Routledge, 2004).

————, 'Mr Strawson on Referring', *Mind*, vol. 66, no. 263 (1957), pp. 385–9.

Ryan, Alan, 'Stuart Newton Hampshire 1914–2004', *Proceedings of the British Academy*, vol. 150 (March 2008), pp. 105–23.

Ryle, Gilbert, 'Autobiographical', in Oscar P. Wood and George Pitcher (eds), *Ryle* (London: Macmillan, 1970), pp. 1–15.

————, *The Concept of Mind* (60th anniversary edn, Abingdon: Routledge, 2009).*

————, 'Fifty Years of Philosophy and Philosophers', *Philosophy*, vol. 51, no. 198 (1976), pp. 381–9.

————, 'G. E. Moore', reprinted in *Collected Papers, Volume 1: Critical Essays* (New York: Barnes & Noble, 1971) pp. 268–71.

————, 'The Genesis of "Oxford" Philosophy', *Linacre Journal*, no. 3 (November 1999), pp. 109–14.

————, 'Introduction', in A. J. Ayer et al., *The Revolution in Philosophy* (London: Macmillan, 1960), pp. 1–11.

————, 'Jane Austen and the Moralists', in *Critical Essays*, Collected Papers vol. 1 (reprint, London: Routledge, 2016), pp. 286–301.

————, *Plato's Progress* (Cambridge: Cambridge University Press, 1975).

————, review of K. R. Popper, *The Open Society and Its Enemies*, in *Mind*, vol. 56, no. 222 (1947), pp. 167–72.

————, review of Martin Heidegger, *Sein und Zeit*, in *Mind*, vol. 38, no. 151 (1929), pp. 355–70.

————, 'Systematically Misleading Expressions', *Proceedings of the Aristotelian Society*, vol. 32, no. 1 (1932), pp. 139–70.

Ryle, John Charles, *Expository Thoughts on the Gospels: St Matthew (For Family and Private Use, With the Text Complete)* (New York: Robert Carter & Brothers, 1860).

————, *Knots Untied: Being Plain Statements on Disputed Points in Religion, from the Standpoint of an Evangelical Churchman* (London: William Hunt, 1874).

Sartre, Jean-Paul, *Existentialism Is a Humanism*, tr. C. Macomber (New Haven: Yale University Press, 2007).

Saunders, Gerda, *Field Notes from My Dementia* (22 June 2017), www.lithub.com/field-notes-from-my-dementia/.

Sbisà, Marina, 'How to Read Austin', *Pragmatics*, vol. 17, no. 3 (January 2007), pp. 461–73.

Schlick, Moritz, *Problems of Ethics*, tr. David Rynin (New York: Dover, 1961).

Schorske, Carl E., *Fin-de-siècle Vienna: Politics and Culture* (London: Weidenfeld and Nicolson, 1979).

Schwenkler, John, *Anscombe's 'Intention': A Guide* (New York: Oxford University Press, 2019).

Scruton, Roger, 'The Man Who Hated Wisdom', *Sunday Telegraph* (2 July 1989).

Seanor, Douglas, and N. Fotion (eds), *Hare and Critics: Essays on Moral Thinking* (Oxford: Clarendon Press, 1988).

Searle, John R., 'Oxford Philosophy in the 1950s', *Philosophy*, vol. 90, no. 2 (April 2015), pp. 173–93.

Shulman, David, *Spring, Heat, Rains: A South Indian Diary* (Chicago: Chicago University Press, 2008).

Sidgwick, Arthur, and Eleanor Mildred Sidgwick, *Henry Sidgwick: A Memoir* (London: Macmillan, 1906).

Sidgwick, Henry, 'A Lecture Against Lecturing', in *Miscellaneous Essays and Addresses* (London: Macmillan, 1904).

Simpson, A. W. Brian, *Reflections on 'The Concept of Law'* (Oxford: Oxford University Press, 2011).

Skidelsky, Robert, *Oswald Mosley* (London: Macmillan, 1975).

Skinner, Quentin, *Visions of Politics, 1: Regarding Method* (New York: Cambridge University Press, 2002).

Slater, John G., and Peter Köllner, 'General Headnote to Part XI', in *The Collected Papers of Bertrand Russell, 11: Last Philosophical Testament 1947–1968*, ed. John G. Slater and Peter Köllner (London: Routledge, 1997), pp. 599–609.

Smith, Sophie, 'Historicizing Rawls', *Modern Intellectual History*, vol. 18, no. 4 (2021), pp. 906–39.

Snow, C. P., *The Two Cultures*, reprinted with an introduction by Stefan Collini (Cambridge: Cambridge University Press, 1993).

Snowdon, Paul, 'Strawson on the Concept of Perception', in Lewis Edwin Hahn (ed.), *The Philosophy of P. F. Strawson* (Chicago: Open Court, 1998), pp. 293–310.

———, 'Strawson, Sir Peter Frederick (1919–2006), philosopher', in the *Oxford Dictionary of National Biography*.

Snowdon, Paul, and Anil Gomes, 'Peter Frederick Strawson', in Edward N. Zalta (ed.), *The Stanford Encyclopedia of Philosophy* (Metaphysics Research Lab, Stanford University, Summer 2021).

Soames, Scott, *Philosophical Analysis in the Twentieth Century, 1: The Dawn of Analysis* (Princeton: Princeton University Press, 2005).

———, *Philosophical Analysis in the Twentieth Century, 2: The Age of Meaning* (Princeton: Princeton University Press, 2005).

Sontag, Susan, *Against Interpretation and Other Essays* (New York: Penguin, 2009).

Spender, Stephen, *World Within World* (Berkeley: University of California Press, 1966).

Spurling, Hilary, 'The Wickedest Man in Oxford', *The New York Times* (24 December 2000).

Stadler, Friedrich, 'Documentation: The Murder of Moritz Schlick', in Friedrich Stadler (ed.), *The Vienna Circle: Studies in the Origins, Development, and Influence of Logical Empiricism* (Vienna: Springer, 2001).

Stebbing, L. Susan, 'Logical Positivism and Analysis', *Proceedings of the British Academy*, vol. 44, no. 19 (1933), pp. 53–87.

———, 'Moore's Influence', in P. A. Schilpp (ed.), *The Philosophy of G. E. Moore* (Evanston: Northwestern University Press, 1942), pp. 517–32.

———, *Thinking to Some Purpose* (Harmondsworth: Penguin, 1939).

Stone, C. G., *The Social Contract of the Universe* (London: Methuen, 1930).

Strawson, P. F., review of Ludwig Wittgenstein, *Philosophical Investigations*, in *Mind*, vol. 63, no. 249 (1954), pp. 70–99.

———, *An Introduction to Logical Theory* (London: Routledge, 1952).

———, 'Ecce Homo! (Epstein)', in *The Threshold, 1935: An Anthology of Verse and Prose from the Public and Secondary Schools of England*, ed. R. W. Moore (London: Selwyn & Blount, 1935), p. 72.

———, 'Ethical Intuitionism', *Philosophy*, vol. 24, no. 88 (1949), pp. 23–33.

———, 'Freedom and Resentment', *Proceedings of the British Academy*, vol. 48 (1962), pp. 187–211.

———, *Individuals: An Essay in Descriptive Metaphysics* (London: Methuen, 1959).*

———, 'Intellectual Autobiography', in Lewis Edwin Hahn (ed.), *The Philosophy of P. F. Strawson* (Chicago: Open Court, 1998), pp. 3–22.

———, 'Introduction', in *Philosophical Logic*, ed. P. F. Strawson (Oxford: Oxford University Press, 1967), pp. 1–16.

———, 'Necessary Propositions and Entailment-Statements', *Mind*, vol. 57, no. 226 (1948), pp. 184–200.

———, 'On Referring', *Mind*, vol. 59, no. 235 (1950), pp. 320–44.†

———, 'The Post-Linguistic Thaw', in *P. F. Strawson: Philosophical Writings*, ed. Galen Strawson and Michelle Montague (Oxford: Oxford University Press, 2011), pp. 71–7.

————, 'Ryle, Gilbert (1900–1976)', in the *Oxford Dictionary of National Biography*.

Stray, Christopher, 'Eduard Fraenkel: An Exploration', *Syllecta Classica*, no. 25 (2014), pp. 113–72.

Stroud, Barry, 'Transcendental Arguments', *Journal of Philosophy*, vol. 65, no. 9 (1968), pp. 241–56.

Taylor, C. C. W., and Mi-Kyoung Lee, 'The Sophists', in Edward N. Zalta (ed.), *The Stanford Encyclopedia of Philosophy* (Metaphysics Research Lab, Stanford University, Fall 2020).

Teichman, Jenny, 'Anscombe, (Gertrude) Elizabeth Margaret (1919–2001), philosopher', in the *Oxford Dictionary of National Biography*.

Urmson, J. O., *Philosophical Analysis: Its Development Between the Two World Wars* (Oxford: Clarendon Press, 1956).

Trevor-Roper, Hugh, *The Wartime Journals*, ed. Richard Davenport-Hines (London: I. B. Tauris, 2012).

Tripodi, Paolo, *Analytic Philosophy and the Later Wittgensteinian Tradition* (London: Palgrave Macmillan, 2020).

Truman, Harry S., *1948: Containing the Public Messages, Speeches, and Statements of the President, January 1 to December 31, 1948* (Ann Arbor: University of Michigan Library, 2005).

Uschanov, T. P., 'Ernest Gellner's Criticisms of Wittgenstein and Ordinary Language Philosophy', in G. N. Kitching and Nigel Pleasants (eds), *Marx and Wittgenstein: Knowledge, Morality and Politics* (London: Routledge, 2002), pp. 23–46.

————, 'The Strange Death of Ordinary Language Philosophy' (April 2001, accessed 12 January 2019), www.helsinki.fi/~tuschano/writings/strange/.

Wilamowitz-Moellendorff, Ulrich von, *Greek Historical Writing and Apollo: Two Lectures Delivered before the University of Oxford, June 3 and 4, 1908*, tr. Gilbert Murray (Oxford: Clarendon Press, 1908).

————, *History of Classical Scholarship*, tr. Alan Harris (Baltimore: Johns Hopkins University Press, 1982).

Voorhoeve, Alex, *Conversations on Ethics* (Oxford: Oxford University Press, 2009).

Warnock, G. J., *English Philosophy since 1900* (Oxford: Oxford University Press, 1958).

————, 'John Langshaw Austin, A Biographical Sketch', in *Symposium on*

J. L. Austin, ed. K. T. Fann (London: Routledge & Kegan Paul, 1969), pp. 3–21.

———, review of Ernest Gellner, *Words and Things*, in *Cambridge Review* (7 November 1959), pp. 129–31.

———, 'Saturday Mornings', in *Essays on J. L. Austin* (Oxford: Clarendon Press, 1973), pp. 31–45.

Warnock, Mary, *A Memoir: People and Places* (London: Duckworth, 2000).

———, 'A Tremendous Coup', in F. A. Flowers III and Ian Ground (eds), *Portraits of Wittgenstein* (London: Bloomsbury, 2018).

Watkins, J. W. N., review of Ernest Gellner, *Words and Things*, in *Ratio*, vol. 3, no. 1 (1960), pp. 106–10.

Waugh, Evelyn, *Brideshead Revisited* (new impression, London: Chapman & Hall, 1952; US edn, New York: Harcourt Brace, 1973).

Winter, P. R. J., 'A Higher Form of Intelligence: Hugh Trevor-Roper and Wartime British Secret Service, Intelligence and National Security', *Intelligence and National Security*, vol. 22, no. 6 (2007), pp. 847–80.

White, Morton, *A Philosopher's Story* (University Park, PA: Penn State Press, 2010).

Williams, Bernard, *Descartes: The Project of Pure Enquiry* (London: Routledge, 2005).

———, 'An Essay on Collingwood', in his *The Sense of the Past: Essays in the History of Philosophy* (Princeton: Princeton University Press, 2009), pp. 341–58.

———, *Essays and Reviews, 1959–2002* (Princeton: Princeton University Press, 2014).

———, *Ethics and the Limits of Philosophy* (London: Fontana, 1985).

———, 'The Hatred of Philosophy', *Isis* (4 December 1957).

———, 'Limpidity and Impudence', *Spectator* (18 May 1961).

———, 'A Mistrustful Animal', *Harvard Review of Philosophy*, vol. 12, no. 1 (2004), pp. 80–91.

———, *Morality: An Introduction to Ethics* (Cambridge: Cambridge University Press, 1972).*

———, 'Nietzsche's Minimalist Moral Philosophy', *European Journal of Philosophy*, vol. 1, no. 1 (1993), pp. 4–14.

———, *On Opera* (London: Yale University Press, 2006).

———, *Problems of the Self* (Cambridge: Cambridge University Press, 1973).

———, 'Replies', in Ross Harrison and J. E. J. Altham (eds), *World, Mind, and Ethics: Essays on the Ethical Philosophy of Bernard Williams* (Cambridge: Cambridge University Press, 1995), pp. 185–224.

—, review of A. J. Ayer et al., *The Revolution in Philosophy*, in *Philosophy*, vol. 33, no. 124 (1958), pp. 65–7.

—, review of G. J. Warnock, *English Philosophy since 1900*, in *Philosophy*, vol. 34, no. 129 (1959), pp. 168–70.

—, 'Ryle Remembered', *London Review of Books* (22 November 1979); reprinted in *Essays and Reviews*, pp. 152–6.

—, The Self and the Future, *Philosophical Review*, vol. 79, no. 2 (April 1970), pp. 161–80.†

—, *Making Sense of Humanity and Other Philosophical Papers 1982–1993* (Cambridge: Cambridge University Press, 1995).

—, *The Sense of the Past* (Princeton: Princeton University Press, 2003).

—, *Shame and Necessity* (Berkeley: University of California Press, 1993).

—, *Truth and Truthfulness* (Princeton: Princeton University Press, 2002).

—, Untitled typescript on education (Patricia Williams's collection).

—, 'Wittgenstein and Idealism', in *Moral Luck* (Cambridge: Cambridge University Press, 1981), pp. 144–63.

Williams, Bernard, and Alan Montefiore (eds), *British Analytical Philosophy* (London: Routledge & Kegan Paul, 1966).

Williams, Bernard, and Michael Tanner, 'Reply', in Michael D. Bayles (ed.), *Ethics and Population* (Cambridge, MA: Schenkman, 1976), pp. 41–51.

Williams, Shirley, *Climbing the Bookshelves: The Autobiography* (London: Virago, 2009).

Williamson, Timothy, *Knowledge and Its Limits* (Oxford: Oxford University Press, 2000).

—, *Modal Logic as Metaphysics* (Oxford: Oxford University Press, 2013).

—, *The Philosophy of Philosophy* (Oxford: Blackwell, 2007).

—, *Vagueness* (London: Routledge, 1994).

Wilson, A. N., letter to the *London Review of Books* (26 February 2009).

Wisdom, John, 'Philosophical Perplexity', *Proceedings of the Aristotelian Society*, vol. 37, no. 1 (1937), pp. 71–88.

Wiseman, Rachael, 'Anscombe on Brute Facts and Human Affairs', *Royal Institute of Philosophy Supplement*, vol. 87 (2020), pp. 85–99.

—, *Routledge Philosophy Guidebook to Anscombe's 'Intention'* (Abingdon: Routledge, 2016).

Wittgenstein, Ludwig, *Tractatus Logico-Philosophicus*, tr. C. K. Ogden and Frank Ramsey (London: Routledge, 1922).

—, 'A Lecture on Ethics', *Philosophical Review*, vol. 74, no. 1 (1965), pp. 3–12.

————, *The Big Typescript: German–English Scholar's Edition: TS 213*
(London: John Wiley & Sons, 2005).

————, *Preliminary Studies for the 'Philosophical Investigations': Generally
Known as the Blue and Brown Books* (2nd edn, Oxford: Blackwell,
1969).

————, *Philosophical Investigations* (3rd edn, Oxford: Basil Blackwell,
1958).

————, *Zettel* (Oxford: Blackwell, 1967).

Ludwig Wittgenstein, Friedrich Waismann, and Brian McGuinness,
*Wittgenstein and the Vienna Circle: Conversations Recorded by Friedrich
Waismann*, ed. Brian McGuinness (Oxford: Blackwell, 1979).

Wolin, Richard, *The Heidegger Controversy: A Critical Reader* (Cambridge,
MA: MIT Press, 1993).

Wollheim, Richard, 'Ayer: The Man, the Philosopher, the Teacher', *Royal
Institute of Philosophy Supplements*, vol. 30, no. 1 (1991), pp. 17–30.

————, 'Ayer, Sir Alfred Jules [Freddie] (1910–1989), philosopher', in the
Oxford Dictionary of National Biography.

————, 'A Bed out of Leaves', *London Review of Books* (4 December 2003).

————, *F. H. Bradley* (Baltimore: Penguin, 1959).

————, 'A Familiar Concept?', *New Statesman* (16 November 1957).

————, review of R. M. Hare, *The Language of Morals*, in *New Statesman
and Nation* (20 December 1952).

————, 'Review: Problems of the Self', *Listener* (26 July 1973).

Woolf, Leonard, *Sowing: An Autobiography of the Years 1880–1904*
(London: Hogarth Press, 1960), pp. 129–30.

Woolf, Virginia, *The Sickle Side of the Moon: The Letters of Virginia Woolf*,
vol. 5 (London: Hogarth Press, 1979).

Index